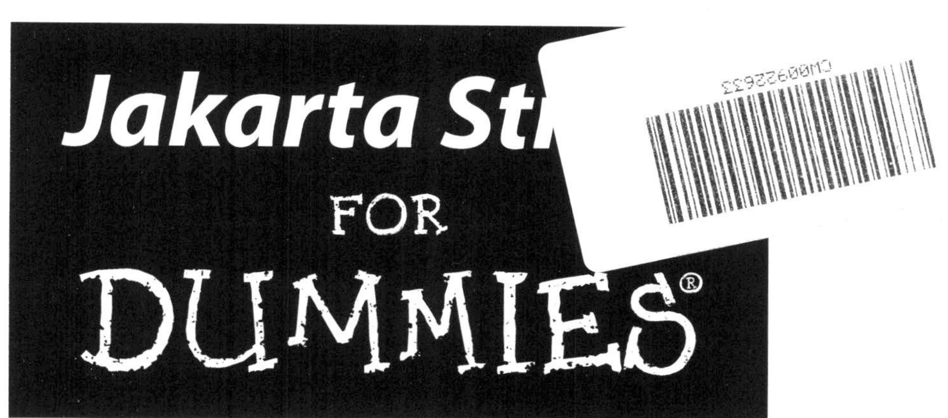

by Mike Robinson and Ellen Finkelstein

Wiley Publishing, Inc.

Jakarta Struts For Dummies®

Published by
Wiley Publishing, Inc.
111 River Street
Hoboken, NJ 07030-5774

Published by Wiley Publishing, Inc., Indianapolis, Indiana

Published simultaneously in Canada

For general information on our other products and services or to obtain technical support, please contact our Customer Care Department within the U.S. at 800-762-2974, outside the U.S. at 317-572-3993, or fax 317-572-4002.

Wiley also publishes its books in a variety of electronic formats. Some content that appears in print may not be available in electronic books.

Library of Congress Control Number: 2004101960

ISBN: 0-7645-5957-5

10 9 8 7 6 5 4 3 2 1

1O/RZ/QT/QU/IN

About the Authors

Mike Robinson has been working in the computing field since, well, when minicomputers were popular. He has a master's degree in computer science and has been an independent Java developer specializing in interactive Web applications since 1998. Mike is an adjunct faculty member in the Computer Science Department at Maharishi University of Management in Fairfield, Iowa. If he had any spare time, he would probably spend it hiking.

Ellen Finkelstein is the author of numerous best-selling computer books on AutoCAD, PowerPoint, Flash, and most recently OpenOffice.org. She writes regular articles on AutoCAD and PowerPoint in magazines, e-zines, and for Web sites. She is an adjunct Instructor of Management, teaching e-business courses to M.B.A. students. She writes at home so that she can take the bread out of the oven on time.

Dedication

To MMY, for explaining the organizing power of Natural Law that sustains the existence and evolution of the entire universe and showing us how to make use of this power in our daily lives to achieve maximum results through minimum effort.

Authors' Acknowledgments

Mike Robinson

First and foremost I have to thank my co-author, Ellen Finkelstein, who initiated me into the ins and outs of writing a book. Ellen is the epitome of cool under the pressure of deadlines. She always manages to have a great sense of humor and shiny outlook regardless of the situation. Thanks for your patience.

Thanks to my wife, Pat, who is always my guiding inspiration.

Ellen Finkelstein

I'd like to start out by thanking Mike Robinson for his extensive knowledge and experience, clear thinking, integrity, sense of responsibility, and great flexibility. Mike is the fountain of knowledge for this book. He is always a pleasure to work with.

Thanks to my husband, Evan, and kids, Yeshayah and Eliyah (who want to see their names in a book), who support me while I'm writing, writing, and writing some more.

Collectively

At Wiley, our esteemed publisher, we'd like to thank Terri Varveris, our acquisitions editor, for her ever-lively support. Both Linda Morris and Susan Pink were our able project editors, keeping track of innumerable details, including chapters, figures, and by how many pages we were over our quota. They kept us on track and made it easy.

Thanks to Peter Just, our friend and colleague, who did a thorough and careful job of technical editing, making sure that our terms and code were correct and that we were consistent and clear. He also contributed the material for Chapter 5.

Publisher's Acknowledgments

We're proud of this book; please send us your comments through our online registration form located at www.dummies.com/register/.

Some of the people who helped bring this book to market include the following:

Acquisitions, Editorial, and Media Development

Project Editors: Susan Pink and Linda Morris

Acquisitions Editor: Terri Varveris

Technical Editor: Peter Just

Editorial Manager: Carol Sheehan

Permissions Editor: Laura Moss

Media Development Manager: Laura VanWinkle

Media Development Supervisor: Richard Graves

Editorial Assistant: Amanda Foxworth

Cartoons: Rich Tennant (www.the5thwave.com)

Production

Project Coordinator: Nancee Reeves

Layout and Graphics: Andrea Dahl, Lauren Goddard, Denny Hager, Lynsey Osborn, Heather Ryan, Jacque Schneider

Proofreaders: Andy Hollandbeck, Carl William Pierce, TECHBOOKS Production Services

Indexer: TECHBOOKS Production Services

Publishing and Editorial for Technology Dummies

Richard Swadley, Vice President and Executive Group Publisher

Andy Cummings, Vice President and Publisher

Mary C. Corder, Editorial Director

Publishing for Consumer Dummies

Diane Graves Steele, Vice President and Publisher

Joyce Pepple, Acquisitions Director

Composition Services

Gerry Fahey, Vice President of Production Services

Debbie Stailey, Director of Composition Services

Contents at a Glance

Table of Contents

Introduction

Welcome to *Jakarta Struts For Dummies,* your plain-English guide to the Java programming framework that everyone is talking about. In this book, we explain how to use Struts to support your Java-based Web development. *Jakarta Struts For Dummies* gives you all the information you need to start using Jakarta Struts — so that you can create better code right away.

About This Book

As if you didn't know, *Jakarta Struts For Dummies* covers Jakarta Struts, the popular, open-source framework for creating Web applications in Java.

We comprehensively explain the features in Jakarta Struts, including the following:

- How Jakarta Struts structures Web application code into three groups — Model, View, and Controller — and how this helps make your code easier to write and maintain
- How Struts works with a Web container, JavaServer Pages, and Java servlets
- Integrating Struts into a Web development environment
- Controlling your application's business logic
- Representing your data, whether a few items or a huge and complex database
- Designing the view — the JavaServer Pages that the application presents to the user
- Internationalizing a Web application and using the internationalization feature to create easy-to-update text content, even if you care about only one language
- Validating data
- How the configuration files hold all the parts together
- Using plug-ins to extend Jakarta's functionality

- Using tag libraries
- Using Java Server faces
- How tiles help you to dynamically create pages
- Securing your application
- Logging for troubleshooting

How to Use This Book

You don't have to read this book from cover to cover. *Jakarta Struts For Dummies* provides just the information you need, when you need it. If you already have your Web development environment set up, you don't need to read all of Chapter 2, for example. However, we do suggest that you skim that chapter to understand the environment we use in the book, so that you can adjust your steps accordingly.

For additional information, don't ignore Part V, where we explain ten helpful extensions to Jakarta Struts and ten ways to get more information. In Part VI, we list the syntax of the Struts-EL and JSTL tag libraries and provide a glossary.

So that you don't have to tire out your fingers, you can find code for this book at `www.dummies.com/go/jakarta`.

Keep *Jakarta Struts For Dummies* handy while you work. You'll find that it's a useful resource.

Foolish Assumptions

We know that you want an easy-to-understand, logical explanation of how to incorporate Jakarta Struts into your programming environment. Our first assumption is that because you're a Web developer, you're not a dummy! We also assume that you know Java and understand how to create JavaServer Pages. You understand also the overall concepts involved in creating a Web application.

You can use any IDE (Integrated Development Environment) that you want, or you can write your code in a simple text editor. However, we chose to use an IDE so that we can give you the specific steps that you need to take to create a complete Web application. That IDE is Eclipse, an open-source, full-featured IDE. If you choose a different IDE, we assume that you understand your IDE well enough to figure out the parallel commands that we provide for Eclipse. Alternatively, you can use Eclipse while you're getting up to speed with Struts and then go back to your previous IDE. Who knows, maybe you'll find that you like Eclipse as much as we do!

Finally, we assume that you know your operating system. We use Windows for this book, but you should be able to use this book with Linux or Mac OS, for example. After all, cross-platform usability is one of the reasons you use Java, isn't it?

Just in case, here a few of the most common PC-to-Mac conversions for keyboard strokes and mouse movements:

PC	*Mac*
Ctrl	Command (⌘)
Right-click	Ctrl-click
Enter	Return
Alt	Option

Conventions Used in This Book

A typographical convention is not a convention of typists. Instead, a typographical convention helps you to know why some text is bold and other is italic so that you can figure out what we're talking about. New terms are in *italic.* Text that you need to type is **bold.** (If the text that you need to type is in an entire sentence that's bold, the text you type is not bold, to create a contrast.) Messages and other text that come from Jakarta Struts are in a special typeface, `like this`. Code in a paragraph uses the same special typeface.

When we say something like "Choose File⇨Save As," it means to click the File menu and then choose Save As from the menu that appears. When we want you to use a toolbar button, we tell you to click the button.

How This Book Is Organized

We start by introducing you to Jakarta Struts and its concepts. We help you collect the pieces you need for a complete Web development environment and then introduce you to a simple Web application. Then we drill deep into the processes you need to understand to use Struts as you create a Web application.

More specifically, this book is divided into five parts. Each part contains two or more chapters, and each part functions as a whole to explain how Jakarta Struts works.

Part I: Getting to Know Jakarta Struts

Part I contains important introductory information about Jakarta Struts, including what it is and how to start using it. Chapter 3 takes you through the steps of creating a simple logon application from beginning to end so that you can get the big picture and understand the details that follow in the rest of the book. You can download all the code from `www.dummies.com/go/jakarta`, giving you more time to understand, place, and deploy the application.

Part II: Starting from the Core

Part II settles into the three groups that make up the Struts framework: the Controller (Chapter 4), the Model (Chapter 5), and the View (Chapter 6). In Chapter 7, we explain how to use the configuration files. This part contains all the concepts that you need to know to use Struts for creating Web applications.

Part III: Expanding Your Development Options

Part III offers some additional tools and techniques that any programmer can use. Chapter 8 covers exception handling. Chapter 9 explains how to use plug-ins. Chapter 10 reviews the tag libraries as well as how to use Java Server faces and create custom tabs. Chapter 11 discusses page composition techniques including server side `includes` and tiles. Chapter 12 is all about securing your application.

Part IV: Putting It All Together

Part IV starts with a chapter on using logging to troubleshoot any problems that might come up. (But that never happens to you, does it?) Then we introduce a music collection application as a thorough example of the process of developing an application using Struts.

Part V: The Part of Tens

No *For Dummies* book is complete without its part of tens — it's a long-standing tradition. Chapter 15 reviews ten helpful extensions to Struts, and Chapter 16 offers you ten ways to find more information about Struts.

Part VI: Appendixes

Throughout the book, we use tags from the Struts-EL and JSTL tag libraries. For your easy reference, Appendix A includes the syntax for all the tags in these libraries. Appendix B is a glossary of the terms we use in this book, just to make sure that you understand what we're saying!

Icons Used in This Book

If you see little pictures in the margins, you've found an icon. Icons highlight special information in the text and let you know if you need to look more carefully or if you can just skip to more important parts.

This icon alerts you to information that you need to keep in mind to avoid wasting time or falling on your face.

Jakarta Struts has some advanced features you may want to know about — or not. This icon lets you know when we get into some heavy details

Tips help you complete a task more easily, quickly, or effectively. Don't skip these.

This icon is telling you to play close attention. Otherwise, you never know what may happen.

Where to Go from Here

Enough of all this talk. Let's move into the real content of this book and start using Jakarta Struts.

If you want, review the table of contents to see which parts interest you. Or just turn the page and start reading. Happy programming. Enjoy!

Part I
Getting to Know Jakarta Struts

In this part . . .

This is where you find out what Jakarta Struts is and what it can do for your Web applications. We explain how Jakarta Struts fits into the architecture of a Web application, including the Web container, Java Server Pages, and Java Servlets. We show you how Jakarta Struts organizes and structures your application for easy coding and maintenance.

In case you don't already have all the pieces necessary to create Web applications, in Chapter 2 we run through the process of obtaining and installing an entire Web development environment. In Chapter 3 we describe a simple Web application created using Jakarta Struts.

Chapter 1

Starting with the Basics

In This Chapter

- Getting an overview of Jakarta Struts
- Creating the structure of a Web application
- Understanding the Model-View-Controller paradigm

Suppose that you're a programmer and your job is creating Web applications. You know the basics of Web applications. You use the Java programming language because of its power and flexibility. To make the Web pages interactive, you create Java Servlets and JavaServer Pages (JSP). You're getting pretty good at what you do, so your Web applications are becoming more complex.

You've heard the buzz about Jakarta Struts and how it can help structure leaner, tighter Web applications. You want to know how you can make use of this powerful programming framework to make your application programming more systematic and consistent, while taking less time. In this chapter, we explain what Jakarta Struts is all about and how it fits into the scheme of a Web application.

What Is Jakarta Struts?

Jakarta Struts is incredibly useful in helping you create excellent Web applications. When you use Jakarta Struts, your applications should work more effectively and have fewer bugs. Just as important (because your time is important), Struts should save you hours and hours of programming and debugging.

As we explain more fully later in this chapter, Struts is a *framework* that structures all the components of a Java-based Web application into a unified whole. These components of a Web application are

- **Java Servlets:** Programs written in Java that reside on a Web server and respond to user requests

- **JavaServer Pages:** A technology for generating Web pages with both static and dynamic content
- **JavaBeans:** Components that follow specific rules, such as naming conventions
- **Business logic:** The code that implements the functionality or rules of your specific application

We provide an overview of the first three items in this chapter. (The business logic varies with each application.)

Jakarta Struts uses a specific *paradigm,* or *design pattern,* to structure your application. You simply fill in the pieces of the structure. The design pattern is called Model-View-Controller (MVC). The MVC design pattern helps you organize the various pieces of the application puzzle for maximum efficiency and flexibility. We explain MVC later in this chapter and expand on the Model, View, and Controller concepts in Chapters 4, 5, and 6.

Structuring a Web Application

We define a *Web application* as a program that resides on a Web server and produces static and dynamically created pages in a markup language (most commonly HTML) in response to a user's request. The user makes the request in a browser, usually by clicking a link on the Web page. Figure 1-1 shows a high-level view of Web architecture. We explain the components of this figure subsequently in this chapter.

To build Web applications, you use Java 2 Enterprise Edition (J2EE), which provides support for Servlets, JSP, and Enterprise JavaBeans (EJB), a distributed, multi-tier, scalable component technology.

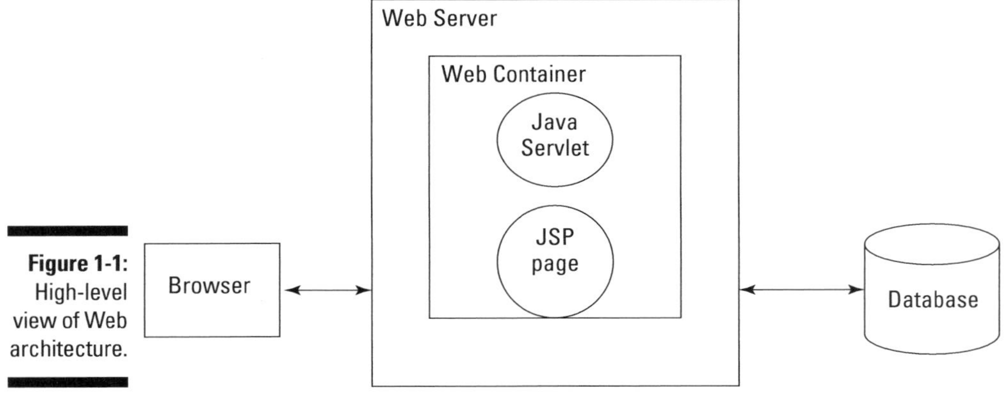

Figure 1-1: High-level view of Web architecture.

Where does Jakarta Struts come from?

To understand what Jakarta Struts is all about, you need to know something about the open-source movement that is its heritage. *Open-source* generally refers to software that the distributor provides at no cost to the user and that includes both the binary (compiled) code and the source code.

You obtain open-source software under a specific license, and the license can vary from one software provider to another. For example, the GNU (`www.gnu.org`) license provides that you must always include the source code if you redistribute the software of the application, whether or not you have made modifications to the original source code. The Apache (`www.apache.org`) license does not require you to provide the source code when you redistribute one of their applications. So open-source software licenses vary — check the license to be sure. For more information on open-source software, take a look at `www.opensource.org`.

Jakarta is one of many projects under the auspices of the Apache Software Foundation (ASF) (`www.apache.org`), formerly known as the Apache Group. The Apache Group was formed in 1995 by a number of individuals who worked together to create one of the most successful examples of an open-source project, the Apache Web Server (used by 64% of the Web sites on the Internet as of October, 2003). In 1999, the Apache Group became the non-profit Apache Software Foundation, to better provide support for its members and a legal presence to protect its resources.

As the popularity of Apache grew, so did ideas for other related open-source applications. Currently 16 software projects are supported by ASF. Actually, *software projects* is a bit of a misnomer because many of these projects have numerous subprojects that are really independent projects in themselves. Creativity is unlimited, so the ideas keep coming!

Jakarta (`jakarta.apache.org`) is one of the principal 16 ASF projects. To quote from their Web site, "Jakarta is a Project of the Apache Software Foundation, charged with the creation and maintenance of commercial-quality, open-source, server-side solutions for the Java Platform, based on software licensed to the Foundation, for distribution at no charge to the public." Struts is one of the 22 subprojects currently listed. Yes, this entire book is about one subproject.

Struts was created by Craig R. McClanahan and donated to ASF in May, 2000. Craig is an employee of Sun Microsystems and is the primary developer of both Struts and Tomcat 4. You can read about Craig and many other Struts contributors at `jakarta.apache.org/struts/volunteers.html`. The Struts 1.0 release had 17 contributors. With release 1.1 that number has jumped to 50. The project was named Struts as a reference to the architectural structures in buildings and homes that provide the internal support. The present version of Struts is 1.1.

A *Web container* is a program that manages the components of a Web application, in particular JSP pages and Java Servlets. A Web container provides a number of services, such as

- **Security:** Restricted access to components, such as password protection
- **Concurrency:** The capability to process more than one action at a time
- **Life-cycle management:** The process of starting up and shutting down a component

Some people use the term *JSP/Servlet container,* which means the same thing as Web container. We favor Web container — it's shorter and easier to type.

Apache Tomcat is an example of a Web container — an open-source *implementation* of the J2EE Java Servlet and JavaServer Pages (JSP) specifications. A *specification* is a document that describes all the details of a technology. The implementation is the actual program that functions according to its specification. In fact, Apache Tomcat is the official reference implementation for the J2EE Java Servlet and JSP specifications. As a result, Apache Tomcat is a popular Web container for Web applications that use JSP and Servlets, including applications that use Struts. We use Tomcat in all the examples in this book. However, many other commercial and open-source Web containers are available.

Typically, a Web container also functions as a Web server, providing basic HTTP (Hypertext Transfer Protocol) support for users who want to access information on the site. When requests are for static content, the Web server handles the request directly, without involving Servlets or JSP pages.

However, you may want your Web pages to adapt in response to a user's request, in which the response is *dynamic.* To generate dynamic responses, the Servlet and JSP portion of the container gets involved. Tomcat has the capability to act as both a Web server and a Web container. However, it also can interact with a standard Web server, such as Apache Web Server, letting it handle all static requests and getting involved only when requests require Servlet and JSP service.

Using Java Servlets

Java Servlets extend the functionality of a Web server and handle requests for something other than a static Web page. They are Java's answer to CGI (Common Gateway Interface) scripts of olden times (5 to 6 years ago). As their name implies, you write Java Servlets in Java and usually extend the `HttpServlet` class, which is the base class from which you create all Servlets. As such, Java Servlets have at their disposal the full functionality of the Java language, which give them a lot of power.

Servlets need to run in a *Web container,* an application that adheres to the Java Servlet Specification. In most cases, the container will support also the JavaServer Pages Specification. You can find a list of products supporting the

Java Servlet and JSP specifications at `java.sun.com/products/servlet/industry.html`. The latest Java Servlet Specification is 2.3, and the latest JavaServer Pages Specification is 1.2.

Creating JavaServer Pages

You use JavaServer Pages to present dynamic information to the user in a Web page. A JSP page has a structure like any static HTML page, but it also includes various JSP tags, or embedded Java *scriptlets* (short Java code fragments), or both. These special tags and scriptlets are executed on the server side to create the dynamic part of the presentation, so that the page can modify its output to reflect the user's request.

What really happens behind the scenes is that the JSP container translates the JSP page into a Java Servlet and then compiles the Servlet source code into runnable byte code. This translation process happens only the first time a user accesses the JSP page. The resulting Servlet is then responsible for generating the Web page to send back to the user.

Each time the JSP page is changed, the Web container translates the JSP page into a Servlet.

Listing 1-1 shows an example of a JSP page, with the JSP-specific tags in **bold.**

Listing 1-1 Sample JSP Page

```
<%@ page  contentType="text/html;charset=UTF-
          8"language="java" %>
<%-- JSTL tag libs --%>
<%@ taglib prefix="fmt" uri="/WEB-INF/fmt.tld" %>
<%-- Struts provided Taglibs --%>
<%@ taglib uri="/WEB-INF/struts-html-el.tld"
          prefix="html" %>
<html:html locale="true"/>
<head>
    <fmt:setBundle basename="ApplicationResources" />
    <title><fmt:message key="loggedin.title"/></title>
</head>
<body>
    <jsp:useBean id="polBean"
          class="com.othenos.purchasing.struts.POListBean"/>
    <H2>
        <fmt:message key="loggedin.msg">
            <fmt:param value='${polBean.userName}' />
        </fmt:message>
    </H2>
</body>
</html>
```

JSP defines six types of tag elements:

- **Action:** Follows the XML (eXtended Markup Language) format and always begins with `<jsp:some action/>`. It provides a way to add more functionality to JSP, such as finding or instantiating (creating) a JavaBean for use later. You see one example of an action tag in line 12 of the code in Listing 1-1.
- **Directive:** A message to the Web container describing page properties, specifying tag libraries, or substituting text or code at translation time. The form is `<%@ the directive %>`. Listing 1-1 has directives on lines 1, 3, and 5.
- **Declaration:** Declares one or more Java variables or methods that you can use later in your page. The tag has this form `<%! declaration %>`.
- **Expression:** Defines a Java expression that is evaluated to a `String`. Its form is `<%= expression %>`.
- **Scriptlet:** Inserts Java code into the page to perform some function not available with the other tag elements. Its form is `<% java code %>`.
- **Comment:** A brief explanation of a line or lines of code by the developer. Comments have the form `<%-- the comment --%>`. Lines 2 and 4 in Listing 1-1 are examples of comments.

Because a JSP file is just a text file, you can create it in just about any kind of text editor. Note that some editors understand JSP syntax and can provide nice features such as formatting and color coding. A few of the bigger ones are Macromedia Dreamweaver (www.macromedia.com/software/dreamweaver/), NetBeans (www.netbeans.org), and Eclipse (www.eclipse.org); the last two are complete Java development environments.

Like Java Servlets, JSP pages must be run in a Web container that provides support for JSP technology, as we explained in the preceding section, "Using Java Servlets."

Using JavaBeans

When you program in Java, you define or use classes that function as a template for objects that you create. A *JavaBean* is a special form of Java class that follows certain rules, including the methods it uses and its naming conventions.

Beans are so useful because they are portable, reusable, and platform independent. Beans are *components* because they function as small, independent programs. JavaBeans *component architecture* defines how Beans are constructed and how they interact with the program in which they are used.

Scope

Scope refers to an area in which an object (such as a Bean or any Java class) can be stored. Scopes differ based on the length of time stored objects are available for reference, as well as where the objects can be referenced from.

In JSP and Struts, scope can be one of four values:

- **Page:** Objects in the page scope are available only while the page is responding to the current request. After control leaves the current page, all objects stored in the page scope are destroyed.
- **Request:** Objects in the request scope are available as long as the current request is being serviced. A request can be serviced from more than one page.
- **Session:** The objects in the session scope last as long as the session exists. This could be until the user logs out and the session is destroyed or until the session times out due to inactivity. Each client using the Web application has a unique session.
- **Application:** The longest lasting scope is the application scope. As long as the application is running, the objects exist. Furthermore, objects in the application scope are available to all clients using the application.

You can call a JavaBean a Bean and everyone will know what you're talking about, as long as you're not discussing coffee.

The JavaBean documentation refers to the rules as *design patterns*. However, this term is more generally used to refer to design patterns such as the Model-View-Controller design pattern. *Naming conventions* is a more appropriate term.

As an example of the special Bean rules, let's look at properties. A Bean's properties that are exposed (public) are available only through the getter and setter methods, because the actual property definition is typically private (available to only the defining class). The properties follow the naming convention that the first letter of the property must be lowercase and any subsequent word in the name should start with a capital letter, such as `mailingAddress`. (We explain getters and setters after Listing 1-2.) Listing 1-2 is an example of a simple Bean.

Listing 1-2 Example of a Simple JavaBean

```
public class SimpleBean implements java.io.Serializable
{
    private String name;

    // public no-parameter constructor
    public SimpleBean()
```

```
    {
    }
    // getter method for name property
    public String getName()
    {
        return name;
    }
    // setter method for name property
    public void setName(String aName)
    {
        name = aName;
    }
}
```

In this example, `String` is the type of property and `name` is the property.

Methods that access or set a property are *public* (available to anyone using the Bean) and also use a certain naming convention. You name these methods as follows:

- To get a property's value, the method must begin with `get` followed by the property name with the first letter capitalized, as in `public String getName();`.These methods are called *getters*.
- To set a property's value, the method must begin with `set` followed by the property name with the first letter capitalized and the value to set the property to, as in `public void setName(String theName);`. These methods are called *setters*.

You should also be familiar with special naming conventions for Boolean and indexed properties. Many additional requirements exist, but they are less important for our situation. See `java.sun.com/docs/books/tutorial/javabeans/index.html` for more information on JavaBean requirements.

You should follow the JavaBean conventions when creating Beans to ensure that the user of the Bean knows how to get information in and out of the component. Classes that use the Beans know that if it's really a Bean, it follows the proper conventions; therefore, the class can easily discover the properties, methods, and events that make up the Bean.

In Struts, you commonly use Beans in Web applications and specifically in a more restricted manner than in the component architecture we just described. You use Beans more often as temporary holding containers for data. For example, suppose that a user requests to see a purchase order. The Web application then does the following:

1. Retrieves a copy of the requested purchase order information from the backend database

2. Builds a `PurchaseOrder` Bean
3. Populates the Bean with the retrieved data
4. Uses the Bean in the JSP page to display the data.

Because the Web application has transferred the data from the backend database to the Web page or for access by the business logic, the Bean is called a *Data Transfer Object* (DTO). A DTO is a design pattern.

Understanding the Model-View-Controller Design Pattern

Although Struts is not a complete application, it can be customized through extension to satisfy your programming needs. By using Struts, you can save hundreds, if not thousands, of hours of programming time and be confident that the underlying foundation is efficient, robust, and pretty much bug-free. When implemented properly, Struts is definitely a boon.

An *application framework* is a skeleton of an application that can be customized by the application developer. Struts is an application framework that unifies the interaction of the various components of a J2EE Web application — namely Servlets, JSP pages, JavaBeans, and business logic — into one consistent whole. Struts provides this unification by implementing the Model-View-Controller (MVC) design pattern. Struts provides an implementation of the MVC design pattern for Web applications. To understand why this is so important, you need to see why MVC is such a useful architecture when dealing with user interactions.

The MVC pattern is the grand-daddy of object-orientated design patterns. Originally used to build user interfaces (UI) in Smalltalk-80, an early object-oriented programming system, it has proved useful everywhere UI's are present. The MVC pattern separates responsibilities into three layers of functionality:

- **Model:** The data and business logic
- **View:** The presentation
- **Controller:** The flow control

Each of these layers is loosely coupled to provide maximum flexibility with minimum effect on the other layers.

What is a design pattern?

The expression "Don't reinvent the wheel" means that you shouldn't try to solve a common problem that many bright people have already faced and solved in a clever and elegant way. For many years, other disciplines (for example, architecture) have recognized that repeating patterns of solutions exist for common problems. In 1995, an often-quoted book called *Design Patterns: Elements of Reusable Object-Oriented Software* by Gamma, Helm, Johnson, and Vlissides (published by Addison-Wesley Publishing Co.) used the same technique to formalize problem-solving patterns in the field of object-orientated design.

A *design pattern* is a blueprint for constructing a time-tested solution to a given problem. It's not a concrete implementation; rather, it's a high-level design of how to solve a problem. Because design patterns are more general than concrete implementations, they are consequently more useful because they have broader applications.

The MVC design pattern

In the MVC design pattern, the Model provides access to the necessary business data as well as the business logic needed to manipulate that data. The Model typically has some means to interact with persistent storage — such as a database — to retrieve, add, and update the data.

The View is responsible for displaying data from the Model to the user. This layer also sends user data to the Controller. In the case of a Web application, this means that both the request and the response are in the domain of the View.

The Controller handles all requests from the user and selects the view to return. When the Controller receives a request, the Controller forwards the request to the appropriate *handler,* which interprets what action to take based on the request. The Controller calls on the Model to perform the desired function. After the Model has performed the function, the Controller selects the View to send back to the user based on the state of the Model's data.

Figure 1-2 shows the relationships among the three layers.

To get an idea of why the MVC pattern is so useful, imagine a Web application without it. Our fictional application consists of just JSP pages, with no Servlets. All the business logic necessary to service a user's request and present the user with the desired results is in those JSP pages. Although this scheme is simpler than an implementation using MVC, it is also difficult to work with for anything but the most trivial application, due to the intermixing of Model, View, and Controller elements.

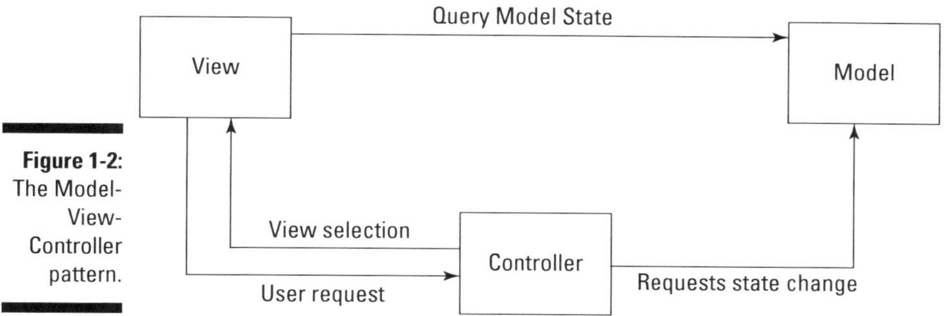

Figure 1-2: The Model-View-Controller pattern.

To illustrate the difference between Web applications that don't use MVC and those that do, think about the difference between Rocky Road and Neapolitan ice cream. Both may be delicious, but if you want to make any changes to Rocky Road, think about how much trouble it would be to switch the almonds for walnuts. The almonds are too deeply embedded in the ice cream to do the switch without affecting everything else. On the other hand, because Neapolitan is cleanly separated into layers, switching one flavor for another is an easy task. Think of Neapolitan as MVC compliant, and Rocky Road as not.

Using the MVC pattern gives you many advantages:

- **Greater flexibility**: It's easy to add different View types (HTML, WML, XML) and interchange varying data stores of the Model because of the clear separation of layers in the pattern.
- **Best use of different skill sets:** Designers can work on the View, programmers more familiar with data access can work on the Model, and others skilled in application development can work on the Controller. Differentiation of work is easier to accomplish because the layers are distinct. Collaboration is through clearly defined interfaces.
- **Ease of maintenance:** The structure and flow of the application are clearly defined, making them easier to understand and modify. Parts are loosely coupled with each other.

How Struts enforces the MVC pattern

The architecture of Struts provides a wonderful mechanism that, when followed, ensures that the MVC pattern remains intact. Although Struts provides a concrete implementation of the Controller part of the pattern, as well as providing the connections between the Controller and Model layers and between the Controller and View layers, it doesn't insist on any particular View paradigm or require that you construct the Model in a particular way.

The Struts Controller

Although Struts does not provide or require any particular Model or View components of the MVC pattern, it does implement the Controller as well as the mechanisms that bind the three layers and allow them to communicate with each other. The primary controller class is a Java Servlet called the `ActionServlet`. This class handles all user requests for Struts-managed URLs. Using information in the configuration files, the `ActionServlet` class then gets the appropriate `RequestProcessor` class that collects the data that is part of the request and puts it into an `ActionForm`, a Bean that contains the data sent from or to the user's form. The final step of the Controller is to delegate control to the specific handler of this request type. This handler is always a subclass of the `Action` class. Figure 1-3 shows how Struts uses the MVC pattern.

The `Action` subclass is the workhorse of the Controller. It looks at the data in the user's request (now residing in an `ActionForm`) and determines what action needs to be taken. It may call on the business logic of the Model to perform the action, or it may forward the request to some other View. The business logic may include interacting with a database or objects across the network or may simply involve extracting some data from an existing JavaBean.

After the necessary action has been performed, the `Action` subclass then chooses the correct View to send back to the user. The View is determined by the current state of the Model's data (the model state) and the specifications you defined in the Struts configuration file. (For an explanation of the configuration file, see the "The Struts configuration file" section later in this chapter). Figure 1-4 shows the principal classes of the Struts Controller.

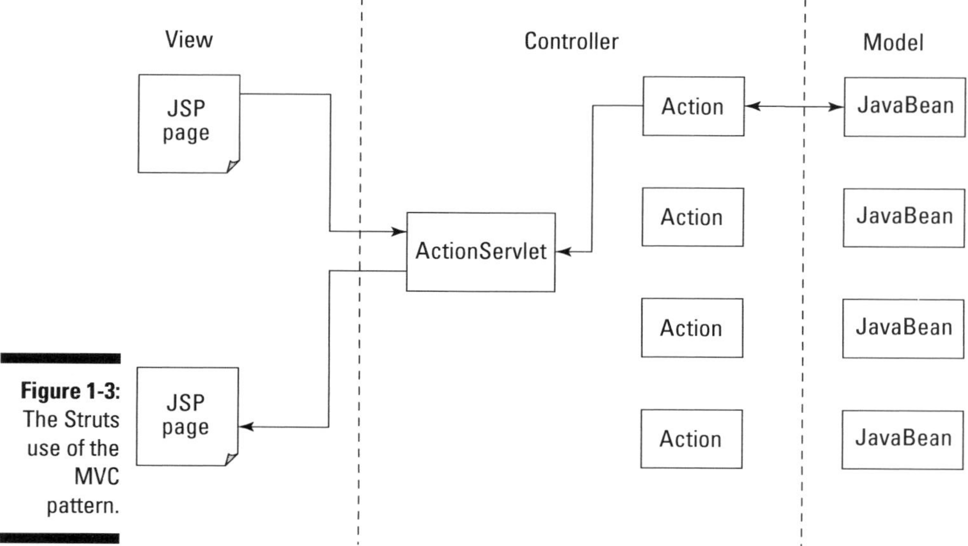

Figure 1-3: The Struts use of the MVC pattern.

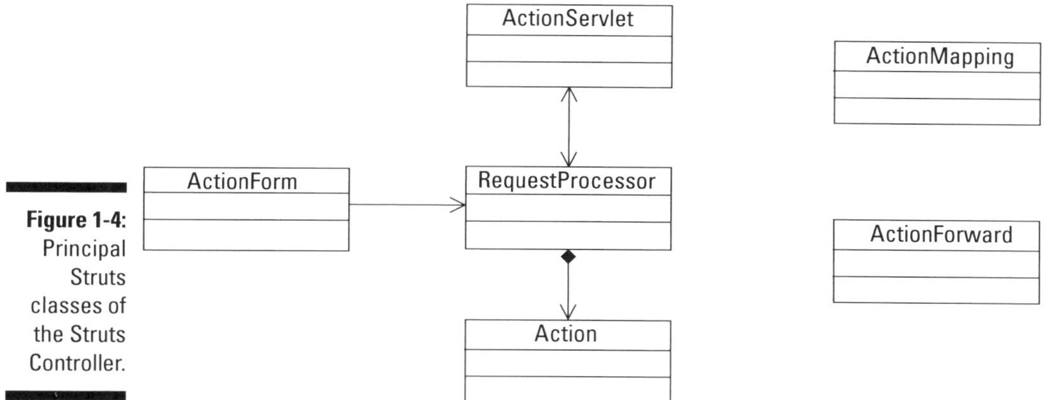

Figure 1-4: Principal Struts classes of the Struts Controller.

The Struts View

As mentioned, Struts does not provide, nor is it dependent on, a specific presentation technology. Many Struts applications use JSP (JavaServer Pages) along with the Struts tag library (Struts and Struts-EL), JSTL (JSP Standard Tag Library), and JSF (Java Server Faces). Some other possibilities are

- Apache Cocoon (`cocoon.apache.org/`)
- Jakarta Velocity templates (`jakarta.apache.org/velocity/index.html`)
- XSLT (eXtensible Stylesheet Language Transformation) (`www.w3.org/TR/xslt`)

The JSP specification provides for the creation of HTML-like tags that extend the functionality of JSP. These custom tags are bundled by their creators into *custom tag libraries* and are accompanied by a descriptor file called a *Tag Library Descriptor* (tld). The Struts and Struts-EL tag libraries are examples of this extended functionality.

Our examples throughout the book use JSP along with Struts-EL, JSTL, and other tag libraries. (For more on tag libraries, see Chapter 10.)

For new projects, the recommendation from the Struts Web site is to use *not* the standard Struts tag libraries, but instead the Struts-EL tag library along with JSTL. The Struts-EL tags library is really a reimplementation of the standard Struts tag library to make it compatible with JSTL's method of evaluating values. However, when a JSTL tag implemented the same functionality, the Struts tag was not reimplemented in the Struts-EL library. See `jakarta.apache.org/struts/faqs/struts-el.html` for full details on the Struts-EL tag library.

The Struts Model

Nothing in Struts dictates how to construct the Model. However, the best practice is to encapsulate the business data and operations on that data into JavaBeans, as we described previously when discussing Data Transfer Objects (in the "Using JavaBeans" section). The data and operations may reside in the same class or in different classes, depending on your application.

The operations represent the business logic that your application is defining. Operations may be the rules that should operate on a particular business entity. For example, if you're writing a purchasing system, part of the business data might be an entity called a Purchase Order. You may encapsulate this data into a class called `PurchaseOrder` as a way of representing the Purchase Order entity. Furthermore, you may choose to place your business rules directly into this class, or you may choose to put the rules into a different class.

The connection between the Controller and Model rests in the code that you write in the `Action` subclasses. The `Action` subclasses contain the analysis of the user's request that determines the interaction (if any) with the Model. Some examples of that interaction are

- Creating a JavaBean (like the `PurchaseOrder` class example above) that in turn accesses a database to populate itself and then makes it available to subsequent Views.
- Referencing a business logic object and asking it to perform some operation based on incoming data from the user.

The `Action` subclass initiates any action required to handle a user's request, thereby creating the connection with the Model.

When formulating a response, the Controller may pass some or all of the Model data to the View through the use of the `ActionForm` Bean. Although this Bean is a data container, it should not be considered part of the Model but rather just a transport mechanism between the Model and the View. Just as often, the View may directly reference the Model's data by referencing one or more of the Beans that belong to the Model.

The standard MVC pattern describes an interaction between the Model and the View so that when the Model's data changes, it can immediately *push* those changes out to the View so the user sees them. However, this is more difficult to achieve in the Web application architecture. Consequently, the View is commonly updated by the user requesting it.

The Struts configuration file

The Struts configuration file performs an important role in structuring your Struts application. Although it is not really part of the Model, View, or Controller, it does affect the functioning of the three layers. The configuration file allows you to define exactly which of your `Action` subclasses should be used under what circumstances and which `ActionForm` should be given to that `Action` subclass. So you specify part of the Controller interaction in the configuration file.

In addition, when the Controller decides which View to return to the user, it chooses the particular View according to specifications in the configuration file. Thus the configuration file actually defines many of the connections between the MVC components. The beauty of the configuration file is that you can change the connections *without* having to modify your code. The configuration file does much more than defining connections, which is why we devote all of Chapter 7 to the configuration file.

Chapter 2

Laying the Groundwork

In This Chapter

- Installing Java
- Installing the Web container
- Choosing a development environment
- Installing Eclipse
- Getting the Tomcat Launcher
- Installing Jakarta Struts
- Testing your application

In this chapter, we explain all the necessary preparations to actually start using Struts. We also specify what you need to do to create the sample Struts application that we introduce in Chapter 3.

To get ready to use Struts, you need to gather several tools, install them, and make sure they're in working order.

You must download and install five items to follow the examples in the book. Each one is free and open source:

- **The Java environment**: Used for development and running the Web container.
- **The Web container application:** We use Jakarta Tomcat because it's the reference implementation for the JSP and Servlet specification, as we explain in Chapter 1.
- **A Java integrated development environment (IDE):** We chose Eclipse, the popular open-source IDE. Eclipse is a fine tool with plenty of features to help the programmer.
- **A plug-in for the IDE:** We use Sysdeo Eclipse Tomcat Launcher to assist in running applications in Tomcat.
- **The Struts framework:** What this entire book is about!

Getting Java

The first step in preparing to use Struts is to ensure that you have an up-to-date version of Java. This is a primary consideration: All your work in Struts depends on having the proper version of Java.

If you already installed a recent version (1.3 or later) of the Java Standard Edition SDK (Software Development Kit), you can skip this step and jump ahead to the next section, "Getting the Web Container." Note that we said SDK, not JRE (Java Runtime Environment). Tomcat, the Web container, requires the compiler in the SDK version to compile the JSP pages.

Downloading and installing Java

Before installing a recent version of Java, you need to uninstall any previous versions. You need at least 120MB of disk space to install the SDK. Windows 2000 or XP users must have administrator privileges to perform the installation.

The exact steps to download and install Java depend on your operating system. To download and install Java in a Windows environment, follow these steps:

1. **Go to** `java.sun.com/j2se/downloads.html`.
2. **Click the link for the latest SDK version of J2SE (1.4.2 as of this writing).**

   The Download page for the version you chose appears, as shown in Figure 2-1.

   You can download many things from this page. The only one you need for this book is the one labeled `Download J2SE v 1.4.2_03`. Ignore the others and choose the SDK for your operating system.
3. **Click the Download link for your operating system.**

   The License Agreement appears.
4. **Read the License Agreement. Scroll down to the bottom and click Accept.**

   The Java installation file link appears.
5. **Click the Java installation file link.**

   The File Download dialog box appears.
6. **Click Save.**

   The Save As dialog box appears.

Release Notes	VIEW	
License	VIEW	
Download J2SE v 1.4.2_03	**JRE**	**SDK**
32-bit/64-bit for Windows/Linux/Solaris SPARC 32-bit for Solaris x86	DOWNLOAD	DOWNLOAD
Installation Instructions	VIEW	VIEW
Third Party License Readme	VIEW	VIEW
ReadMe	VIEW	VIEW
Release Notes	VIEW	VIEW
License for all platforms	VIEW	VIEW
J2SE v 1.4.2 Documentation		
J2SE 1.4.2 Documentation	DOWNLOAD VIEW	
Installation Instructions for Documentation	VIEW	
License	VIEW	
Solaris OS Patches	**Solaris SPARC**	**Solaris x86**
Patches	DOWNLOAD	DOWNLOAD
Other Downloads		
Java Cryptography Extension (JCE) Unlimited Strength Jurisdiction Policy Files	DOWNLOAD	

Figure 2-1: The Download page for J2SE.

7. **Choose a location for the installation file and then click Save.**

   Jot down the location — you'll need it later.

8. **When the download is complete, locate and double-click the installation file.**

   The InstallShield Wizard opens.

9. **Follow the instructions in the InstallShield Wizard to install Java Standard Edition SDK.**

To test your installation, display a command prompt as follow. In Windows, choose Start➪(All) Programs➪Accessories➪Command Prompt. Type the following command:

```
java -version
```

Java responds with the version information about the SDK you just installed, as shown in Figure 2-2.

When installing the Java SDK, two JREs are installed by default. One JRE is in the home directory of the SDK and is considered private. The other JRE is generally installed in the Program Files directory of the system volume. This second JRE is considered the public JRE.

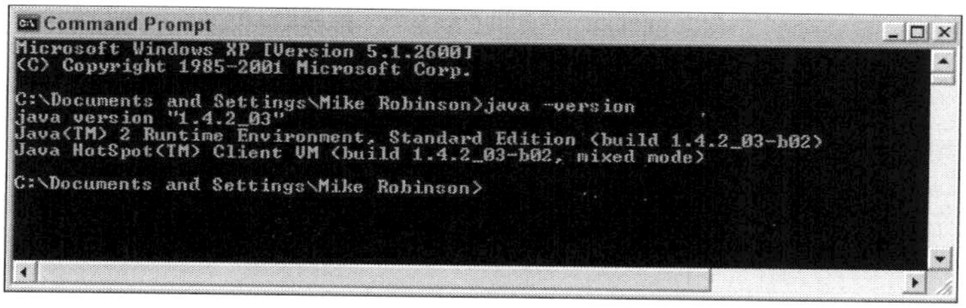

```
Command Prompt
Microsoft Windows XP [Version 5.1.2600]
(C) Copyright 1985-2001 Microsoft Corp.

C:\Documents and Settings\Mike Robinson>java -version
java version "1.4.2_03"
Java(TM) 2 Runtime Environment, Standard Edition (build 1.4.2_03-b02)
Java HotSpot(TM) Client VM (build 1.4.2_03-b02, mixed mode)

C:\Documents and Settings\Mike Robinson>
```

Figure 2-2: Testing your J2SE installation.

Setting the Java Home environment variable

If you want to follow our examples by using Tomcat as the Web container, you also need to set an environment variable so that Tomcat can find and use the Java environment. This variable is `JAVA_HOME`, and you set it to the installed location of the SDK.

The procedure for setting this variable depends on your operating system. To set this variable in Windows 2000 and XP, follow these steps:

1. **Choose Start⇨Control Panel.**

   If you're using the Classic theme, choose Start⇨Settings⇨Control Panel.
2. **Double-click the System icon.**
3. **Click the Advanced tab.**
4. **Click the Environment Variables button.**
5. **In the System Variables section, click the New button.**

   The Edit System Variable dialog box appears.
6. **In the Variable Name text box, type** JAVA_HOME.
7. **In the Variable Value text box, type the full path to the installation folder, as shown in Figure 2-3.**
8. **Click OK three times to close all the dialog boxes and the Control Panel.**

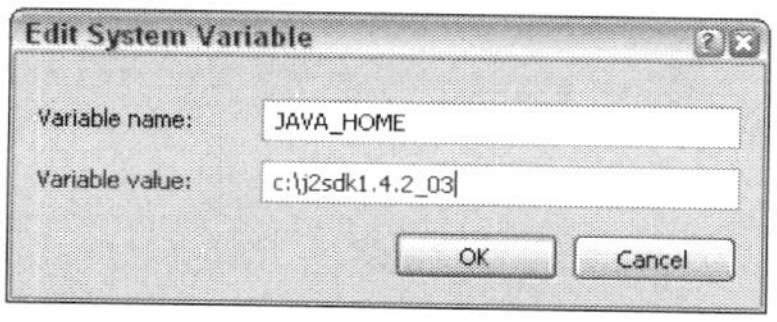

Edit System Variable
Variable name: JAVA_HOME
Variable value: c:\j2sdk1.4.2_03
OK Cancel

Figure 2-3: Setting the JAVA_HOME environmental variable.

Getting the Web Container

For the examples of Web applications in this book, we assume that you're using the Tomcat Web container, version 4.1.*x*. Of course, you can choose whatever container you please, as long as it supports the Servlet 2.3 and JSP 1.2 specifications.

Downloading Tomcat to Windows

To download Tomcat to Windows NT, 2000, or XP, follow these steps:

1. **Go to** `jakarta.apache.org/tomcat/index.html`**.**
2. **In the Downloads menu on the left, click the Binaries link.**

   The Binary Downloads page appears.
3. **Scroll down (quite a bit) until you see the Tomcat 4.1.29 KEYS link.**

   Tomcat 4.1.29 is the latest version as of this writing.

   Each Tomcat link includes KEYS and PGP links. Each binary version of Tomcat (in fact, all Jakarta project binaries) is digitally signed by the developers. To verify that the binary version you download is intact, you download the public KEY. Then you use the public domain PGP program to check the key against the PGP signature. To see how to do this, take a look at `www.apacheweek.com/issues/01-06-01`. You can verify Tomcat if you want, or you can simply download Tomcat without verification.
4. **Click one of the links below the Tomcat 4.1.29 KEYS link.**

   We suggest choosing the Tomcat 4.1.29.exe link instead of the 4.1.29.zip link because the `.exe` file automatically installs shortcuts for starting and stopping Tomcat. The File Download dialog box appears.
5. **Click the Save button.**

   The Save As dialog box opens.
6. **Choose a location for the file and then click Save.**

   Remember where you put the downloaded file.

Installing Tomcat under Windows

After you download the Tomcat installation file, you need to install Tomcat. The instructions vary according to your operating system. Here we provide instructions for Windows. After these steps, we refer you to online resources that provide installation instructions for Linux and Mac OS.

To install Tomcat under Windows, follow these steps:

1. **Double-click the installation file.**

   A dialog box appears, explaining that Tomcat has found your Java installation.

2. **Click OK.**

   The License Agreement opens.

3. **Read the License Agreement and then click the I Agree button.**

   The Installation Options dialog box appears, shown in Figure 2-4.

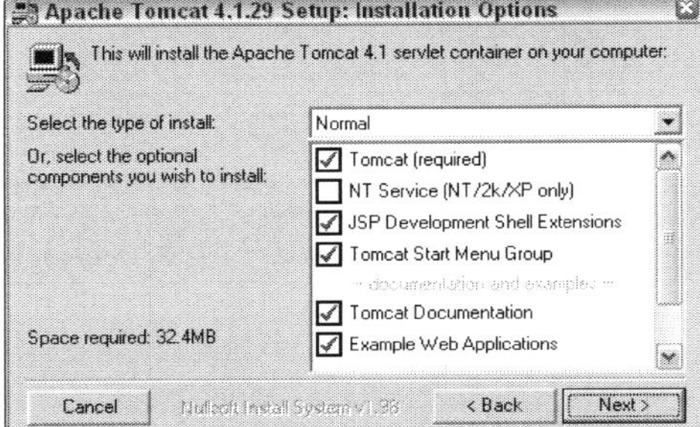

Figure 2-4: The Installation Options dialog box.

4. **Keep the default installation values and then click Next.**

   The Installation Directory dialog box appears.

5. **Change the path so that Tomcat is in the root of the drive and rename the folder by replacing the blank space between *Tomcat* and *4.1* with a hyphen or an underscore, as shown in Figure 2-5.**

   Sometimes we experience problems with DOS commands when the path name contains blank spaces; eliminating blank spaces reduces the chance for problems later.

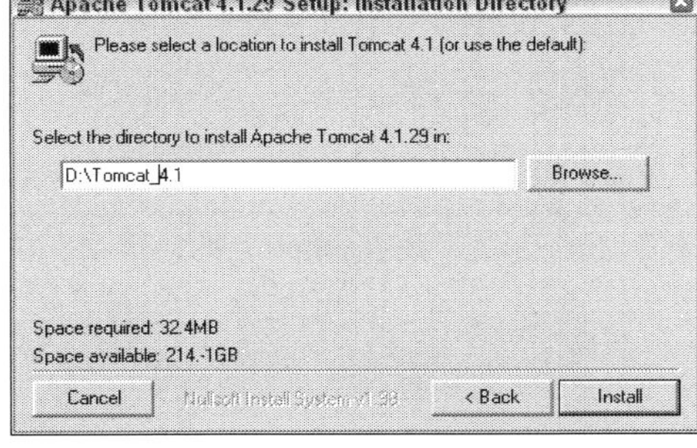

Figure 2-5: Setting the installation directory.

6. **Click the Install button.**

   The Installer puts the files into the location you specified. Then the Testing Installer Options dialog box appears.

7. **If you don't have a Web server program installed and running, change the port from 8080 to 80.**

   If you already have a Web server such as Apache or IIS, just leave the port number at 8080.

   The standard Web server port is 80 and consequently does not need to be specified in the browser URL. If you leave the port at 8080, remember that all requests to Tomcat must specify port 8080. For example, you need to enter `http://localhost:8080/index.jsp` instead of `http://localhost/index.jsp` to display the index.jsp page in your browser.

8. **In the Password text box, type a password and then click Next.**

   The Setup program completes the Tomcat installation.

9. **Click Close.**

Congratulations! You successfully installed Tomcat.

Installing Tomcat under Linux or Mac OS X

If you need to install Tomcat on Linux, refer to the instructions at the following:

```
www.cymulacrum.net/tomcat/tomcat_install.html#2
```

Be sure to download the full Tomcat, not just the LE (Lite) version.

Installing Tomcat on OS X is a snap. Refer to the documentation on the Apple Developers site at `developer.apple.com/internet/java/tomcat1.html`.

Port numbers

Ports are numbered network connectors that a computer uses to communicate using the Internet's Transmission Control Protocol (TCP). Generally, port numbers 0 through 1023 are reserved for well-known functions such as ftp or telnet.

For Web applications, remember that port 80 is reserved for HTTP protocol (Web server) communications.

Ports from 1024 through 49151 are registered ports. This means those port numbers must be registered with Internet Corporation for Assigned Names and Numbers (ICANN), much like domain names must be registered. Port 8080 is registered for use for the Tomcat Web server application.

Port numbers from 49152 through 65535 can be used by anybody for any reason.

Starting and testing Tomcat

After you install Tomcat, you should start it and test it. To start Tomcat, choose Start➪(All) Programs➪Apache Tomcat 4.1➪Start Tomcat. The Start Tomcat screen appears, as shown in Figure 2-6.

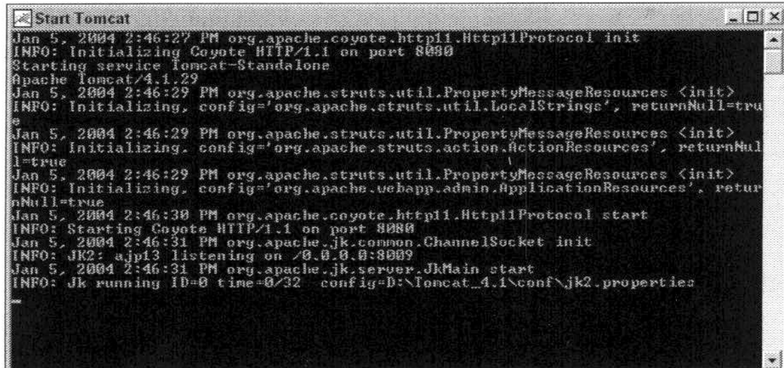

Figure 2-6: The Start Tomcat screen.

To test that Tomcat is running, open your favorite browser and type the following URL:

```
http://localhost
```

If you see the page shown in Figure 2-7, Tomcat is installed and running properly.

If the Tomcat home page does not appear, you probably didn't change the port to 80 in Step 7 in the "Installing Tomcat under Windows" section. To change the port, follow these steps:

1. **Navigate to tomcat-4.1\conf\server.xml.**
2. **Open the** `server.xml` **file with a text editor, such as Notepad.**
3. **Use the Find function (in Notepad, choose Edit➪Find) to find 8080.**
4. **Click Find Next to find the next instance of 8080.**

   You see the statement `port="8080"`.
5. **Change 8080 to 80.**
6. **Save and close the** `server.xml` **file.**
7. **Restart the Tomcat server.**
8. **Try typing** http://localhost **in your browser again.**

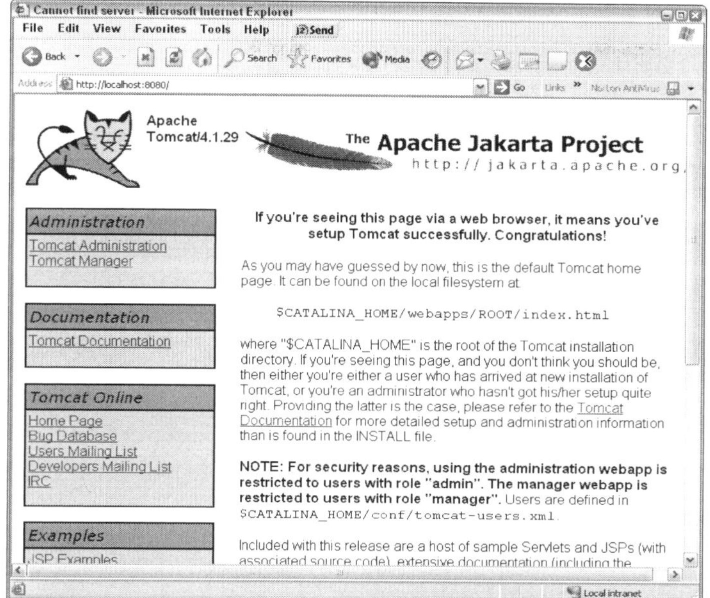

Figure 2-7: The default Tomcat home page.

Choosing Your Development Environment

An integrated development environment (IDE) is a tool for writing and editing programming code. However, choosing an IDE is up to you. Some people are minimalists and prefer to simply use a good editor. Others like to have everything built into their development environment. You can find tools out there for every taste and budget.

We like Eclipse (`www.eclipse.org`). Although Eclipse is definitely not for the minimalists, it's not bloated with tons of features you never use. Eclipse has all the necessities you might want in a development environment, including a great editor, compiler, and debugger. Support for building and deploying applications is built-in with the Ant program.

Ant is a Java-based build tool that makes building and deploying applications a one-step process. If you're not familiar with Ant, see `ant.apache.org`. Like Struts, Ant is an Apache open-source project.

And if Eclipse doesn't offer all the functionality you want or need, chances are someone has written a plug-in that does. (A *plug-in* is a program that provides additional functionality and plugs in to the main application.) You can find plug-ins that manage a Tomcat environment, interface with your favorite source-code control program, or offer any of a hundred other actions that extend Eclipse. Oh, and did we mention that Eclipse is an open-source project? There's no charge for it or most of its plug-ins.

If you already have a favorite tool and it satisfies your requirements, you shouldn't change it. If you do want to try something else but Eclipse is not for you, try one of the dozens of Java IDEs available. Some are free and all are easy to find on the Internet. Here are a few of the more popular ones:

- **Borland JBuilder:** Borland offers Enterprise, Professional, and Personal versions of JBuilder. The Personal version is free. Go to `www.borland.com/jbuilder/index.html`.
- **IBM WebSphere Studio:** Built on Eclipse technology, WebSphere Studio expands functionality by combining enterprise-level project management, advanced Java development, visual editors, Web infrastructure management, and support for Web services. Visit `www-3.ibm.com/software/info1/websphere/index.jsp`.
- **IntelliJ IDEA:** This IDE, at `www.intellij.com/idea`, has received a lot of good reviews from developers around the world, so don't ignore it when researching your choices.
- **NetBeans:** Released into open-source in July of 2000 by Sun Microsystems, NetBeans at `www.netbeans.org`, is full-featured and used by many developers.

Downloading and Installing Eclipse

To download Eclipse, follow these steps:

1. **Go to `www.eclipse.org/downloads/index.php`.**
2. **To find the proper download server, click the link for your part of the world.**
3. **Click the link for the version of Eclipse you want to download.**

   The current production version as of this writing is 2.1.2. You see the page for the version you chose.
4. **Click the HTTP or FTP link (you can download using either method) for your operating system and follow the instructions to complete the download.**

If you use plug-ins, be careful about upgrading to the latest and greatest version of Eclipse. Developers sometimes don't update their plug-ins to run with the latest Eclipse version for weeks or months after the version release date.

To install Eclipse, use a decompression program such as WinZip to extract the `eclipse-SDK-2.1.2-win32.zip` file directly to a root of a drive (for example, C:\). An Eclipse folder structure is created automatically. (Don't worry — all those files don't go into your root!)

To run Eclipse, double-click the `eclipse.exe` file, which is in the Eclipse folder that the extraction creates. For further information, read the `eclipse\readme\readme_eclipse.html` file. For easy access, you probably want to create a shortcut to the `eclipse.exe` file.

Getting the Tomcat Launcher Plug-in for Eclipse

If you decide to use Eclipse, you should think about installing at least one plug-in that can help you work easily with Tomcat. The Sysdeo Eclipse Tomcat Launcher plug-in at `www.sysdeo.com/eclipse/tomcatPlugin.html` is a great addition that has the following features and benefits:

- Lets you start and stop the Tomcat Web container from Eclipse.
- Lets you register the Tomcat process with the Eclipse debugger. This is invaluable when the time comes to test your code running in Tomcat.
- Is free and open source.

You can read about the other features of the plug-in on the Web site.

Be sure to install Tomcat, as explained in the "Getting the Web Container" section, before installing this plug-in.

Downloading and installing the Tomcat Launcher plug-in

To download the Sysdeo Eclipse Tomcat Launcher, follow these steps:

1. **Go to** `www.sysdeo.com/eclipse/tomcatPlugin.html`**.**
2. **Scroll to the Download section and click the link for the version that you want to download.**

   You can download the latest version, which may be a beta version, or the latest final release. We use version 2.1.
3. **Save the** `.zip` **file in any temporary folder or directory.**
4. **Make sure Eclipse is *not* running.**

5. **Use WinZip or a similar decompression utility to decompress the `.zip` file.**

   Decompress the file into the `eclipse\plugins` folder, assuming that `eclipse` is the folder where you installed the Eclipse application.

Placing the extracted files in the `plugins` folder installs the plug-in.

Configuring the Tomcat Launcher plug-in

When you've installed the Tomcat plug-in, you can configure it.

You must install the Tomcat Web container before you can install the Tomcat plug-in.

Follow these steps to configure the Tomcat plug-in:

1. **Start Eclipse, by double-clicking the eclipse`.exe` file or the Eclipse shortcut, if you created one.**
2. **To activate the plug-in, choose Window⇨Customize Perspective from the Eclipse menu.**

   The Customize Perspective dialog box opens. Before continuing, be sure the current perspective is Java. If it is, the dialog box will have this sentence across the top — "Select the items to be displayed in the current perspective (Java)."
3. **Click the plus sign (+) next to Other, and then click the Tomcat check box to select it, as shown in Figure 2-8. Click OK to close the dialog box.**
4. **To let the plug-in know where Tomcat is installed, choose Window⇨ Preferences to open the Preferences dialog box.**

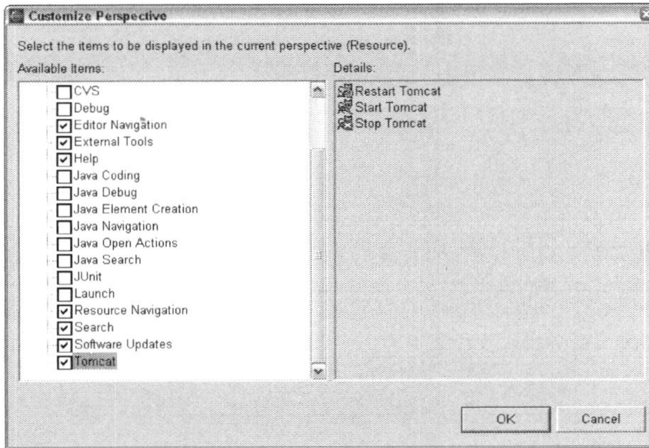

Figure 2-8: Activating the Tomcat plug-in in Eclipse.

5. **In the list on the left side of the dialog box, click the Tomcat item.**
6. **In the Tomcat Home text box, type the path to the folder where you installed Tomcat or click the Browse button to navigate to and select the folder.**
7. **At the top of the Preferences dialog box, use the Tomcat Version radio buttons to choose the version of Tomcat that you're using, as shown in Figure 2-9.**

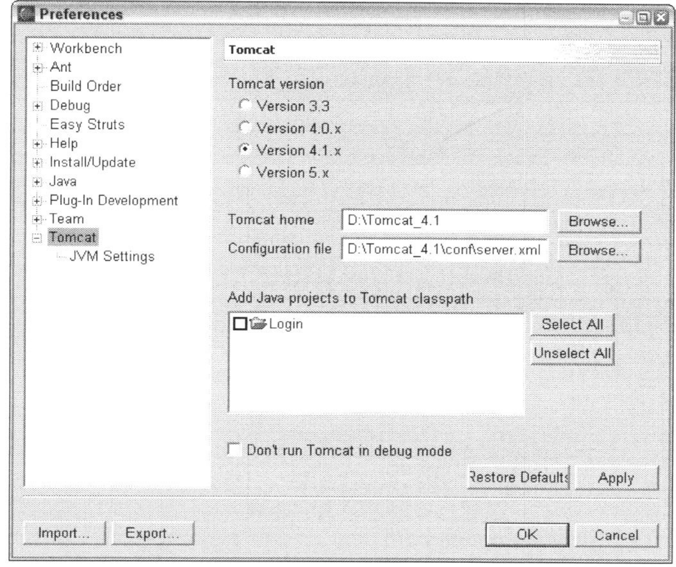

Figure 2-9: Specifying the location of the Tomcat installation.

8. **To set the SDK's JRE for Eclipse, click the plus sign (+) next to the Java item in the list on the left side of the Preferences dialog box.**
9. **Click the Installed JREs item and check the panel on the right side of the dialog box to make sure that the JRE that's selected is from the SDK.**

   You can tell whether the JRE is from the SDK because the location points to the path where the SDK was installed. (See Figure 2-10.) The plug-in launches Tomcat using the default JRE checked in the Eclipse Preferences window. Because Tomcat needs the SDK to perform properly, you need to ensure that the private JRE in the SDK is used as the Eclipse default JRE. If the JRE is not from the SDK, you need to add the private JRE to the list. To add another JRE, see the information after these steps.

10. **To make sure that the plug-in works, click the Start Tomcat button on the Eclipse toolbar.**

    You see startup messages in the Console window, as shown at the bottom of Figure 2-11.

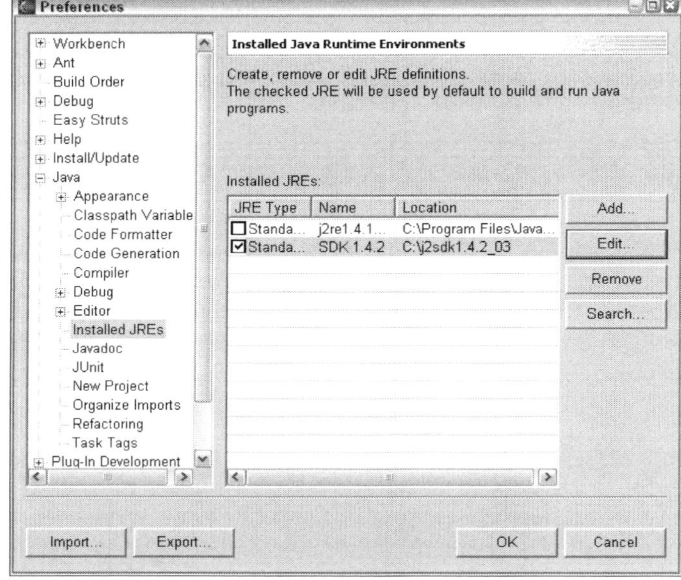

Figure 2-10: Checking to make sure that Eclipse lists your Java SDK as the default JRE.

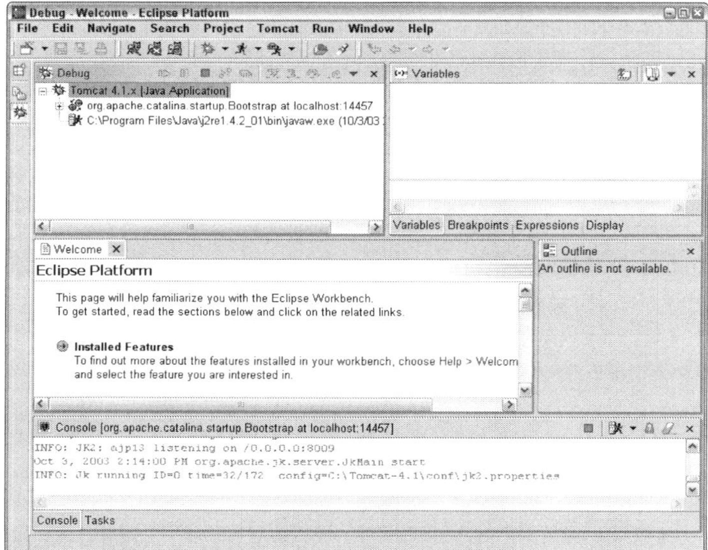

Figure 2-11: Starting Tomcat from Eclipse.

11. **To test Tomcat, open your Internet browser and type** http://localhost **in your browser's address window.**

    You see the Tomcat startup page (refer to Figure 2-6).

If the JRE you saw listed in Step 9 was not the SDK you installed, follow these steps to add another JRE to the list:

1. **In the Preferences dialog box, click the Add button.**

   The Create JRE dialog box appears.

2. **In the JRE Name text box, type a name for the new JRE, such as SDK 1.4.2.**

3. **In the JRE Home Directory text box, type the path where you installed the SDK or click the Browse button to navigate to and select the SDK directory, as shown in Figure 2-12.**

4. **Click OK to save your addition.**

5. **In the Installed JREs dialog box, click to select the box next to the JRE you just created.**

   Refer to Figure 2-10.

6. **Click OK to close the Preferences dialog box.**

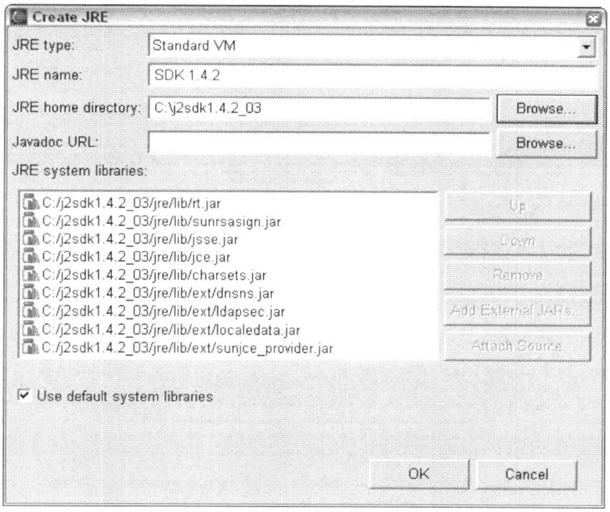

Figure 2-12: Adding a new JRE to Eclipse.

Getting Struts

When you have a fully functioning development environment as well as a ready-to-go Web container, you're ready to get Struts and set it up for use.

Getting the Struts source code

If you want the Struts source code for some reason, go to `jakarta.apache.org/struts/acquiring.html`. First click the Prerequisites link in the Acquiring Struts section to make sure that you have all the prerequisite software. Then return to the Acquiring Struts section and click the Struts Source Code Distribution link to get the source code.

No prerequisites are required for the binary version if you're using a Java JRE version 1.4 or better. If you intend to use a Java JRE version earlier than 1.4, you need to get an XML parser. Sun Microsystems provides the JXML (Java XML) reference (example) implementation at `java.sun.com/xml`, or you can get the Xerces XML parser at `xml.apache.org`.

Put the parser into the Struts/lib directory after installing Struts,. The simplest route is to use the latest version of Java (SDK 1.4.2 as of this writing), as explained in the "Downloading and installing Java" section, earlier in this chapter.

As of this writing, Struts is in release version 1.1. Although a later version might be available by the time you get around to downloading, we suggest that you use version 1.1 because this book is based on that version. After you feel comfortable with 1.1, you can easily upgrade to the latest version.

Downloading Struts

The first step in getting started with Struts is to download the code. To download Struts, follow these steps:

1. **Go to the Jakarta download area at** `jakarta.apache.org/site/binindex.cgi`.
2. **Scroll down to the Struts item.**
3. **If you're a Windows user, click the 1.1 zip link. If you use Unix, click the 1.1 tar.gz link.**

   These links are for the binary versions. For the instructions that follow, we assume that you download the binary version.

For an explanation of the KEYS and PGP links that you find on the site, see the "Downloading Tomcat to Windows" section earlier in this chapter.

Reviewing the components of Struts

Struts is not installed like a regular application — by itself, it's only a framework that forms the basis of an application. So the closest step to installing is to put the Struts components into their proper positions in the Web application directory structure. We will do this in Chapter 3 when we build our first Struts application.

When you finish downloading the Struts file, decompress it to a temporary folder. Navigate to that directory. Inside you see three files and three folders:

- `INSTALL`: This file outlines special installation notes for Web containers other than Tomcat. You can safely ignore this file if you're using the Tomcat Web container.
- `LICENSE`: This file defines the terms by which you can use this software.
- `README`: This file explains how to install Struts, step by step. You may need to refer to the `README` file if you run into any problems, but the following sections should be sufficient for most of your purposes.
- `contrib/`: This folder contains the Struts-EL tag library, which we use to build the applications in this book.
- `lib/`: This folder contains the Struts framework, all the library files needed by the framework, and the tag library definitions.
- `webapps/`: This folder contains documentation and examples of how to use the various components of Struts. The documentation and examples are in the form of `WAR` files — compressed Web applications that automatically expand when you put them into a Web container.

Libraries

The libraries we use in the examples in this book are all in the `contrib/struts-el/lib` folder rather than the `lib` directory because we use the EL version of the tag library. These are all JAR files (Java ARchive), the common way to store compressed files in Java. For more information about the EL version of the tag library, see Chapter 1.

Following are the libraries we use:

- `commons-beanutils.jar`: Provides various utilities to make working with JavaBeans easy.
- `commons-collections.jar`: Special-purpose implementations of various collections not implemented in the standard JDK.

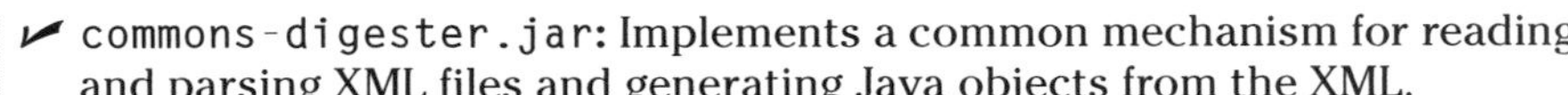

- commons-digester.jar: Implements a common mechanism for reading and parsing XML files and generating Java objects from the XML.
- commons-fileupload.jar: Implements the functionality that allows users to upload files to Web applications.
- commons-lang.jar: Provides a host of helper utilities for the java.lang API, most notably String manipulation methods, basic numerical methods, object reflection, creation and serialization, and System properties.

The acronym API stands for Application Programming Interface. The API specifies the rules by which a programmer can make requests to another application.

- commons-logging.jar: Implements the generic logging functionality to make use of various logging libraries.
- commons-validator.jar: Provides the validation mechanism to validate user input.
- jakarta-oro.jar: Implements regular expressions using the Perl5 syntax.

Perl5 is a widely used scripting language for creating Web applications. Its implementation of regular expressions is considered the de facto standard.

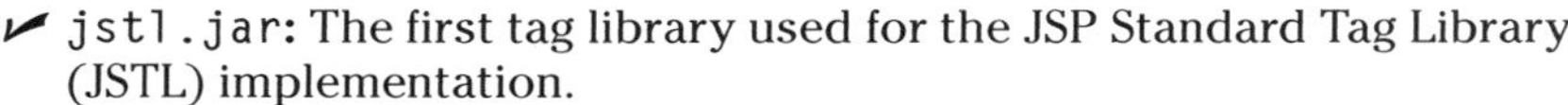

- jstl.jar: The first tag library used for the JSP Standard Tag Library (JSTL) implementation.
- standard.jar: The second tag library used for the JSTL implementation.
- struts-el.jar: Implements the standard Struts tag library using the Expression Language (EL) defined by JSTL. Only those functions from the original tag library that do not have a functional equivalent in JSTL are implemented.
- struts.jar: Contains all the classes that make up the Struts framework.
- struts-legacy.jar: Contains references to classes removed from Struts 1.1. Used for backward compatibility.

Tag Library Definition

In addition to the libraries in the preceding list, Struts has a set of standard tag libraries that it uses. These libraries are represented by files with .tld extensions. (The tld stands for Tag Library Definition.) To find more detail about tag libraries, see Chapter 10.

Documentation and examples

Struts comes with numerous Web applications that provide examples of how to use components in the Struts framework as well as documentation on

Struts. You can find these examples in the `webapps` folder. Web applications are normally packaged as WAR files (Web ARchive). A WAR file is similar to a JAR file and includes all the files that make up your Web application. The Web applications that come with a Struts distribution are

- `struts-blank.war`: A starting point to begin your own application.
- `struts-documentation.war`: A copy of all the documentation found on the Struts Web site.
- `struts-example.war`: An example application that uses most of the features found in Struts.
- `struts-exercise-taglib.war`: Test pages for the various tags of the standard Struts tag library.
- `struts-upload.war`: An example application that shows how to upload files with Struts.
- `struts-validator.war`: An example application that provides examples of how to use the Validator framework.
- `tiles-documentation.war`: Documentation on how to use tiles. For more information on tiles, see Chapter 11.

Testing Your Web Application Development Environment

Before starting to use Struts, you need to test all your tools to make sure everything works as expected. Don't skip this step: Before you create a Web application using Struts (we show you how to create one in Chapter 3), you need to be confident that Tomcat runs as you expect it to:

1. **Start Eclipse by double-clicking either the** `eclipse.exe` **file or a shortcut (if you made one).**

2. **If Tomcat is not yet started, start the Tomcat server from Eclipse by clicking the Start Tomcat button in the Eclipse toolbar.**
3. **Make sure Tomcat is running properly by using your browser to open the Tomcat Web page at** `http://localhost`.

   You should see the Tomcat startup page (refer to Figure 2-6).

   If Tomcat doesn't open properly, make sure that Tomcat was not running previously. Click the useful Restart Tomcat button on the Eclipse toolbar. Clicking this button stops Tomcat if it's currently running and then starts it again. If Tomcat is not running, clicking the button just starts it.

4. **To install your first Web application, the Struts documentation, carefully copy the** `struts-documentation.war` **file from the** `jakarta-struts-1.1\webapps` **folder to the** `Tomcat-4.1\webapps` **folder.**

   Tomcat automatically decompresses and starts the Web application. Is the Struts documentation really a Web application? Well, yes, it is. It's just not a *Struts* Web application. However, installing this application both tests that Tomcat is working properly and gives you an opportunity to look at the Struts documentation.

5. **To test that you have successfully installed the Struts documentation, type** http://localhost/struts-documentation **in your browser.**

   You see the page shown in Figure 2-13. From this page, you can find most of the documentation found at the Struts Web site.

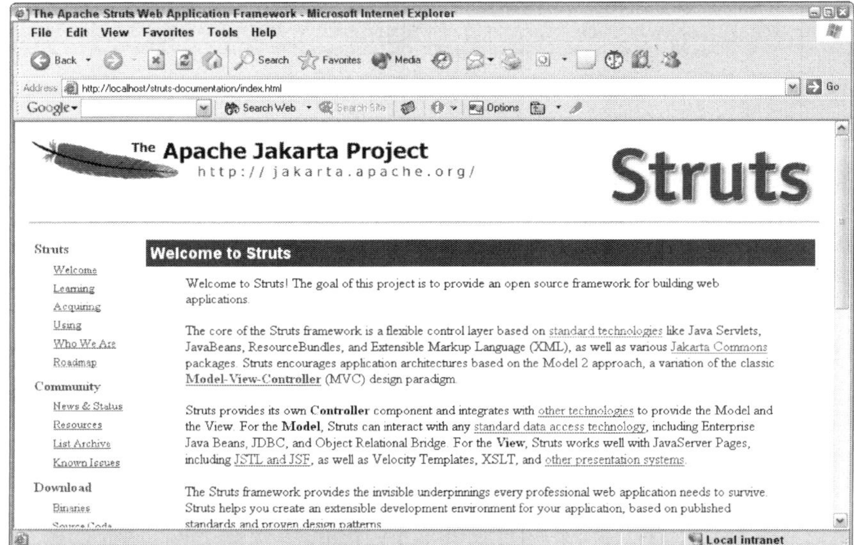

Figure 2-13: The Struts documentation page.

6. **Copy the** `struts-example.war` **file from the** `jakarta-struts-1.1\webapps` **folder to the** `Tomcat-4.1\webapps folder.`

   Tomcat automatically decompresses and starts the Web application. This Web application *is* a Struts Web application.

7. **To test the installation, type** http://localhost/struts-example **in your browser.**

This sample (shown in Figure 2-14) is an incomplete Struts application that allows users to register and maintain a set of mail servers subscriptions so they can read mail from any subscribed server. Click the A Walking Tour of the Example Application link to explore the example further.

Figure 2-14: The Struts example application page.

Now you have all of the tools you need, installed and in working order, as well as the Struts documentation available as a Web application on Tomcat. You are finally ready to create your first Web application using Struts — the topic of Chapter 3.

Chapter 3

Creating a Simple Web Application with Struts

In This Chapter

- Specifying a simple Struts application
- Creating the application structure
- Working with the JavaServer pages
- Adding the formbean
- Creating the JavaBean
- Creating an Action class
- Modifying the configuration files
- Testing the application

In this chapter, you create a simple Struts application from start to finish. This application may seem fairly trivial, but it exposes you to the major components involved in a Struts application and gives you an introduction to the interaction of these components. We assume that you understand the basics of how Struts can create simpler, more flexible, and easier to maintain Web applications. If you feel that you need a primer, see Chapter 1. We also assume that you have available a complete Web development environment on your computer. If not, see Chapter 2 for instructions.

We start by analyzing the requirements for a Log In application, and then we create the application. For each piece of the application, we show you the code and then explain the code. Because you already know Java, we emphasize the parts of the code that are specific to Struts. Finally, we provide instructions for putting the code in its proper place, so that by the end of the chapter you have a complete application.

Designing Your First Struts Application

The Login application is simple but still provides you with experience with Struts. We set certain minimum design specifications to create a Web application based on the Struts framework:

- At least one View component
- In the Controller, a subclass of at least one `Action` class that provides specific processing functionality for the application
- In the Controller, a subclass of the `ActionForm` associated with every View component that submits data
- For the Model, at least one JavaBean to represent the data presented in each View
- For the configuration files, the required updating

The Login application serves as the entry point to a more complex Music Collection application that you build in Chapter 14. By itself, the Login application does nothing of value. However, it provides with a good starting point for understanding the development of Struts applications.

The Login application could be written in a simpler way without using Struts, but that would defeat the purpose of explaining the essentials of a Struts application without a lot of complications.

Application requirements

When you design an application, you need to consider what you need to accomplish and assess the requirements. In this case, the requirements for a Login application are pretty straightforward, as follows:

- You want a Log In page that accepts a user's name and password as input.
- You want to be able to verify that name and password against a repository of name and password combinations.
- If the application can verify the user's input against the repository data, the application tells the user so by displaying a Success page.
- If the user's input is rejected, the application tells the user and asks the user to try logging in again.

Now that you have stated the requirements, you can list the steps that you need to take to fulfill the requirements of the application. These steps are as follows:

1. **The application displays the Log In page with user name and password fields.**
2. **The user types a name and password and clicks the Log In button.**
3. **The application checks the submitted values against a repository of acceptable values.**
4. **If the name and password are valid (the combination can be found in the data repository), the user is forwarded to a Log In Was Successful page and a welcome message appears containing the user's name.**
5. **If the name and password are not valid (the combination can't be found in the data repository), the Log In page is redisplayed with an appropriate error message.**

Determining which components to use

In analyzing the requirements, you see that you need not just one View but two. Each View requires a JSP page. (For more information on JSP pages in a Struts application, see "Creating JavaServer Pages" in Chapter 1.) One JSP provides the initial Log In page, and the other JSP is the Successful Log In page. The first JSP contains a form that has the username and password fields. The second JSP needs only a message indicating that the user has logged on successfully.

For the Controller, you need one specialized `Action` class to handle the request from the Log In page and one specialized `ActionForm` class to hold the request data.

The Model needs a JavaBean that serves as the data repository. The JavaBean contains a list of username and password combinations for authorized users and the methods required to operate on that list.

Finally, to make the necessary connections between the components, you need to configure and set up the `struts-config.xml` and `web.xml` files, the two principal configuration files for each Struts application,

Putting Everything in Place

Now that you know your requirements and the steps to include, you need to set up your development environment so that you can work on this project. In this example, we use Eclipse and explain step-by-step how to create the initial environment for the project. This is not intended to be a tutorial on using Eclipse; that task would require another book. However, we do point out the minimum set of Eclipse features that you need to initialize, create, build, and debug the example applications.

If you're using a different IDE, you need to take similar steps for your IDE. For more information on using various IDEs with Struts, see "Choosing Your Development Environment" in Chapter 2.

Creating the project in Eclipse

When you start to create a program, the first task is to create a *project*. Creating a project specifies the folder that contains all the files for your Web application. To create a project, follow these steps:

1. **Start Eclipse.**

   For information on starting Eclipse, see "Downloading and Installing Eclipse" in Chapter 2. If you're using a different development environment, look at the end of this section for instructions on how the final application structure should look.

2. **To set up the most appropriate display in Eclipse, choose Window➪Open Perspective➪Java.**

   Your work area now displays the JAVA perspective and should look like Figure 3-1. The Perspectives feature of Eclipse helps customize the display for your current needs. For more information, see the "Perspectives in Eclipse" sidebar.

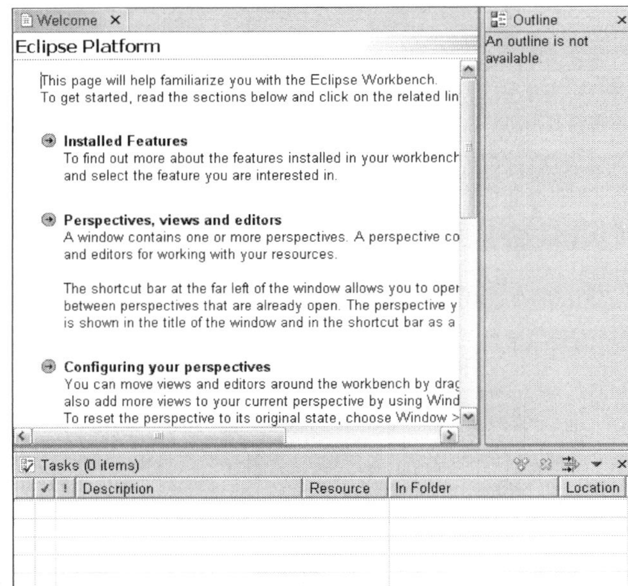

Figure 3-1: The Eclipse work area with the JAVA perspective.

Perspectives in Eclipse

Eclipse has a feature called *perspectives* that allows you to change the overall arrangement of the work area to suit your current task. For example, the Java perspective is suited for editing and compiling source files. The Java perspective displays various panes called *views* in Eclipse. Do not confuse these views with a View in the MVC design pattern. The various views show you the project file hierarchy, the source code of the file being edited, the output console, and an outline of the source file denoting all methods and fields of the current source file. The perspective can be modified to show different views depending on your current needs. Another perspective is the Debug perspective, which displays debugging information about the currently running program. This powerful feature of Eclipse helps make the developer's task easier.

3. **To create a project, choose File⇨New⇨Project.**

   The New Project dialog box appears.

4. **In the left pane, click Java from the list of Wizards. In the right pane, choose Java Project from the project list. Click Next.**

5. **In the Project Name text box, type** Login**, as shown in Figure 3-2.**

   Leave the Use Default check box selected so that the contents of the project go into the default `c:\eclipse\workspace` folder.

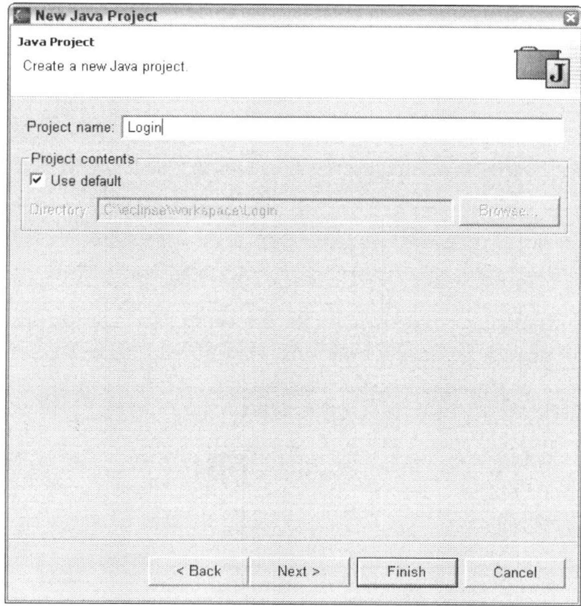

Figure 3-2: The New Java Project dialog box.

6. **Click the Finish button.**

   Now you should have a project named Login displayed in the Package Explorer view of the Eclipse window.

Setting up the application folders

Now you need to create a folder structure to hold all the files. Part of this structure is important only while you're developing your application. The other part is important when you're ready to deploy your application to the Web container.

To create the folder structure, follow these steps:

1. **To create a special folder in the project to hold your Java source files, right-click the Login project folder item in the Package Explorer view and choose New⇨Source Folder.**

   The New Source Folder dialog box opens.

2. **In the Folder Name text box, type** source **and click the Finish button.**
3. **To add a regular folder to the project, right-click the Login project folder item in the Package Explorer view and choose New⇨Folder.**

   The New Folder dialog box opens.

4. **In the Folder Name text box, type** WEB-INF **and then click the Finish button.**

   This is the folder where most of your Web application will reside. For more information about the `WEB-INF` folder and the folder structure for Web applications, see the "Web Application Folder Structure" sidebar.

5. **In the Package Explorer view, right-click the `WEB-INF` folder item and choose New⇨Folder.**
6. **In the Folder Name text box, enter** classes **and then click the Finish button.**
7. **Repeat Steps 5 and 6 to add the `lib` folder in the `WEB-INF` folder.**

   Your folder structure should now look like Figure 3-3. If you're using another IDE, create the same folder structure using the tools in your IDE.

Another entry appears in the `Login` folder: `JRE System Library`. This folder is created automatically when you create your project and contains all the Java JAR files needed for a Java project. If the JRE System Library doesn't appear, Eclipse may be filtering it from the display. See the next section on setting Eclipse filters.

Web application folder structure

A J2EE Web application has a particular folder structure. It starts with the application's folder (for example, the Login folder for the Login application) and contains at least the WEB-INF folder. The WEB-INF folder is required and must reside in the root of the Web application's folder.

The WEB-INF folder contains at least two other folders, the classes and lib folders. All Java class files that make up your application as well as any property files that the application uses reside in the classes folder. The lib folder contains all the library files, including tag libraries, which your application needs. The root level of the WEB-INF folder contains all the configuration files and tag library descriptor files.

One of the key points about the WEB-INF folder is that the Web container hides it. That means that as far as the browser is concerned, the WEB-INF folder doesn't exist. This is an important security feature.

Other folders that might be typically found in the application folder are folders for organizing other files used by the Web pages, such as images, JavaScript, CSS (cascading style sheets), and applets. All the files in these folders are typically meant to be accessible by a browser. HTML and JSP pages may or may not reside in a separate folder, depending on the number of pages that make up the application.

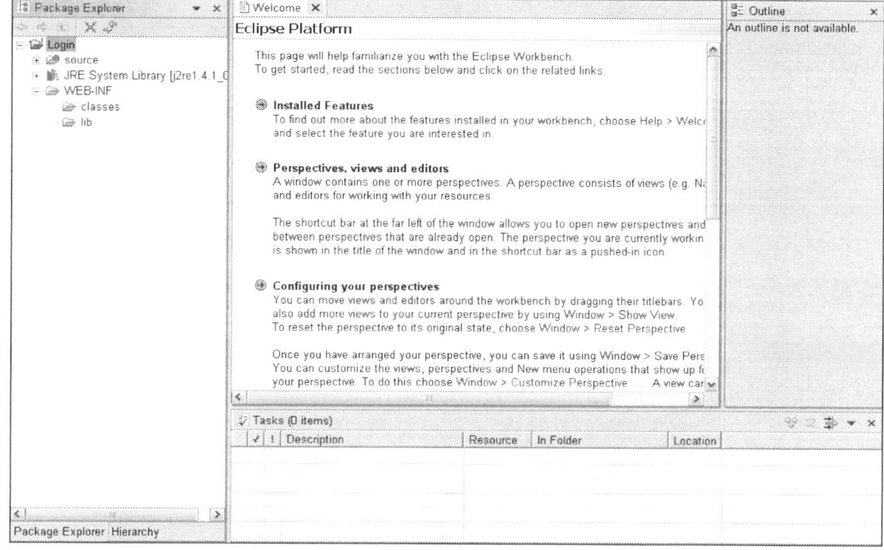

Figure 3-3: The folder structure in the Package Explorer of Eclipse.

Importing the Struts files

At this point you need to bring the Struts files into your project structure. In this phase, you do the following:

- Import all the library files into the `WEB-INF/lib` folder.
- Import the tag library description files into the `WEB-INF` folder.

You don't absolutely have to import these files, because you're going to inform Eclipse about the files in a different but related step. However, having the parts to your Web application in the proper folder structure makes it easier to deploy the application to Tomcat.

Library files

To import the library files, follow these steps:

1. **In the Package Explorer view, right-click the `WEB-INF/lib` folder and choose Import.**

   The Import dialog box opens.

2. **In the list of import sources, double-click File System.**
3. **Click the Browse button next to the From Directory text box and use the Import from Directory dialog box to navigate to and select the `jakarta-struts-1.1/contrib/struts-el/lib` folder. Click OK.**

   Your folder may be different if you downloaded the Struts files to a different location. All the `.jar` files appear in the right-hand pane of the Import dialog box.

4. **Select the check boxes of all the `.jar` files.**

   Refer to Figure 3-4. Don't forget to scroll down to display all the `.jar` files.

5. **Click Finish.**

After you've imported the library files, you can see that the Package Explorer view is cluttered with the new additions. To hide these library files from the view, click the drop-down menu at the top of the Package Explorer view and choose Filters. In the Java Element Filters dialog box (see Figure 3-5), scroll to the bottom and select the Referenced Libraries items. Click OK. This hides from view all libraries referenced by the project. The use of filters is a nice way to eliminate clutter.

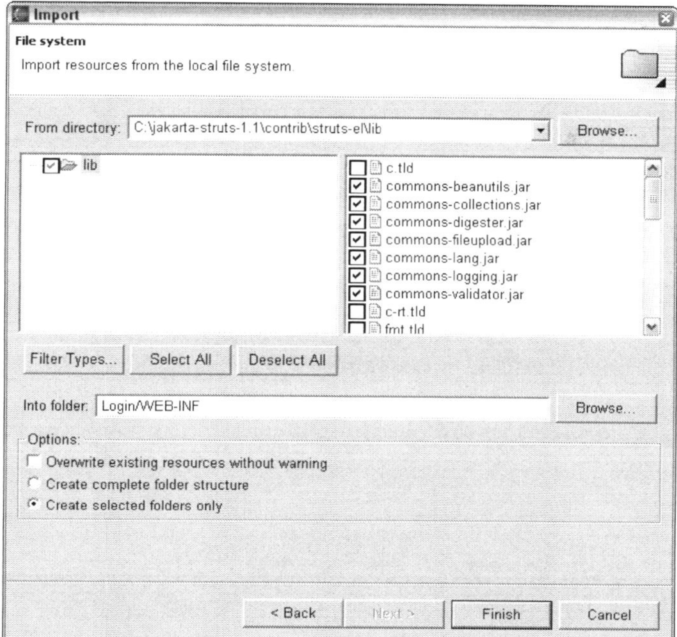

Figure 3-4: Importing the library files.

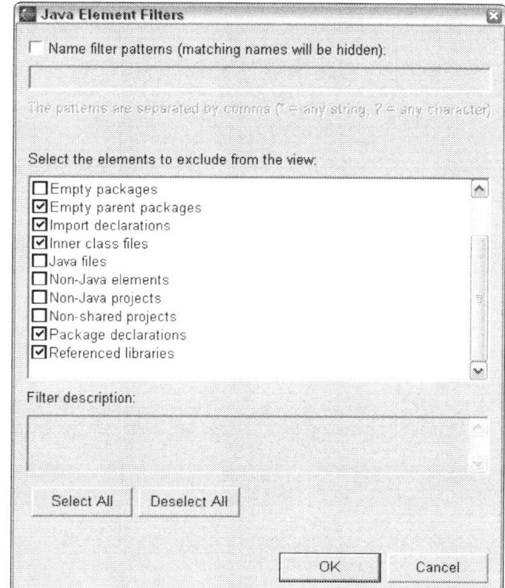

Figure 3-5: The Java Element Filters dialog box.

Tag library description files

To import the tag library description (`.tld`) files, follow these steps:

1. **In the Package Explorer view, right-click the `WEB-INF` folder and choose Import.**

   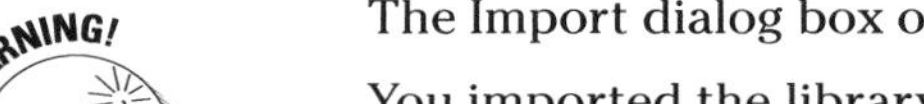

   The Import dialog box opens.

   You imported the library files into the `WEB-INF/lib` folder, but the `.tld` files go into the `WEB-INF` folder.

2. **In the list of import sources, double-click File System.**
3. **Click the Browse button next to the From Directory text box and use the Import from Directory dialog box to navigate to and select the `jakarta-struts-1.1/contrib/struts-el/lib` folder. Click OK.**

   Your folder may be different if you downloaded the Struts files to a different location. All the `.tld` files appear in the right pane of the Import dialog box.

4. **Select the check boxes of the following `.tld` files, ignoring the others because they're not needed for your project:**
   - `c.tld`
   - `fmt.tld`
   - `sql.tld`
   - `struts-bean-el.tld`
   - `struts-html-el.tld`
   - `struts-logic-el.tld`
   - `x.tld`
5. **Click Finish.**

   Your folder structure should now look like Figure 3-6.

Configuring Eclipse to use the library files

Now that you have the `.jar` files imported to Eclipse, you need to tell Eclipse how to find them for compiling. This process is equivalent to putting the files on the classpath for the application.

Classpath and Build Path refer to the same thing: the path or paths used by the application to search for certain files (generally Class files).

To tell Eclipse about the `.jar` files, follow these steps:

1. **In the Package Explorer view of Eclipse, right-click the project folder name (`Login` in our example) and choose Properties.**

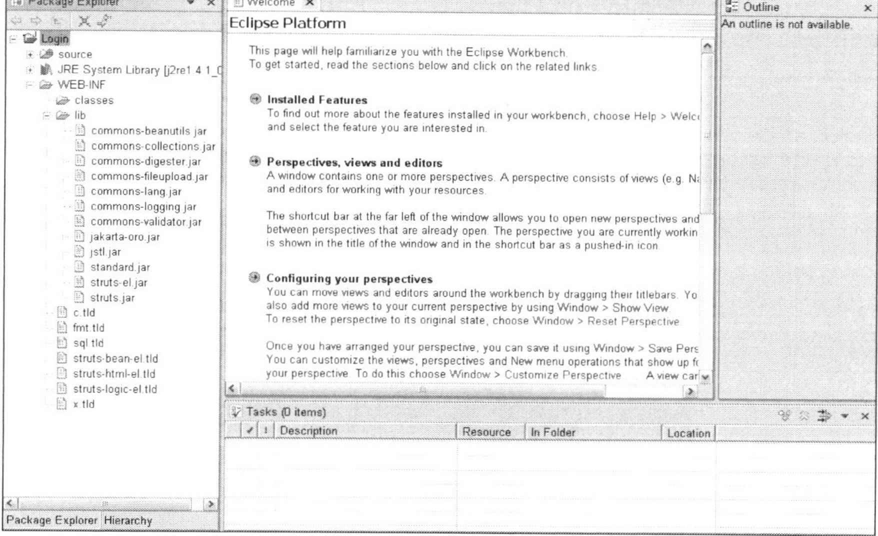

Figure 3-6: The folder structure in the Package Explorer view of Eclipse.

The Properties for Login dialog box appears. (*Login* is the name of the project in our example. If you named your project differently, the dialog box uses the name of your project.)

2. **In the list of items in the left pane, choose Java Build Path.**
3. **On the right side of the dialog box, click the Libraries tab.**

   The dialog box looks like Figure 3-7.

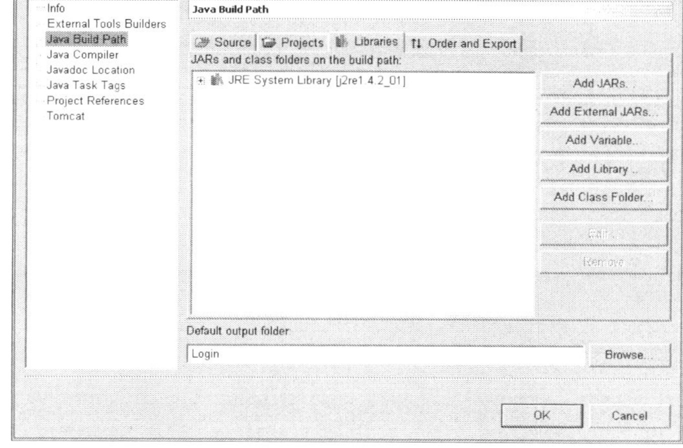

Figure 3-7: The Libraries tab of the Properties for Login dialog box.

4. **Click the Add JARs button.**

   The JAR Selection dialog box appears.

5. **Navigate to `Login/WEB-INF/lib` folder and select all `.jar` files displayed there. Click the Open button.**

   All the `.jar` files are now in the build path of the Login project. You need to add one more `.jar` file to be complete.

6. **Click the Add External JARs button.**

   Note that this is the External Jars button.

7. **Navigate to the `Tomcat-4.1/common/lib` folder, and select the `servlet.jar` file. Click Open.**

   The `servlet.jar` files adds the all the Java Servlet classes to your build path. The Java Servlet classes are necessary because they're not included in the Standard Edition of Java (just the J2EE version). The set of libraries associated with the project should now look like Figure 3-8.

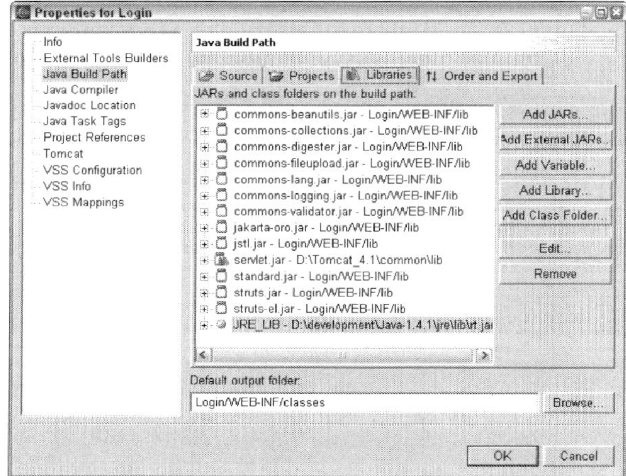

Figure 3-8: The complete set of libraries for the project.

8. **To close the Properties of Login dialog box, click OK.**

You're now ready to begin creating your JSP pages.

Downloading the Login project

Before you move on, you might want to download all the code for the Login project to avoid having to type it. To get the files, go to `www.dummies.com/go/jakarta` and click the Login.zip link. Save `Login.zip` to a temporary folder. After the file is downloaded, unzip it into a new folder. `Login.zip` contains the eight files that we describe in the next sections:

- `login.jsp`
- `loggedin.jsp`
- `LoginForm.java`
- `LoginBean.java`
- `LoginAction.java`
- `web.xml`
- `struts-config.xml`
- `ApplicationResources.properties`

Creating the JavaServer Pages

As explained in the "Determining which components to use" section earlier in this chapter, the Login application requires two JSP pages. The first is for the user to enter the necessary login information, and the second is to notify the user that the log-in process was a success.

For each of the two JSP pages, we show you what the final page will look like when the application is complete. Then we list and explain the code. Finally, we explain the steps that you need to complete to create the pages.

In the "Downloading the Login project" sidebar in this chapter, we explain how to download all the project files from the For Dummies Web site. So if you don't like to type, follow those instructions to avoid typing the files into Eclipse manually.

The login.jsp page

The Login application presents the `login.jsp` page when the system needs to authenticate the user. The `login.jsp` page has one field for a username and one field for a password. The password field displays bullets instead of the entered text. The page contains one button to submit the entries to the server. Everything is simple and straightforward!

Figure 3-9 shows what the page will look like. You need to complete several more steps before you can display your own `login.jsp` page, as explained in the next sections of this chapter.

Setting a default editor for JSP files

You can set the default editor (the editor that opens when you double-click the file) for JSP pages to be Eclipse's built-in text editor instead of the default editor (Wordpad on our system). Follow these steps to associate JSP files with the Eclipse text editor:

1. **Choose Window⇨Preferences.**

   The Preferences dialog box appears.

2. **In the left pane, double-click the Workbench item.**
3. **In the left pane, click File Associations.**
4. **In the File Associations pane, click the top Add button.**
5. **In the New File Type dialog box, type** *.jsp **and then click OK.**

   This action adds a new file type, JSP, so that we can add an association for it.

6. **In the File Associations pane of the Preferences dialog box, be sure that the new entry is selected, and then click the lower Add button.**

   The Editor Selection dialog box appears.

7. **Scroll down and select the Text Editor item, and then click OK.**

   This action associates Eclipse's editor with the JSP file type.

8. **Click the OK button in the Preferences dialog box.**

Now when you double-click a JSP file in the Package Explorer, the Eclipse Text Editor opens to edit it.

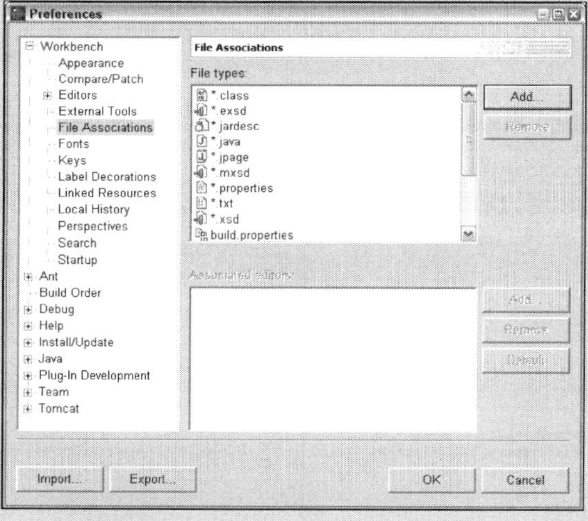

Figure 3-9: The login.jsp page.

The complete code for the login page is in Listing 3-1. The numbers to the left of each line are not part of the code. We refer to these numbers when we explain the code.

Listing 3-1 login.jsp

```
1  <%@ page contentType="text/html;charset=UTF-8" language="java" %>

2  <%-- JSTL tag libs --%>
3  <%@ taglib prefix="fmt" uri="/WEB-INF/fmt.tld" %>

4  <%-- Struts provided Taglibs --%>
5  <%@ taglib prefix="html" uri="/WEB-INF/struts-html-el.tld" %>

6  <html:html locale="true"/>
7  <head>
8      <fmt:setBundle basename="ApplicationResources" />
9      <title><fmt:message key="login.title"/></title>
10  </head>
11  <body>
12  <html:errors property="login"/>
13  <html:form action="login.do" focus="userName">
14      <table align="center">
15          <tr align="center">
16              <td><H1><fmt:message key="login.message"/></H1></td>
17          </tr>
18          <tr align="center">
```

```
19             <td>
20                 <table align="center">
21                     <tr>
22                         <td align="right">
23                             <fmt:message key="login.username"/>
24                         </td>
25                         <td align="left">
26                             <html:text property="userName"
27                                        size="15"
28                                        maxlength="15" />
29                            <html:errors property="userName" />
30                         </td>
31                     </tr>
32                     <tr>
33                         <td align="right">
34                             <fmt:message key="login.password"/>
35                         </td>
36                         <td align="left">
37                             <html:password property="password"
38                                            size="15"
39                                            maxlength="15"
40                                            redisplay="false"/>
41                             <html:errors property="password" />
42                         </td>
43                     </tr>
44                     <tr>
45                         <td colspan="2" align="center">
46                             <html:submit>
47                                 <fmt:message key="login.button.signon"/>
48                             </html:submit>
49                         </td>
50                     </tr>
51                 </table>
52             </td>
53         </tr>
54     </table>
55 </html:form>
56 </body>
56 </html>
```

The first thing to point out is the use of specialized Struts tag libraries. This page uses two libraries. The first is a JSTL tag library, `fmt`, which formats data and provides localized message information. The second is a Struts specific tag library, `struts-html-el`, that inserts various HTML elements into the page. The other Struts-specific items are on the following lines:

- Lines 3 and 5: Standard JSP directives for including tag libraries in the page. The `prefix` attribute references the library tags throughout the code.
- Line 6: Generates the top-level `<html>` element and specifies that the HTTP header will determine the locale to be used to set the language preferences. This tag has implications when you want your Web

application to handle more than one language. For more information about internationalization (I18N), see Chapter 6. Also see the "Using message resources" section later in this chapter.

- Line 8: Identifies to the JSP page the name of the message resource file. This tag is from the JSTL `fmt` tag library. Other ways to identify the message resource file exist, but this method is straightforward.
- Line 9: Now that the code has identified the message resource file, you can reference the key-value pairs in the file. This line is another tag that will retrieve the value associated with the key named `login-title`. That value will be displayed as text in the title bar of the browser window.
- Line 12: If the submitted data contains an error, this tag is used to display the error. Actually, this tag displays a specific error associated with the `login` property. Any such error is detected by the validation process and an error message is generated. (See Chapter 6 for more information on validation.)
- Line 13: Generates the `html <form>` tag. The `action` attribute sets the form submission to the URL `login.do`. Any URL with the `.do` extension is automatically routed to the `ActionServlet`. We specify the extension when we set up the `web.xml` configuration file towards the end of this chapter. The other attribute is `focus`, which tells the browser in which field to put the initial focus.
- Lines 26 and 37: Create the two form fields, `userName` and `password`. One thing to point out about the `password` field is the use of the `redisplay` attribute. When this attribute is set to `false`, the value of the `password` field is not redisplayed if the page is redisplayed. This attribute is important for security. Although the `password` value will contain asterisks if the page is redisplayed, the user could view the source code of the page to see the full text of `password`.
- Lines 29 and 41: These error messages are just like the one on line 12, except these error messages are specific for each of the fields. If one or both of the errors arise, the messages are displayed next to the field in which the error occurs.

The `login.jsp` file illustrates some of the advantages of Struts applications. Error messages generated in the Controller are displayed in appropriate locations on the page through the interaction of the struts tag libraries and the Controller code. In addition, static text (such as titles, labels, and buttons) is never used directly. Instead, Struts inserts the text from a message resource file. This eases the job of maintaining JSP pages.

At this point, if you downloaded the Login project files from the *For Dummies* Web site (see instructions in the preceding section) you can import the `login.jsp` file into Eclipse or you can use the manual method of typing. We have instructions for both.

Importing login.jsp into Eclipse

Follow these four steps to import `login.jsp` into Eclipse:

1. **In the Package Explorer view, right-click the Login project and choose Import.**

   The Import dialog box appears.

2. **Choose File System and then click the Next button.**
3. **Click the Browse button next to the From Directory text box and navigate to and select the folder where you put the Login files that you downloaded. Click OK.**
4. **Select the login.jsp check box and then click the Finish button.**

That's all there is to it.

Entering login.jsp by typing it in

If you decide to enter the `login.jsp` file the labor-intensive way, you can type `login.jsp` into the project manually at this point by following these steps:

1. **In the Package Explorer View, right-click the Login project and choose New⇨File.**

   The New File dialog box appears.

2. **In the File Name text box, type** login.jsp **and then click Finish.**

   Because login.jsp is a JSP file and not a Java file, the default editor appears unless you have reset the default editor. (See the "Setting a default editor for JSP files" sidebar.)

3. **Type Listing 3-1, but do not include the line numbers.**
4. **To save your changes, choose File⇨Save.**

The loggedin.jsp page

The `loggedin.jsp` page is just a validation to the user that the system has accepted the username and password combination. This page is even simpler that the `login.jsp` page. The only interesting feature of the page is the insertion of the user's name in the welcome message. Figure 3-10 shows what the page looks like when displayed.

The complete listing for loggedin.jsp is shown in Listing 3-2.

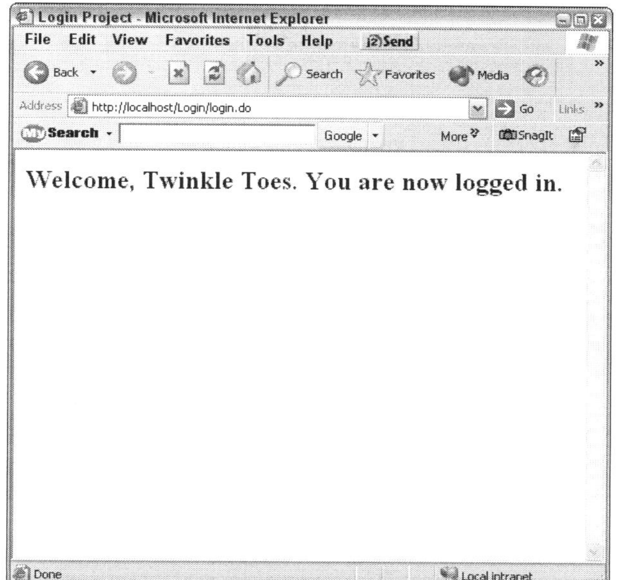

Figure 3-10: The loggedin.jsp page.

Listing 3-2 loggedin.jsp

```
1   <%@ page contentType="text/html;charset=UTF-8" language="java" %>

2   <%-- JSTL tag libs --%>
3   <%@ taglib prefix="fmt" uri="/WEB-INF/fmt.tld" %>

4   <%-- Struts provided Taglibs --%>
5   <%@ taglib uri="/WEB-INF/struts-html-el.tld" prefix="html" %>

6   <html:html locale="true"/>
7   <head>
8       <fmt:setBundle basename="ApplicationResources" />
9       <title><fmt:message key="loggedin.title"/></title>
10   </head>
11   <body>
12       <H2>
13       <fmt:message key="loggedin.msg">
14           <fmt:param value='${requestScope.userName}' />
15       </fmt:message>
16       </H2>
17   </body>
18   </html>
```

This page uses the same two tag libraries as the `login.jsp` page described in the preceding section. The two new things used on this page are both on lines 13–15:

- The message you want to display has a mechanism to accept one or more parameters. This is useful when you want to vary the content of a message. The application does not know the user's name in advance but knows it at runtime. You need to provide that name when the page is run so that you can personalize the message to the user. To do so, we add a placeholder to the message in the message resource file (see the "Using message resources" section later in the chapter):

  ```
  loggedin.msg=Welcome, {0}. You are now logged in.
  ```

  The value has a placeholder `{0}` that indicates that the first parameter that is passed should be substituted for the `{0}`. Line 14 specifies the first and only parameter.
- The `loggedin.jsp` page references values in *implicit objects* (objects already defined by the Web container) using JSTL expression language. (See Chapter 10 for more details on JSTL.) In this case, you are using the `requestScope` object, which represents the current request you're processing. In the `LoginAction` class (we explain the `LoginAction` class in the following section, "Creating an Action"), you specifically put the user's name into the request when you validate the user. The user's name is referenced by the `userName` key. So on line 14, you're getting the user's name from the request and passing it to `loggedin.msg` as the first parameter. This personalizes the logged-in message.

You can enter `loggedin.jsp` into Eclipse by either importing or typing, as shown next.

Importing loggedin.jsp into Eclipse

Follow these four steps to import `loggedin.jsp` into Eclipse:

1. **In the Package Explorer view, right-click the Login project and choose Import.**
2. **Choose File System and then click the Next button.**
3. **Click the Browse button next to the From Directory text box and navigate to and select the folder where you put the Login files that you downloaded. Click OK.**
4. **Click the loggedin.jsp check box and then click the Finish button.**

Entering loggedin.jsp by typing it in

Follow these steps to manually enter `loggedin.jsp` into the project:

1. **In the Package Explorer View, right-click the Login project and choose New⇨File.**

   The New File dialog box appears.
2. **In the File Name text box, type** loggedin.jsp **and then click Finish.**

3. **Type Listing 3-1 but do not include the line numbers.**
4. **To save your changes, choose File⇨Save.**

Using message resources

Message resources are a means to separate text from the application's code. Keeping the text separate from the code makes it easier to change the text later, which makes the application easier to maintain.

One of the key mechanisms to handle I18N is to put any text that will be displayed for the user into a message resource file. The format for this file is simply a set of key-value pairs, where the *key* is used as the reference and the *value* is what is displayed. For example:

```
login.message=Please Log In!
```

In this example, `login.message` is the key and `Please Log In!` is the value. The Login application has a message resource file that contains all the text that will be displayed on the two JSP pages. Even if I18N was not a concern (maybe your application will be used only internally by your company), using message resources is still a good idea. For maintenance, it is generally better not to embed static text in your code. By centralizing static text in an external file, you can easily make changes to text without disturbing the code.

In the Login application, the name of the message resource file is `ApplicationResources.properties`. Listing 3-3 shows the key-value pairs that the Login application requires. Lines that begin with a number sign (#) are comments.

Listing 3-3 ApplicationResources.properties

```
# Resources for Login Project

# Struts Validator Error Messages
# These two resources are used by Struts HTML tag library
# to format messages. In this case we make sure that errors
# are red so that they can be noticed.
errors.header=<font color="red">*
errors.footer=</font>

#errors associated with the Login page
error.username.required=username is required.
error.password.required=password is required.
error.login.invalid=The system could not verify your username
           or password. Is your CAPS LOCK on? Please try
           again.

#login page text
```

```
login.title=Login Project - Log In, Please
login.message=Please Log In!
login.username=username:
login.password=password:
login.button.signon=Log In

#loggedin page text
loggedin.title=Login Project
loggedin.msg=Welcome, {0}. You are now logged in.
```

The `errors.header` and `errors.footer` are special keys that the `html:errors` tag uses if they are defined. When displaying an error message, the `html:errors` tag will preface the error messages with whatever value is associated with the `errors.header` key. After the error messages are displayed, `html:errors` displays the value found in the `errors.footer` key.

At this point, enter the file into Eclipse using one of the following two methods.

Importing ApplicationResources.properties into Eclipse

To import the `ApplicationResources.properties` file into the project, follow these steps:

1. **In the Package Explorer view, right-click the `source` folder and choose Import.**

   The Import dialog box appears.

2. **Choose File System and then click the Next button.**
3. **Click the Browse button next to the From Directory text box and navigate to and select the folder where you put the Login files that you downloaded. Click OK.**
4. **Select the ApplicationResources.properties check box and then click the Finish button.**

Entering ApplicationResources.properties manually into Eclipse

To enter the `ApplicationResources.properties` file into the project manually, follow these steps:

1. **In the Package Explorer view, right-click the `source` folder and choose New⇨File.**
2. **In the File Name text box, type** ApplicationResources.properties **and click Finish.**
3. **Type Listing 3-3.**

   Do not include the line numbers.

4. **To save your changes, choose File⇨Save.**

Any message resource file or other file that you might use needs to be on the classpath so that the application can find it. Because the message resource file is located in the source folder, whenever the project gets rebuilt, it will get moved by the build process to the `classes` folder. Everything in the `classes` folder is considered on the classpath.

Making the Formbean

The `ActionForm` class is part of the Struts Controller. (For more information on the `ActionForm` class, see the "Struts Controller" section in Chapter 1.) The `ActionForm` class is associated with a particular View, but could service multiple Views, if necessary. `ActionForm` is an abstract class, so you always use a subclass to create a specific version for your View.

The main purpose of the `ActionForm` subclass is to hold the properties of the submitted form. Therefore, it has the properties of a JavaBean and is called a formbean. You need to reference every form property you need in the `ActionForm` subclass, such as text fields, radio buttons, and hidden properties. In addition, for each property defined, there should be getter and setter methods appropriate to Beans.

Listing 3-4 shows the formbean, `LoginForm.java`.

Listing 3-4 LoginForm.java

```
package dummies.struts;

import javax.servlet.http.HttpServletRequest;

import org.apache.struts.action.ActionError;
import org.apache.struts.action.ActionErrors;
import org.apache.struts.action.ActionForm;
import org.apache.struts.action.ActionMapping;

public class LoginForm extends ActionForm
{
   private String userName;
   private String password;

   public void reset(ActionMapping mapping, HttpServletRequest request)
   {
      password = "";
      userName = "";
   }

   public ActionErrors validate(ActionMapping mapping,
                                HttpServletRequest request)
   {
```

```
18       ActionErrors errors = new ActionErrors();

19       if((userName == null) || (userName.length() < 1))
20          errors.add("userName", new ActionError("error.username.required"));
21       if((password == null) || (password.length() < 1))
22          errors.add("password", new ActionError("error.password.required"));

23       return errors;
24    }
25    public String getPassword() {
26       return password;
27    }

28    public String getUserName() {
29       return userName;
30    }

31    public void setPassword(String string) {
32       password = string;
33    }

34    public void setUserName(String string) {
35       userName = string;
36    }
37}
```

In the example application, you create a subclass of `ActionForm` so you can create a specific version named `LoginForm`. The `LoginForm` is tied to the `login.jsp` View through the `struts-config.xml` file (see the section "Configuring Struts with struts-config.xml"). The main purpose of `LoginForm` is to hold the properties of the submitted form. In the case of the `login.jsp` page, you have two fields: the `userName` and `password` fields. As a result, the associated `LoginForm` needs two properties with the same names as the fields, as well as the getter and setter methods for those properties. In Listing 3-4, you can see the properties in lines 9 and 10 and the getter and setter methods for those two properties below line 24.

Two additional methods can be overridden by the subclass:

- `reset` **method:** Can be used to initialize the form's properties (and anything else you may want) and is called with each new request. In lines 13 and 14 of Listing 3-4, you set the properties back to the empty string.
- `validate` **method:** Is called after the `ActionServlet` populates the form with the request properties and before the form is passed to a particular `Action` class for processing. This method is one way that form validation can take place to ensure that the user has entered appropriate and acceptable data. Line 18 creates an empty `ActionErrors` object, which is the return value for the method. Line 19 and 21 are tests to ensure that the user enters something for the `userName` and `password` fields. If not, the code creates an `ActionError` object and adds it to

ActionErrors. Note that when adding ActionError, the code specifies a particular key so that the JSP page will know where to display the error. Here is an example from the login.jsp file:

```
<html:text property="userName"  size="15" maxlength="15" />
<html:errors property="userName" />
```

Note that the html:errors tag has a property attribute with the value of userName, which matches the key associated with the ActionError in line 19. The ActionError itself is given a message resource key to indicate which message should be displayed.

The validate method is a nice feature of the ActionForm because it provides the developer with a way to immediately validate user input. The Struts framework will test for errors; if any are detected it redisplays the page with appropriate error messages to the user.

To enter the LoginForm.java file into the project manually, you must create the dummies.struts package (packages are a way to organize source code and the resulting class files into logical units), reset the output folder, and then type the source code. These procedures are described in the next three sections.

Creating the packages

The LoginForm.java, LoginAction.java, and LoginBean.java files need to go into the source folder of the project. However, they must be part of the dummies.struts package, so first create the packages in the source folder. To create the dummies and struts packages in the source folder, follow these steps:

1. **Open Eclipse or your IDE.**

   The instructions that follow are for Eclipse.

2. **Right-click the source folder and choose New⇨Package.**
3. **In the Name text box, type** dummies.struts.
4. **Click Finish.**

   You should now see the package in the source folder.

5. **If you don't see the package, do the following:**
   a. **Click the Menu down arrow at the upper-right of the Package Explorer window and choose Filters.**
   b. **In the Java Element Filters dialog box, deselect the Empty Packages check box.**
   c. **Click OK.**

   The dummies.struts package should now be visible.

Compiling in Eclipse

Compiling the Java source code into class files is an automatic process in Eclipse. When you save a Java source file, it is automatically compiled into a class file. Compilation errors are denoted with a red circle with a white x in the center, located in the left margin next to the problematic line of code. The class file is saved in the default output folder. This location can be set as a property of the project, as explained in the "Setting the default output folder" section. Syntax checking is performed in real time, as you type. Syntax errors are denoted with a red line under the code in question.

Setting the default output folder

Before entering any Java source files in Eclipse, set the default output folder for the class files to `WEB-INF/classes` in the Login project. To set the default output folder, follow these steps:

1. **In the Package Explorer view, right-click the Login project and choose Properties.**

   The Properties for Login dialog, box appears. If your project has a different name, your project name appears instead of Login in the name of the dialog box.

2. **In the list in the left pane, choose the Java Build Path item.**
3. **Click the Source tab.**
4. **In the Default Output Folder text box at the bottom of the dialog box, type** Login/WEB-INF/classes.

   You can also click the Browse button, use the Folder Selection dialog box to navigate to the `Login/WEB-INF/classes` folder, and click OK.

5. **Click the OK button.**

   You see the message "The output folder has changed. OK to remove all generated resources from '/Login/bin'?".

6. **Go ahead and click the Yes button.**

Now whenever a Java file is compiled, the resulting class file goes in the `classes` folder. This makes it easier to deploy the application.

Importing the LoginForm.java file

To import the `LoginForm.java` file, follow these steps.

1. **In the Package Explorer view, right-click the** `dummies.struts` **package in the source folder and choose Import.**

2. **Choose File System and then click the Next button.**
3. **Click the Browse button next to the From Directory text box and navigate to and select the folder where you put the Login files that you downloaded. Click OK.**
4. **Select the LoginForm.java check box and then click the Finish button.**

Manually entering the LoginForm.java source code

To manually enter the `LoginForm.java` file into Eclipse, follow these steps:

1. **In the Package Explorer View, right-click the** `dummies.struts` **package in the source folder and choose New➪Class.**

   The New Java Class dialog box appears.
2. **In the Name text box, type** LoginForm.
3. **In the Superclass text box, type** org.apache.struts.action.ActionForm.

   Refer to Figure 3-11.
4. **Click Finish.**
5. **Type Listing 3-4 into the newly created** `LoginForm.java` **file.**

   Don't include the line numbers.
6. **To save your changes, choose File➪Save.**

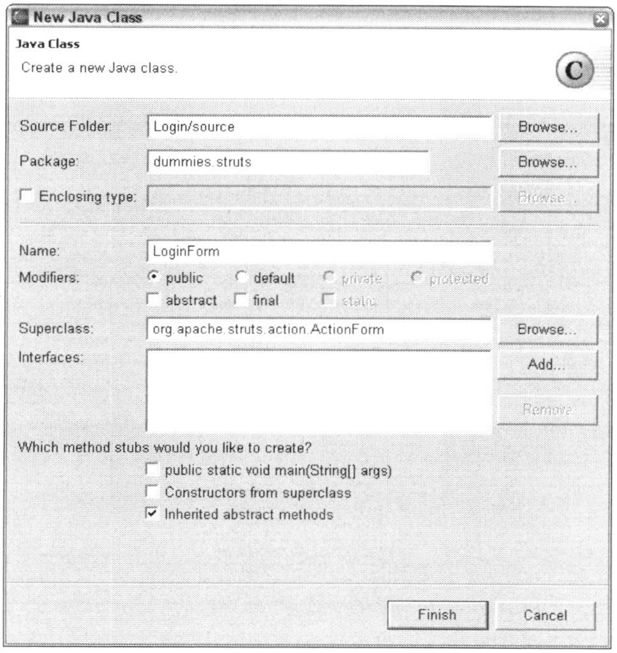

Figure 3-11: Use the New Java Class dialog box to create the LoginForm class.

Adding a JavaBean

The JavaBean represents the Model group and holds the `userName` and `password` data for all allowable users. One method validates a particular `userName` and `password` combination against the repository of usernames and passwords. It's straightforward. In practice, sometimes the Model group has a combination of JavaBeans and other classes that go to make up the business logic of the application. The JavaBean is shown in Listing 3-5.

Listing 3-5 LoginBean.java

```
package dummies.struts;

import java.util.HashMap;

public class LoginBean
{
  private HashMap validUsers = new HashMap();

  /**
   * Constructor for LoginBean
   * Initializes the list of usernames/passwords
   *
   */
  public LoginBean()
  {
     validUsers.put("Twinkle Toes","tt");
     validUsers.put("administrator","admin");
     validUsers.put("Barbara Smith","smitty");
  }

  /**
   * determine if the username/password combination are
   * present in the validUsers repository.
   * @param userName
   * @param password
   * @return boolean true if valid, false otherwise
   */
   public boolean validateUser(String userName, String password)
   {
      if(validUsers.containsKey(userName))
      {
         String thePassword = (String)validUsers.get(userName);
         if(thePassword.equals(password))
            return true;
      }
      return false;
   }
}
```

The JavaBean has the following noteworthy characteristics:

- Lines 4–9: The `LoginBean` constructor creates the data repository as a `HashMap` with the `userName` as the key and the `password` as the value.
- Lines 10–19: The `validateUser` method takes `userName` and `password` as parameters and then checks to see whether `userName` is even present in `HashMap`. If not, it returns `false`. If `userName` is there, it gets the `password` from the `HashMap` associated with `userName` (line 14) and compares it with the `password` entered by the user (line 15). If they match, the `userName` and `password` combination is authenticated and the method returns `true` (line 16). Otherwise, it returns `false`.

Importing the LoginBean.java file

To import the `LoginBean.java` file, follow these steps.

1. **In the Package Explorer view, right-click the `dummies.struts` package in the source folder and choose Import.**
2. **Choose File System and then click the Next button.**
3. **Click the Browse button next to the From Directory text box and navigate to and select the folder where you put the Login files that you downloaded. Click OK.**
4. **Select the LoginBean.java check box and then click the Finish button.**

Manually entering the LoginBean source code

1. **In the Package Explorer View, right-click the `dummies.struts` package in the source folder and choose New⇨ Class.**

   The New Java Class dialog box appears.
2. **In the Name text box, type** LoginBean.
3. **Leave the Superclass field as-is because you're not creating a subclass.**
4. **Click Finish.**
5. **Type Listing 3-5 into the newly created `LoginBean.java` file.**

   Do not include the line numbers.
6. **To save your changes, choose File⇨Save.**

Creating an Action

The `Action` class is called `LoginAction`. Remember that the purpose of the `Action` subclass is to process the user's request. Listing 3-6 creates the `LoginAction` class.

Listing 3-6 LoginAction.java

```
package dummies.struts;

import javax.servlet.http.HttpServletRequest;
import javax.servlet.http.HttpServletResponse;

import org.apache.struts.action.Action;
import org.apache.struts.action.ActionError;
import org.apache.struts.action.ActionErrors;
import org.apache.struts.action.ActionForm;
import org.apache.struts.action.ActionForward;
import org.apache.struts.action.ActionMapping;
1public class LoginAction extends Action
2{
3   public ActionForward execute(ActionMapping mapping,
4                                ActionForm form,
5                                HttpServletRequest request,
6                                HttpServletResponse response)
7   throws Exception
8   {
      // create a new LoginBean with valid users in it
9      LoginBean lb = new LoginBean();

      // check to see if this user/password combination are valid
10      if(lb.validateUser(((LoginForm)form).getUserName(),
                        ((LoginForm)form).getPassword()))
11      {
12         request.setAttribute("userName",((LoginForm)form).getUserName());
13         return (mapping.findForward("success"));
14      }
15      else      // username/password not validated
      {
         // create ActionError and save in the request
16         ActionErrors errors = new ActionErrors();
17         ActionError error = new ActionError("error.login.invalid");
18         errors.add("login",error);
19         saveErrors(request,errors);

20         return (mapping.findForward("failure"));
21      }
22   }
23}
```

In the `LoginAction` class, note the following items:

- Line 9: Instantiates a `LoginBean`. (See the "Adding a JavaBean" section for the `LoginBean` description.) The `LoginBean` represents the Model and holds the data regarding authorized users.
- Line 10: Passes `userName` and `password` from the `LoginForm` to the LoginBean's `validateUser` method and asks whether the `userName` and `password` combination is valid. If the code on line 10 returns `true` (the `userName` and `password` combination is valid), the code puts the

userName into the Request scope for use by the loggedin.jsp page on line 12.

- Line 13: Gets an ActionForward object for the name success and returns control to RequestProcessor. The mapping.findForward (success) call retrieves the path mapped to the success name. This mapping is set up in the struts-config.xml file. (See the "Configuring Struts" section for details.)
- Lines 16 and 17: If the validation fails, the code creates an ActionErrors object with an error message.
- Line 18: Like the validate method of the LoginForm class, a key for the error is specified when adding the ActionError so that the JSP page knows where the error message should be displayed.
- Line 19: Saves the ActionErrors into the request object using the saveErrors method of the Action superclass.
- Line 20: Returns an ActionForward object with the real path that's mapped to failure; control is then returned to RequestProcessor.

Notice the minimum dependency between the Controller (LoginAction) and the Model (LoginBean) in lines 9 and 10. The code instantiates the LoginBean and then call its validateUser method. You have no idea what goes on in the LoginBean and really don't need to care. The LoginBean could be querying a remote database and performing many steps of validation when you call the validateUser method. This is what MVC is trying to achieve: minimum coupling (dependencies) between the Model, View, and Controller. With minimum dependency, you gain increased flexibility and maintainability in your code.

Importing the LoginAction.java file

To import the LoginAction.java file, follow these steps:

1. **In the Package Explorer view, right-click the dummies.struts package in the source folder and choose Import.**

   The Import dialog box appears.
2. **Choose File System and click the Next button.**
3. **Click the Browse button next to the From Directory text box and navigate to and select the folder where you put the Login files that you downloaded. Click OK.**
4. **Select the LoginAction.java check box and click the Finish button.**

Manually entering the LoginAction source code

If you want to manually enter the code, follow these steps:

1. **In the Package Explorer View, right-click the dummies.struts package in the source folder and choose New⇨ Class.**

The New Java Class dialog box appears.

2. **In the Name text box, type** LoginAction.
3. **In the Superclass text box, type** org.apache.struts.action.Action.
4. **Click Finish.**
5. **Type Listing 3-6 into the newly created** `LoginAction.java` **file.**

   Do not include the line numbers.
6. **To save your changes, choose File⇨Save.**

Configuring Struts

To complete the application, you need to configure the Web container and Struts. It is through the configuration files that we tie all the parts together. First you configure the Web container so that it knows about the application.

Defining web.xml

Defining the `web.xml` file makes the Web container aware of your application and how to run the application. Listing 3-7 shows the `web.xml` configuration file.

Listing 3-7 web.xml

```
<?xml version="1.0" encoding="ISO-8859-1"?>

<!DOCTYPE web-app
 PUBLIC "-//Sun Microsystems, Inc.//DTD Web Application 2.2//EN"
 "http://java.sun.com/j2ee/dtds/web-app_2_2.dtd">

<web-app>

    <!-- Action Servlet Configuration -->
    <servlet>
        <servlet-name>action</servlet-name>
            <servlet-class>org.apache.struts.action.ActionServlet
            </servlet-class>
            <init-param>
                <param-name>config</param-name>
                <param-value>/WEB-INF/struts-config.xml</param-value>
            </init-param>
            <load-on-startup>1</load-on-startup>
```

```
    </servlet>

    <!-- Action Servlet Mapping -->
    <servlet-mapping>
        <servlet-name>action</servlet-name>
        <url-pattern>*.do</url-pattern>
    </servlet-mapping>

    <!-- The Welcome File List -->
    <welcome-file-list>
        <welcome-file>login.jsp</welcome-file>
    </welcome-file-list>

    <!-- JSTL Tag Library Descriptor -->
    <taglib>
       <taglib-uri>/WEB-INF/c.tld</taglib-uri>
       <taglib-location>/WEB-INF/c.tld</taglib-location>
    </taglib>

    <taglib>
      <taglib-uri>/WEB-INF/fmt.tld</taglib-uri>
      <taglib-location>/WEB-INF/fmt.tld</taglib-location>
    </taglib>

    <taglib>
      <taglib-uri>/WEB-INF/sql.tld</taglib-uri>
      <taglib-location>/WEB-INF/sql.tld</taglib-location>
    </taglib>

   <taglib>
      <taglib-uri>/WEB-INF/x.tld</taglib-uri>
      <taglib-location>/WEB-INF/x.tld</taglib-location>
    </taglib>

    <!-- Struts Tag Library Descriptors -->
    <taglib>
      <taglib-uri>/WEB-INF/struts-bean-el.tld</taglib-uri>
      <taglib-location>/WEB-INF/struts-bean-el.tld</taglib-location>
    </taglib>

    <taglib>
      <taglib-uri>/WEB-INF/struts-html-el.tld</taglib-uri>
      <taglib-location>/WEB-INF/struts-html-el.tld</taglib-location>
    </taglib>

    <taglib>
      <taglib-uri>/WEB-INF/struts-logic-el.tld</taglib-uri>
      <taglib-location>/WEB-INF/struts-logic-el.tld</taglib-location>
    </taglib>
</web-app>
```

Here's what you should know about this `web.xml` file:

- Lines 8–16: Define the Struts controller, the `ActionServlet`.
- Line 9: The `ActionServlet` is referred to by the name `action`.
- Line 10: Contains the class name.
- Line 12: Passes one parameter named `config` to the Servlet.
- Line 13: The value of the parameter is the path to the `struts-config.xml` file).
- Line 15: Indicates that this Servlet should be the first one to be started when the application starts. Right now there's only one Servlet, so the order doesn't make much difference. However, when there are many Servlets in an application, the starting order is important.
- Lines 18–21: Tell the container that for every URL that the container encounters for this application context that ends in `.do`, it should route the request to the `action` Servlet.

  The application *context* is simply a name used to refer to a particular Web application. In our case, the context is Login.
- Lines 23–25: Define the file to display if the user enters the context in the browser without specifying a particular file, for example, `http://localhost/Login`. In this case, the `login.jsp` page will be displayed by default.
- Lines 27–42: Define the use of certain JSTL tag libraries and specifies where to find the library definition files. The URI in the definition is referred to in the JSP file when specifying the use of a tag library. For example, the following directive is from a JSP file that specifies the use of JSTL's formatting library. Note that the `uri` in the directive must match the `uri` defined for the library in the `web.xml` file on line 32.

  ```
  <%@ taglib prefix="fmt" uri="/WEB-INF/fmt.tld" %>
  ```
- Lines 44–55: Define the use of certain Struts-EL tag libraries and specifies where to find the library definition files.

Importing web.xml into Eclipse

Follow these four steps to import `web.xml` into Eclipse:

1. **In the Package Explorer view, right-click the `WEB-INF` folder and choose Import.**
2. **Choose File System and click the Next button.**
3. **Click the Browse button next to the From Directory text box and navigate to and select the folder where you put the Login files that you downloaded. Click OK.**
4. **Select the web.xml check box and click the Finish button.**

Entering the web.xml file into Eclipse

To manually enter the `web.xml` file into Eclipse, follow these steps:

1. **In the Package Explorer View, right-click the `WEB-INF` folder and choose New➪ File.**

   The New File dialog box appears.
2. **In the File Name text box, type** web.xml **and then click Finish.**
3. **Type the text from Listing 3-7.**

   Do not include the line numbers.
4. **To save your changes, choose File➪Save.**

Configuring Struts with struts-config.xml

You now need to configure Struts with the `struts-config.xml` file. At this point, you're going to make the connection between the Views, Forms, and Actions. For the Login application you configure three items: the `LoginForm`, the mapping for the `/login` path, and the message resource file. Listing 3-8 shows the `struts-config.xml` file.

Listing 3-8 struts-config.xml

```
<?xml version="1.0" encoding="ISO-8859-1" ?>

<!DOCTYPE struts-config PUBLIC
          "-//Apache Software Foundation//DTD Struts Configuration 1.1//EN"
          "http://jakarta.apache.org/struts/dtds/struts-config_1_1.dtd">

<!-- This is the Struts configuration file for the Login application -->
<struts-config>
   <!-- ========== Form Bean Definitions ================================= -->
   <form-beans>
       <form-bean name="loginForm"
                  type="dummies.struts.LoginForm"/>
    </form-beans>

    <!-- ========== Action Mapping Definitions ========================== -->
    <action-mappings>
        <action path="/login"
                type="dummies.struts.LoginAction"
                name="loginForm"
                scope="request"
                input="/login.jsp"
                validate="true">
          <forward name="failure" path="/login.jsp"/>
          <forward
              name="success" path="/loggedin.jsp"/>
```

```
22       </action>
23    </action-mappings>

24    <!-- ========== Message Resources Definitions ======================== -->
25     <message-resources null="false"
26                        parameter="ApplicationResources"/>
27</struts-config>
```

Struts-config.xml has the following notable lines:

- Line 9: Uses the `<form-bean>` tag to give LoginForm a name you can refer to later in the struts-config file. You must define every form-bean that you intend to use in an application, using the `<form-beans>` tag. The Login application has only one formbean, LoginForm.
- Line 10: Specifies the full class name of the form and closes the tag.
- Line 13: Starts the section on action mappings. The Action Mapping Definitions section defines which Action subclass should be called when a particular path is referenced in a URL. Because you have only one Action subclass (LoginAction), you have only one mapping to define.

  Remember that in the web.xml file we specified, all URLs with a .do extension should be routed to ActionServlet. Each path defined for an action in the struts-config file will have the .do extension in the URL. The Struts Controller will strip the extension to get the path. That path will be used to determine which action should be called.
- Line 14: Begins the one action definition. The path attribute specifies which path will result in the LoginAction class being called.
- Line 15: Defines the full class name of the LoginAction.
- Line 16: Specifies which form-bean should be associated with this action. In this case, the code uses the loginform defined earlier.
- Line 17: Specifies that the scope of the form-bean should be the request scope. In other words, where should the form-bean exist? The other option is the session scope. You would use the session scope if you want the form to persist between requests, such as when you have a multi-page form.
- Line 18: Specifies that the login.jsp page populates form-bean.
- Line 19: Calls the validate method of form-bean. Specifying false would mean not to call the validate method, and validation would need to occur through another means. (For more information about other means of validation, see Chapter 6).
- Lines 20 and 21: Contain the actual mapping between a logic name and a path. Line 20 specifies the failure name when forwarding to the login.jsp page. Line 21 specifies the success name when forwarding to the loggedin.jsp page. The use of these mappings provides flexibility without having to change code. You may decide to use a different JSP for

success at some point. Rather than having to search your code for all instances of /loggedin.jsp and change it to the new JSP, you could simply change the path here in the struts-config file. All references to success in your code would now point to the new JSP rather than the old page. Here is a line from LoginAction that shows how the mapping is used:

```
return (mapping.findForward("success"));
```

- Line 25: Defines the message resources. Line 25 specifies that the key be displayed instead of the value if a key is encountered that can't be found in the property file. If you use true instead of false, the behavior will be to use an empty string. The parameter attribute defines the name of the property file to use for the message resource. It's assumed that the file's extension is properties.

The struts-config.xml file represents the definition of the parts of the application to the Struts framework, how the parts are connected with each other, and the flow of control. It allows Struts to use your code without you having to modify the Struts code directly. This is a big plus in terms of the application's flexibility and ease of maintenance.

Importing struts-config.xml into Eclipse

Follow these four steps to import struts-config.xml into Eclipse:

1. **In the Package Explorer view, right-click the WEB-INF folder and choose Import.**

   The Import dialog box appears.

2. **Choose File System and click the Next button.**
3. **Click the Browse button next to the From Directory text box and navigate to and select the folder where you put the Login files that you downloaded. Click OK.**
4. **Select the struts-config.xml check box and click the Finish button.**

Entering the struts-config.xml file into Eclipse

To enter the struts-config.xml file into Eclipse manually, follow these steps:

1. **In the Package Explorer view, right-click the WEB-INF folder and choose New⇨File.**

   The New File dialog box appears.

2. **In the File Name text box, type** struts-config.xml **and then click Finish.**
3. **Type Listing 3-8.**

   Do not include the line numbers.

4. **To save your changes, choose File⇨Save.**

Creating the project in other development environments

If you're not using Eclipse as your development environment, you still need to follow the basic steps as described throughout this chapter. To summarize, you need to

1. Create the folder structure used for a Web application.
2. Put all the JAR and TLD files into the proper folders.
3. Set up your classpath to include all the library files described in this chapter.
4. Download the Project files from the Web site.
5. Copy the various project files into the proper folders as explained in the "Web application folder structure" sidebar.
6. Compile the Java source files and put the class files into the `classes` folder.

Now you have the all the files necessary for the project. Your Package Manager View should look like Figure 3-12.

If you're using a development environment other than Eclipse, check out the "Creating the project in other development environments" sidebar.

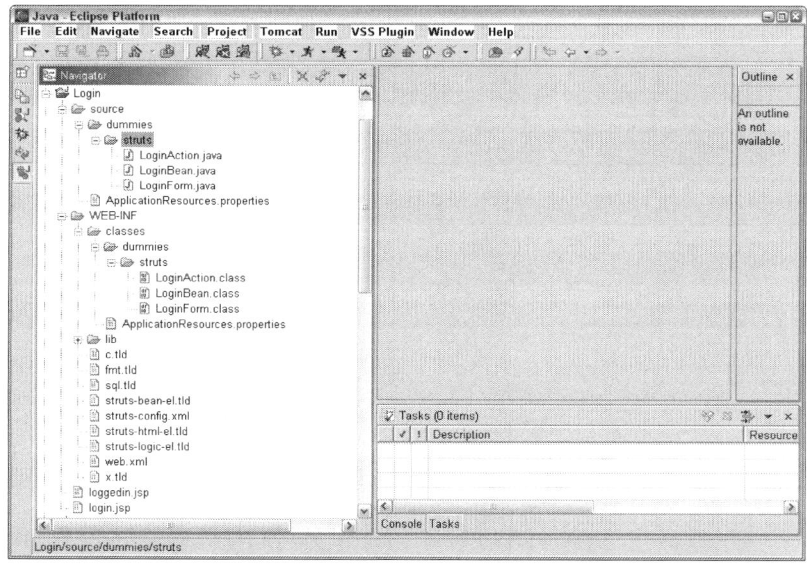

Figure 3-12: The Package Manager after importing the project files.

Strutting Your Stuff: Running the Application

The time has come to see your Login project in operation. The last step before proceeding is to compile the Java source files. Before compiling, be sure you have set the default output folder to point to `WEB-INF/classes`, as explained in "Creating the packages" earlier in this chapter.

To compile your source code, choose Project⇨Rebuild Project. This command generates the class files and puts them in the `classes` folder, preserving the structure of the `dummies/struts` package.

At this point, your folder structure should look like Figure 3-13. If your folder structure is different, review the appropriate part of Chapter 3 to see what step you missed. Once everything is in place, you can continue here.

Deploying the Login application

The folder structure you created for the development process is also the structure that the Web container requires for Web applications. Deploying the application is just a matter of copying a few files and folders to the `webapps` folder in the `Tomcat` application folder. To copy the required files and folders, follow these steps:

1. **In Windows Explorer, go to the `webapps` subfolder of your Tomcat folder and create a `Login` folder to hold your Web application files.**
2. **In Windows Explorer, go to the `workspace` folder of the `Eclipse` folder and open the `Login` folder.**
3. **In the window with the `workspace` folder, select the two JSP files and the `WEB-INF` folder in the `Eclipse` folder and Ctrl-drag to copy (not move) them to the `Login` folder in `Tomcat-4.1/webapps`.**

You have just deployed your application.

Testing the application

The Login application is complete, and you should now test it. To test the application, follow these steps:

1. **Open Eclipse.**
2. **If you're not sure that Tomcat is running, click the Tomcat Restart icon.**

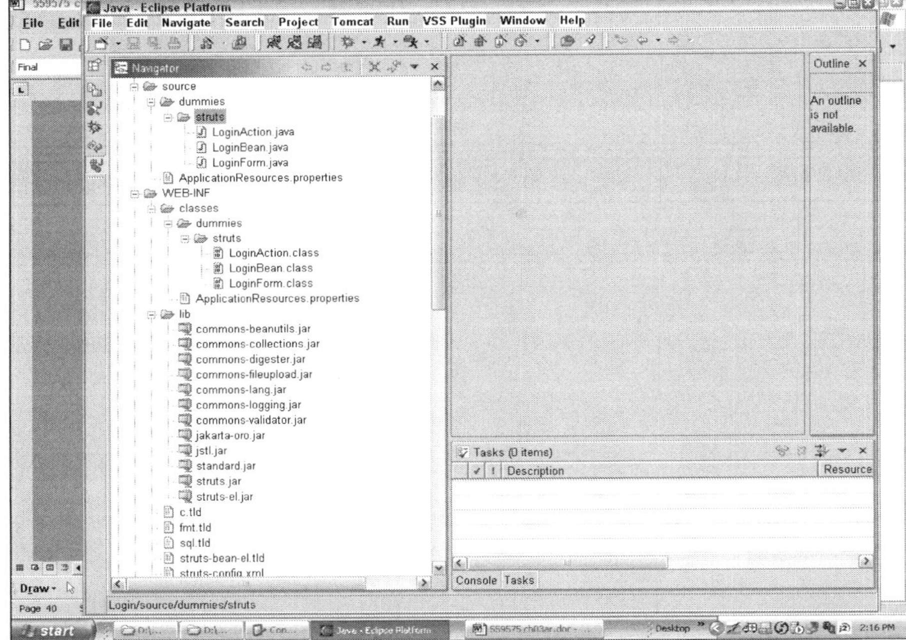

Figure 3-13: The final folder structure for the Login project.

3. **In your favorite Web browser, type the application's URL:** `http://localhost/Login`.

   (Because the application defines a default page, you do not need to enter `login.jsp`.) You see the login page, as shown in Figure 3-9.

4. **To test the validation process, click the Log In button without entering any information,.**

   The application should respond with error messages next to both the username and password fields, as shown in Figure 3-14.

5. **Try the application again, this time supplying either a password or a username, but not both.**

   Again, you should see an error message next to the field missing data.

6. **Try logging in with a bad username or password, and then click the Log In button.**

   This time the error message should appear at the top of the page because it is a more general error than the previous ones.

7. **Type a valid username and password (as defined in `LoginBean`) and then click Log In.**

Figure 3-14: Login errors for missing information.

For example, try **Twinkle Toes** as the username and **tt** as the password. The `loggedin.jsp` page should appear (see Figure 3-10) and the user's name should be embedded in the message.

Congratulations on completing your first Struts Web application.

Debugging with Eclipse

In Chapter 2 we discussed the Tomcat plug-in for Eclipse and mentioned how it registers the Eclipse debugger with Tomcat, allowing you to debug all your Web application code from the Eclipse environment.

It is beyond the scope of this book to describe the Eclipse environment in any depth. But let's take a few minutes to explore how you can use the debugging feature to troubleshoot your Web applications.

Setting a breakpoint

You can easily set a breakpoint in your Java source code by double-clicking the gray area to the left of the line where you want to stop. To try this out, follow these steps:

1. **In the Package Explorer view in Eclipse, double-click the** `LoginAction.java` **file.**

   The `LoginAction.java` file opens in the Eclipse editor.

2. **To set a breakpoint in the first line of the** `execute` **method where you instantiate a copy of the** `LoginBean`**, double-click the margin to the left of that line of code.**

   Refer to Figure 3-15.

3. **Go back to your browser and reenter the** `http://localhost/Login` **URL to display** `login.jsp` **again.**

4. **Type an invalid username and password, and then click Log In.**

   This action ensures that the `LoginAction` code is executed and that you will therefore come to the breakpoint that you just set.

5. **Return to Eclipse.**

   Notice that Perspective has changed from the Java Perspective to the Debug Perspective. Eclipse now displays Views that are more appropriate for the task at hand.

6. **Use the debugger icons at the top of the Debug View or the equivalent menu items in the Run menu to step through your code.**

For further information about debugging under Eclipse, look at the debugging topics in Eclipse Help.

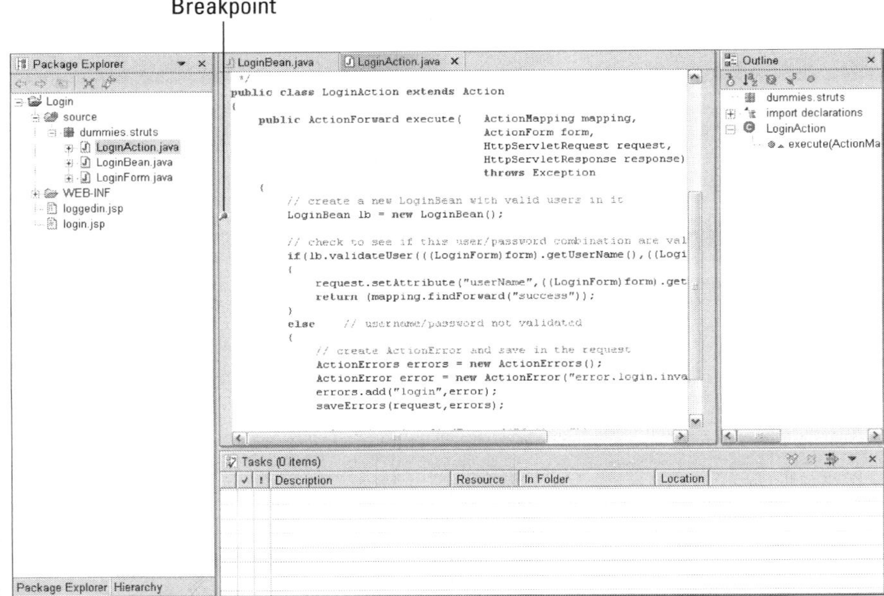

Figure 3-15: LoginAction.java in the Editor with the breakpoint set.

Part II
Starting from the Core

"Give him air! Give him air! He'll be okay. He's just been exposed to some raw HTML code. It must have accidently flashed across his screen from the server."

In this part . . .

This is where you delve into the three parts of Struts: the Controller, the Model, and the View. Chapter 4 explains the Controller and how you use it to make your Web application execute the business logic that you require. Chapter 5 discusses the Model, which represents your data. Chapter 6 covers the View, so that your viewers can see the results of all your great work. Finally, Chapter 7 explains the Struts and Web container configuration files that you need to use to make sure all the sections of your code stay connected.

Chapter 4

Controlling with the Controller

In This Chapter

- Working with the Struts Controller classes
- Understanding the ActionServlet
- Using the RequestProcessor
- Creating the Action classes

When you created a Web application using Java in the olden days, you probably started to write Servlets to service your JSP pages, or in Struts terminology, your views. In these enlightened times, you can use the Struts Controller classes to help you fly through the development process. In this chapter, we explain the Struts Controller classes and show you how they can keep you organized.

Understanding the Struts Controller Classes

The Struts Controller layer of the MVC design pattern makes up the majority of the classes in the Struts framework. This is to be expected because Struts is not tied to any particular View or Model implementation. (We explain this in more detail in the "How Struts enforces the MVC pattern" section in Chapter 1.) Regarding the View or Model implementation, the Struts architecture is flexible and can adapt to many possibilities. Therefore, the emphasis in Struts is in the area of implementing the set of classes that go to make up the Controller.

The Struts Controller contains 41 classes and an additional 17 utility classes as of this writing. The principal Controller classes are shown in the UML diagram in Figure 4-1. (UML stands for Unified Modeling Language and is the most common diagramming methodology for software design.) The following section provides a brief description of each of the classes. Later in the chapter, we provide more detail.

The principal Controller classes are as follows:

- `ActionServlet`: A subclass of `javax.servlet.http.HttpServlet`, like most Servlets. The `ActionServlet` handles all requests to the Struts framework whose URL ends in `.do`. The use of `.do` to indicate that Struts should handle the request was defined in the `web.xml` file we create in Chapter 3.
- `RequestProcessor`: The workhorse of the Controller, whose main functions are to gather all necessary resources for a request by using the configurations in the `struts-config.xml` file and pass control to the proper `Action` subclass.
- `Action`: A generic abstract class to handle specific requests from the client, that is, the user. You always subclass this class (creating new subclasses such as `MyAction1`, `MyAction2`, `...` `MyAction`*N*) for the particular needs of the request.

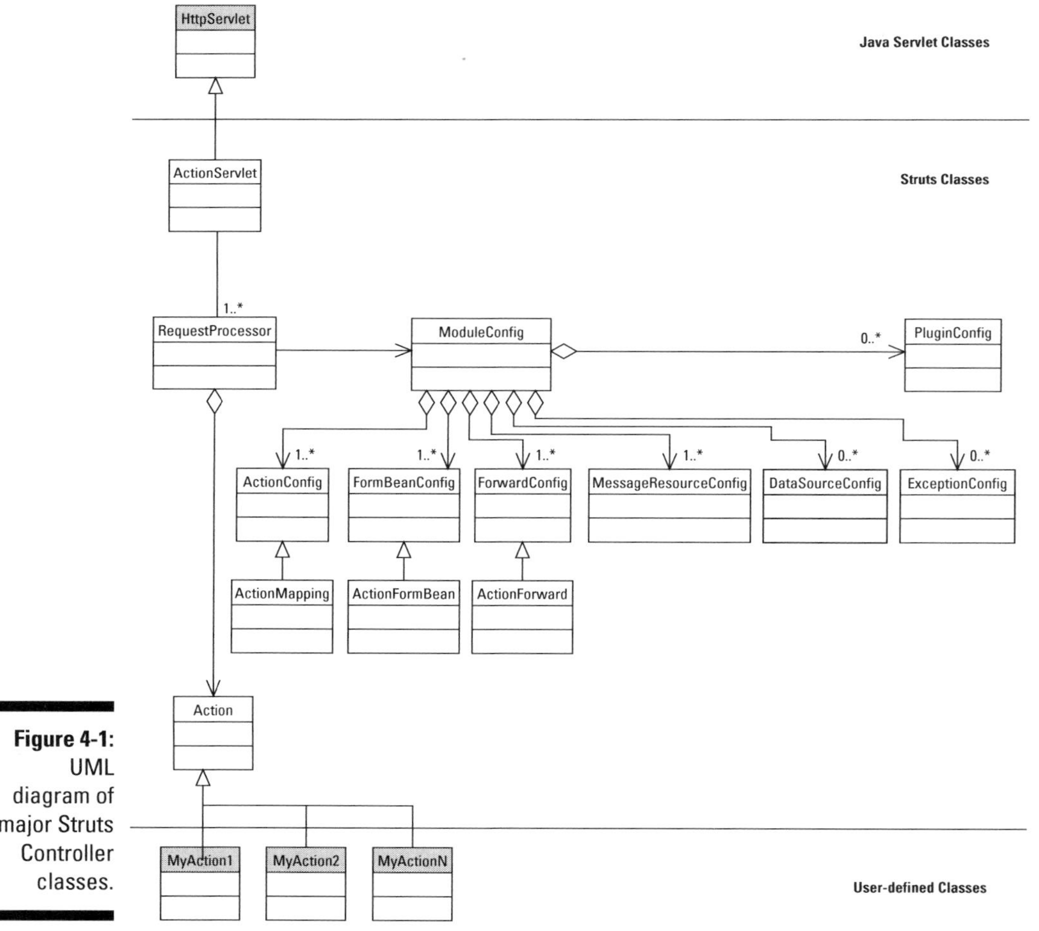

Figure 4-1: UML diagram of major Struts Controller classes.

- ModuleConfig: A class containing all the configuration information for each module in the application. Much of this configuration information is represented in the classes that follow.
- ActionConfig **and** ActionMapping: These classes contain all the mapping information needed to map a particular request to a particular Action class. ActionMapping extends ActionConfig.
- FormBeanConfig **and** ActionFormBean: These classes represent a FormBean. ActionFormBean extends FormBeanConfig.
- ForwardConfig **and** ActionForward: These classes represent destinations to which an Action might direct the RequestProcessor to forward or redirect a request. ActionForward extends ForwardConfig. Struts will create an ActionForward class for each forward definition in the struts-config.xml file.
- MessageResourcesConfig: Represents MessageResources associated with a module of a Struts application. For example, in the Login application created in Chapter 3, MessageResourcesConfig would contain the contents of the ApplicationResources.properties file.
- DataSourceConfig: Represents datasource elements in the struts-config file. DataSources are implementations of the javax.sql.DataSource interface that provide database connection management and pooling. See Chapter 5 for more information.
- ExceptionConfig: Represents exception elements in the struts-config file. An exception element defines how Struts will react to particular types of exceptions.
- PluginConfig: Represents plug-in elements in the struts-config file. See Chapter 9 for more information on plug-ins.

Working with the Master Controller — the ActionServlet

The ActionServlet class is the front-line soldier in the Struts Controller and is responsible for handling all requests that come to the Web application. Frankly, the ActionServlet doesn't do very much, but it's still important because it is the first to act.

In this chapter, we mention the classes of the Struts Controller in some detail to give you more understanding of their purpose. Because Struts is an open-source project, the source code is available to you, the developer, to use as needed for the particulars of your application. Therefore, if you need the ActionServlet (or any other Struts class) to do something different, you simply have to implement a subclass and add the new functionality.

Starting the Servlet

When the Web container starts, it looks in the web.xml file of each Web application it is serving and starts the described Servlets in the prescribed order as defined in web.xml. Generally, the ActionServlet is the first Servlet started in a Struts application.

Because the ActionServlet is just like any other Servlet, it overrides the init method of its parent class, HttpServlet. The Web container calls the init method to allow the Servlet to initialize whatever resources the Servlet needs to run. ActionServlet does the bulk of its work during this initialization phase. This phase creates all the resources needed by the Servlet and the modules.

An application can be made of one or more modules. Each module represents a logical set of functionality that together makes the application a whole. Smaller applications generally have only one module. (The sample Login application in Chapter 3 has just the default module.) But if the project is larger, with numerous developers or teams, dividing the application into separate modules makes it easier for the different groups to work on the application without running into each other. Each module has its own struts-config.xml file. ActionServlet must be made aware of additional modules. This is accomplished in the ActionServlet configuration found in the web.xml file. For example, if you want to have a separate module named purchasing that's configured in its own struts-config.xml file, you add that information as follows to the web.xml file:

```
<servlet ...>
     <!--default module -->
<init-param>
  <param-name>config</param-name>
  <param-value>/WEB-INF/struts-config.xml</param-value>
</init-param>
     <!--purchasing module -->
<init-param>
  <param-name>config/purchasing</param-name>
  <param-value>/WEB-INF/struts-config-purch.xml</param-value>
</init-param>
</servlet>
```

The default module is defined by the struts-config.xml file while the purchasing module uses the struts-config-purch.xml for configuration. To switch from one module to another, use the SwitchAction mechanism (described later in the chapter) or use the module name in the forward definition, as in this example:

```
<action ... >
  <forward name="success"
           contextRelative="true"
```

```
            path="/Purchasing/index.do"
            redirect="true"/>
</action>
```

Following are the major steps that `ActionServlet` takes at initialization time. These initialization steps are also shown in Figure 4-2.

1. **Creates the message resources used internally by `ActionServlet`.**

   These are different than the message resources used by each module. We discuss message resources briefly in the "Using message resources" section of Chapter 3 and discuss them further in Chapter 6.

2. **Defines some of the global characteristics of the application, including the location of the `struts-config.xml` file.**

   Normally the `struts-config.xml` file is in the `WEB-INF` folder. However, you can define the `struts-config.xml` file to be in some other location. You specify this in the `web.xml` file, which passes the new location as a parameter to `ActionServlet`.

Threads and Servlets

One important aspect of Servlet technology is that it creates only one instance of the Servlet. Even so, the Servlet can handle multiple requests simultaneously because each request is handled by an individual thread. A *thread* is an instance of execution of the program's code. Java Servlets (and any Java class) can support multiple threads running simultaneously, which is great when you have many people using your Web application at the same time. The only catch is that you have to write your Servlet code to be thread-safe.

For write *thread-safe code,* you need to ensure that no conflict occurs when multiple clients run the code simultaneously. What kind of conflict *could* occur? For example, if you define instance or class variables that could be used by a method in the class, what happens if two threads attempt to modify and then read the same variable? Let's say that thread 1 modifies instance variable x to the value 19 and thread 2 then changes the value to 44. Then thread 1 reads the value to perform some additional operation. It should read 19 but instead reads 44. Uh oh! Your client pays $44 for that $19 tee shirt. The wrong result occurs because of this conflict.

How do you make sure that each thread finds the right variable value? In the case of Servlets, you just make sure you do not use class or instance variables. (The exception would be if the class or instance variables were initialized at startup and then used in a read-only fashion.) Use only local variables in each method because local variables are unique for each thread. You can apply this method to other classes that you want to make thread-safe. Another technique for thread-safety is the use of the `synchronized` keyword. See

```
java.sun.com/docs/books/
    tutorial/essential/threads/
```

to find out more about Java threads, including the `synchronized` keyword.

In previous versions of Struts, `ActionServlet` also set the debug level. However, it is now recommended that you set the debug level in the underlying logging implementation. We talk more about logging in Chapter 13.

3. **Sets up the Servlet mapping that determines how this `ActionServlet` is accessed.**

   This retrieves information from the `web.xml` file about the name used for this `ActionServlet` and what URL pattern it handles. These values are stored in the Application context, or scope.

4. **Creates the `ModuleConfig` instance for the first (and possibly only) module in the application.**

5. **Initializes the message resources for each module.**

   Each module can have one or more message resource files defined in the Struts configuration file. These files are read into memory during initialization.

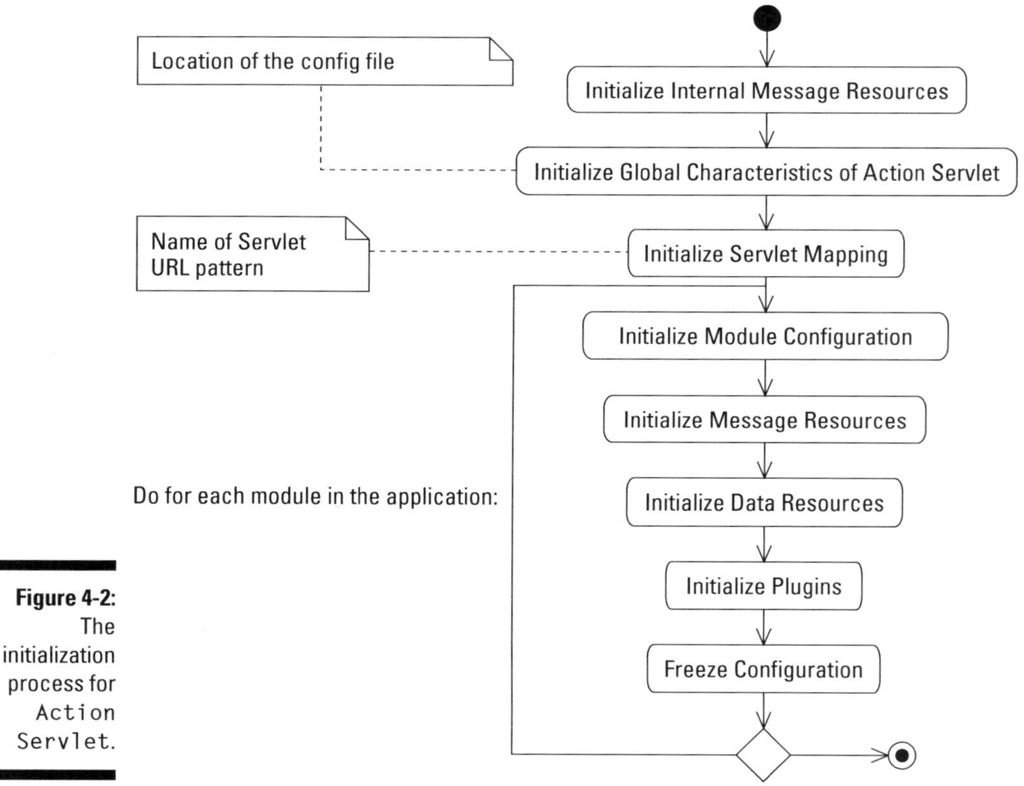

Figure 4-2: The initialization process for `ActionServlet`.

Because message resource files are read into memory during initialization, any changes that you make to a message resource file after the application starts do not take effect until the next startup.

6. **Initializes the data resources for this module.**

   If data resources are defined for your application, they're initialized at this step. (See Chapter 5 for more information on data resources.)

7. **Initializes the plug-ins for this module.**

   If plug-ins are defined for your application, they're initialized at this step. (See Chapter 9 for more information on plug-ins.)

8. **Freezes the configuration for this module.**

   The `ModuleConfig` object is marked as initialized and nonchangeable. Any attempt to change the configuration settings for the `ModuleConfig` object will result in an error.

9. **Repeats Steps 4 through 8 for any additional modules.**

Processing requests

After `ActionServlet` is initialized, it is ready for its main purpose: handling user requests. When a request comes in from the client, the Web container routes the request to `ActionServlet`. How do you know this? Step 3 in the `ActionServlet` initialization process, just listed, states that the `web.xml` file defines the URL pattern that this Servlet handles. Any request for the application must have the defined pattern in its URL (usually `*.do`), and therefore the Web container routes the request to the `ActionServlet`.

Every request is handled by the `process` method. The `process` method first adds `ModuleConfig` and `MessageResources` to the request. If the application has more than one module, the module's particular `ModuleConfig` and `MessageResources` are used. Then `ActionServlet` gets the `RequestProcessor` instance for the module being called and calls the `process` method of `RequestProcessor`, the real workhorse of request processing in Struts.

That's it. `ActionServlet` is finished — at least until the next request comes in or the container shuts down.

Shutting down the Servlet

When it's time to shut down the application, the Web container calls the `ActionServlet`'s `destroy` method to notify `ActionServlet` of the impending shutdown. This is a standard method of the `HttpServlet` class that `ActionServlet` overrides. During the execution of this method, `ActionServlet` releases any resources generated during the initialization phase — module resources, datasource resources, internal message resources, and the logger resource.

Working with the Controller's Helper — RequestProcessor

We've all seen work sites where a bunch of people are digging a ditch. One person is standing around watching and making a few comments, while the others are down in the hole feverishly digging with their shovels. That's the relationship between `ActionServlet` and `RequestProcessor`. `ActionServlet` tells `RequestProcessor`, "dig here," and `RequestProcessor` does most of the work.

`ActionServlet` calls the `RequestProcessor`'s `process` method to handle the incoming request. The `process` method then performs a series of steps, gathering resources for the request, calling the specific actions that act on the request, and finally forwarding or redirecting the response to the appropriate destination. Following are the detailed steps taken by `RequestProcessor` for each request it handles:

1. **Wraps the request in a special wrapper if the request's content type is `multipart/form-data`.**

   Struts includes a library to provide file upload services. You put that library (`commons-fileupload.jar`) in the `WEB-INF/lib` folder. When a user uploads a file, the file has a special content type of `multipart/form-data`. When the `RequestProcessor` finds a request with that special type, it puts the request in a special wrapper class so that the request can be processed more easily.

2. **Gets the path in order to select the mapping.**

   `RequestProcessor` determines from the request URL the path that caused the request and then uses that path in Step 7 to determine which `ActionMapping` to select.

3. **Selects the `Locale` for the request in the session scope, if configured to do so.**

   By default, the `Locale` of the request is set into the session scope. To change it, you would need to specify a different `ControllerConfig` class in the `struts-config.xml` file and set the `locale` attribute to `false`.

   A `Locale` represents a user's language and geographical region. By knowing the `Locale`, the application can customize the language and regional formatting for values such as dates and money.

4. **Sets the content type for the response, if configured to do so in the `struts-config` file.**

   Otherwise, the content type is the standard `text/html`. This can be changed by specifying a different `ControlConfig` class and setting the `contentType` attribute to another valid value.

5. **Sets a no-cache header to disallow caching of the page, if configured to do so.**

   By default, caching is allowed. To disallow caching, you must specify a different `ControllerConfig` class and set the `noCache` attribute to `true`.

6. **Performs custom preprocessing, if defined in a subclass.**

   The `processPreprocess` method is a *hook* (an empty method designed to be overridden) to allow developers to add custom preprocessing logic to each request. To make use of preprocessing, you need to subclass the `RequestProcessor` class and override the `processPreprocess` method. This is described more fully in Chapter 9.

7. **Gets the `ActionMapping` instance to use.**

   Based on the path used for the request, `RequestProcessor` looks up the `ActionMapping` instance. `ActionMapping` determines which of the `Action` classes to call to process the request.

8. **Checks security roles for this action to make sure that the user can perform it.**

   The Web container has a built-in security architecture that each application can use. If the application uses the built-in security, the `struts-config` file defines how to use it. This step verifies that the current user can perform any specific action.

9. **Gets the `ActionForm` instance associated with the request.**

   `RequestProcessor` gets `ActionForm` associated with this action based on `ActionMapping`. If `ActionForm` does not yet exist, `RequestProcessor` creates it.

10. **Populates `ActionForm`.**

    Uses the parameters from the request to populate `ActionForm`.

11. **Validates `ActionForm`.**

    If you're using standard form validation, `RequestProcessor` calls the `ActionForm`'s `validate` method now. If validation has any errors, `RequestProcessor` forwards control back to the input form from which the request came.

12. **Processes a `forward` or `include` if specified in `ActionMapping`.**

    If you have used a `forward` or `include` attribute in the action mapping, `RequestProcessor` processes them at this point. One of these two attributes is used if you do not specify an `Action` method to receive control. We define these attributes in Chapter 7.

13. **Calls the `execute` method on the specific `Action` class.**

    Finally, the `Action` class gets to do its stuff. At this point, the code we have written to handle this request gets executed. When it is finished, it returns an instance of `ActionForward`.

14. **Forwards or redirects to the destination specified by `ActionForward`.**

    The last step in the request processing is to forward or redirect the user to the specified destination, usually a JSP page.

Each module that the application has defined has one `RequestProcessor` instance. Each `RequestProcessor` has a reference to `ModuleConfig` for that module. Figure 4-1 shows the relationship between `RequestProcessor` and `ModuleConfig`. The `ModuleConfig` class has all the necessary information (mappings, datasources, forwards, exceptions, formbeans, message resources, plug-ins, and prefix) to fully describe each module

Getting Down to Work: Extending ActionClass

When you start to work with the `Action` class you *have* to extend the Struts framework to accommodate the particular needs of your application. `Action Servlet` and `RequestProcessor` *can* be extended, if you want. But you *must* extend the `Action` class for two reasons:

- The `Action` class is a Struts class that must be subclassed to be used.
- `Action` subclasses are the only way for you to process a user's request. After all, you're the only one who knows how you want to respond to your users.

`Action` subclasses must be thread-safe, as we explain in the "Threads and Servlets" sidebar in this chapter, because `RequestProcessor` creates only one instance of each `Action` subclass. If more than one user requests at the same time that the same action be performed, the one instance of the `Action` class will be called on to do multiple tasks. Therefore, you must use only local variables (class or instance variables that are read-only would also be safe).

When a request comes in, `RequestProcessor` needs to know which `Action` subclass should have control. `RequestProcessor` finds the necessary information from the `ActionMapping` instance that relates the request URL with a particular `Action` class. The `ActionMapping` instance also indicates which `ActionForm` should be used with the request. You provide the necessary information for `ActionMapping` when you define the action mappings in the `struts-config` file. (See Chapter 7 for more on action mappings.)

Using the execute method

`RequestProcessor` calls the `execute` method when it is ready to pass control to the `Action` class. This method is the principal worker method in the class. In the `execute` method you define all the operations that are necessary to handle the request. However, you should not embed all logic in the `execute` method. In fact, if you need to apply some business rules or operations, you should create a separate set of business objects. If you follow the MVC model, the Model should be responsible for business logic and data manipulation. The Controller just makes decisions about the flow of control.

The `Action` class can do anything you want it to do. Well, it can't tap dance or wear a top hat. Typically, the `Action` class performs the following steps:

1. **Verifies the user.**

   If this `Action` is a protected operation (requiring authorization), the first thing `Action` should do is to verify the user's authorization. (If you're using Web-container-based security, you hand over user verification to the Web container.) Verification could take many forms depending on what kind of authorization scheme you use. We talk more about security issues in Chapter 12.

2. **Determines which action needs to be performed and performs the action.**

   If the action is simple and straightforward, you need only one action. Sometimes, you may have two or more choices depending on some form parameter. For example, you may have a page that displays a list of all purchase orders for a particular user. Let's say that the page contains a button that enables the user to display the purchase orders for a particular date. You have one `Action` class that handles both the initial request and subsequent requests for particular purchase orders. In your `execute` method, you need to know whether to display all purchase orders for the user or perform a search based on a particular date. Therefore, you need to check a form parameter to determine which operation to perform.

3. **Sets or updates the necessary attributes that the destination page will need.**

   This may mean putting a JavaBean into one of the scopes, or it may mean updating a formbean so that when the page is redisplayed it has the updated values.

4. **Returns an appropriate `ActionForward` object to display the proper View.**

   The `ActionForward` object will have all the information needed for the `RequestProcessor` to determine where to forward control.

Listing 4-1 shows some of the highlights of the `Action` class. Comments throughout the listing explain the purpose of the code.

Listing 4-1 Example of an Action Class

```
public class POListAction extends Action
{
    public ActionForward execute(ActionMapping mapping,
                                 ActionForm form,
                                 HttpServletRequest request,
                                 HttpServletResponse response)
        throws Exception
    {
        // Extract attributes we will need from the session
        HttpSession session = request.getSession();
        // If validated, user will be in the session
        User user = (User) session.getAttribute(Constants.USER_KEY);
        // Get the POListBean, if it exists
        POListBean polBean = (POListBean)
              session.getAttribute(Constants.POLIST_KEY);
        // ensure user has logged on, otherwise make them
        if (user == null)
        {
            return (mapping.findForward("logon"));  // make user logon
        }
        // ensure we have a POListBean, otherwise create one
        if (polBean == null)
        {
            polBean = new POListBean();
        }
        // the action value will determine what we need to do
        POListForm polForm = (POListForm) form;
        String action = polForm.getAction();
        // if null, first time to the form - just get the user's POs
        if ((action == null))
        {
            polBean.findAll(user);      // get all the user's pos
        }
        // Action == Find - do a search
        else if(action.equals("find"))

        {
            // perform the search for the specified purchase orders
            polBean.findPurchaseOrders( polForm.getFind(),
                                        polForm.getFilter(),
                                        polForm.getFrom(),
                                        polForm.getTo(),
                                        user);
        }
        // save the updated bean
        session.setAttribute(Constants.POLIST_KEY, polBean);
        return (mapping.findForward("success"));
    }
}
```

The listing performs the four common steps of the Action class, as follows:

- Lines 1, 2, 4, and 5: Validate the user.
- Lines 9, 10, and 12: Determine the action to perform and then perform that action.
- Line 14: Sets the attribute that the destination page will need.
- Line 15: Returns the proper ActionForward object to call the destination page.

Predefined Action classes

Struts has five predefined Action classes for developers to use. Why would you want to use these classes? In the appropriate situation, these classes can save you a lot of time. These classes are explained in the next few sections.

ForwardAction

The ForwardAction class is useful when you're trying to integrate Struts into an existing application that uses Servlets to perform business logic functions. You can use this class to take advantage of the Struts controller and its functionality, without having to rewrite the existing Servlets. Use ForwardAction to forward a request to another resource in your application, such as a Servlet that already does business logic processing or even another JSP page. By using this predefined action, you don't have to write your own Action class. You just have to set up the struts-config file properly to use ForwardAction.

The configuration to use ForwardAction is almost identical to regular Action class configurations except you use the parameter attribute to specify where the request should be forwarded to instead of the forward attribute. The following code example is from the Struts API documentation:

```
<action path="/saveSubscription"
        type="org.apache.struts.actions.ForwardAction"
        name="subscriptionForm"
        scope="request"
        input="/subscription.jsp"
        parameter="/path/to/processing/servlet"/>
```

The type attribute is the full class name of the ForwardAction class. The parameter attribute is pointing to the path of the resource you want to forward control to. The other attributes are like normal action definitions.

IncludeAction

Like ForwardAction, the IncludeAction class is useful when you want to integrate Struts into an application that uses Servlets. Use the IncludeAction class to include another resource in the response to the request being processed. All that you have to do is set up the struts-config file properly to use IncludeAction, no extension of the class is necessary. The following code example is from the Struts API documentation:

```
<action path="/saveSubscription"
        type="org.apache.struts.actions.IncludeAction"
        name="subscriptionForm"
        scope="request"
        input="/subscription.jsp"
        parameter="/path/to/included/resource" />
```

The type attribute is the full class name of the IncludeAction class. The parameter attribute is pointing to the path of the resource you want to include. The other attributes are like normal action definitions.

SwitchAction

The SwitchAction class provides a means to switch from a resource in one module to another resource in a different module. SwitchAction is useful only if you have multiple modules in your Struts application. The SwitchAction class can be used as is, without extending.

To switch to another resource in a different module, set up an action path using SwitchAction in the struts-config file, as shown in this code snippet:

```
<action path="/toModule"
        type="org.apache.struts.actions.SwitchAction"  />
```

Then whenever you want to accomplish a switch, you use the /toModule path in your URL along with two parameters:

- The prefix parameter indicates which module you want to switch to.
- The page parameter indicates which URL gets control after switching modules.

For example, if you want to switch to the purchasing.do URL in module2, your URL might look like this:

```
http://localhost/toModule.do?prefix=/module2&page=/
        purchasing.do
```

When you switch back to the default module, use an empty string for the prefix parameter, as in the following URL:

```
http://localhost/toModule.do?prefix=&page=/index.do
```

DispatchAction

The DispatchAction class is for developers who want to have numerous similar actions in a single Action class. You may have a View that offers the user many possible actions to perform. For example, suppose that you have a page with a list of purchase orders that the user can sort, void, or print. These actions all relate to the list of purchase orders, so you might implement a single `Action` class to handle the possible actions. Rather than crowd the `execute` method with a series of if-then-else statements, you may opt to create separate methods that each handle one possible action from the user. The `DispatchAction` class is abstract and must be extended to be used.

In the purchasing order example, you could create a separate method (`sort`, `print`, and `void`) for each of the possible actions. These methods would need the same method signature as the standard `execute` method found in the `Action` class. This shows the `execute` method signature:

```
public ActionForward execute(ActionMapping mapping,
                             ActionForm form,
                             HttpServletRequest request,
                             HttpServletResponse response)
                      throws Exception
```

Your three method signatures would look just like the `execute` method signature, down to the fact that your new methods return an `ActionForward` object. Following is an example of how to define the `sort` method signature:

```
public ActionForward sort(ActionMapping mapping,
                          ActionForm form,
                          HttpServletRequest request,
                          HttpServletResponse response)
                   throws Exception
```

When you extend the `DispatchAction` class, do not override the `execute` method. That method is now responsible for calling one of your defined `action` methods.

The final step is to configure `strut-config` to make use of `DispatchAction`. The configuration is just like configuring any action except for the `parameter` attribute. The value of the `parameter` attribute defines the name of the request parameter that will pass along the name of the method to be executed. If you want to call the `sort` method for the `polist` action, you use the following URL:

```
http://localhost/myapp/polist.do?method=sort
```

Here is an example for configuring `DispatchAction`:

```
<action path="/polist"
        type="org.example.POListAction"
        name="polistForm"
        scope="request"
        input="/polist.jsp"
        parameter="method"/>
```

The type attribute is the full class name of the extended DispatchAction class. The parameter attribute names the request parameter method. The other attributes are like normal action definitions.

LookupDispatchAction

The predefined LookupDispatchAction is similar to DispatchAction, in that you define in one Action multiple methods that handle similar actions. The difference between LookupDispatchAction and DispatchAction is that the actual method that gets called in LookupDispatchAction is based on a lookup of a key value instead of specifying the method name directly. The LookupDispatchAction class is abstract and must be extended to be used.

The entry into the configuration file is similar to DispatchAction. The parameter attribute contains the name of the request parameter. This time, however, the value in the parameter is not a method name but a key used to look up the method name:

```
<action path="/test"
        type="org.example.MyLookupAction"
        name="MyForm"
        scope="request"
        input="/test.jsp"
        parameter="action"/>
```

The type attribute is the full class name of the extended LookupDispatchAction class. The parameter attribute names the request parameter action. The remaining attributes are defined like any other standard action definition.

Because the method to be looked up is based on a key value, LookupDispatchAction is more suited to an application that contains multiple submit buttons with the same name (but different labels and different actions) on a single page, as in the code segment that follows:

```
1<html:form action="/test">
2    <html:submit property="action">
3        <bean:message key="button.add"/>
4    </html:submit>
5    <html:submit property="action">
6        <bean:message key="button.delete">
7    </html:submit>
8</html:form>
```

In this code, all tags are custom tags from the Struts tag libraries. In particular, notice that lines 2 and 5 are defining a submit button whose name is action. Lines 3 and 6 define how the buttons are labeled and also what value is submitted when the button is clicked. When the form is submitted, action will be a request parameter and the button's label will be the value.

Assume that the following keys are part of the ApplicationResources.properties file:

```
button.add=Add Record
button.delete=Delete Record
```

In this example, if the first button is clicked, the action parameter contains the Add Record string. If the second button is clicked, the action parameter contains Delete Record.

You extend LookupDispatchAction in a manner similar to how you extend DispatchAction:

- You do not override the execute method.
- You need to create your specialized methods to handle each of the actions to be serviced. These methods need to have the same method signature as the execute method.
- You must create a protected method named getKeyMethodMap that returns a Map. In the implementation of the method, you need to create a HashMap and enter key-value pairs. The key corresponds to the keys used in defining the buttons on your forms. The value is the name of the associated method to invoke.

The following code shows an example of implementing getKeyMapMethod:

```
protected Map getKeyMethodMap()
{
    Map map = new HashMap();
    map.put("button.add", "add");     // add is the method to invoke
    map.put("button.delete", "delete"); // delete is the method to invoke
    return map;
}
```

The following code shows how the add and delete methods would look. Note that they return an ActionForward object just like the execute method does:

```
   public ActionForward add(ActionMapping mapping,
          ActionForm form,
          HttpServletRequest request,
          HttpServletResponse response)
          throws IOException, ServletException
   {
       // do add logic here. . .
       return mapping.findForward("success");
   }

   public ActionForward delete(ActionMapping mapping,
          ActionForm form,
          HttpServletRequest request,
          HttpServletResponse response)
```

```
        throws IOException, ServletException
{
    // do delete logic here. . .
    return mapping.findForward("success");
}
```

The final step in understanding how the pieces of the `LookupDispatchAction` puzzle come together is to know that the `execute` method gets the value of the `action` parameter and then uses that value to find the associated key in the message resources. After the `execute` method finds the key, the key is used to look up the method name in `Map`, which the `getKeyMethodMap` method returned. The `execute` method goes through the following steps:

1. **Gets the name of the parameter that contains the key by looking in the `ActionMapping`.**

   This is defined in the preceding action configuration example to be `action`.

2. **Gets the value of the `action` parameter from the request.**

   In the example, this is either `Add Record` or `Delete Record`.

3. **Using the message resources associated with this application, looks up the key for the value retrieved from the `action` parameter.**

   In the example, the key could be `button.add` or `button.delete`.

4. **Using the retrieved key, looks up the method name from the `Map` built by `getKeyMethodMap`.**

   In the example, the resulting name is `add` or `delete`.

5. **Calls the method.**

Action Forms

While the `ActionForm` class is part of the Controller, we postpone its discussion until we talk about Views in Chapter 6. It is the function of `ActionForm` to move information between the View and the Controller.

Now that you have seen what the Struts Controller does, you can appreciate the benefit of using this framework instead of trying to write your own. The Struts Controller is an elegant, simple, and extensible design that provides maximum flexibility in creating Web applications that cover the gamut of possibilities from relatively simple to complex, enterprise level, multideveloper products.

Chapter 5
Creating the Model

In This Chapter

- What is the Model?
- Using business objects
- Working with the Model
- Getting a database server
- Using an IDE and Web container with your database server
- Using MySQL
- Connecting the Model to a database
- Using connection pooling

For those of you who think the Model is related to a fashion show, you're in the wrong book. We're talking about the Model part of the MVC design pattern. It would be an oversimplification to say that the Model is just about the business data. Yet the Model represents the business domain more than the View does, and certainly more than the Controller does and typically you use the Model in Jakarta Struts to help you connect your Web site with a database. In this chapter, we explain how to connect your user with your data.

Understanding the Model

The Model holds and manages the business data and all the business functions related to the data. The Model also provides implementations for accessing and modifying the business data that can be invoked by the View or the Controller.

To manage all that data, the Model usually includes at least one instance of some persistent data store, most commonly a relational database server. However, the Model could interact with many different databases and types of data sources anywhere in the world. How the Model represents the business data and logic is transparent to the View and the Controller. They don't need to know whether the data resides on the same server as the Web container or on another server somewhere in Australia. They need to know only the interface of the Model to access the various business functions and data items.

Just imagine a banking application that allows users to access their banking information and withdraw money from thousands of ATMs anywhere in the world. Now you have an idea of how complex the Model can become.

By separating the Model from the View and the Controller, you can share the business data and logic across many different applications and different types of applications, such as Web applications, client-server applications, and even Business-to-Business (B2B) applications. For example, in a B2B application, your Model layer may interact with the business functions of another organization such as a credit card processing center. This flexibility creates a powerful architecture in which systems can grow and expand with a business — you can easily extend and scale systems to accommodate future demands.

In Chapter 3 we introduce a simple Login application that doesn't even have a database, containing just one business object, the `LoginBean`. In this chapter, we enhance the Login application example by connecting it to a database as shown in Figure 5-1.

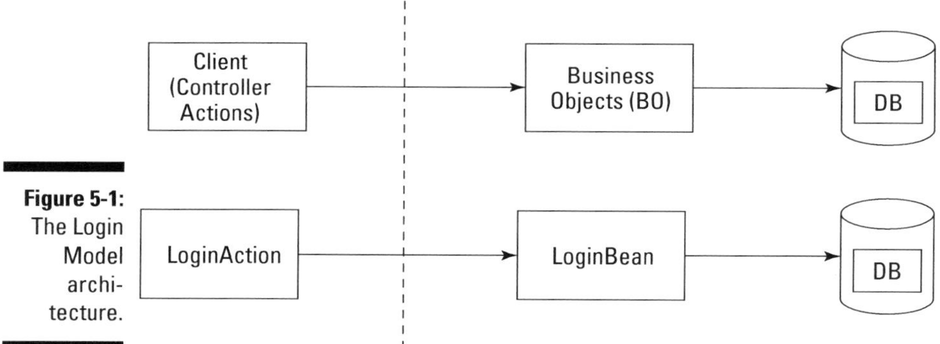

Figure 5-1: The Login Model architecture.

Working with Business Objects

A business object represents a real-world entity — it can be a person, a place, a thing, or a concept. Business objects are taken directly from the business domain that you're analyzing. Therefore, not only programmers, but the people working in the business departments, can relate to these terms and the ideas they represent. In this manner, business objects provide a common ground in which developers and domain experts can discuss and define the requirements for developing a software application and are the starting point for designing any object-oriented system.

In object-oriented programming, a developer implements business objects by creating classes that hold the data related to a particular business object and also by defining the operations that can be performed on that data, all in one programming language structure. In Java, you use either regular JavaBeans for simple implementations of business objects or Enterprise JavaBeans (EJB) for implementing business objects as distributed components that users can access over the network.

Some good examples of business objects are Customer, Order, and Product. Business departments can easily understand these terms, so that these terms should definitely become objects in a related software application. The `LoginBean` from Chapter 3 is not a business object in the sense of representing an entity, because it defines a business function performed on a `User` business object. In this chapter, we refine the Login application a little bit to better fit the business object definition.

Meeting requirements for business objects

Sun Microsystems has defined a set of guidelines for developing enterprise architectures with Java called the J2EE Blueprints (`java.sun.com/blueprints`). The Enterprise JavaBeans (EJB) technology, which is an ideal platform for implementing business objects, addresses all of Sun's requirements. However, not all Web applications are complex enough to justify the investment in expertise and money to include an EJB application server. EJB is definitely worth investigating further, however, if you plan on taking your Struts application to the next level.

For more information on EJB, read *Enterprise JavaBeans For Dummies* by Mac Rinehart (published by Wiley). Also refer to `java.sun.com/products/ejb`.

In this chapter, we focus on only the following requirements for business objects:

- **Maintaining state:** Retain the value of data between method invocations and throughout the process of shutting down and restarting the Web application.
- **Reusability:** A business object is general to the entire business, and you should be able to reuse the object in different components of the same application or in other applications. For example, an order fulfillment application, a customer service application, and a billing application could all use the same `Customer` business object. After you define the `Customer` object, you should not need to reimplement the object in each application.

- **Shared data:** Most business objects maintain their state in some kind of database. Many users share the data in the database and the business object provides the means to access and manipulate the shared data.

Adding helper classes

In addition to defining business objects that represent real-world entities, you need to create additional classes, called *helper* classes. These classes perform the various business functions in the Model layer.

Helper classes are implementations of objects that you add during the design phase. These classes do not directly represent real-world concepts that business people can relate to. Their purpose is to improve the flexibility and structure of the programming code. Some examples of helper classes follow:

- A special data class that holds a set of related data items for the purpose of handing it from one subsystem to the next.
- A specialized class or set of classes that implements lower-level functions for the sake of efficiency. If you tried to implement these functions in the business objects, you would end up with bloated classes that would be hard to maintain.
- A list of business objects, for the purpose of providing functionality related to a set of customers or all customers.

Using JavaBeans

The consensus is that data should be represented as a JavaBean, because JavaBeans offer many advantages through their well-defined component architecture. The creators of both JSP and the Struts framework made it easy to present data that is encapsulated in a JavaBean. Many specialized tags and classes help you to extract data from a data object that follows a certain naming convention — and following a certain naming convention is the hallmark of a JavaBean.

Implementing the Model

Struts itself doesn't provide much support for implementing the Model portion of a Web application, other than the support for datasource implementations. In a Struts application, the `Action` classes use JavaBeans to access business data or to request the execution of a specific business function. That, however, is their only interaction with the Model layer. The underlying mechanics of the Model, such as database interactions, data representation, and data manipulation, needs to be implemented by you, the developer.

Achieving persistence

Persistence means that the lifetime of the data outlasts the lifetime of the application. The data continues to exist after the application or even the computer has been shut down. Next time the application starts, the same data is still available. We're sure that you don't want your data to disappear whenever your users close their browsers. By definition, business objects must be persistent. They represent vital business data, such as bank accounts and transactions that must be accessible beyond individual invocations of the software application.

You can achieve persistence in many ways, but all approaches result in a system that writes the data to some kind of permanent storage device, usually a hard drive.

More often then not, you gain persistence by connecting the Web application to a relational database management system (RDBMS). Other alternatives are object-oriented databases or file-based repositories.

Many vendors provide relational database management systems. Some of the more popular ones are

- Microsoft SQL Server (`www.microsoft.com /sql`)
- MySQL (`www.mysql.com/products/mysql/index.html`)
- Oracle (`www.oracle.com/ip/deploy/database/oracle9i`)
- Sybase (`www.sybase.com/products`)

MySQL is an open-source implementation of a relational database that is free for noncommercial use. We use MySQL in the examples in this chapter. You can use any other type of database that you're familiar with, but note that all the examples show how to perform certain functions using MySQL.

Getting MySQL

To add the capability of persistence to a Struts application, you need the following items:

- **A relational database management server:** We chose MySQL, which is open-source and free for noncommercial use.
- **A database driver:** A driver is necessary for the Java application to connect to the database server. The driver is usually a Java class (it can be written in another language) that implements the low-level details establishing and maintaining connections to a particular database implementation. MySQL provides a Java Database Connectivity (JDBC) driver called MySQL Connector/J.

- **A database connection pool:** In this chapter, we start by using direct JDBC calls to access the database, which works fine for a small Web application. For larger systems, however, this approach could create resource conflicts and poor performance. A connection pool that manages and reuses a certain number of connections to the database server is a better solution. At the end of this chapter, we introduce the Jakarta Commons Database Connection Pooling (DBCP) implementation.

Downloading and installing MySQL

If you want to work through our examples in MySQL, follow these steps to download and install the program (on Windows NT, 2000, or XP):

1. **Go to `www.mysql.com`.**

   The various MySQL products are listed on the main page.

2. **Under the Database Server heading, select the Production version, which is 4.0.16 as of this writing.**

   The MySQL download page appears.

3. **Scroll down until you see all versions listed, ordered by operating system. When you find your operating system, click the Download link.**

   - If the File Download dialog box appears, click the Save button, choose a location for the file, and click Save. Remember where you put the downloaded file. Then extract the downloaded file to a temporary folder, using WinZip or some other decompression utility.
   - If the file immediately starts to download and opens in your decompression application (such as WinZip), extract the files to a temporary folder.

4. **Double-click the `Setup.exe` file and follow the installation instructions.**

   By default, MySQL installs in `C:\mysql`. You can safely accept all the defaults, including the Typical installation option in the Setup Type window.

You've set up your database server.

Downloading MySQL Connector/J

For your Java application to connect to the MySQL database server, you need a driver that your program can use. If you're using a database other than MySQL, contact your vendor for information on available JDBC drivers. To download the MySQL Connector/J to Windows NT, 2000, or XP, follow these steps:

1. **Go to** `www.mysql.com`.
2. **Select the Production link for the Connector/J product.**

   Version 3.0.9 is the latest version as of this writing. The Connector/J download page appears.
3. **Scroll down until you see the Sources and Binaries heading. Click the Download link for the zip version.**
   - If the File Download dialog box opens, click the Save button, choose a location for the file, and then click Save. Remember where you put the downloaded file. Then extract the downloaded file to a location of your choosing, using WinZip or some other decompression utility.
   - If the file immediately starts to download and opens in your decompression application (such as WinZip), extract the files to a location of your choice.

Next we add this driver to the classpath of Eclipse and Tomcat so that our Web application knows where to find it.

Setting Up Your IDE and Web Container

Before you can connect to the database, you need to add the appropriate library files to your IDE (if you're using one) and to your Web container. In general, you need to take the following steps:

1. Add the `mysql-connector-java-3.0.9-stable-bin.jar` file to the classpath of your development environment.
2. Add the `mysql-connector-java-3.0.9-stable-bin.jar` file to the Web container you're using. It should go into the `webapps/`*`yourapp`*`/WEB-INF/lib` folder.

If you want to follow along with the example that we presented in Chapter 3, you can continue to use Eclipse as your IDE and Tomcat as your Web container and follow the steps in the next two sections. Or you can apply the appropriate steps to your own development environment and just read on.

Importing the class library into Eclipse

To use the MySQL Connector/J driver in Eclipse, you need to import the library file so that you can write and compile code in Eclipse. For more information on using Eclipse, see Chapter 3.

To import the library file, follow these steps:

1. **Start Eclipse.**
2. **Right-click the** `WEB-INF/lib` **folder in the Package Explorer view and choose Import.**

   The Import dialog box opens.
3. **In the list of import sources, double-click the File System item.**
4. **Click the Browse button next to the From Directory text box and use the Import from Directory dialog box to navigate to the** `mysql-connector-java-3.0.9-stable` **folder. Click OK.**

   All the `.jar` files appear in the right pane of the Import dialog box.
5. **Select the check box for the** `mysql-connector-java-3.0.9-stable-bin.jar` **file.**
6. **Click Finish.**

After you import the `.jar` file to your IDE, you need to add the file to the build path so that your IDE knows that you want to use it during compilation. This process is equivalent to putting the files on the classpath for the application. Here we explain how to add the `.jar` file to the build path in Eclipse:

1. **Right-click the Login project in the Package Explorer view and choose Properties.**
2. **In the Properties for Login (or your application's name), choose the Java Build Path item.**
3. **Click the Libraries tab.**
4. **Click the Add External JARs button.**

   The JAR Selection dialog box appears.
5. **Navigate to the** `eclipse\workspace\Login\WEB-INF\lib` **folder.**
6. **Select the** `.jar` **file you just imported and then click Open.**
7. **Click OK.**

Adding the class library to Tomcat

The preceding set of steps took care of being able to write and compile code that accesses the database. To run this code under your Web container, you need to copy the class library into your Web container application environment.

To copy the class library into the Tomcat Web application environment, follow these steps:

1. **Open Windows Explorer.**
2. **In your `WEB-INF\lib` folder, select the `.jar` file that you just imported into your IDE.**

   To follow along with the example, go to `eclipse\workspace\Login\WEB-INF\lib` and select the `mysql-connector-java-3.0.9-stable-bin.jar` file. (Whew! That's a long file name!)
3. **Copy the `mysql-connector-java-3.0.9-stable-bin.jar` file to the `WEB-INF\lib` folder of your application in your Web container.**

   To follow along with the example, copy the `mysql-connector-java-3.0.9-stable-bin.jar` file to the `Tomcat\webapps\Login\WEB-INF\lib folder`. Make sure to press Ctrl as you drag the file so that you copy it instead of moving it.

Working with MySQL

So far in this chapter, we've explained how to install a database server and add some class libraries to your project. These steps are necessary but by themselves don't change anything. Before your Web application can connect to your database, you need to do the following:

1. Create a database.
2. Create at least one table.
3. Put some data into the table.

In this section, we use MySQL to explain how to do the following:

- Start the MySQL database server
- Create a database called `musiccollection`
- Create a table called `users`
- Insert three records into the `users` table

MySQL provides an implementation of the Structured Query Language (SQL), which is an industry standard used by most major RDBMS vendors. (That's why the program is called MySQL.) SQL provides commands for creating and retrieving data from a relational database.

All about SQL

SQL, which stands for Structured Query Language, defines a set of commands to manipulate a relational database system. SQL commands can be divided into two main sublanguages:

- **Data Definition Language (DDL):** Used to create and destroy databases and database objects such as tables, fields, and indexes. Some of the commands are `CREATE DATABASE`, `CREATE TABLE`, `DROP DATABASE`, and `DROP TABLE`.
- **Data Manipulation Language (DML):** Used to create, retrieve, and modify the data in the database. Some important commands are `INSERT`, `UPDATE`, `DELETE`, and `SELECT`.

By the way, the American National Standards Institute (ANSI) declared that the correct pronunciation of SQL is "S-Q-L." However, database professionals commonly pronounce it "see-kwel." We don't care how you say it.

Although meant to be a standard, each database vendor implements their own proprietary flavor. For example, Oracle uses PL/SQL and Microsoft SQL Server uses Transact-SQL. These flavors are all based on the industry standard ANSI SQL but add certain functions that often make some tasks easier. The best practice is to not be tempted into using those extensions and stick to the ANSI compliant SQL in your applications, because that ensures that your applications will be portable to other database implementations.

MySQL also has a number of extensions or changes to the ANSI standard SQL. However, you can run MySQL in ANSI mode by adding the `--ansi` argument to the command line when starting the MySQL server:

```
C:\>mysqld-max-nt --ansi
    --standalone
```

See the section "Starting and stopping MySQL" for more information on starting the MySQL server.

SQL has been around for quite a while, so you can find plenty of literature on the Web (one such Web site is `www.devshed.com/Server_Side/MySQL`) as well as a number of good books. The MySQL installation includes a good tutorial on using MySQL and SQL. If you installed MySQL in `C:\mysql` you can find the tutorial at `C:\mysql\Docs\manual.html#Tutorial`.

Starting and stopping MySQL

Assuming that you installed MySQL on your C: drive in a folder called `mysql`, open a command prompt window as shown in Figure 5-2 and type the following:

```
C:\>cd mysql\bin
C:\MYSQL\BIN>mysqld-max-nt --standalone
```

The first line changes the current folder to the `mysql\bin` folder where all the mysql applications reside. The second line starts the MySQL version for Windows and specifies that MySQL should not be started as a Windows service (`--standalone`).

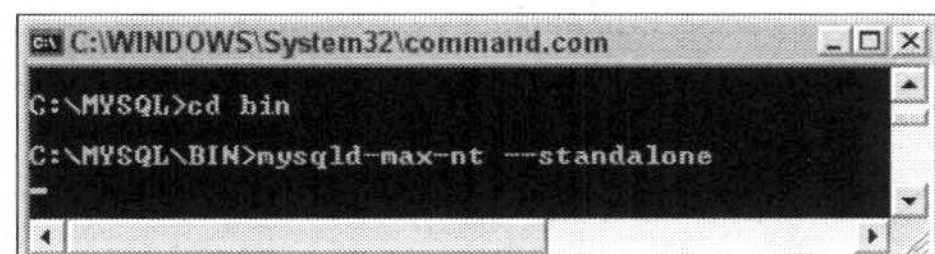

Figure 5-2: Starting the MySQL database server.

You don't see another command prompt because MySQL is still running in that command window. That command cursor just keeps blinking until you close MySQL. You need to open another command window to give commands to MySQL.

To stop the MySQL server, open another command prompt window as shown in Figure 5-3 and type the following:

```
C:\MYSQL\BIN>mysqladmin shutdown
```

In case you were wondering, yes, you do need to open another command prompt window. The window in which you started MySQL is not usable, because it is waiting for MySQL to quit before it will allow any further commands to be issued.

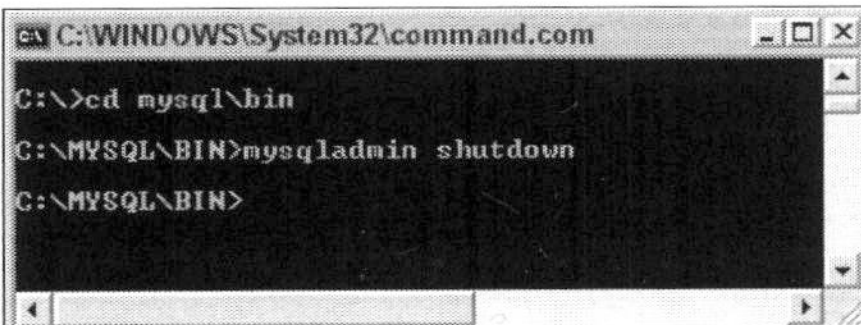

Figure 5-3: Shutting down the MySQL database server.

All the MySQL programs are located in the `C:\mysql\bin` folder. To avoid having to change to that folder each time you want to execute one of those commands, you may find it more convenient to add that folder to the system path, as follows:

1. **Choose Start➪Control Panel.**

   If you're using Classic view, choose Start➪Settings➪Control Panel instead.

2. **Double-click the System icon.**
3. **Click the Advanced tab.**

4. **Click the Environment Variables button.**
5. **In the System Variables section, select the system variable named Path.**
6. **Click the Edit button.**

   The Edit File System Variable dialog box appears.
7. **Move the cursor to the end of the Variable Value field and type a semicolon (;) and then the path to the MySQL bin folder.**

   For example, you might type **;c:\mysql\bin.**
8. **Click the OK button three times to close all the dialog boxes and the Control Panel.**

Creating a database

The next step is to create a database in your RDBMS. In this section, we explain how to create a database in MySQL. MySQL provides a command-line tool for manipulating databases, tables, and data. Open a new command prompt window and type the following boldface text to create a database and a table as shown in Figure 5-4. (You may need to restart MySQL if you stopped it in the preceding section.)

```
C:\>cd mysql\bin
C:\MYSQL\BIN>mysql
mysql> create database musiccollection;
mysql> show databases;
```

When you enter the `mysql` command, MySQL responds with its own `mysql>` prompt. The next command, `create`. . . creates an empty database called `musiccollection`. We use this name, because in Chapter 14 we describe a larger application that manages a collection of music CDs.

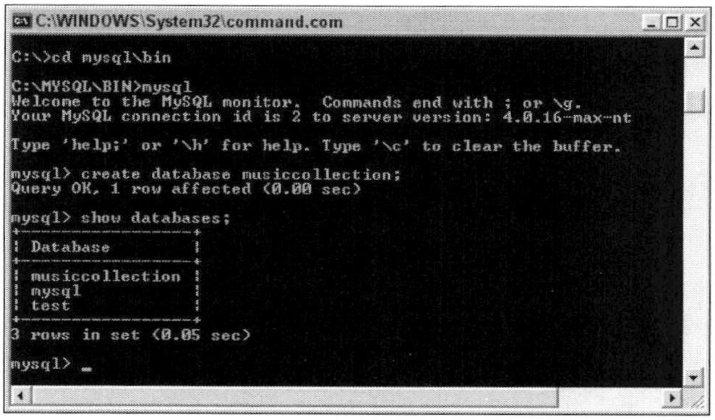

```
C:\>cd mysql\bin

C:\MYSQL\BIN>mysql
Welcome to the MySQL monitor.  Commands end with ; or \g.
Your MySQL connection id is 2 to server version: 4.0.16-max-nt

Type 'help;' or '\h' for help. Type '\c' to clear the buffer.

mysql> create database musiccollection;
Query OK, 1 row affected (0.00 sec)

mysql> show databases;
+-----------------+
| Database        |
+-----------------+
| musiccollection |
| mysql           |
| test            |
+-----------------+
3 rows in set (0.05 sec)

mysql> _
```

Figure 5-4: Running the MySQL command-line interface.

Don't forget the semicolon after each command before pressing the Enter key. Otherwise, MySQL will not execute your command because it thinks that you want to continue the command on the next line. This is the default behavior. You can still type a semicolon on the next line and then press Enter to execute your command — a useful technique for entering long commands.

After you type the `show databases;` command, you see displays a list of all databases that exist in this database server. MySQL usually has two already called `test` and `mysql`. You should also see your newly created `music collection` database.

Your database is not too useful yet. To actually store data in your database, you need to create at least one database table.

Creating a table in MySQL

After you create a database, you need to create a table. If you're using MySQL to create a table in the `musiccollection` database, type the following at the `mysql>` prompt:

```
mysql> use musiccollection;
mysql> create table users (username varchar(20), password
          varchar(20));
mysql> show tables;
```

When you want to execute a command on any of your databases, you always need to tell MySQL which database you want to work on. You accomplish this with the `use musiccollection` command, which switches MySQL to that database. All commands entered after the `use` command perform their task on that database.

The next command creates a simple table called `users` with two fields, a username and a password. The `varchar(20)` that you see after each field name is the data type and size of each field. `varchar` is a variable-length string in MySQL, in this case with a maximum length of 20 characters.

The `show tables` command lists all tables in the current database.

Inserting data in the users table

The next step is to add data to your table. To add the example data to a table in MySQL, type the following at the `mysql>` prompt, after specifying the database to use, as explained in the preceding section:

```
mysql> insert into users (username, password) values
         ("admin", "secret");
mysql> insert into users (username, password) values ("john",
         "dummy");
mysql> insert into users (username, password) values ("barb",
         "struts");
```

The insert SQL command allows you to insert data into a table. These entries insert three records in the users table with different usernames and passwords.

Note that the commands we explain here are sufficient only for the simplest of systems. An industrial-strength application would require you to create indexes for better performance, manage users and permissions, create views, and so on. In a real-world development team, usually at least one person, designated as the database administrator, specializes in designing and tuning the database servers.

Executing queries

To test that you have created the table and data successfully, you can select all the rows in the users table by typing in the following SQL select statement, after specifying the database to use, as explained in the "Creating a table in MySQL" section:

```
mysql> select * from users;
```

Using SQL scripts

You may have noticed by now that typing all those commands on the mysql command line is tedious, especially if you make a mistake and have to retype your entry. Another approach is to write all your SQL commands in a text file and then pass the text file to the mysql program. MySQL then executes all the commands in that file. We provide the SQL for this chapter in a text file at the *Jakarta Struts For Dummies* Web site at www.dummies.com/go/jakarta.

To use an SQL script called musiccollection.sql, type the following

```
C:\>cd mysql\bin
C:\MYSQL\BIN>mysql
    < musiccollection.sql
```

The musiccollection.sql file creates the musiccollection database, which creates the table users, and populates the table with three records of username and password combinations.

This command assumes that the musiccollection.sql file is located in the same folder as the mysql program. If that is not the case, you need to type the full pathname location of the script file on your hard disk.

This command displays all records in the `users` table. The asterisk (*) indicates that you want to see all fields. You could specify particular field names if you want to limit the query. For example:

```
select username from users
```

shows only the username field but not the passwords field.

Figure 5-5 shows the command prompt window with the SQL commands discussed in the previous few sections.

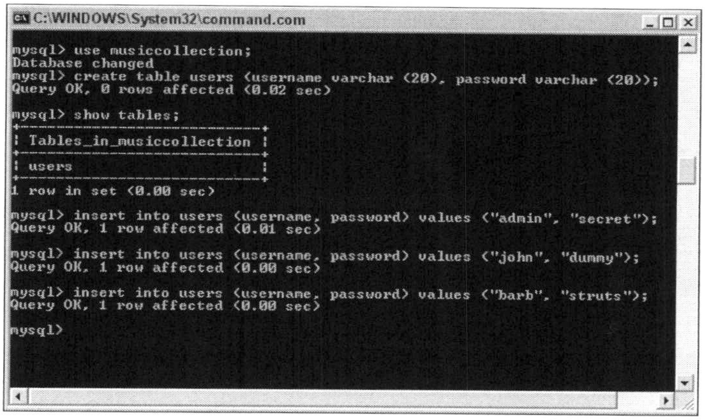

```
C:\WINDOWS\System32\command.com
mysql> use musiccollection;
Database changed
mysql> create table users (username varchar (20), password varchar (20));
Query OK, 0 rows affected (0.02 sec)

mysql> show tables;
+---------------------------+
| Tables_in_musiccollection |
+---------------------------+
| users                     |
+---------------------------+
1 row in set (0.00 sec)

mysql> insert into users (username, password) values ("admin", "secret");
Query OK, 1 row affected (0.01 sec)

mysql> insert into users (username, password) values ("john", "dummy");
Query OK, 1 row affected (0.00 sec)

mysql> insert into users (username, password) values ("barb", "struts");
Query OK, 1 row affected (0.00 sec)

mysql>
```

Figure 5-5: Creating a database and table in MySQL.

Exiting the MySQL command tool

To exit the MySQL command line tool, type **quit** or **exit** at the `mysql>` prompt. MySQL responds, "Bye." You don't have to say "Bye" back, although you can if you want.

Connecting the Model to the Database

In Chapter 3, for simplicity, we used an example of a JavaBean containing hard-coded data. Hard-coding data is not a useful way to implement a Web application — or any application for that matter. To make the Login application practical, you need to add a persistent data repository — a database — and make `LoginBean` work with that database.

To upgrade the Login application, you need to implement a new version of the `LoginBean`. The View and Controller components of this application do not have to change. This gives you a little taste of the power of a layered architecture: A change to the Model implementation requires no change in the other layers!

Working with JDBC

JDBC stands for Java Database Connectivity and is Java's way of connecting to many types of databases. Using JDBC keeps the application code independent of the specific database implementation.

The JDBC class library is included in the J2SE distribution in the `java.sql` and `javax.sql` packages. The only missing piece is the vendor-specific implementation of the `java.sql.Driver` interface. These driver classes are available for most major database products and act as the connector between your application and the database you're using.

Listing 5-1 shows a modified implementation of `LoginBean` using JDBC calls to connect to the MySQL database and then query the `users` table.

Listing 5-1 LoginBean.java Using JDBC

```
package dummies.struts;

import java.sql.Connection;
import java.sql.DriverManager;
import java.sql.ResultSet;
import java.sql.SQLException;
import java.sql.Statement;

public class LoginBean
{
   public boolean validateUser(String username, String password)
   {
       boolean valid = false;
       Connection con = null;
       Statement stmt = null;
       ResultSet rs = null;
       try
       {
           Class.forName("com.mysql.jdbc.Driver");

           con = DriverManager.getConnection(
             "jdbc:mysql://localhost/musiccollection", "", "");

           stmt = con.createStatement();

           rs = stmt.executeQuery(
             "SELECT * FROM Users " +
             "WHERE username = '" + username + "' " +
             "AND password = '" + password + "'");
```

```
26
27             if (rs.next())
28                 valid = true;
29         }
30         catch (ClassNotFoundException e) {
31             e.printStackTrace();
32         }
33         catch (SQLException e) {
34             e.printStackTrace();
35         }
36         finally {
37             try { if (rs != null) rs.close(); } catch (SQLException e) {};
38             try { if (stmt != null) stmt.close(); } catch (SQLException e) {};
39             try { if (con != null) con.close(); } catch (SQLException e) {};
40         }
41         return valid;
42     }
43 }
```

By comparing this code to Listing 3-5 in Chapter 3, you can see that the usernames and passwords are no longer hard-coded. Instead, you find JDBC calls to connect to the database server and to find the requested username in the database. If the username is found and the password matches, the `validateUser()` method returns `true`. Let's look at some of these lines in more detail:

- Line 19: Loads the appropriate JDBC driver class for this particular database type. This is the only database-vendor-specific reference. For complete portability, you would usually store this string in a configuration file that you read at startup.
- Line 21: Establishes a connection to the database. This line is equivalent to logging into the MySQL database. The first parameter is the connection string to the database. The `jdbc:mysql:` prefix specifies the protocol to use (which is JDBC in this case) and the type of data source to access (which is MySQL in this example). The rest is the path to the database server and the database name. If your database server were on a different machine than your Web application, you would use the IP address for the server followed by the database name.

  Note that the last two parameters of Line 21 are empty strings. This is where you put the database username and password, respectively, that you want to use for the query. You haven't defined any database users for your database yet, so at this point anyone can connect. Not very secure and not to be imitated in a real application!
- Line 23: After you acquire a connection, you need to create an SQL statement, which is an instance of the `java.sql.Statement` class. You use the statement object to execute an SQL command on the database server.
- Line 25: After the statement has been created, you can execute it by invoking the `executeQuery()` method and passing it the desired SQL

query string. The `executeQuery()` method returns an object of type `java.sql.ResultSet`, which can hold zero or more rows of data from the database table that you're querying.

- Lines 27 and 28: Because the username should be unique in this database, you can expect at most one row to be returned. If you got one row back, the username and password are valid and the `validateUser()` method returns `true`.
- Lines 37–39: You should always clean up when you're finished. Because you created the database connection in this method, you should close the connection here as well.

It is important to close the statement before closing the connection because some JDBC drivers will throw an exception if the connection is closed and the statement is still open.

This version of `the LoginBean` is a great improvement to the one we used in Chapter 3, but it's a bit inefficient. Because the entire code to connect to the database is in the `validateUser()` method, a new connection is created every time this method is invoked. This is expensive in terms of computer time and resources and can affect server performance when too many users are executing queries.

It would be better to open and the close the database connection outside the `invalidateUser()` method and even outside the `LoginBean` class. One or more connections could be opened when the application starts and then reused while the application is running. You could write your own connection-pooling mechanism or use one that has already been proven. We look at this technique later in this chapter, in the "Pooling Connections" section.

You can now run the Login application. When you enter the username and password, `LoginBean` verifies that the entry is valid.

Retrieving multiple records

`LoginBean`, in line 27 of Listing 5-1, accesses `ResultSet` but does not retrieve any data. In that case it was not necessary because the `users` table doesn't provide any other fields than the ones we're using in the query. In Listing 5-2, we add another method called `getAllUsers()` to the `LoginBean` class to demonstrate how you can retrieve data from `ResultSet` and pass it back to the View. We also wanted two more fields — `age` and `status` to add more personal information about the user. If you want to follow along with the example, type the following MySQL commands to add these two fields to the database table:

```
mysql> alter table users add column age int default 0;
mysql> alter table users add column status varchar(10)
         default 'active';
```

The `getAllUsers()` method is shown in Listing 5-2.

Listing 5-2 LoginBean.getAllUsers()

```
//...package declaration and other import statements...

import java.util.ArrayList;

public class LoginBean
{
   //... validateUser() method ...

   /**
    * Retrieve a list of all users.
    * @return ArrayList containing a list of Transfer Objects (TO) of type
    * UserTO. Returns an empty ArrayList if none where found.
    */
   public ArrayList getAllUsers()
   {
       ArrayList users = new ArrayList();

       Connection con = null;
       Statement stmt = null;
       ResultSet rs = null;
       try
       {
         // ... database connection code ...

           rs = stmt.executeQuery(
             "SELECT username, password, age, status " +
             "FROM Users ");

           while (rs.next())
           {
               // Retrieve one user record at a time
               String username = rs.getString(1);
               String password = rs.getString(2);
               int age = rs.getInt(3);
               String status = rs.getString(4);

               // Create new user transfer object
               UserDTO user = new UserDTO(username, password, age, status);

               // Add user to list of users
               users.add(user);
           }
       }

      // ... catch and finally blocks ...

      return users;
   }
}
```

Object-to-relational mapping frameworks

The problem of storing objects in a relational database is similar to putting a square peg in a round hole. They just don't match. Data belonging to an object is determined in part by the relationships the object has with other objects in the hierarchy of objects. On the other hand, in a relational database, you relate data by providing a common field among tables of data.

When making an object persistent by storing its data in a relational database, the common technique is to combine the hierarchy into one table. Therefore, the superclass may be duplicated in many tables. Another approach is to break the data out of each class of objects and insert the data into a separate table.

Likewise, when reconstituting the objects from table data, the programmer must know how the relationships are defined in the database table and reconstruct the objects based on a series of queries.

Don't you wish you could just use an object-oriented database instead? Then you would not have these problems because both the application code and the database would support the object-oriented paradigm. However, at the present time, relational databases are still more widely used and accepted. It may be a few more years before OODBMS (Object Orientated Database Management System) will rival RDBMS.

In the `LoginBean` example, we had to do the mapping between the users table and `UserDTO` ourselves. That wasn't too bad, but what if you have many database tables and more complex objects that have many relationships to other objects. Implementing the mapping logic would become quite a task.

Well, there's good news: *Object-to-relational mapping* (ORM) frameworks strive to solve this mismatch issue. ORMs are tools that do the mapping for you. Some create Java classes that you can use to access the database. Others use XML definitions of your business objects to map them to the database structure.

You can map your Java objects to relational database tables using several expensive ORM as well as a few free ones. You might want to investigate the following free ones:

- Object Relational Bridge (OJB) at `db.apache.org/ojb`
- Castor at `castor.exolab.org`
- Expresso at `www.jcorporate.com`

The following lines are of interest:

- Line 1: Because you're retrieving not just one record but potentially many, you need to use a collection class from the Java class library called `ArrayList` to hold the row data.
- Line 12: The `getAllUsers()` method returns an object of type `ArrayList` containing all the user records.
- Line 22: The `select` statement now lists the names of the fields that you want to retrieve instead of just using an asterisk to get all fields. In this way, you can match each field in `ResultSet` to a particular field in the database.

- Line 24: Uses a `for` loop to cycle through the result set. With each iteration, you retrieve one row from the users table.
- Lines 27–30: For each row, the code first assigns the value of each field to a separate variable. The `ResultSet` class provides getter methods to retrieve values of various data types. Most of the fields are of type `String`, so the code uses the `getString()` method. However, the `age` field is an integer, so it uses the `getInt()` method.

  These getter methods take care of the type casting for you, but if you use the wrong method, you'll get a runtime exception. Notice that each method takes a number as an argument. The number signifies the order of the fields as shown in the `select` statement. Another version of each getter method allows you to pass the field name, for example, `getString("username")`. However, using numbers to specify fields is generally recommended. If the field name changes in the database, you would have one less place where you have to modify your code to accommodate that change.
- Line 33: Creates a user Data Transfer Object (DTO), as shown in Listing 5-3. A DTO is a design pattern that helps improve performance and keep the data structures used in the persistence layer hidden from the business logic and presentation layers. The object-oriented paradigm encourages many calls to get various data items from an object. However, that is inefficient when accessing a relational database because each method call translates to a network transaction. Hence, the code uses transfer objects to retrieve all the data for an object at once and then package it into a DTO before passing it back to the other layers.
- Line 36: Each user DTO that you create must be added to `ArrayList`.
- Line 40: Finally, you return the list of user objects. You could write another Controller action to use the `getAllUsers()` method and then display the results in another JSP page.

Listing 5-3 UserDTO.java

```
package dummies.struts;

import java.io.Serializable;

/**
 * User Transfer Object (TO). Previously called Value Object (VO)
 * or sometimes Data Transfer Object (DTO).
 */
public class UserDTO implements Serializable
{
    private String username = null;
    private String password = null;
    private int age = 0;
    private String status = null;
```

(continued)

Listing 5-3 ***(continued)***

```

    public UserDTO(String username, String password, int age, String status)
    {
        this.username = username;
        this.password = password;
        this.age = age;
        this.status = status;
    }

    public String getUsername() {
        return username;
    }

    public String getPassword() {
        return password;
    }

    public int getAge() {
        return age;
    }

    public String getStatus() {
        return status;
    }
}
```

For more information on JDBC, see Sun's JDBC home page at `java.sun.com/products/jdbc` and Sun's Java Tutorial Trail on JDBC Database Access at `java.sun.com/docs/books/tutorial/jdbc/index.html`.

Pooling Connections

Creating and removing a connection to a data source is an expensive proposition in terms of time and computer resources. Therefore, you should try to minimize these operations to keep data-access processing efficient. So someone cleverly asked, "Why not keep a collection of live connections hanging around, and when a request for a database access comes up, just give the requester one of the live connections from the pool? When the requester has completed the database request, the connection goes back into the pool for someone else to use."

In JDBC 2.0, a definition for a connection pooling interface was added, but an implementation was not included. Instead of writing your own implementation, you can use one provided by a vendor. We use the implementation of the Jakarta Commons DBCP project.

Jakarta Commons DBCP

The Jakarta Commons DBCP (database connection pooling) project provides an implementation of the JDBC 2.0 connection pool specification.

Jakarta Commons DBCP is built on another project, the Jakarta Commons Pool. The Jakarta Commons Pool implements a general object pooling mechanism that can pool any kind of object. Commons DBCP reuses this generalized object pooling implementation to provide a data source connection pooling mechanism.

Each project has its respective home page, where you can find more information on what the project is and how to use it. Those home pages are `jakarta.apache.org/commons/dbcp/` and `jakarta.apache.org/commons/pool/`. However, you can also go directly to the Jakarta Binary Downloads Page to download these — and all other Jakarta projects.

To download Jakarta Commons DBCP and Pool for Windows NT, 2000, or XP, follow these steps:

1. **Go to** `jakarta.apache.org/site/binindex.cgi`.
2. **Scroll down to the Commons DBCP entry, and click its 1.1.zip link.**
   - If the File Download dialog box appears, click the Save button, choose a location for the file, and click Save. Remember where you put the downloaded file. Then use WinZip or some other decompression program to unzip the file to a location of your choosing.
   - If the file immediately begins to download and WinZip or another decompression program opens with the files, extract the files to a location of your choosing.
3. **Go to** `jakarta.apache.org/site/binindex.cgi`.
4. **Scroll down to the Commons Pool entry and click its 1.1.zip link.**
   - If the File Download dialog box appears, click the Save button, choose a location for the file, and click Save. Remember where you put the downloaded file. Then use WinZip or some other decompression program to unzip the file to the root of a drive.
   - If the file immediately begins to download and WinZip or another decompression program opens with the files, extract the files to a location of your choosing.
5. **Add the DBCP class library,** `commons-dbcp-1.1.jar`**, and the Pool class library,** `commons-pool-1.1.jar`**, to both Eclipse and Tomcat.**

   See the "Setting Up Your IDE and Web Container" section, earlier in this chapter, for instructions.

The implementation class for the connection pool we use is called `BasicDataSource`. An older implementation called `GenericDataSource`, is now *deprecated* (outdated) and will be removed from Struts 1.2. However, Struts 1.1 still references the `GenericDataSource` class, even when you use `BasicDataSource`.

When running your Web application, the first time you make a reference to the datasource you'll get a runtime error message. The message will say that Struts can't find the `GenericDataSource` class. To remedy this, make sure you're including the `struts-legacy.jar` class library file to your Eclipse and Tomcat setup. You can find this library file in the `jakarta-struts-1.1/lib` folder.

Using connection pooling

Listing 5-4 shows the example `LoginBean` rewritten to make use of the connection pooling capability.

Listing 5-4 LoginBean.java

```
package dummies.struts;

import java.sql.Connection;
import java.sql.ResultSet;
import java.sql.SQLException;
import java.sql.Statement;

import javax.sql.DataSource;

public class LoginBean
{
    private DataSource dataSource = null;

    public LoginBean(DataSource dataSource)
    {
        this.dataSource = dataSource;
    }

    public boolean validateUser(String username, String password)
    {
        boolean valid = false;

        Connection con = null;
        Statement stmt = null;
        ResultSet rs = null;
        try
        {
            con = dataSource.getConnection();
```

```
29
30            stmt = con.createStatement();
31
32            rs = stmt.executeQuery(
33                "SELECT * FROM Users " +
34                "WHERE username = '" + username + "' " +
35                "AND password = '" + password + "'");
36
37            if (rs.next())
38                valid = true;
39        }
40        catch(SQLException e) {
41            e.printStackTrace();
42        }
43        finally {
44            try { if (rs != null) rs.close(); } catch (SQLException e) {};
45            try { if (stmt != null) stmt.close(); } catch (SQLException e) {};
46            try { if (con != null) con.close(); } catch (SQLException e) {};
47        }
48        return valid;
49    }
50 }
```

The only new lines in this code are the ones in bold. They replace the more tedious way of connecting using a driver manager. Also, this class no longer contains any data-source-specific code, making it more general and reusable. Also note the following:

- Line 8: Note that `import java.sql.DriverManager` is no longer there. Instead, we now import the `javax.sql.DataSource` class.
- Lines 14–17: The `LoginBean` class no longer creates the connection itself. Instead, at construction time, a reference to a `DataSource` object is passed to the `LoginBean` class, which stores it in an `instance` variable on line 12.
- Line 28: The only thing to do to acquire a database connection is to call `getConnection()` on the `DataSource` object.

For the connection pooling to work, you have to make a change to the `LoginAction` class. In Eclipse, locate the `LoginAction.java` file. Look for the line:

```
LoginBean lb = new LoginBean();
```

Change this line to look like the following:

```
LoginBean lb = new LoginBean(getDataSource(request,
         "musiccollection"));
```

This change takes care of passing a `DataSource` object reference to `LoginBean`.

Configuring the data source in Struts

You have to make one more change and that is to register the data source in the struts configuration file, `struts-config.xml`, which is located in the `WEB-INF` folder.

Add the data source definition as shown in lines 2 through 15 of Listing 5-5 to the beginning of the `struts-config.xml` file, just after the first element in the file, `<struts-config>`.

Listing 5-5 struts-config.xml Data Source Definition

```
1  <struts-config>
2    <!-- ========== Data Source Definitions =============================== --
         >
3    <data-sources>
4        <data-source key="musiccollection"
5        type="org.apache.commons.dbcp.BasicDataSource">
6            <set-property property="description" value="Music Collection
             Database"/>
<set-property property="driverClassName" value="com.mysql.jdbc.Driver"/>
8            <set-property property="username"
             value="theDatabaseUserName"/>
9            <set-property property="password"
             value="theDatabaseUserPassword"/>
10           <set-property property="url"
11                   value="jdbc:mysql://localhost/musiccollection"/>
12           <set-property property="maxCount" value="8"/>
13           <set-property property="minCount" value="2"/>
14            </data-source>
15        </data-sources>
  ...
</struts-config>
```

Within the `<data-sources>` element, you can define as many data sources as you want. To access them, you use the key parameter for the `<data-source>` element. Notice in lines 8 and 9 that you need to replace *theDatabaseUserName* and *theDatabaseUserPassword* with the appropriate values for connecting to your own database.

When requesting a data source in your web application's `Action` classes, you can use the provided `getDataSource()` method. The method takes two arguments, the request object and a key string:

```
getDataSource(request, "musiccollection");
```

This method call returns a reference to the data source we defined in Listing 5-5. You could now add additional data-source declarations with different keys and then access each as you need it. This procedure makes managing multiple data sources and connection pools easy.

After you update the `struts-config.xml` file in your workspace, make sure you copy this file to the Tomcat `webapps\Login\WEB-INF` folder.

Whenever you change an application configuration file (`web.xml`, `struts-config.xml`, or any of the property files), you need to restart Tomcat before the changes can take place.

That's all you have to do. You can run your application again. However, as a user, you won't notice any difference. As a developer, you can rest assured that your Struts application will be able to handle a much greater load while still performing well.

For more information on configuring a data source in Struts, look at the Struts online documentation at the following address:

```
jakarta.apache.org/struts/userGuide/configuration.
        html#data-source_config
```

Chapter 6

Designing the View

In This Chapter

- Choosing a View technology
- Creating applications for an international audience
- Connecting the View and the Controller
- Using the `DynaActionForm` class for automation

If you want your application's users to see your beautiful work, you need to create a visual component for your application. In the Struts implementation of the MVC pattern, you have complete flexibility to choose the View technology of your choice. After you choose a technology, you need to implement it. In this chapter, we discuss some View options, how to create applications for an international clientele, and how to connect the View to the Controller.

Choosing JSP or an Alternative

Struts doesn't care what View architecture you choose to use. Most developers use the JSP architecture, but this is not a requirement. However, Struts does distribute a comprehensive tag library that you can use with JSP pages to make writing the JSP pages easier.

Other view creation possibilities may better fit your needs. The following sections explain a sampling of your options.

Template engines

Template engines are characterized by a separation of the page design from page data. This methodology offers several advantages over plain vanilla JSP, such as

- More flexibility in site design
- Easier design development for graphics people
- Greater control of the consistency of the site appearance

In the following sections, we discuss three template engines.

Apache Cocoon and the Cocoon plug-in

The Apache Cocoon project is a Web application framework built on the premise of *separating concerns,* that is, separating presentation from logic from data. Apache Cocoon contains *pipelines* (a particular path for the flow of transformations) that create XML data from various sources and then transform that data into various presentation technologies through the use of XSL (eXtensible Stylesheet Language) stylesheets. Cocoon offers a wide range of possible transformations, including JSP, Velocity, FreeMarker, PHP, and XSP. For more information see `cocoon.apache.org`.

The Cocoon plug-in allows Struts to pass forwards to Cocoon for transformation in one of Cocoon's pipelines. (A *forward,* more exactly known as an `ActionForward`, is a mechanism that defines the passing of control to another resource, usually a JSP page or a servlet.) See `struts.sourceforge.net/struts-cocoon/index.html` for more information.

Jakarta Velocity and VelocityStruts

Velocity is a Jakarta project — a Java-based template engine that provides a simple scripting language to create pages. No Java code is allowed in the pages. For further information on Jakarta Velocity, see `jakarta.apache.org/velocity.html`.

VelocityStruts is an extension to Struts that seamlessly marries the Struts Framework to Velocity. With the VelocityStruts extension, developers can forward a request to a Velocity template instead of to a JSP page. The nice thing about this method is that you are not forced to choose between one technology or the other. You can mix and match as you see fit. To find out more about VelocityStruts, see `jakarta.apache.org/velocity/tools/struts/`.

FreeMarker

FreeMarker generates text output (anything from HTML to PDF files) based on templates. The FreeMarker templates are essentially page designs that contain no application logic, only page design information. This provides a clean separation of concerns between page designers and application programmers. The framework works with Struts out-of-the-box and replaces the use of JSP and JSP tag libraries as presentation technologies.

FreeMarker is an open source project. Further information on FreeMarker can be found at `freemarker.sourceforge.net`.

XML tools

The advantage of an XML document is that you can use XSL stylesheets to transform the document into virtually any other type of document for presentation. This transformation process is advantageous for sites that need to offer many forms of display to the user. For example, you may want to let the user view a purchase order in HTML, PDF, or plain text. This section describes two tools that integrate with Struts to provide XML and XSL services.

StrutsCX

The StrutsCX framework replaces JSP with XSLT (eXtensible Stylesheet Language Transformations). StrutsCX outputs well-formed XML that can then be transformed into any number of presentation markup languages (HTML, CSV, PDF, WML, and so on) using XSL stylesheets. See `it.cappuccinonet.com/strutscx/index.php` for more information on StrutsCX.

stxx

The four letters *stxx* are an acronym for Struts for Transforming XML with XSL. The stxx technology bills itself as an extension to the Struts framework that allows an action to return an XML document that will be transformed into the final presentation form by XSL or Velocity. The purpose of this system is to provide an alternative presentation technology to JSP. However, you can still use JSP alongside stxx. Take a look at `stxx.sourceforge.net` to find out more.

Internationalization

The world of today is much closer than the world of a decade ago, and the world of tomorrow will be even closer. This shrinking of boundaries is due in part to the instant communication now available to most citizens and organizations. Communication is further enhanced by the creation of virtual representations of people and organizations through the use of the World Wide Web.

When you plan an application for the Web, you need to keep in mind the audience for the application. If there is any chance that the application might be used by people from different locales, you should plan to design for that possibility right from the start.

I18N is a lazy (or smart) person's way of saying Internationalization: *I,* plus 18 characters in between, plus *N.* Some clever person, whose typing was probably challenged like ours, decided to make a challenging word more acceptable. As they say, necessity is the mother of invention.

Creating multinational applications

When creating a Web application that supports multiple locales, you need to consider how to present information in the preferred language and customary formatting style of your audience. Customary formatting style refers to locale-sensitive information such as dates, times, numbers, and currency.

Struts displays I18N text and images through the use of message resources and specialized tag libraries. We touch briefly on these capabilities in Chapter 3 in the "The login.jsp page" section, where we describe the creation of JSP pages for our sample Login Web application. The JSTL tag libraries provide the means to format dates, times, and numbers in the locale-specific style. (We address formatting for locales separately in Chapter 10.)

To create applications with multilanguage capabilities, you work with two aspects of Jakarta Struts: the resource bundle properties file and the tag libraries to reference the resource bundles.

Creating the resource bundle properties file

The *resource bundle* contains all the text that the application will display to the user. The file can have any name that you choose but should have an extension of `.properties`. The file may also contain image *locations* if you want to display different images for different locales. The text and images might be one or more of the following:

- Labels on fields and buttons
- Titles of pages or sections and page content
- Messages to tell the user something
- Icons that indicate an action to be performed

Any content that you need to localize must be in the resource bundle.

Each entry of text or image location requires a key that identifies that text or image location. For example, the following illustrates a key and the key's associated value.

```
defaultdisk=My Disk
```

The `defaultdisk` key is used to look up the text value of `My Disk`.

Sometimes it may be convenient to divide the key-value pairs into different files, especially if you have multiple developers or modules in your application. The only requirement is that you set them up properly in the `struts-config` file, as we explain in the next section.

Configuring the message resources

To tell Struts about your message resources (or resource bundles), you need to create a `<message-resources>` tag in the `struts-config` file and specify the context in `the web.xml` file. In the `struts-config` file, the `<message-resources>` tag has five possible attributes:

- `className`: Optional. The fully qualified name of the configuration class. This value defaults to `org.apache.struts.config.MessageResourcesConfig`. Use this attribute only if you subclass `MessageResourcesConfig`.
- `factory`: Optional. The fully qualified name of `MessageResourcesFactory`. This value defaults to `org.apache.struts.util.PropertyMessageResourcesFactory`. Use this attribute only if you subclass `PropertyMessageResourcesFactory`.
- `key`: Optional. The attribute key to store this bundle in the Servlet context. The key defaults `to org.apache.struts.action.MESSAGE`. If you use multiple resource bundles in your application, you should set a different key for each one. In the application, you would use the key to indicate which bundle to select.
- `null`: Optional. Determines how to display missing resources. The default value is `true` and displays missing resources as `null`. If you set the value to `false`, the missing resource is displayed as `???`*`key`*`???`. This option is useful during development because it helps you to spot missing resources.
- `parameter`: Required. The name of the resource bundle. This is the name of the message resource file, minus the `.properties` extension.

Here is an example of a `message-resources` tag in the `struts-config` file:

```
<!-- ========= Message Resources Definition ================== -->
<message-resources null="false" parameter="ApplicationResources"/>
```

This tag specifies the name of the resource bundle as `ApplicationResources`. Because the `null` parameter is set to `false`, if the referenced resource is missing, you see a display like this: `???`*`key`*`???`.

If you have two resource bundles, you need to also define a key for each to reference them properly in your application. Here is an example of configuring the message resources for two resource bundles:

```
<!-- ========= Message Resources Definitions ================== -->
<message-resources  key="purchasing" parameter="PurchasingResources"/>
<message-resources  key="vendors"  parameter="VendorResources"/>
```

In this example, a key is associated with each resource bundle. When you need to reference one of the bundles, you must specify the bundle's key as well, for example, using the JSTL tag `<fmt:message>`. We show examples of the `<fmt:message>` tag in the next section.

The `web.xml` file also needs to be set up to know about the resource bundles. Otherwise you're required to specify the resource bundles in the JSP page using special JSTL tags. To set up the `web.xml` file, add the following snippet to the beginning of the file:

```
<web-app>
    ...
1   <context-param>
2       <param-name>
3           javax.servlet.jsp.jstl.fmt.localizationContext
        </param-name>

4       <param-value>
5           ApplicationResources
        </param-value>
    </context-param>
    ...
</web-app>
```

You can specify only the default resource bundle in the `web.xml` file. If you use more than one resource bundle, you must specify the nondefault bundle name in the JSTL tags.

In the preceding code, note the following:

- Line 1: Adds a context parameter tag. The context represents the scope called `application`. All key-value pairs stored in the context are available everywhere in the application.
- Line 2: Adds the parameter name tag for the context.
- Line 3: Specifies the complete class name of the context parameter. In this case, we're defining the context parameter to be the class that represents `FMT_LOCALIZATION_CONTEXT` used by the JSTL tag library.

  JSTL has numerous configuration items that contain the default values for such settings as locale, resource bundle, time zone, and SQL datasource. The `FMT_LOCALIZATION_CONTEXT` contains the default resource bundle and its associated locale. This resource bundle will be used for all message lookups unless an alternate is specified in the JSP page. See Chapter 10 for more information on JSTL.
- Line 4: Adds the parameter value tag for the context.
- Line 5: Specifies the name of the resource bundle to be included in `FMT_LOCALIZATION_CONTEXT`. In this case, the name is `ApplicationResources`.

The position of tags in the `web.xml` file is important. For example, the `<context-param>` tag must come before the `<servlet>` tag.

Using the tag library to display messages

When you've defined and configured your message resources, the next step is to integrate them into your JSP pages. Both the Struts-EL and JSTL tag libraries provide such functionality. The Struts-EL library has a tag designed for I18N called the `<bean:message>` tag. However, because the JSTL tag library also has tags to use for I18N — `<fmt:message>` and `<fmt:parameter>` — we'll use them. The creators of Struts have recommended using JSTL whenever possible.

Whenever you want to display text in your JSP page, rather than putting the text statically in an HTML tag such as `<Title>This is the Title Page </Title>`, you can instead use the `<fmt:message>` tag and retrieve the text from the resource bundle. For example, suppose that you have defined the title of the page in a resource bundle by using a key of `homepage.title`:

```
homepage.title=This is the Title Page
```

The `<fmt:message>` tag would look like this:

```
<fmt:message key="homepage.title" />
```

And your HTML would now look like this:

```
<title><fmt:message key="homepage.title" /></title>
```

If you have more than one resource bundle defined in `struts-config`, you need to specify another tag when you want to reference the non-default resource bundle. The `<fmt:setBundle>` or `<fmt:bundle>` tag needs to specify the name of the resource bundle subsequent `<fmt:message>` tags will reference. See Chapter 10 for more information on these tags.

Creating parameterized messages

Besides defining plain text messages in the message resource file, you can also create parameterized messages. This is a great feature if you need to insert specific information into a message at runtime. Struts supports messages with up to four parameters (`{0}` through `{3}`). In Chapter 3, we develop a message resource file containing an example of a parameterized message. Here is the parameterized message from that example:

```
loggedin.msg=Welcome, {0}. You are now logged in.
```

This message's placeholder, `{0}`, indicates that the first parameter that gets passed should replace the `{0}`. When you specify the use of the message in the JSP page, the tag looks like this:

```
<fmt:message key="loggedin.msg">
    <fmt:param value='${requestScope.userName}' />
</fmt:message>
```

The parameter that is being passed is the user's name, which will replace the {0} when the message is output to the page.

Setting up message resource files for different locales

The final step when preparing your application for I18N is to create additional resource bundles for each locale that you intend to support. Each locale needs a two-character language specifier. In addition, you may choose to further refine the locale with a two-character country code. For example, fr refers to the French language in general and fr_CA references French as used in Canada and fr_FR is French as used in France.

You don't need to add additional files to any configuration. Assuming that you have defined the default resource bundle name in the struts-config file, you append the locale specifier to the default resource name to find any locale-specific bundle. For example, if ApplicationResources is the default resource bundle name, ApplicationResources_fr is the name used for the French language version of the resource bundle.

Here are the full definitions of the two bundles. Lines starting with a number sign (#) are comments.

The following is from the ApplicationResources.properties file:

```
# default locale messages
greetings=Hello.
farewell=Goodbye.
inquiry=How are you?
```

The following is from the ApplicationResources_fr.properties file:

```
# French locale messages
greetings=Bonjour.
farewell=Au revoir.
inquiry=Comment allez-vous?
```

For a list of all language codes, see

```
ftp.ics.uci.edu/pub/ietf/http/related/iso639.txt
```

For a list of all two-digit country codes, see

```
userpage.chemie.fu-berlin.de/diverse/doc/ISO_3166.html
```

You can also reference resource bundles in your server-side Java code. We show section examples in the "Mediating between the View and the Controller" section, later in this chapter.

An I18n example

The Login application you create in Chapter 3 is an ideal candidate for internationalization. Everything is set up to take advantage of I18N; all that you need to do is to create a new message resource file. To see I18N in action, simply make a copy of the `ApplicationResources.properties` file and name it `ApplicationResources_de.properties` to create a message resource file for German. Then edit the `ApplicationResources _de.properties` file to look like Listing 6-1.

Listing 6-1 The German Version of the ApplicationResources File

```
# Resources for Login Project

# Struts Validator Error Messages
# These are special resources that the Struts tag library
# uses to format messages. In this case we make sure that
# errors are red so that they can be noticed.
errors.header=<font color="red">*
errors.footer=</font>

#errors
error.username.required=Benutzername notwendig.
error.password.required=Passwort notwendig.
error.login.invalid=Das System konnte Ihren Benutzernamen und
          Passwort nicht bestñtigen. Haben Sie die Feststell-
          Taste an? Bitte versuchen Sie es nochmal.

#login page
login.title=Anmeldungsprojekt - Bitte, anmelden
login.message=Bitte anmelden
login.username=Benutzername:
login.password=Passwort:
login.button.signon=Anmeldung

#loggedin page
loggedin.title=Anmeldungsprojekt
loggedin.msg=Willkommen, {0}. Sie sind jetzt angemeldet.
```

Copy the `ApplicationResources _de.properties` file into the `WEB-INF/classes` folder of the Login application in the Tomcat `webapps` folder. Then restart Tomcat.

In your Web browser, you must set the default language to German. When you do so, the browser tells the Web server the user's preferred language.

Setting the language preference in Internet Explorer

To set the default language in Internet Explorer 6.0, follow these steps:

1. **Choose Tools⇨Internet Options.**

   The Internet Options dialog box appears.

2. **Click the General tab.**
3. **At the bottom of the General tab, click the Languages button.**

   The Language Preference dialog box appears.
4. **Click the Add button.**

   The Add Language dialog box appears, as shown in Figure 6-1.

Figure 6-1: Internet Explorer's Add Language dialog box.

5. **Scroll down to find the language you want to set as a default.**

   To follow along with the example, look for an entry for German. There should be several, one for each country that speaks German. Because the resource bundle in this example is for German in general and not for a particular country, you can choose any German option.
6. **Select the language option you want, and then click OK.**

   You are returned to the Language Preference dialog box, as shown in Figure 6-2.
7. **Select the new German entry and click the Move Up button until the German entry is at the top.**

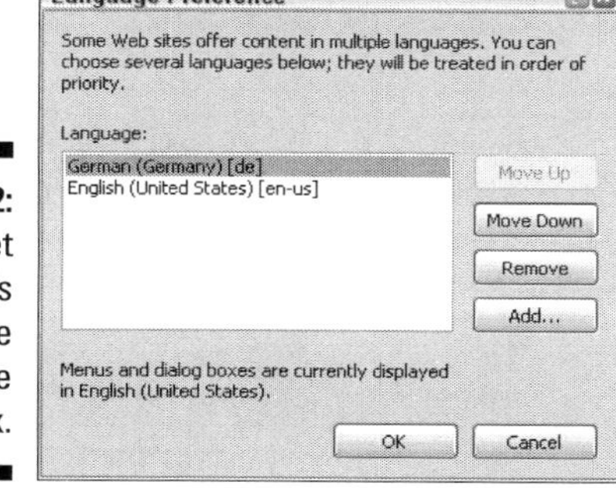

Figure 6-2: Internet Explorer's Language Preference dialog box.

When this test is over, be sure to delete the German entry unless you want to see your Web sites in German from now on. Re-open the Language Preference dialog box, choose the German entry, and click the Remove button. Click OK to close the dialog box.

8. **Click OK twice to close both open dialog boxes.**

Internet Explorer is ready to go. Other versions of Internet Explorer use a similar mechanism to set the language preference.

Setting the language preference in Netscape Navigator

To set the language default in Netscape 7.0, follow these steps:

1. **Choose Edit⇨Preferences.**

   The Preferences dialog box appears.

2. **In the Category pane, click the arrow next to Navigator.**
3. **Click the Languages option.**

   The Languages Panel appears on the right, as shown in Figure 6-3.

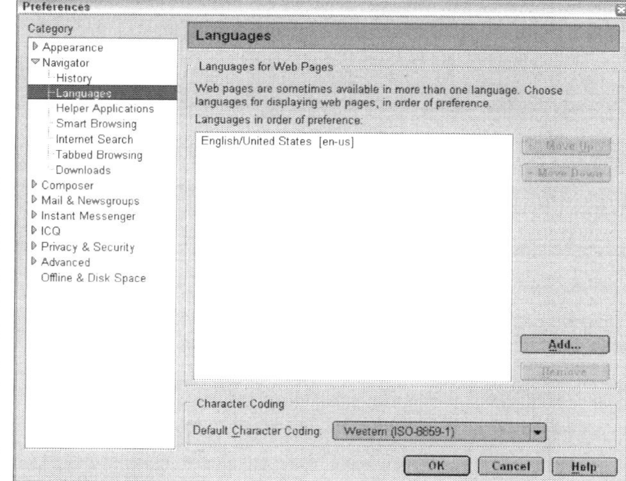

Figure 6-3: Netscape Navigator's Preferences dialog box with the Languages option selected.

4. **Click the Add button.**

   The Add Language dialog box appears.

5. **Scroll down to find and select the language that you want.**

   To follow along with the example, choose any German item.

6. **Click OK to close the dialog box.**

7. **In the Languages pane of the Preferences dialog box, select the German entry and then click the Move Up button until the German entry is at the top.**
8. **Click OK to close the Preferences dialog box.**

Netscape is ready to go. Other versions of Netscape Navigator set the language preference in a similar fashion.

Testing the internationalized application

In your browser, type the URL for the Login page (`http://localhost/Login`). The initial page should now be displayed in German, as shown in Figure 6-4.

Figure 6-4: The Login page displayed in German.

Enter a valid user name and password, and then log in. The normal logged-in message should now be displayed in German. Neat!

Using one source for String type constants

You may not think your application really needs I18N if only people in your company will see it. Nevertheless, you should consider using the I18N mechanism described in the previous sections for another reason — consolidating textual content for ease of maintenance. Often, especially for larger applications, the same textual content is displayed in many places throughout the application. During the lifetime of the application, you may need to change the text to meet some unforeseen need or demand of the marketplace.

For example, each page may have a button with the label OK. After the application has been in production for a while, usability experts may conclude that OK is confusing for some people and a better button label would be Save. To make that change, you would have to search all pages for instances of OK buttons and change the labels to Save. You might easily miss one or more instances.

If all the displayed text comes from message resources, however, you can easily find the reference to the OK button in the message resources and make one change there. This change will propagate throughout the application automatically when you restart the application. The maintenance is easy and there's no chance of missing an occurrence. Do less and accomplish more!

Mediating between the View and the Controller

When users fill out a form on a Web page, you need to collect that data for processing in the `Action` subclass that will handle the request. You create the movement of form data from the View to the Controller by using a formbean. Here we discuss the role of formbeans in detail.

A *formbean* is an extension of the `ActionForm` abstract class. The purpose of the formbean is to provide a consistent container to store the View's form data for presentation to the Controller. That being the case, the formbean requires little content — just the View's properties and their associated getter and setter methods. And that's the way it should be. The formbean shouldn't contain business logic or any other specific methods. The formbean is a data transfer mechanism — that's all.

When defining the properties of the formbean, you need to take into account that the form properties in the View are always `String` types. Even if the content displayed is a numerical value, such as 129.09, the content is always a string. The data may not be stored as a string in the backend database, but it's always displayed using strings in an HTML form. As a result, you may need to perform the following:

- When a form is submitted, convert the string into its numeric format after it's taken out of the formbean.
- Before a View is presented, convert the data from a numeric value to a string before populating the formbean.

We've found one exception when using the Struts tag library. The Struts tag for displaying an HTML check box assumes that the underlying value in the formbean is a boolean primitive type. However, when the HTML form is submitted or displayed, the check box uses a string value to determine whether the check box was or should be checked. The bottom line is that when using ungrouped check boxes on a form, the formbean property type should be boolean, not String.

Configuring the formbean

Listing 6-2 contains the configuration file for the example Login application. For more information on this application, see Chapter 3, where we discuss how to configure formbeans in the `struts-config` file. In this section, we explain the file from the angle of how it mediates between the View and the Controller.

Listing 6-2 struts-config.xml

```
<?xml version="1.0" encoding="ISO-8859-1" ?>

<!DOCTYPE struts-config PUBLIC
          "-//Apache Software Foundation//DTD Struts Configuration 1.1//EN"
          "http://jakarta.apache.org/struts/dtds/struts-config_1_1.dtd">

<!-- This is the Struts configuration file for Login example application -->
<struts-config>
    <!-- ========== FormBean Definitions ================================= -->
    <form-beans>
        <form-bean name="loginForm"
                   type="dummies.struts.LoginForm"/>
     </form-beans>

     <!-- ========== Action Mapping Definitions ========================== -->
     <action-mappings>
         <action path="/login"
                 type="dummies.struts.LoginAction"
                 name="loginForm"
                 scope="request"
                 input="/login.jsp"
                 validate="true">
                 <forward name="failure" path="/login.jsp"/>
                 <forward name="success" path="/loggedin.jsp"/>
         </action>
      </action-mappings>

      <!-- ========== Message Resources Definitions ===================== -->
       <message-resources null="false"
                          parameter="ApplicationResources"/>
</struts-config>
```

Note the following items in Listing 6-2:

- Line 9: Uses the `<form-bean>` tag to give `LoginForm` a name that you can refer to later in the `struts-config` file. You must define every `FormBean` that you intend to use in an application, using the `<form-bean>` tag. The Login application has only one `FormBean`, `LoginForm`.
- Line 10: Specifies the full class name of the form and closes the tag. Lines 9 and 10 tell the Controller how to create the formbean at runtime.
- Line 16: Specifies which formbean should be associated with this action. In this case, the code uses the `loginform` defined in line 9.
- Line 17: Specifies that the scope of the formbean should be the `request` scope. In other words, where should the formbean exist? The default scope is `request`, so this line is not really required. The other possibility is the `session` scope.
- Line 18: Specifies that the `login.jsp` page populates the formbean.
- Line 19: Specifies that the `validate` method of the formbean should be called. `False` would mean not to call the `validate` method, and validation would need to occur through some another means. (For more information about other means of validation, see the "Validating the Data" section later in this chapter).

Interactions with the formbean

The steps of the Controller's interaction with the formbean are presented in Chapter 4 in the "Working with the Controller's Helper-RequestProcessor" section. Here is a summary of the pertinent steps `RequestProcessor` takes when handling `ActionForm`:

1. **Gets the `ActionForm` associated with the request.**

   `RequestProcessor` gets the `ActionForm` associated with this action based on `ActionMapping`. If `ActionForm` doesn't exist, `RequestProcessor` creates it. `RequestProcessor` then calls the `reset` method of `ActionForm`.

2. **Populates `ActionForm`.**

   The `ActionForm` is populated with the parameters received from the request.

3. **Validates `ActionForm`.**

   If you're using standard form validation (`validate="true"`), `RequestProcessor` calls the `ActionForm's validate` method now. If the validation has any errors, `RequestProcessor` forwards control back to the page from which the request came.

4. **Calls the `execute` method on the specific `Action` class.**

   Finally, the `Action` class gets to do its stuff.

Preparing the form with the reset method

The standard `reset` method does nothing by default. This is appropriate because the `reset` method would know nothing about the properties of your formbean. You have the responsibility to write the appropriate code to set all your form properties back to their default state.

Why is resetting property values necessary? Actually, you don't need to reset values if your formbean is stored in the request scope because the formbean gets reinstantiated for each new request anyway. However, if you elect to store the formbean in the `session` scope, you need to make sure that the values from the previous use are cleared before using the formbean again because each new request uses the same copy of the formbean.

Resetting property values generally consists of setting the values back to null, or the empty string. Here is an example from our Login application:

```
public void reset(ActionMapping mapping,
                  HttpServletRequest request)
{
    password = "";
    userName = "";
}
```

Indexing data

If you need to display multiple rows of the same type of data, you may also need to define indexed properties in your formbean. An example would be the display of rows of purchase-order line-item information. You can define indexed properties by using standard Java arrays, Collections, or Maps. You use the various tag libraries to reference this data, which we discuss in Chapter 10.

A *Collection* is an interface and the root definition of a set of classes that hold groups of data objects. A *Map* is also an interface and root definition of a group of classes that hold data as keys mapped to values. The implementations of Collection and Map vary depending on how the objects or key values are stored. Developers choose a particular implementation of a Collection or Map based on the needs of the application. For example, you need to consider whether the data needs to be sorted or unsorted, whether or not the access needs to be thread safe, and whether or not duplicate values are allowed. See the Java SDK API documentation for details.

Validating data

Frequently, JSP pages have forms for the user to complete. The required information could be as simple as a user name and password, or you could have a complex order-entry form. You often want to make sure that the data the user entered is valid before trying to process the data. For example, if the user enters a date, you should verify that the date meets all the criteria of a valid date before passing the value to a database. The data may not be in the proper format for a date. Or the date might be in the proper format but too far in the future or past to be acceptable.

The standard mechanism for validating form data is to override the `validate` method in the `ActionForm` class and to enter there all the logic necessary to determine whether or not the form data is acceptable. `RequestProcessor` calls this method immediately before calling the execute method in the `Action` instance.

Listing 6-3 shows an example of overriding the `validate` method.

Listing 6-3 Overridden Validate Method from a Login formbean

```
1 public ActionErrors validate(ActionMapping mapping,
                               HttpServletRequest request)
2 {
     // create an empty ActionErrors instance
3    ActionErrors errors = new ActionErrors();

     // test for presence of user name
4    if((userName == null) || (userName.length() < 1))
5        errors.add("userName", new ActionError("error.username.required"));
     // test for presence of password
6    if((password == null) || (password.length() < 1))
7        errors.add("password", new ActionError("error.password.required"));
     // test for proper password length
8    else if ((password.length < 5) || (password.length > 8))
9        errors.add("password", new ActionError("error.password.length"));

     // return the ActionErrors object
10   return errors;
11 }
```

In Listing 6-3, note the following:

- Line 3: Creates an empty `ActionErrors` object, which is the return value for the method.
- Lines 4 and 6: Test to ensure that the user actually enters something for the `userName` and `password` fields.
- Line 8: Tests to make sure that the password is a proper length (5 to 8 characters).

If any test fails, the code creates an `ActionError` object and adds it to the `ActionErrors` instance. When creating the `ActionError` instance, a message resource key is passed to indicate which message should be displayed.

Note that when adding ActionError to ActionErrors, the code specifies a particular key (either username or password) so that the JSP page will know where to display the error.

Declarative form validation

Another way to perform validation is to use the declarative mechanism found in the Validator plug-in. The Validator plug-in is discussed in Chapter 9.

Notifying Users of Problems

Whether validating a form or testing logical operations, you need a common way to notify the user of the problem when an error arises. ActionError and ActionErrors are Struts classes created for that purpose.

ActionError is a subclass of ActionMessage that holds an error message that will be returned to the user. You specify the message by using a key of a message resource. If the message is parameterized, you can add the values for the parameters to ActionError. A message can have up to four parameters.

Here are examples of ActionError constructors using the message resource file in Listing 6-2:

```
// constructor with just the message's key
ActionError ae = ActionError("error.username.required");
// constructor with key and one parameter
ActionError ae =
           ActionError("error.username.required","Mike");
```

ActionErrors is a subclass of ActionMessages and is a wrapper class used to hold one or more instances of ActionError. Two constructors are possible — one creating an empty ActionErrors and the other creating an ActionErrors with the same messages as those in another instance of ActionErrors. Here are examples of the two constructors:

```
// empty constructor
ActionErrors aes = new ActionErrors();
// constructor taking an ActionErrors instance
ActionErrors aes2 = new ActionErrors(aes);
```

When you need to add an ActionError to the ActionErrors instance, use the add method. Its signature is

```
public void add(String property, ActionError error)
```

where `property` refers to the form entry that the error is indicating. For general errors that apply to the entire form, use `ActionErrors.GLOBAL_ERROR`. For an error specific to a particular field, use the `property` value of the field.

In our example application, Login, we tied specific errors to the `userName` and `password` properties in the `validate` method of the `LoginForm` class.

```
// create ActionErrors instance
ActionErrors errors = new ActionErrors();
if((userName == null) || (userName.length() < 1))
    // if a username error, create ActionError
    // and tie it to UserName
    errors.add("userName", new
            ActionError("error.username.required"));
if((password == null) || (password.length() < 1))
    // if a password error, create ActionError
    // and tie it to password
    errors.add("password", new
            ActionError("error.password.required"));
return errors;
```

In the `login.jsp` page of the Login application, we took advantage of the `error` property value to display the particular error next to the appropriate field. Here are two segments from that page. Notice the correspondence between the property of the `html:text` tag, the property of the `html:errors` tag, and the property used in the preceding `errors.add` methods.

```
<html:text property="userName"
           size="15"
           maxlength="15" />
<html:errors property="userName" />
<html:password property="password"
               size="15"
               maxlength="15"
               redisplay="false"/>
<html:errors property="password" />
```

`ActionMessages` and `ActionMessage` can be used just like `ActionErrors` and `ActionError`. However, in the JSP file, the `<html:messages>` tag should be used instead of `<html:errors>`. In general, `ActionMessages` are informative messages to the user and `ActionError` is an error message. For example, you may want to inform the user when a requested operation gets performed successfully, such as when a record gets inserted into the database without error.

Mediating Automatically

Although `ActionForms` are useful for conveying request information to the Controller from the presentation page, they're sometimes a hassle if the form contains only simple data that you want to gather. Struts has a slick mechanism to dynamically create the necessary formbean without the developer having to extend the ActionForm class. This mechanism can be used by creating definitions in the struts-config file. The principal Struts class that you use is called the DynaActionForm.

Configuring the DynaActionForm class

Configuring a DynaActionForm is not much different from configuring a regular ActionForm. The definition still goes in a <form-bean> tag in the struts-config file. However, rather than specifying your extended ActionForm class for the type attribute, you use the full class name of the DynaActionForm class. In addition, you specify the form properties that will be implemented by the formbean. Listing 6-4 is an example of how to implement LoginForm (from the Login example application in Chapter 3) as a DynaActionForm instead of an Action form.

Listing 6-4 Configuring DynaActionForm

```
1 <form-bean name="loginForm"
2           type="org.apache.struts.action.DynaActionForm">
3    <form-property name="userName"
4                   type="java.lang.String"
5                   initial=""/>
6    <form-property name="password"
7                   type="java.lang.String"
8                   initial=""/>
9 </form-bean>
```

Listing 6-4 has the following noteworthy items:

- Line 2: Declares the class to instantiate to be the DynaActionForm class.
- Lines 3–5: Define one property named userName of type String whose initial value is the empty string.
- Lines 6–8: Define another property, password, also of type String and with an initial value of the empty string.

As you can see, the configuration of a DynaActionForm and an ActionForm are similar. Note that when you are using DynaActionForm, you must make some changes to the Action class when referencing DynaActionForm values. These changes are described in the next section.

Differences between ActionForm and DynaActionForm

Although ActionForm and DynaActionForm are similar, you do need to take into account a few differences. The following differences stand out:

- The DynaActionForm doesn't have reset or validate methods available. (They exist but they're both empty methods.) Intuitively, it makes sense that reset is not present; DynaActionForms are generated with each request, so there's no need to reset values.
- If you want a DynaActionForm and you also need to call a reset or validate method, you must subclass DynaActionForm and override the reset or validate method. But if you go to that much trouble, you might as well stick with the ActionForm class.

  The alternative to subclassing the DynaActionForm to perform validation is to use the Validator plug-in. We discuss this mechanism in Chapter 9.
- The formbean properties are referenced differently in the Action class. DynaActionForm properties are no longer simple scalar values that can be referenced with getter and setter methods. Using these methods will not work because the formbean is created dynamically by reading the formbean configuration properties. Consequently, the form's properties are put into a Map structure and referenced by the property name. This means that in the Action class, rather than referencing the username value like this:

  ```
  String user = ((LoginForm)form).getUserName();
  ```

  You must now use the Map syntax of providing a key to do the lookup:

  ```
  String user =
          (String)((DynaActionForm)form).get("userName");
  ```
- You reference a form property in a JSP page differently. Assuming that you're using the Struts-EL or JSTL tag library, you reference a property of a standard formbean using the expression language (EL) syntax, like this:

  ```
  ${formbean.property}
  ```

  But because a DynaAction formbean has all the properties stored in a Map structure, you must reference them by using a slightly different syntax, such as

  ```
  ${dynabean.map.property}
  ```

Chapter 7

Setting the Configuration

In This Chapter

- Using configuration files
- Developing the Web container configuration
- Showing an example of Web container configuration
- Developing the Struts framework configuration
- Showing an example of a Struts configuration

When you've finished creating the Model, View, and Controller sections of your Web application, you need to tie all the parts together. Like a kid who puts on his shoes without taking the time to tie his shoelaces — he quickly falls on his face — your Web application won't go anywhere without the configuration files. We describe many configuration examples throughout the previous six chapters. In this chapter, we bring it all together and cover all aspects of configuring Struts.

Stringing the Parts Together

The Struts framework offers a lot of flexibility for developers putting together Web applications. The configuration files are instrumental in implementing much of that flexibility by enabling you to

- Fine-tune the functioning of the various components of the framework
- Specify the developer components that you're adding
- Define how to treat the added components
- Specify what happens in case of errors
- Include I18N information
- Extend the framework

When you set up your Struts application, you need to consider two configuration files: web.xml and struts-config.xml. The web.xml file defines the pieces of your Struts application that the Web container needs to know about. The struts-config.xml informs the Struts framework about the pieces of the Struts application that you've added to the framework.

Editing the Web Container Configuration File

The Web container reads the web.xml file to discover specific information about the application, in particular what kind of resources it contains. You can find the definition of the specification we're using for web.xml in the Java Servlet Specification version 2.3. You can download this specification from Sun's Web site at

```
java.sun.com/products/servlet/download.html
```

This section is not a complete description of the web.xml specification. Instead, we cover only the parts of the specification that directly relate to Struts.

A Document Type Definition (DTD) file defines the XML grammar used in an XML document. The web.xml file has a particular DTD associated with it. That DTD is too long to be included in this book. To see the entire DTD, look at the Java Servlet Specification version 2.3 mentioned previously or go to java.sun.com/dtd/web-app_2_3.dtd. However, we describe some of the DTD to help explain the basic structure of a web.xml file.

Reading a DTD: An overview

The DTD provides a concise definition of the rules for specifying a particular type of XML document. The rules are extensive. Here we define the minimal set of rules that you need to know to make sense of the DTD grammar discussed in this chapter. What are commonly referred to as *tags* in an XML document are known as *elements* in the XML grammar. You define elements through the following syntax:

```
<!ELEMENT element-name ...>
```

where . . . could be a text value or other elements.

The simplest form for an element definition is an element that's defined to have only a textual value, as shown here:

```
<!ELEMENT element-name #PCDATA>
```

The #PCDATA marker refers to parsed character data, but essentially means plain text. If an element contains one other element, describe it in parentheses, like this:

```
<!ELEMENT element-name (other-
    element-name)>
```

It may be that the defined element can contain several other elements. For example, following is the syntax for containing three other elements:

```
<!ELEMENT element-name (other-
    element-name1, other-
    element-name2, other-
    element-name3)>
```

The elements contained in the element you're defining can be optional, mandatory, or appear multiple times. To specify those qualities, follow these rules:

- If an element is optional but can occur only once, follow it with a ?
- If an element is mandatory and can occur one or more times, follow it with a +
- If an element is optional but can occur multiple times, follow it with a *
- If an element appears without any of the previous markers, it is considered mandatory but can appear only once

When an element is defined to contain other elements, the sequence of the appearance of each element in the DTD must be the same as in the definition.

Elements can have *attributes* that are a further qualification of the element. You define an attribute with the following syntax:

```
<!ATTLIST element-name
    attribute-name attribute-
    type default-declaration>
```

The element-name is the element name that you defined in the <!ELEMENT definition. The attribute-name is the name that refers to the attribute. The attribute-type refers to what type of value that you can present for the attribute. Finally, default-declaration determines whether or not the attribute is required.

The attribute-type can be one of several values. For example, if the attribute-type is CDATA, the attribute can take any text value. Another possibility is an *entity* (a shortcut to a commonly used value) that you define elsewhere in the DTD. To define the entity, use the following syntax:

```
<!ENTITY % ent-name "value-
    string">
```

An example of an entity definition is

```
<!ENTITY % ClassName "CDATA">
```

The entity is referenced as %ClassName;. An example of an attribute definition that uses an entity is the following:

```
<!ATTLIST form-bean  name
    %BeanName;       #REQUIRED>
```

You can enforce attributes also through the use of an optional default-declaration value. For example, you can place #REQUIRED or #IMPLIED at the end of the definition. #REQUIRED means that the attribute must be defined for the element; #IMPLIED means the attribute is optional.

All valid web.xml files must contain the following DOCTYPE declaration, indicating the version of the DTD to use:

```
<!DOCTYPE web-app PUBLIC "-//Sun Microsystems, Inc.//DTD Web
Application 2.3//EN" "http://java.sun.com/dtd/
          web-app_2_3.dtd">
```

The root tag of the web.xml file is <web-app>. This tag is always the first tag that you place in the web.xml file. The following DTD segment defines how you use the tag and lists all the possible other tags in it:

```
<!ELEMENT web-app (icon?, display-name?, description?,
distributable?, context-param*, filter*, filter-mapping*,
listener*, servlet*, servlet-mapping*, session-config?,
mimemapping*,welcome-file-list?, error-page*, taglib*,
resource-env-ref*, resource-ref*, security-constraint*,
login-config?,security-role*, env-entry*, ejb-ref*,
ejb-local-ref*)>
```

For more information about the syntax of a DTD, see the sidebar, "Reading a DTD: An overview." We show a complete example of a `web.xml` file at the end of this section.

The ServletContext configuration tag

Each Web container provides an implementation of the `ServletContext` interface for each Web application running in the Web container. Any servlet can reference the `ServletContext` object, which can store and reference objects by any servlet in the application. The `ServletContext` has a lifetime as long as the application is running. Store in the `ServletContext` any data elements that need to be available on a global basis for the life of the application.

The tag for inserting values into the `ServletContext` is `<context-param>`. The DTD syntax for the tag is

```
<!ELEMENT context-param (param-name, param-value,
           description?)>

<!ELEMENT param-name (#PCDATA)>
<!ELEMENT param-value (#PCDATA)>
<!ELEMENT description (#PCDATA)>
```

In the DTD syntax, you include the following items:

- `<param-name>` defines the name that references the param-value
- `<param-value>` is the value of the attribute
- `<description>` is an optional tag that provides descriptive text about the parent element

The following shows an example of the tag's use:

```
<context-param>
    <param-name>
        javax.servlet.jsp.jstl.fmt.localizationContext
    </param-name>
    <param-value>
        ApplicationResources
    </param-value>
</context-param>
```

In the example, we place into the ServletContext one parameter named javax.servlet.jsp.jstl.fmt.localizationContext with a value of ApplicationResources. When you use the JSTL tag library, you can define the default resource bundle in the web.xml file with this technique. In this way, you do not have to reference the resource bundle in the JSP when you need to retrieve messages from the resource bundle. (For more information about this technique, see "Configuring the message resources" in Chapter 6.)

Listener configuration

Application listeners are a new feature in the Servlet 2.3 specification. Their inclusion allows application developers to be aware of various servlet events regarding the ServletContext and HttpSession objects. In particular, developers can receive notification of lifecycle events for either object or changes to attributes stored in either object.

The tag for defining a listener is <listener>. The syntax for the tag is

```
<!ELEMENT listener (listener-class)>
<!ELEMENT listener-class (#PCDATA)>
```

In this syntax, <listener-class> is the fully qualified name of the Java class that implements one of the Listener interfaces.

Following is an example of the tag's use:

```
<listener>
    <listener-class>
        com.othenos.purchasing.common.SessionManager
    </listener-class>
</listener>
```

In the example we define one listener class named com.othenos.purchasing.common.SessionManager. The creation of an application listener class is more fully described in Chapter 9.

ActionServlet configuration

In a Struts application, you always have at least one servlet to declare and possibly others. The servlet definition section of web.xml allows you to define many of the key features of the servlet, in particular the fully qualified class name and how the servlet will be referenced.

The tag that defines a servlet is <servlet>. The syntax for the tag is

```
<!ELEMENT servlet (icon?, servlet-name, display-name?,
    description?,(servlet-class|jsp-file), init-param*,
    load-on-startup?, run-as?, security-role-ref*)>
<!ELEMENT icon (small-icon?, large-icon?)>
<!ELEMENT servlet-name (#PCDATA)>
<!ELEMENT display-name (#PCDATA)>
<!ELEMENT description (#PCDATA)>
<!ELEMENT servlet-class (#PCDATA)>
<!ELEMENT jsp-file (#PCDATA)>
<!ELEMENT init-param (param-name, param-value, description?)>
<!ELEMENT load-on-startup (#PCDATA)>
<!ELEMENT run-as (description?, role-name)>
<!ELEMENT security-role-ref (description?, role-name, role-
            link?)>
```

In this syntax, you use the following tags:

- <icon>: An optional tag that provides small and large icons to represent the Web application in a GUI tool.
- <servlet-name>: Sets the name that refers to the servlet instead of the more verbose class name.
- <display-name>: An optional tag that defines a short name intended to be displayed in GUI tools.
- <description>: An optional tag that provides descriptive text about the parent element.
- <servlet-class>: Must define the fully qualified name of the servlet class. You must specify either this tag or the following jsp-file tag.
- <jsp-file>: Must contain the full path to the JSP file beginning with /.
- <init-param>: An optional tag that contains one name-value pair that is passed to the servlet at initialization. The tag can be repeated multiple times. The requirements of the specified servlet determine the possible parameters.
- <load-on-startup>: An optional tag that specifies to the Web container the order of loading and initializing the servlets. Use a value of 0 or any positive integer to load the servlets in order from smallest integer to largest. Otherwise, the Web container can load the servlets in whatever order it wants.
- <run-as>: An optional tag that overrides the security identity that this servlet used to call an Enterprise JavaBean (EJB).
- <security-role-ref>: An optional tag that defines a mapping between the name of a role called from a servlet and the name of a security role defined for the Web application.

An example of servlet configuration follows:

```
<servlet>
    <servlet-name>action</servlet-name>
    <servlet-class>org.apache.struts.action.ActionServlet
    </servlet-class>
    <init-param>
        <param-name>config</param-name>
        <param-value>/WEB-INF/struts-config.xml</param-value>
    </init-param>
    <load-on-startup>1</load-on-startup>
</servlet>
```

You can supply numerous initialization parameters to ActionServlet using the <init-param> tag.

When you specify the value of a parameter, you need to enclose it in quotation marks.

Here is the current list of parameters:

- **config**: Context-relative path to the XML resource containing the configuration information for the default module. This may also be a comma-delimited list of configuration files. ActionServlet loads each file in turn, and its objects are appended to the internal data structure. The default is /WEB-INF/struts-config.xml.

  If you define an object of the same name in more than one configuration file, the last one loaded wins.

- **config/${module}**: Context-relative path to the XML resource containing the configuration information for the application module that will use the specified prefix (/${module}). You can repeat this as many times as you need for multiple application modules.
- **convertNull**: Forces simulation of the Struts 1.0 behavior when populating forms. If set to true, the numeric Java wrapper class types (such as java.lang.Integer) default to null (rather than 0). The default is false.
- **rulesets**: Comma-delimited list of fully qualified class names of additional org.apache.commons.digester.RuleSet instances that should be added to the Digester that will be processing struts-config.xml files. By default, only the RuleSet for the standard configuration elements is loaded.
- **validating**: Uses a validating XML parser to process the configuration file (strongly recommended). The default is true.

ActionServlet mapping

The servlet mapping tag defines the mapping between a URL pattern and a servlet. With it, the Web container will recognize that the servlet is responsible for handling all requests that follow the specified URL pattern.

The tag that defines the servlet mapping is `<servlet-mapping>`. The syntax for the tag is

```
<!ELEMENT servlet-mapping (servlet-name, url-pattern)>
<!ELEMENT servlet-name (#PCDATA)>
<!ELEMENT url-pattern (#PCDATA)>
```

In the syntax for the servlet mapping tag, you use the following items:

- `<servlet-name>`: Refers to the name that you gave the servlet when you defined it using the `<servlet>` tag. (For more information, see the "ActionServlet Configuration" section.)
- `<url-pattern>`: Specifies the URL pattern to associate with the servlet name used in `<servlet-name>`.

An example of servlet mapping follows:

```
<servlet-mapping>
    <servlet-name>action</servlet-name>
    <url-pattern>*.do</url-pattern>
</servlet-mapping>
```

This servlet mapping informs the Web container that any URL that ends in `.do` should pass to the servlet whose name is `action`. You can use any pattern, but `*.do` is common in Struts applications. The servlet associated with the name `action` was defined by the `<servlet>` tag in the preceding section of this chapter.

Adding in the tag libraries

You need to define tag libraries, like the ones that are part of the Struts-EL package, in the `web.xml` file so that the application can use them.

To define tag libraries, use the `<taglib>` tag. The syntax for the tag is

```
<!ELEMENT taglib (taglib-uri, taglib-location)>
<!ELEMENT taglib-uri (#PCDATA)>
<!ELEMENT taglib-location (#PCDATA)>
```

In this tag, you use the following items:

- <taglib-uri>: Describes a URI, relative to the location of the web.xml document, identifying a tag library used in the application. This URI will be used in the JSP page to reference the tag library.
- <taglib-location>: Contains the location (as a resource relative to the root of the Web application) of the Tag Library Description file for the tag library.

An example of the use of the <taglib> follows:

```
<taglib>
    <taglib-uri>jstl-c</taglib-uri>
    <taglib-location>/WEB-INF/c.tld</taglib-location>
</taglib>
```

This example defines the location of the Tag Library Descriptor as /WEB-INF/c.tld and defines /jstl-c as the URI to use to reference the taglib in a JSP page.

Then in the JSP page, you reference the taglib as follows:

```
<%@ taglib prefix="c" uri="jstl-c" %>
```

The sequence of tags in an XML document is important and must be followed. For example, in the web.xml file, you can't define the <servlet-mapping> tag before you define the <servlet> tag. If you have configuration errors at startup time, be sure to check the sequence of your tag definitions. Make sure they follow the sequence that you defined in the DTD for the XML file in question.

A complete example of a web.xml file

Listing 7-1 is a complete example of a web.xml file taken from the MusicCollection application we build in Chapter 14.

Listing 7-1 A Complete Example of a web.xml File

```
<?xml version="1.0" encoding="ISO-8859-1"?>

<!DOCTYPE web-app
  PUBLIC "-//Sun Microsystems, Inc.//DTD Web Application 2.2//EN"
  "http://java.sun.com/j2ee/dtds/web-app_2_2.dtd">

<web-app>
```

(continued)

Listing 7-1 *(continued)*

```
  <!-- Action Servlet Configuration -->
    <servlet>
      <servlet-name>action</servlet-name>
      <servlet-class>org.apache.struts.action.ActionServlet</servlet-class>
      <init-param>
        <param-name>config</param-name>
        <param-value>/WEB-INF/struts-config.xml</param-value>
      </init-param>
      <load-on-startup>1</load-on-startup>
    </servlet>

  <!-- Action Servlet Mapping -->
  <servlet-mapping>
    <servlet-name>action</servlet-name>
    <url-pattern>*.do</url-pattern>
  </servlet-mapping>

  <!-- The Welcome File List -->
  <welcome-file-list>
    <welcome-file>home.jsp</welcome-file>
  </welcome-file-list>

  <!-- JSTL Tag Library Descriptor -->
  <taglib>
    <taglib-uri>jstl-c</taglib-uri>
    <taglib-location>/WEB-INF/c.tld</taglib-location>
  </taglib>

  <taglib>
    <taglib-uri>jstl-fmt</taglib-uri>
    <taglib-location>/WEB-INF/fmt.tld</taglib-location>
  </taglib>

  <!-- Struts Tag Library Descriptors -->
  <taglib>
    <taglib-uri>/WEB-INF/struts-bean-el.tld</taglib-uri>
    <taglib-location>/WEB-INF/struts-bean-el.tld</taglib-location>
  </taglib>

  <taglib>
    <taglib-uri>/WEB-INF/struts-html-el.tld</taglib-uri>
    <taglib-location>/WEB-INF/struts-html-el.tld</taglib-location>
  </taglib>

  <taglib>
    <taglib-uri>/WEB-INF/struts-logic-el.tld</taglib-uri>
    <taglib-location>/WEB-INF/struts-logic-el.tld</taglib-location>
  </taglib>

</web-app>
```

Modifying the Struts Configuration File

The Struts configuration file, struts-config.xml, is similar to the web.xml configuration file for the Web container except that it informs the Struts framework about the components the developer is adding to the framework and how to use these components.

The struts-config.xml file, like web.xml, has a DTD file that defines the acceptable grammar for laying out the configuration. Each struts-config.xml file must begin with a DOCTYPE indicating the version of the DTD to use. The following example specifies version 1.1 of the Struts Configuration DTD:

```
<!DOCTYPE struts-config PUBLIC "-//Apache Software
          Foundation//DTD Struts Configuration 1.1//EN"
"http://jakarta.apache.org/struts/dtds/struts-
          config_1_1.dtd">
```

The root tag of the struts-config.xml file is <struts-config>. The <struts-config> tag is always the first tag in the struts-config.xml file. The following code defines the use of this tag and all the possible other tags in it. The DTD syntax for the struts-config tag is shown here:

```
<!ELEMENT struts-config (data-sources?, form-beans?,
global-exceptions?, global-forwards?, action-mappings?,
controller?, message-resources*, plug-in*)>
```

We show a complete example of a struts-config file at the end of this section.

DataSource configuration

The Struts framework can take direct advantage of implementations of the javax.sql.DataSource interface to provide database connections and pooling for Web applications. Some Web container providers or database vendors may offer a pooling mechanism that implements the javax.sql.DataSource interface. Such a mechanism might be your first choice. If not, take a look at the Jakarta Commons DBCP package as a possibility. This package is a DataSource implementation and offers connection pooling when you use it with the Jakarta Commons Pool package. For more information about DataSources, see Chapter 5.

If you must support more than one database, you can enter each database as a datasource in the datasources configuration. The tag for inserting datasources is <data-sources>. The DTD syntax for the tag follows:

```
<!ELEMENT data-sources (data-source*)>
<!ELEMENT data-source (set-property*)>
<!ATTLIST data-source  className   %ClassName;     #IMPLIED>
<!ATTLIST data-source  key         %AttributeName; #IMPLIED>
<!ATTLIST data-source  type        %ClassName;     #IMPLIED>

<!ELEMENT set-property  EMPTY>
<!ATTLIST set-property  property   %PropName;      #REQUIRED>
<!ATTLIST set-property  value      CDATA           #REQUIRED>
```

In this tag, you use the following two tags, each with a set of attributes that follow:

- <data-source>: Defines the datasource implementation and the key that references it.
  - className: The configuration bean for this DataSource object. If specified, the object must be a subclass of the default configuration bean. The default is org.apache.struts.config.DataSourceConfig.
  - key: Servlet context attribute key that locates this datasource. The default is org.apache.struts.action.DATA_SOURCE. In our examples we use the application name, such as musiccollection. The application module prefix (if any) is appended to the key (${key}$prefix}).

    The application module prefix includes the leading slash. For example, the musiccollection datasource key for a module named foo is musiccollection/foo.
  - type: Fully qualified Java class name for this datasource object. The class must implement DataSource [javax.sql.DataSource], and the object must be configurable entirely from JavaBean properties.
- <set-property>: Provides a series of name-value pairs that you can use to initialize the datasource.
  - property: Name of the JavaBeans property whose setter method will be called.
  - value: String representation of the value to which this property will be set, after suitable type conversion.

Your choice of parameters depends on the datasource implementation that you choose to work with. If you're using the Commons DBCP package, for example, look at jakarta.apache.org/commons/dbcp/configuration.html for details of the properties you can set.

Listing 7-2 shows an example of the tag's use for the Commons DBCP taken from the example application in Chapter 14.

Listing 7-2 Using the data-sources Tag for the Commons DBCP Package

```
  <data-sources>
1   <data-source key="musiccollection"
             type="org.apache.commons.dbcp.BasicDataSource">
2     <set-property property="description"
             value="Music Collection Database"/>
3     <set-property property="driverClassName"
             value="com.mysql.jdbc.Driver"/>
4     <set-property property="username" value="root"/>
5     <set-property property="password" value="bigmoma"/>
6     <set-property property="url"
             value="jdbc:mysql://localhost/musiccollection" />
7     <set-property property="maxCount" value="8"/>
8     <set-property property="minCount" value="2"/>
    </data-source>
  </data-sources>
```

In Listing 7-2, note the following:

- Line 1: Defines `org.apache.commons.dbcp.BasicDataSource` as the fully qualified class name of the implementation of the `javax.sql.DataSource` interface. In addition, the example defines `musiccollection` as the key to use to look up the datasource from the application scope.
- Lines 2-8: Defines the set of parameters to pass to the DataSource implementation.

Formbean configuration

You need to define the formbean in the `struts-config` file. We also discussed formbeans extensively in Chapters 3 and 6.

The tag for inserting formbeans is `<form-beans>`. The DTD syntax for the tag follows:

```
<!ELEMENT form-beans (form-bean*)>
<!ATTLIST form-beans type          %ClassName;      #IMPLIED>
```

```
<!ELEMENT form-bean   (icon?, display-name?, description?,
                      set-property*, form-property*)>
<!ATTLIST form-bean   className     %ClassName;      #IMPLIED>
<!ATTLIST form-bean   dynamic       %Boolean;        #IMPLIED>
<!ATTLIST form-bean   name          %BeanName;       #REQUIRED>
<!ATTLIST form-bean   type          %ClassName;      #REQUIRED>
```

```
<!ELEMENT icon (small-icon?, large-icon?)>
<!ELEMENT large-icon    (%Location;)>
<!ELEMENT small-icon    (%Location;)>
<!ELEMENT display-name  (#PCDATA)>
<!ELEMENT description   (#PCDATA)>
<!ELEMENT set-property  EMPTY>
<!ATTLIST set-property  property   %PropName;      #REQUIRED>
<!ATTLIST set-property  value      CDATA           #REQUIRED>
<!ELEMENT form-property (set-property*)>
<!ATTLIST form-property className  %ClassName;     #IMPLIED>
<!ATTLIST form-property initial    CDATA           #IMPLIED>
<!ATTLIST form-property name       %PropName;      #REQUIRED>
<!ATTLIST form-property size       %Integer;       #IMPLIED>
<!ATTLIST form-property type       %ClassName;     #REQUIRED>
```

You use the following notation in the DTD file:

- <form-beans>: Starts the section where all the formbeans are defined.
- <form-bean>: Defines a formbean to be used in the application. The tag has the following attributes:
    - className: The configuration bean for this formbean object. If specified, the object must be a subclass of the default configuration bean. The default is org.apache.struts.config.FormBeanConfig.
    - dynamic: This attribute is deprecated. This information is now determined dynamically based on the specified implementation class.
    - name: The unique identifier for this form bean. Referenced by the <action> element to specify which formbean to use with its request.
    - type: Fully qualified Java class name of the ActionForm subclass to use with this formbean.
- <icon>: Defines a large-icon or a small-icon or both that you can use to represent this formbean in a GUI tool.
- <display-name>: Defines a name to be associated with this formbean in a GUI tool.
- <description>: Contains descriptive text about the formbean for display in GUI tools.
- <set-property>: Allows you to pass parameters to the formbean. See the "DataSource configuration" section earlier in this chapter for more details on <set-property>.

- <form-property>: Used when the formbean is a class or subclass of DynaActionForm. The tag has the following attributes:
  - className: The configuration bean for this form property object. If specified, the object must be a subclass of the default configuration bean. The default is org.apache.struts.config.FormPropertyConfig.
  - initial: String representation of the initial value for this property. If you don't specify a value, primitives are initialized to zero and objects are initialized to the zero-argument instantiation of that object class. For example, Strings are initialized to "".
  - name: The name of the JavaBean property described by this element.
  - size: The number of array elements to create if the value of the type attribute specifies an array but does not specify a value for the initial attribute.
  - type: Fully qualified Java class name of the field underlying this property, optionally followed by [] to indicate that the field is indexed.

Listing 7-3 shows an example of a formbean definition.

Listing 7-3 A Formbean Definition

```
<form-beans>
1  <form-bean name="loginForm"
2             type="org.apache.struts.validator.DynaValidatorForm">
3    <form-property name="email"
4                   type="java.lang.String"
5                   initial=""/>
6    <form-property name="password"
7                   type="java.lang.String"
8                   initial=""/>
9  </form-bean>
... other form beans can be defined here
</form-beans>
```

Note the following sections of Listing 7-3:

- Lines 1–9: Define a DynaValidatorForm bean.
- Line 1: Defines the name of the form to be loginForm.
- Line 2: Indicates that the form is based on the DynaValidatorForm class.

- Lines 3–5: Specify that one property of the form is named `email`, of type String, with an initial value of "".
- Lines 6–8: Specify that one property of the form should be named `password`, of type String, with an initial value of "".

Global exceptions

You need to declare any global exceptions in the `struts-config` file. In this section, we discuss how to set up the configuration for global exceptions. For a full discussion of the ins and outs of declarative exception handling, see Chapter 8.

The tag for inserting global exceptions is `<global-exceptions>`. The DTD syntax for the tag is

```
<!ELEMENT global-exceptions (exception*)>
<!ATTLIST global-exceptions id   ID       #IMPLIED>

<!ELEMENT exception (icon?, display-name?, description?,
                     set-property*)>
<!ATTLIST exception bundle       %AttributeName; #IMPLIED>
<!ATTLIST exception className    %ClassName;     #IMPLIED>
<!ATTLIST exception handler      %ClassName;     #IMPLIED>
<!ATTLIST exception key          CDATA           #REQUIRED>
<!ATTLIST exception path         %RequestPath;   #IMPLIED>
<!ATTLIST exception scope        CDATA           #IMPLIED>
<!ATTLIST exception type         %ClassName;     #REQUIRED>
```

You use the following items for the global-exceptions tag:

- `<global-exceptions>`: Marks the beginning of all global exception definitions.
- `<exception>`: Starts the definition of one exception. The attributes of the tag follow:
    - `bundle`: Servlet context attribute for the message resources bundle associated with this handler. The default attribute is the value specified by the string constant declared at `Globals.MESSAGES_KEY`. The default is `org.apache.struts.Globals.MESSAGES_KEY`.
    - `className`: The configuration bean for this `ExceptionHandler` object. If specified, `className` must be a subclass of the default configuration bean. The default is `org.apache.struts.config.ExceptionConfig`.

- handler: Fully qualified Java class name for this exception handler. The default is org.apache.struts.action.ExceptionHandler.
- key: The key to use with this handler's message resource bundle that will retrieve the error message template for this exception.
- path: The module-relative URI to the resource that completes the request and response if this exception occurs.
- scope: The context (request or session) that accesses the ActionError object for this exception. The default is request.
- type: Fully qualified Java class name of the exception type to register with this handler.

Here is an example of the tag's use:

```
<global-exceptions>
  <exception bundle="ApplicationResources"
        key="error.RuntimeException"
        path="/baderror.jsp"
        handler="dummies.struts.music.CustomExceptionHandler"
        type="java.lang.RuntimeException" />
</global-exceptions >
```

The example describes one global exception of type RuntimeException that supplies a message based in the error.RuntimeException resource bundle key. The error is handled by a specialized exception handler class, CustomExceptionHandler. The destination is a custom error page named baderror.jsp.

Global forwards

Global forwards define a set of ActionForward objects available to all Action objects as a return value. Any ActionForward of the same name that is defined in an <action> tag overrides the global ActionForward.

The tag for inserting global forwards is <global-forwards>. The DTD syntax for the tag is

```
<!ELEMENT global-forwards (forward*)>
<!ELEMENT forward (icon?, display-name?, description?,
                   set-property*)>
<!ATTLIST forward className       %ClassName;     #IMPLIED>
<!ATTLIST forward contextRelative %Boolean;       #IMPLIED>
<!ATTLIST forward name            CDATA           #REQUIRED>
<!ATTLIST forward path            %RequestPath;   #REQUIRED>
<!ATTLIST forward redirect        %Boolean;       #IMPLIED>
```

The DTD syntax for the <global-forwards> tag has the following properties:

- <global-forwards>: Begins the definitions of one or more global forwards.
- <forward>: Defines ActionForward. The attributes of the tag follow:
  - className: Fully qualified Java class name of ActionForward subclass to use for this object. The default is org.apache.struts.action.ActionForward.
  - contextRelative: Set this to true if, in a modular application, the path attribute starts with a slash (/) and should be considered relative to the entire Web application rather than the module. The default is false.
  - name: The unique identifier for this forward. Referenced by the Action object at runtime to select — by its logical name — the resource that should complete the request/response.
  - path: The module-relative or context-relative path to the resources that this ActionForward encapsulates. If the path is context-relative when used in a modular application, set the contextRelative attribute to true. This value should begin with a slash (/) character.
  - redirect: Set to true if a redirect instruction should be issued to the user-agent so that a new request is issued for this forward's resource. If true, the sendRedirect method of HttpServletResponse is called. If false, the forward method of RequestDispatcher is called instead. The default is false.

An example of the tag's use is

```
<global-forwards>
    <forward name="logon"
             path="/logon.jsp"/>
</global-forwards>
```

This simple example sets up a global forward of the name "logon" that forwards control to the resource on the path "/logon.jsp".

Action mapping

Action mappings describe a set of ActionMapping objects. Each ActionMapping object associates an Action object with a path and various other attributes. Exactly one ActionMapping is represented by an action tag.

The tag for inserting actions is <action-mappings>. The DTD syntax for the tag is shown here:

```
<!ELEMENT action-mappings (action*)>
<!ATTLIST action-mappings type  %ClassName;     #IMPLIED>

<!ELEMENT action (icon?, display-name?, description?,
                  set-property*, exception*, forward*)>
<!ATTLIST action attribute      %BeanName;      #IMPLIED>
<!ATTLIST action className      %ClassName;     #IMPLIED>
<!ATTLIST action forward        %RequestPath;   #IMPLIED>
<!ATTLIST action include        %RequestPath;   #IMPLIED>
<!ATTLIST action input          %RequestPath;   #IMPLIED>
<!ATTLIST action name           %BeanName;      #IMPLIED>
<!ATTLIST action parameter      CDATA           #IMPLIED>
<!ATTLIST action path           %RequestPath;   #REQUIRED>
<!ATTLIST action prefix         CDATA           #IMPLIED>
<!ATTLIST action roles          CDATA           #IMPLIED>
<!ATTLIST action scope          %RequestScope;  #IMPLIED>
<!ATTLIST action suffix         CDATA           #IMPLIED>
<!ATTLIST action type           %ClassName;     #IMPLIED>
<!ATTLIST action unknown        %Boolean;       #IMPLIED>
<!ATTLIST action validate       %Boolean;       #IMPLIED>
```

The <action-mappings> tag uses the following attributes:

- <action-mappings>: Defines the beginning of a set of actions.
- <action>: Represents one ActionMapping object. The attributes of the tag follow:
  - attribute: Name of the request-scope or session-scope attribute that accesses the ActionForm bean, if it's other than the bean's specified name. This attribute is optional if name is specified but otherwise is not valid.
  - className: The fully qualified Java class name of the ActionMapping subclass to use for this action mapping object. Defaults to the type specified by the enclosing <action-mappings> element or to org.apache.struts.action.ActionMapping if not specified.
  - forward: Module-relative path of the servlet or other resource that processes this request, instead of the Action class specified by type. You can specify one of the following: forward, include, or type.
  - include: Module-relative path of the servlet or other resource that processes this request, instead of the Action class specified by type. You must specify one of the following: forward, include, or type.

- input: Module-relative path of the action or other resource that gets control if a validation error occurs. Valid only if you specify the name attribute. If you specify the name attribute and the input bean returns validation errors, you must specify this attribute. On the other hand, if you specify the name attribute and the input bean does not return validation errors, this attribute is optional.
- name: Name of the formbean, if any, associated with this action mapping.
- path: The module-relative path of the submitted request, starting with a slash (/) character and without the filename extension if you are using extension mapping.

Never include a period in your path name. ActionServlet considers a period the beginning of a filename extension and will not be able to locate your Action.

- parameter: General-purpose configuration parameter that you can use to pass extra information to the Action object selected by this action mapping.
- prefix: Prefix used to match request parameter names to ActionForm property names, if any. Optional if you have specified the name attribute; otherwise, the prefix attribute is not allowed.
- roles: Comma-delimited list of security role names that are allowed access to this ActionMapping object.
- scope: The context ("request" or "session") used to access the ActionForm bean, if any. This attribute is optional if you specify the "name" attribute; otherwise, it's not valid.
- suffix: Suffix used to match request parameter names to ActionForm bean property names, if any. This attribute is optional if you specify the name attribute; otherwise it's not valid.
- type: Fully qualified Java class name of the Action subclass [org.apache.struts.action.Action] that will process requests for this action mapping. This attribute is not valid if you have specified the forward or include attribute. You must specify forward, include, or type.
- unknown: Set to true if this object should be configured as the default action mapping for this module. If a request does not match another object, it will be passed to the ActionMapping object with unknown set to true. You can mark only one ActionMapping as unknown in a module. The default is false.
- validate: Set to true if you want to call the validate method of the ActionForm bean before calling the Action object for this action mapping. Set to false if you don't want to call the validate method. The default is true.

Listing 7-4 shows an example of the <action-mapping> tag's use.

Listing 7-4 An Example of the <action-mapping> Tag

```
 <action-mappings>
1  <action path="/home"
2          type="dummies.struts.music.LoginAction"
3          name="loginForm"
4          scope="request"
5          input="/home.jsp"
6          validate="true">
7    <forward name="failure" path="/home.jsp"/>
8    <forward name="success" path="/musiclist.do"/>
9    <forward name="join" path="/join.jsp"/>
   </action>
 </action-mappings>
```

Here's an explanation of Listing 7-4:

- Line 1: Defines the path for this `ActionMapping` as `"/home"`. The actual URI used to invoke this action is `/home.do` because `*.do` was defined as the URL pattern in `web.xml`.
- Line 2: Specifies that the `Action` class is `POAction` and will be called for each request.
- Line 3: Associates `"loginForm"` as the formbean to be used with requests.
- Line 4: Specifies that the formbean be stored in the `request` object.
- Line 5: Indicates that control should be returned to `home.jsp` in the event of a validation error.
- Line 6: Calls the `validation` method of the formbean.
- Lines 7–9: Define forwards to be used by the `Action` class.

Controller configuration

You can make changes in the configuration of the `ActionServlet` through the use of the `controller` tag. You can configure quite a few qualities of the `ActionServlet` through this tag. Most applications can skip configuring the controller and simply use the default values.

The tag for inserting a new controller is `<controller>`. The DTD syntax for the tag is shown here:

```
<!ELEMENT controller (set-property*)>
<!ATTLIST controller bufferSize     %Integer;     #IMPLIED>
<!ATTLIST controller className      %ClassName;   #IMPLIED>
<!ATTLIST controller contentType    CDATA         #IMPLIED>
<!ATTLIST controller debug          %Integer;     #IMPLIED>
```

```
<!ATTLIST controller forwardPattern CDATA          #IMPLIED>
<!ATTLIST controller inputForward   %Boolean;      #IMPLIED>
<!ATTLIST controller locale         %Boolean;      #IMPLIED>
<!ATTLIST controller maxFileSize    CDATA          #IMPLIED>
<!ATTLIST controller memFileSize    CDATA          #IMPLIED>
<!ATTLIST controller multipartClass %ClassName;    #IMPLIED>
<!ATTLIST controller nocache        %Boolean;      #IMPLIED>
<!ATTLIST controller pagePattern    CDATA          #IMPLIED>
<!ATTLIST controller processorClass %ClassName;    #IMPLIED>
<!ATTLIST controller tempDir        CDATA          #IMPLIED>
```

The `<controller>` tag defines any changes to `ActionServlet`. The list of possible attributes is as follows:

- `bufferSize`: The size of the input buffer used when processing file uploads. The default is `4096`.
- `className`: Fully qualified Java class name of the `ControllerConfig` subclass for this controller object. If you specify this attribute, the object must be a subclass of the default class. The default is `org.apache.struts.config.ControllerConfig`.
- `contentType`: Default content type (and optional character encoding) for each response. The Action, JSP, or other resource that receives the request may override this attribute. The default is `text/html`.
- `debug`: Debugging detail level for this module. The default is 0. This attribute is deprecated. Instead, you should configure the logging detail level in your underlying logging implementation. For more information on logging, see Chapter 13.
- `forwardPattern`: Replacement pattern defining how the `path` attribute of a `<forward>` element is mapped to a context-relative URL when it starts with a slash (and when the `contextRelative` property is `false`). This value may consist of any combination of the following:
  - `$M`: Replaced by the prefix of this module.
  - `$P`: Replaced by the `path` attribute of the selected `forward` element.
  - `$$`: Displays a literal dollar sign.
  - `$x`: `x` is any character not defined previously in this list. Currently disregarded, but reserved for future use.

  The default `forwardPattern` is `$M$P`.
- `inputForward`: Set to `true` if you want the input attribute of `<action>` elements to be the name of a local or global ActionForward, which will then be used to calculate the ultimate URL. Set to `false` to treat the input parameter of `<action>` elements as a module-relative path to the resource to be used as the input form. The default is `false`.
- `locale`: Set to `true` if you want to store a `Locale` object in the user's session if not already present. The default is `true`.

- maxFileSize: The maximum size (in bytes) of a file that the application accepts as a file upload. You can express this attribute as a number followed by a K, M, or G, for kilobytes, megabytes, or gigabytes, respectively. The default is 250M.
- memFileSize: The maximum size (in bytes) of a file whose contents are retained in memory after uploading. Files larger than this threshold are written to some alternative storage medium, typically a hard disk. Can be expressed as a number followed by a K, M, or G, for kilobytes, megabytes, or gigabytes, respectively. The default is 256K.
- multipartClass: The fully qualified Java class name of the multipart request handler class that you want to use with this module. The default is org.apache.struts.upload.CommonsMultipartRequestHandler.
- nocache: Set to true if you want the controller to add HTTP headers for tell the Web server not to cache responses from this module. The default is false.
- pagePattern: Replacement pattern defining the mapping of the page attribute of custom tags to a context-relative URL of the corresponding resource. This value may consist of any combination of the following:
  - $M: Replaced by the prefix of this module.
  - $P: Replaced by the value of the page attribute.
  - $$: Displays a literal dollar sign.
  - $x: x is any character not defined previously in this list. This value is currently disregarded, but reserved for future use.

  The default pagePattern is MP.
- processorClass: The fully qualified Java class name of the RequestProcessor subclass to be used with this module. The default is org.apache.struts.action.RequestProcessor.
- tempDir: Temporary working directory to use when processing file uploads. The default is {Directory provided by servlet container}.

An example of the tag's use is shown here:

```
<controller processorClass =
    "com.othenos.purchasing.common.CustomRequestProcessor"/>
```

This example shows the installation of a new RequestProcessor subclass. This replaces the original RequestProcessor reference in ActionServlet.

Message resource configuration

To insert message resources, use the <message-resources> tag. For more information on message resources, their use and configuration, see Chapters 3 and 6.

The DTD syntax for the tag is as follows:

```
<!ELEMENT message-resources (set-property*)>
<!ATTLIST message-resources className %ClassName;    #IMPLIED>
<!ATTLIST message-resources factory   %ClassName;    #IMPLIED>
<!ATTLIST message-resources key     %AttributeName; #IMPLIED>
<!ATTLIST message-resources null       %Boolean;      #IMPLIED>
<!ATTLIST message-resources parameter CDATA          #REQUIRED>
```

The `<message-resources>` tag defines a message resource bundle to be made available to the Web application. The `parameter` attribute is required and refers to the file name of the resource bundle. The following are attributes of the tag:

- `className`: The configuration bean for this message resources object. If you specify this attribute, the object must be a subclass of the default configuration bean. The default is `org.apache.struts.config.MessageResourcesConfig`.
- `factory`: Fully qualified Java class name of the `MessageResourcesFactory` subclass to use for this message resources object. The default is `org.apache.struts.util.PropertyMessageResourcesFactory`.
- `key`: Servlet context attribute key that locates the message resources bundle. The default attribute is the value that the string constant `Globals.MESSAGES_KEY` specifies, which happens to be `org.apache.struts.action.ACTION_MESSAGE`. The application module prefix (if any) is appended to the key (`${key}${prefix}`).

  The application module prefix includes the leading slash. For example, `org.apache.struts.action.MESSAGE/foo` references the default message resource bundle for a module named `foo`.
- `null`: Set to `true` if you want your message resources to return a null string for unknown message keys. Set to `false` to return a message with the bad key value in the form of ???key???.
- `parameter`: Configuration parameter to be passed to the `createResources` method of the `PropertyMessageResourcesFactory` object or its subclass.

Here is an example of the tag's use:

```
<message-resources null="false"
                   parameter="ApplicationResources"/>
```

In this example, we specify a message resource bundle named `"ApplicationResources"`. In addition, we specify that if a particular resource key can't be found, the application should display the `"???`*key*`???"` message, as shown in Figure 7-1.

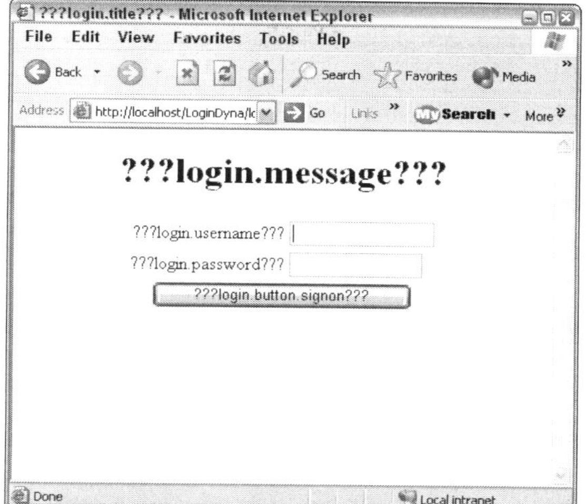

Figure 7-1: A message resource is missing, so the application displays lots of question marks.

Plug-in configuration

You can extend the functionality of Struts through the use of plug-ins, such as the Validator plug-in. We discuss the use of plug-ins fully in Chapter 9. To use plug-ins, the Struts framework must learn about them through the plug-in tag that you place in the `struts-config` file.

The tag for inserting plug-ins is `<plug-in>`. The DTD syntax for the tag is

```
<!ELEMENT plug-in (set-property*)>
<!ATTLIST plug-in className %ClassName; #REQUIRED>
```

The DTD syntax for the `<plug-in>` tag has one attribute — `<plug-in>` — that defines the plug-in that you want to include by requiring the `className` attribute. The `className` attribute specifies the fully qualified Java class name of the plug-in class and must implement `[org.apache.struts.action.PlugIn]`. Some plug-ins require parameters; others don't. If you need parameters, specify them by using the `set-property` tag.

Here is an example of the tag's use:

```
<plug-in
  className="org.apache.struts.validator.ValidatorPlugIn">
    <set-property property="pathnames"
                  value="/WEB-INF/validator-rules.xml,
                         /WEB-INF/validation.xml"/>
</plug-in>
```

In this example, we define the Validator plug-in. This plug-in requires one parameter, "pathnames". This parameter specifies the paths to find its configuration files: validator-rules.xml and validation.xml.

Complete example of a struts-config.xml file

In this chapter, we've broken the struts-config.xml file into itty-bitty pieces to provide you with all the details you need. Now is the time to put Humpty Dumpty back together again. Listing 7-5 is a complete example of a working struts-config.xml file taken from the example application we create in Chapter 14. The comments in the file help to delineate all the sections that we've discussed.

Listing 7-5 A Complete Example of the struts-config.xml File

```
<?xml version="1.0" encoding="ISO-8859-1" ?>

<!DOCTYPE struts-config PUBLIC
          "-//Apache Software Foundation//DTD Struts Configuration 1.1//EN"
          "http://jakarta.apache.org/struts/dtds/struts-config_1_1.dtd">

<!-- This is the Struts configuration file for MusicCollection application -->

<struts-config>
  <!-- ========== DataSource Definitions ================================= -->
  <data-sources>
    <data-source key="musiccollection"
                 type="org.apache.commons.dbcp.BasicDataSource">
      <set-property property="description" value="Music Collection Database"/>
      <set-property property="driverClassName" value="com.mysql.jdbc.Driver"/>
      <set-property property="username" value="root"/>
      <set-property property="password" value="bigmoma"/>
      <set-property property="url"
                    value="jdbc:mysql://localhost/musiccollection" />
      <set-property property="maxCount" value="8"/>
      <set-property property="minCount" value="2"/>
    </data-source>
  </data-sources>

  <!-- ========== Form Bean Definitions ================================= -->
  <form-beans>
    <form-bean name="loginForm"
               type="org.apache.struts.validator.DynaValidatorForm">
      <form-property name="email"
                     type="java.lang.String"
                     initial=""/>
```

```
    <form-property name="password"
                   type="java.lang.String"
                   initial=""/>
  </form-bean>

  <form-bean name="joinForm"
           type="org.apache.struts.validator.DynaValidatorForm">
    <form-property name="email"
                   type="java.lang.String"
                   initial=""/>
    <form-property name="password"
                   type="java.lang.String"
                   initial=""/>
    <form-property name="password2"
                   type="java.lang.String"
                   initial=""/>
    <form-property name="fname"
                   type="java.lang.String"
                   initial=""/>
    <form-property name="lname"
                   type="java.lang.String"
                   initial=""/>
  </form-bean>

  <form-bean name="musiclistForm"
           type="org.apache.struts.action.DynaActionForm">
    <form-property name="action"
                   type="java.lang.String"
                   initial=""/>
  </form-bean>

  <form-bean name="albumForm"
           type="org.apache.struts.validator.DynaValidatorForm">
    <form-property name="album"
                   type="java.lang.String"
                   initial=""/>
    <form-property name="artist"
                   type="java.lang.String"
                   initial=""/>
    <form-property name="year"
                   type="java.lang.String"
                   initial=""/>
    <form-property name="type"
                   type="java.lang.String"
                   initial=""/>
    <form-property name="category"
                   type="java.lang.String"
                   initial=""/>
    <form-property name="description"
                   type="java.lang.String"
                   initial=""/>
```

(continued)

Listing 7-5 *(continued)*

```
      <form-property name="userid"
                     type="java.lang.String"
                     initial=""/>
      <form-property name="id"
                     type="java.lang.String"
                     initial=""/>
      <form-property name="action1"
                     type="java.lang.String"
                     initial=""/>
      <form-property name="years"
                     type="java.util.ArrayList" />
      <form-property name="types"
                     type="java.util.ArrayList" />
      <form-property name="categories"
                     type="java.util.ArrayList" />
    </form-bean>
  </form-beans>

  <!-- ========== Global Exception Definitions ============================== -->
  <!-- key value will be taken from the ModuleException instance -->
  <global-exceptions>
    <exception bundle="ApplicationResources"
               key=""
               path="/error.jsp"
               handler="dummies.struts.music.CustomExceptionHandler"
               type="org.apache.struts.util.ModuleException" />
    <exception bundle="ApplicationResources"
               key="error.RuntimeException"
               path="/baderror.jsp"
               handler="dummies.struts.music.CustomExceptionHandler"
               type="java.lang.RuntimeException" />
  </global-exceptions>

  <!-- ========== Action Mapping Definitions ============================== -->
  <action-mappings>
    <action path="/home"
            type="dummies.struts.music.LoginAction"
            name="loginForm"
            scope="request"
            input="/home.jsp"
            validate="true">
      <forward name="failure" path="/home.jsp"/>
      <forward name="success" path="/musiclist.do"/>
      <forward name="join" path="/join.jsp"/>
    </action>
    <action path="/join"
            type="dummies.struts.music.JoinAction"
            name="joinForm"
            scope="request"
            input="/join.jsp"
            validate="true">
```

```
      <forward name="cancel" path="/home.jsp"/>
      <forward name="failure" path="/join.jsp"/>
      <forward name="success" path="/welcome.jsp"/>
    </action>
    <action path="/musiclist"
            type="dummies.struts.music.MusicListAction"
            name="musiclistForm"
            scope="request"
            input="/musiclist.jsp"
            validate="false">
      <forward name="logoff" path="/logoff.do"/>
      <forward name="newalbum" path="/album.do"/>
      <forward name="success" path="/musiclist.jsp"/>
    </action>
    <action path="/album"
            type="dummies.struts.music.AlbumAction"
            name="albumForm"
            scope="request"
            nput="/album.jsp"
            validate="false">
      <forward name="cancel" path="/musiclist.do"/>
      <forward name="success" path="/musiclist.do"/>
      <forward name="new" path="/album.jsp"/>
      <forward name="failure" path="/album.jsp"/>
    </action>
    <action path="/logoff"
            type="dummies.struts.music.LogoffAction"
            scope="request"
            validate="false">
      <forward name="success" path="/home.jsp"/>
    </action>

  </action-mappings>

  <!-- ========== Controller Definition ============================== -->
  <controller processorClass="dummies.struts.music.CustomRequestProcessor" />

  <!-- ========== Message Resources Definitions =========================== -->
  <message-resources null="false"
                     parameter="ApplicationResources"/>

  <!-- ========== Plugin Definitions ============================ -->
  <plug-in className="org.apache.struts.validator.ValidatorPlugIn">
    <set-property property="pathnames"
          value="/WEB-INF/validator-rules.xml,/WEB-INF/validation.xml"/>
  </plug-in>
  <plug-in className="dummies.struts.music.StartupManager" />

</struts-config>
```

Part III
Expanding Your Development Options

"What I'm looking for are dynamic Web applications and content, not Web innuendoes and intent."

In this part . . .

Part III provides you with all the pieces that you need to complete your Struts-enabled Web application. Chapter 8 deals with exception handling. Chapter 9 covers a number of useful plug-ins that can streamline your work. Chapter 10 explains the Struts tag libraries and how to use them. Chapter 11 is all about page composition techniques. Last but not least is Chapter 12, which explains the tools in Struts for securing your application.

Chapter 8

Exceptions to the Rule

In This Chapter

- Understanding the Java exception mechanism
- Choosing an exception strategy
- Writing `Exception` classes
- Using chained exceptions
- Asserting yourself
- Handling exceptions on your own
- Using Struts declarative exception handling
- Extending the Struts default exception handler
- Handling `RuntimeExceptions`

You may be the eternal optimist, but sooner or later all applications have problems (generally both sooner *and* later). These problems could be the result of actions outside your responsibility (for example, a network failure), or they may be the result of coding errors. Regardless of the degree of effort made to eliminate errors, they do appear — even in the best software products. Therefore, you need to have a plan in place to react to errors as they occur so that the application can recover and continue to function properly or, at the very least, shut down in a graceful way.

You can find interesting statistics on how many programming errors occur per 1000 lines of code (KLOC). In a recent article in Software Development, Watts Humphry, the father of the Capability Maturity Model (CMM) (see `www.sei.cmu.edu/tsp/watts-bio.html`) described the average number of bugs found in various organizations that are certified at one of the five CMM levels (see `www.sei.cmu.edu/cmm/cmm.sum.html`). The lowest-ranking CMM organizations (level 1) have no formal development process in place. The highest ranking CMM organizations (level 5) have the most mature and organized development process in place. Level 1 organizations averaged 7.5 defects per KLOC, whereas level 5 averaged 1.05 per KLOC.

Fortunately, you're programming in Java, which has an excellent problem notification and handling mechanism built in.

Java Errors and Exceptions

Problems that can occur in Java are defined in a class hierarchy with the `Throwable` class as the king. The `Throwable` class has two subclasses: the `Error` class and the `Exception` class. See Figure 8-1 for an abbreviated class hierarchy.

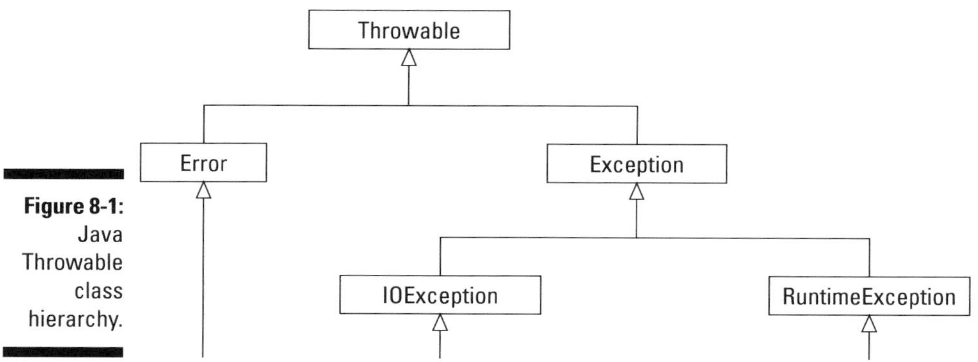

Figure 8-1: Java Throwable class hierarchy.

The `Error` class and its descendents (at least 25 subclasses) represent serious errors from which recovery is not an option. The application should not try to handle these types of errors because they're usually outside the scope of the application and typically indicate a problem in the Java Virtual Machine (JVM).

The `Exception` class and its descendents (at least 55 subclasses) represent errors that the application should make an attempt to handle. The `Exception` class has two lineages: the `IOException` and the `RuntimeException` classes.

The `Exception` class, the `IOException` class, and its descendents make up the checked exceptions. With a *checked* exception, the application programmer must catch the exception in a `try/catch` block or *throw* (cause) a similar exception. The compiler insists upon it! Every other descendent of the `Throwable` class falls into the category of an unchecked exception.

Try/catch block

In a `try/catch` block, the `try` block contains the code that may throw a checked exception. The `catch` block contains the reference to the exception that could be thrown. The `catch` block contains also the code that reacts to the exception. Here is an example of a simple `try/catch` block:

```
try
{
    some code that could throw the ExceptionType
}
catch( ExceptionType e)
{
    handle the exception here
}
```

If your code in the `try` block performs some action that causes an exception to be thrown, control moves immediately to the code in the `catch` block.

You're not required to catch unchecked exceptions. However, if they're not caught, your application terminates. The unchecked exceptions descended from the `Error` class should not be caught, because they're not recoverable anyway. However, the `RuntimeException` class and its descendents should be caught. Later in this chapter, we show a mechanism uses Struts to catch the infamous `RuntimeException` and it descendents.

Throwing exceptions

Methods throw checked exceptions when

- An error condition occurs in the code and the method can not or will not recover from it.
- An exception is thrown by a called method and the calling method can not or does not want to handle it.

To let the compiler know that the method may throw an exception, the method specifies in the `throws` clause the type of exception(s) it might throw. For example, the following code illustrates a method that might throw an `IOException`:

```
public void getTransfers(String token) throws IOException
{
    some code ...
}
```

If certain conditions arise, the method may throw an `IOException` in the code by creating an instance of the exception and then use the `throw` keyword to actually throw it. Here's the preceding example illustrating how this might be accomplished:

```
public void getTransfers(String token) throws IOException
{
    some code ...
```

```
    // oops. some condition occurred which makes
    // us want to throw an exception
    if(some condition)
        throw new IOException();

    some further code ...
}
```

The method can also call another method that throws an IOException. Rather than catching the exception, this method simply passes the exception up the call chain to the next method.

Wrapping it up in finally

What happens if you absolutely, positively have to do something regardless of whether or not an exception is thrown? You can use a third block for that purpose called the finally block, which can be used only in the try/catch block. The finally block is guaranteed to always execute regardless of whether or not an exception was thrown.

To see how you might use the finally block, suppose that you're performing some database operation in the try block that throws a SQLException. Before making the database call, you get a database connection. You want to release the connection under all circumstances; otherwise it is a nonrecoverable resource. Listing 8-1 shows some code that doesn't guarantee that the connection will always be released.

Listing 8-1 A try/catch Block in Need of a finally Block

```
public Map getCompanies() throws ModuleException
{
   HashMap companies = null;
   Connection conn = null;
   try
   {
       conn = dbConnMgr.getConnection();
       DBFactory dbf = DBFactory.getDBFactory();
       DBUtility dbu = dbf.getDBUtility();
       companies = dbu.getCompanies(conn); // retrieve companies from database
       conn.close();
   }
   catch (SQLException se)
   {
       ModuleException me = new ModuleException("error.company.select");
       throw me;
   }
   return companies;
}
```

You do not have to understand the details of this code, just the fact that in the `try` block (lines 5–12), we are getting a database connection and then performing some operations that could throw a `SQLException`. Here's the problem — if the code in lines 7–10 throws the exception, the release of the connection in line 11 would not take place. The connection would be left in limbo, so to speak.

To circumvent this situation, you can add a `finally` block to the code, which is guaranteed to always execute no matter what happens (unless the program exits). The code in Listing 8-2 has the `finally` block added.

Listing 8-2 A try/catch Block Using a finally Block

```
1 public Map getCompanies() throws ModuleException
2 {
3     HashMap companies = null;
4     Connection conn = null;
5     try
6     {
7         conn = dbConnMgr.getConnection();
8         DBFactory dbf = DBFactory.getDBFactory();
9         DBUtility dbu = dbf.getDBUtility();
10        companies = dbu.getCompanies(conn); // retrieve companies from database

11    }
12    catch (SQLException se)
13    {
14        ModuleException me = new ModuleException("error.company.select");
15        throw me;
16    }
17    finally
18    {
19        try
20        {
21            conn.close();
22        }
23        catch(SQLException se)
24        {
25            log.error("Could not close the connection. " + se.getMessage());
26        }
27    }
28    return companies;
29 }
```

We moved the line of code that releases the connection from the `try` block to the `finally` block (line 21). This example is a more complex than usual because executing line 21 (`conn.close`) could also result in a `SQLException` being thrown. Therefore, we have to wrap the line in a `try/catch` block also. Generally, statements in the `finally` block do not cause exceptions.

This review is not intended to be a comprehensive look at how to deal with exceptions in Java. For more detail information on Java Exceptions visit the Java Tutorial at

```
java.sun.com/docs/books/tutorial/essential/exceptions/index.html
```

Another good article on exceptions is at

```
www.developer.com/java/article.php/10922_1455891_1
```

Exception Strategies

Dealing with exceptions is an important part of creating robust applications (Web or otherwise). So you need to have a good strategy in place for those times when things don't go according to plan. In this section, we talk about ways of handling those "oops" situations.

Catching exceptions

Don't just have an empty `catch` block to satisfy the compiler. Do something useful. Exceptions are your friends. They're messengers that bring you valuable information about the cause of trouble. It's a good idea is to extract the information out of the exception and save it somewhere, such as to the system console or a log file. We talk in more detail about logging in Chapter 13.

Here are some useful possibilities for the `catch` block:

- Extract and save the relevant information from the exception
- Throw a new exception more relevant to your application
- Throw a new exception, chaining the original exception to the new one (see "Using Chained Exceptions")

Exception information

Every exception contains at least two pieces of valuable information that you can extract. The first is the detailed message describing the exception. You can get this by the method call `getMessage`:

```
String theMessage = exception.getMessage();
```

The second piece of information in every exception is the stack trace, which provides you with the calling history from the current method to the method that started the process. You can retrieve this information in a couple of ways.

The easiest way is just to use the `printStackTrace` method, which outputs the trace to the standard error device (usually the Java console).

```
exception.printStackTrace();
```

Following is a typical stack trace output:

```
java.lang.IllegalArgumentException: Invalid context path: webpurchasing
    at org.apache.catalina.core.StandardHostDeployer.remove
       (StandardHostDeployer.java:458)
    at org.apache.catalina.core.StandardHost.remove(StandardHost.java:852)
    at org.apache.catalina.startup.HostConfig.undeployApps(HostConfig.java:758)
    at org.apache.catalina.startup.HostConfig.stop(HostConfig.java:738)
    at org.apache.catalina.startup.HostConfig.lifecycleEvent
       (HostConfig.java:360)
    at org.apache.catalina.util.LifecycleSupport.fireLifecycleEvent
       (LifecycleSupport.java:166)
    at org.apache.catalina.core.ContainerBase.stop(ContainerBase.java:1221)
    at org.apache.catalina.core.ContainerBase.stop(ContainerBase.java:1233)
    at org.apache.catalina.core.StandardService.stop(StandardService.java:554)
    at org.apache.catalina.core.StandardServer.stop(StandardServer.java:2225)
    at org.apache.catalina.startup.Catalina.start(Catalina.java:543)
    at org.apache.catalina.startup.Catalina.execute(Catalina.java:400)
    at org.apache.catalina.startup.Catalina.process(Catalina.java:180)
    at sun.reflect.NativeMethodAccessorImpl.invoke0(Native Method)
    at sun.reflect.NativeMethodAccessorImpl.invoke
       (NativeMethodAccessorImpl.java:39)
    at sun.reflect.DelegatingMethodAccessorImpl.invoke
       (DelegatingMethodAccessorImpl.java:25)
    at java.lang.reflect.Method.invoke(Method.java:324)
    at org.apache.catalina.startup.Bootstrap.main(Bootstrap.java:203)
```

If you're not using the `printStackTrace` method (maybe because you're using a log file), you can still output the stack trace information programmatically. See the `logExceptionChain` method defined in Listing 8-3 for an example of how to do this.

Some exceptions may have additional pieces of information available (such as. `SQLException`), so be sure to check the exception's API. You can find this in the Java API documentation under the `java.lang.Exception` class.

Writing Your Own Exception Classes

Sometimes the members of the `Throwable` class hierarchy may not adequately describe the type of exception that your code needs to throw. For example, you may be expecting a list to be of a particular length. When you find that it's not the proper length, what exception do you throw? `IOException`? `NoSuchFieldException`? In looking through the 55 or so possibilities, you may find that none of them describe your particular error. In this instance, it makes more sense to create your own exception class by extending `Exception` rather than use an exception that inadequately describes the situation.

Some programmers think it's better to create an exception class by extending `RuntimeException`, because it's unchecked and would, therefore, not require a `try/catch` block or a `throws` clause in the method signature. However, this technique is frowned upon because the compiler will not complain if you do not try to catch the exception (and possibly recover). A better idea is to extend one of the checked exceptions: `Exception`, `IOException`, or one of its descendents.

Struts provides one specialized exception class, `ModuleException`. This exception creates and stores an `ActionError` instance using the key that you pass to the constructor. `ActionError` comes into play when `ExceptionHandler` recognizes that the exception is an instance of `ModuleException`. `ExceptionHandler` retrieves `ActionError` directly from `ModuleException`. If the exception is not an instance of `ModuleException`, `ExceptionHandler` creates an `ActionError` instance based on the key in the exception declaration and the message found in the exception. (We discuss `ExceptionHandler`, a Struts class for exception handling, in the "Declarative Exception Handling" section later in this chapter.)

Using Chained Exceptions

The *chained exception* mechanism is a new feature starting with Java version 1.4. You can think of it as exception piggy-backing. One exception may contain another exception. Why would you want to use chained exceptions? It may be that your code has caught an exception of one type (say `SQLException`), but doesn't handle the exception other than to log it. Instead, it throws a new exception (say `Exception`). Normally, this means that all the information included in `SQLException` (for example, the stack trace) is lost when the new `Exception` is thrown. However, starting with Java version 1.4, you have the option of chaining the original exception with the new one.

In the following example, when constructing the `Exception`, we can add `SQLException` to it, thereby *chaining* `SQLException` to `Exception`. Here is a code snippet showing how to do this:

```
catch (SQLException se)
{
    Exception e = new Exception("A database error
          occurred",se);
    throw e;
}
```

In the `Exception` constructor, the `"A database error occurred"` string is the message associated with `Exception` and `se` is the cause.

That's nice, but what can you do with it? You don't have to do anything. However, when handling an exception, you now have the option of finding out whether it contains any additional chained exceptions. A new method in the Throwable hierarchy is getCause, which returns the Throwable that caused the current Throwable. This means you can programmatically retrieve the entire history of the exception and output the information to a log or system console. See the logExceptionChain method in Listing 8-3 for an example of how to retrieve chained exception information.

A helpful article on the chained exceptions feature of Java version 1.4 can be found at

```
javaboutique.internet.com/tutorials/Chained_Exceptions
```

Asserting Yourself

Another form of defensive programming is the use of assertions. *Assertions* can be characterized as lazy exceptions, in the sense that an assertion behaves somewhat like an exception yet takes a lot less code on the part of the programmer. The following example clarifies this technique. Suppose that you've written a method that gets a reference to a poList object and then uses the reference to update information in the list:

```
public void updateList()
{
    ... do something here to get a reference to a poList
          object

    // assert that we actually got the reference to poList
    assert poList != null;

    ... continue on with processing the poList
}
```

Under almost all conditions, you will get the reference (in this example, to a poList object) successfully. To cover the unlikely possibility that you can't get the reference, you assert that poList should not be null at this point. If it turns out to be null, an AssertionError is thrown.

The assert statement has two forms. The first form is as follows:

```
assert expression1;
```

where expression1 evaluates to a boolean. The second form is

```
assert expression1 : expression2;
```

where expression2 evaluates to a value.

The main difference between these two forms is that the first form throws `AssertError` without any message, but the second form uses `expression2` as the message in `AssertError`.

When compiling code with assertions, you must have JDK 1.4 or greater. Otherwise, the compiler will not allow the use of the `assert` statement.

If you're using the Eclipse IDE, you need only version 1.4 JRE or better installed and 1.4 selected as the compiler compliance level. To make sure that the compiler compliance level is set correctly, do the following:

1. **Choose Window⇨Preferences.**

   The Preferences dialog box appears.

2. **On the left side of the screen, choose Java. Click the plus sign (+) next to Java to see the other options.**
3. **Click Compiler.**

   The Complier dialog box appears.

4. **Choose the Compliance and Classfiles tab. Make sure that the Compiler compliance level is set to 1.4 (see Figure 8-2).**

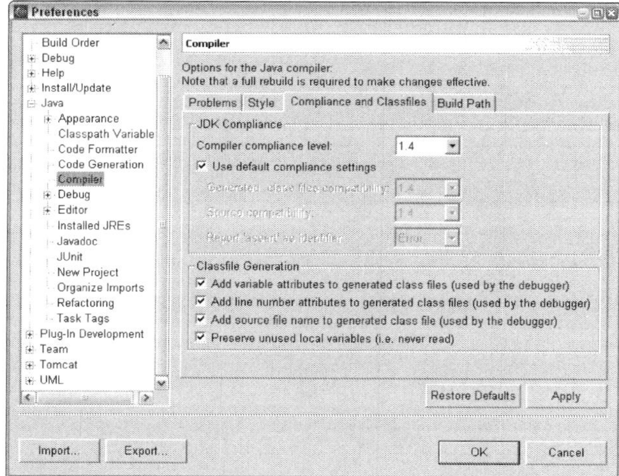

Figure 8-2: The compiler compliance setting.

If you're using the command line to invoke the compiler, use the `source 1.4` command-line option to ensure that the compiler will accept `assert` statements.

The `assert` statements are interesting because you can turn them on and off at runtime. Assertions are turned off by default. To turn assertions on, use the `-ea` or `-enableassertions` command-line switch when starting the program. For example:

```
java -ea myProgram
```

turns on (enables) assertion checking in `myProgram`.

When developing and testing, assertions are valuable debugging tools for shaking out error conditions. But in production code, these conditions should no longer exist. If some doubt exists about whether to use an assertion or throw an exception, consider whether the condition could arise in a production state or not. If it could, throw the exception.

To find out more about assertions and their use, look at the following Web site:

```
java.sun.com/j2se/1.4.1/docs/guide/lang/assert.html#intro
```

Handling Exceptions Yourself

You have two choices for exception handling in Struts: use declarative exception handling (explained in the next section) or handle the exceptions yourself.

In Struts, the `Action` classes are the most likely candidates for handling exceptions because they're generally the root class of other classes that you might have written for your application. Therefore, the `Action` class should probably catch all checked exceptions.

The handling of all exceptions in the `Action` class should be pretty much the same:

1. **Save information about the exception.**
2. **Recover from the error condition, if possible.**
3. **If necessary, provide the user with a clear and concise message that explains what has happened and what the user should do (if anything) to correct the problem.**
4. **When it is not possible to recover from the error, fail in a graceful way.**

These four steps are discussed in this section.

Saving information

As mentioned, exceptions contain valuable information. The first step in handling exceptions is to extract and save the information. What you extract will depend on the type of error you're handling. For example, the error is an `SQLException`, you might want to get the SQL string and save it. You can save the information by printing to the console through the use of `System.out.println` or `exception.printStackTrace` (or both). The other possibility is to save the information to a log file. We discuss logging in Chapter 13.

Recovering from errors

When an error occurs, you have to determine whether or not you can recover from the condition and continue processing. The recovery is application specific. Sometimes recovery may be as simple as reinitializing a variable and trying again. Other times, it may mean undoing a series of steps and then informing the users of the failure and asking them to try again.

Inform the user

To continue processing, the user may need to be notified of the situation. This notification might be by means of messages that appear on the normal presentation page that the user would normally receive. In particular, if the user has submitted unacceptable data, you should provide a message indicating what needs to be corrected.

Another possibility is to forward the user to a specialized presentation page that details more general errors. For example, the page could let the user know that the data just submitted could not be saved due to an error in the network and ask the user to try again.

Fail gracefully

If recovery from the exception is not possible, failure should occur as gracefully as possible. Perhaps the situation affects the state of only one user. For example, data stored in the user's session may have become corrupted or suspect, and recovery of the data may not be practical. In that case, one choice is to log the user off the system and invalidate the user's session. In effect, this choice makes the user start over.

More serious scenarios might mean accepting no further connections until the responsible party can assess the situation.

Declarative Exception Handling

Struts offers some help with exception handling through the exception declarative tags of the `struts-config.xml` file. In the "Global exceptions" section in Chapter 7, we explain that the `<global-exceptions>` and `<exception>` tags in the `struts-config.xml` file are useful for exception handling.

The `execute` method of the `Action` class can throw an exception of type `Exception`. Doing so allows exceptions to be handled by `RequestProcessor`, which determines whether the exception has been declared in the configuration file through the `<exception>` tag. If so, the exception handler class that was defined is called. `org.apache.struts.action.ExceptionHandler` is used by default. However, you can also create your own subclass of `ExceptionHandler` — for details, see the "Extending the ExceptionHandler" section

`ExceptionHandler` is then responsible for preparing information to be forwarded to the presentation layer. Specifically, `ExceptionHandler` gets or creates `ActionError` with the exception information and puts it into an `ActionErrors` object. `ExceptionHandler` then determines where to pass control by using `ActionForward`. Figure 8-3 shows this process graphically.

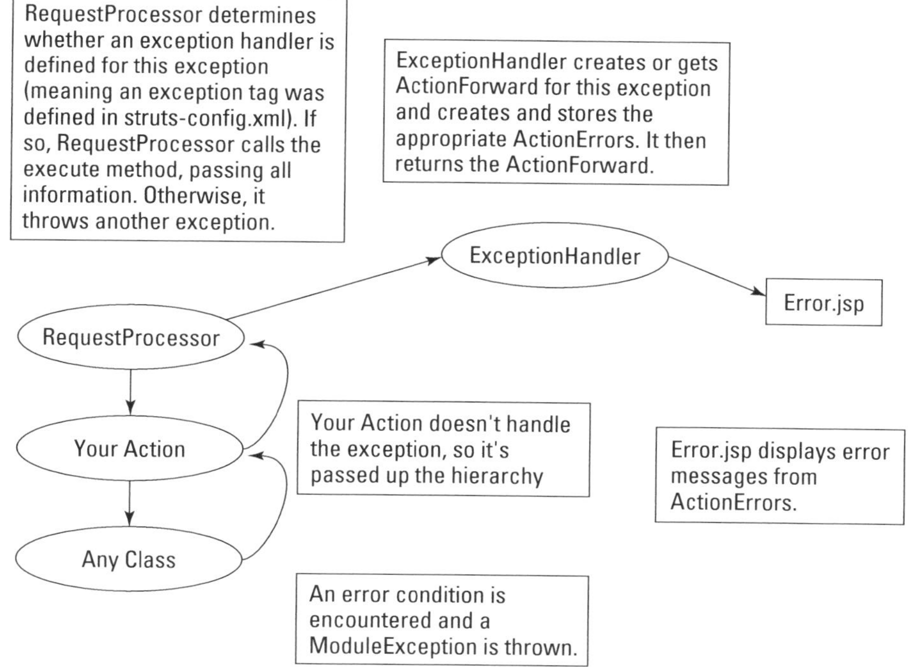
RequestProcessor determines whether an exception handler is defined for this exception (meaning an exception tag was defined in struts-config.xml). If so, RequestProcessor calls the execute method, passing all information. Otherwise, it throws another exception.
ExceptionHandler creates or gets ActionForward for this exception and creates and stores the appropriate ActionErrors. It then returns the ActionForward.
ExceptionHandler
Error.jsp
RequestProcessor
Your Action
Your Action doesn't handle the exception, so it's passed up the hierarchy
Error.jsp displays error messages from ActionErrors.
Any Class
An error condition is encountered and a ModuleException is thrown.

Figure 8-3: The flow of declarative exception processing.

Declaring the exception

To see how the declaration is defined, let's first take a look at the <exception> tag. (See Chapter 7 for the complete definition of the <exception> tag's attributes.) The <exception> tag allows you to specify a particular exception type that will be handled by Struts. The <exception> tag has two required attributes: key and type. The key attribute defines the message resource key that will be put into the ActionError object for the exception. The type attribute refers to the fully qualified class name of the particular exception type to be handled. An example of an exception definition follows:

```
<exception key="error.db.general"
          type="com.othenos.purchasing.common.DBException" />
```

If the path attribute is not defined, ExceptionHandler uses the input attribute of the action definition where the exception was thrown.

Global or local exception handling

Exceptions can be defined globally for the entire application or locally for a particular Action. In this respect, exceptions are similar to forwards. If you choose to define an exception globally and that exception type occurs in any Action in your application, it's handled in the manner defined in the global definition. One caveat: if the exception type is also defined locally for a particular Action, the local definition takes precedence.

To define an exception globally, simply place the exception definition in the <global-exceptions> tags. For example, you could specify the preceding exception example as global in this manner:

```
<global-exceptions>
    <exception key="error.db.general"
               type="com.othenos.purchasing.DBException" />
</global-exceptions>
```

And you could also define the same exception in an Action definition to make it local to the Action, as shown here:

```
<action path="/home"
        type="com.othenos.purchasing.struts.HomeAction"
        scope="request"
        validate="false">
    <forward name="success" path="/index.jsp"/>
    <exception key="error.db.myaction"
               type="com.othenos.purchasing.DBException" />
</action>
```

If DBException occurs, ExceptionHandler determines whether the exception occurred in HomeAction. If the exception occurred in HomeAction, the error.db.myaction key is used to create ActionError. Otherwise, the error.db.general key defined for the global exception is used. Of course, you can differentiate the two exceptions much further by using additional attributes, such as defining different ExceptionHandlers or destination paths.

Extending ExceptionHandler

Struts provides a plain-vanilla ExceptionHandler class that is useful as it is. However, if you're interested in additional capabilities, you need to extend the ExceptionHandler class. Some of the more commonly desired features might be to

- Log error information before passing control to the presentation layer
- Send an e-mail to one or more people responsible for the application
- Handle chained exceptions

Your subclass of ExceptionHandler needs to override the execute method and potentially the storeException method. The execute method is where you need to put your customized functionality, as shown in Listing 8-3.

Listing 8-3 Extending the ExceptionHandler Class

```
public class CustomExceptionHandler extends ExceptionHandler
{
    Log log = LogFactory.getLog(CustomExceptionHandler.class);
    // commons logging reference

    /**
     * Handle the exception. Standard execute method with addition of
     * logging the stacktrace.
     */
    public ActionForward execute(
        Exception ex,
        ExceptionConfig ae,
        ActionMapping mapping,
        ActionForm formInstance,
        HttpServletRequest request,
        HttpServletResponse response)
        throws ServletException
    {
        // write the exception information to the log file
        logExceptionChain(ex);
        // process the exception as normal
        return super.execute(ex, ae, mapping, formInstance, request, response);
```

(continued)

Listing 8-3 *(continued)*

```
    }
    /**
     * logging exception stack trace, including chained exceptions
     * modified from version by Keld H. Hansen
     * http://javaboutique.internet.com/tutorials/Chained_Exceptions/
     *
     * @param thr
     */
    private void logExceptionChain(Throwable thr)
    {
        StackTraceElement[] s;
        Throwable t = thr;
        StringBuffer errorMsg = new StringBuffer("\nException chain (top to
              bottom):\n");
        while (t != null)
        {
            errorMsg.append("------------------------------\n");
            s = t.getStackTrace();
            StackTraceElement s0 = s[0];
            errorMsg.append(t.toString());
            errorMsg.append("  at " + s0.toString() + "\n");
            if (t.getCause() == null)
            {
                errorMsg.append("------------------------------\n");
                errorMsg.append("Complete traceback (bottom to top):\n");
                for (int i = 0; i < s.length; i++)
                errorMsg.append("  at " + s[i].toString() + "\n");
            }
            t = t.getCause();
        }
        log.error(errorMsg.toString());
    }
}
```

To let Struts know about the new CustomExceptionHandler, you need to add it to one or more of the <exception> tag definitions. In our previous example, you would just need to add the handler attribute with the fully qualified class name of the custom handler, as shown here (taken from the example application in Chapter 14):

```
<exception
   key=""
   path="/error.jsp"
   handler="dummies.struts.music.CustomExceptionHandler"
   type="org.apache.struts.util.ModuleException" />
```

Now whenever ModuleException occurs, CustomExceptionHandler processes the exception. Note that the key defined for ModuleExeception is empty. This is because the message key is placed in ModuleException when it is created. We do not omit the key attribute because it is required.

If you want all exceptions to be handled by `CustomExceptionHandler`, just change the `type` attribute to the root class of all exceptions, `java.lang.Throwable`.

Handling RuntimeExceptions in Struts

`RuntimeExceptions` and its descendents are unchecked exceptions. Therefore, you don't have `try/catch` blocks that try to trap and recover from the exceptions. However, it's bad form to let the exception propagate back to the user so that the user sees the raw stack trace information in the browser.

You can use the declarative exception mechanism to catch `RuntimeExceptions` and display a more reasonable page when exceptions occur. The first step is to create the global exception definition for `RuntimeException` in the `struts-config.xml` file, as shown here (the example is from the MusicCollection application in Chapter 14):

```
<global-exceptions>
    <exception  bundle="ApplicationResources"
        key="error.RuntimeException"
        path="/baderror.jsp"
        handler="dummies.struts.music.CustomExceptionHandler"
        type="java.lang.RuntimeException" />
</global-exceptions>
```

The `error.RuntimeException` key is used to retrieve the error message to display on the presentation page. The `path` attribute specifies the path to `baderror.jsp` to display if the `RuntimeException` occurs.

The second step is to define the JSP page that will display the error message to the user. Listing 8-4 is an example of the content of such a page. (The entire page is defined in Chapter 14.)

Listing 8-4 Snippets from the baderror.jsp Page

```
<%@ include file="taglibs.jsp" %>
<fmt:setBundle basename="ApplicationResources" />
<table>
<tr>
  <td align="center" colspan="2" style="font-family: 'MS Reference Sans
          Serif', 'Verdana Ref', sans-serif;font-size: 18px;color:red;">
    <fmt:message key="error.RuntimeException"/>
  </td>
</tr>
<tr>
  <td width="55" align="left">
```

(continued)

Listing 8-4 *(continued)*

```
11    <img  src="images/annoy.gif" name="annoy" width="54" height="54"
             border="0">
12  </td>
13  <td>
14  <html:link page="/logoff.do">
15    <fmt:message key="goto.logoff"/>
16  </html:link>
17  </td>
18</tr>
19</table>
```

Figure 8-4 shows the `baderror.jsp` page as it would appear to the user.

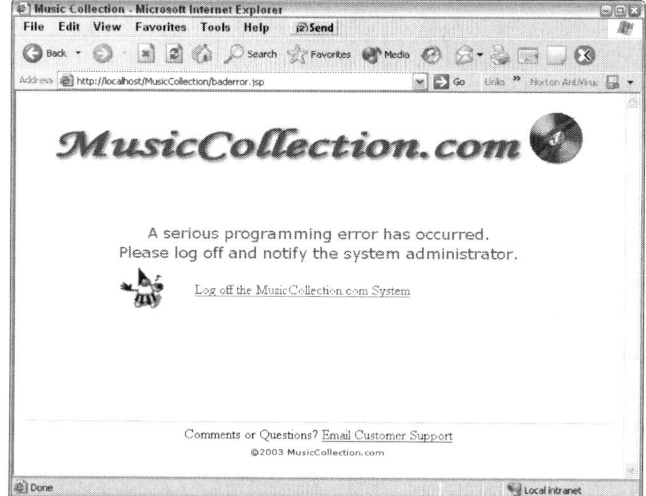

Figure 8-4: The baderror page.

The key parts of the JSP snippet are lines 6 and 14–16:

- Line 6: Defines the error message to be displayed to the user.
- Lines 14–16: Define a link that the user can click to log off the application. In practice, you may have already logged the user off the system. Programmatically logging the user off the system would be easy to do if you were using a customized version of the `ExceptionHandler` class.

Chapter 9

Getting Friendly with Plug-ins

In This Chapter

- Understanding the PlugIn interface
- Creating and configuring a plug-in
- Using the Validator plug-in

An application often needs to initialize certain resources when starting up and release resources when shutting down. If you're writing a standard application, initializing and releasing resources are not much of an issue because you have complete control over the code that's responsible for startup and shutdown. However, these functions are not as simple with a Struts Web application because `ActionServlet` gets startup and shutdown notifications from the Web container.

You could extend `ActionServlet` to add custom startup and shutdown actions, but that's messy — the number of actions could be large and unrelated. Fortunately, the Struts developers have anticipated the need to control startup and shutdown by including a plug-in architecture with the Struts framework. In this chapter, we explain how to use and implement plug-ins.

Using the PlugIn Interface

If you need custom startup or shutdown actions, you can simply create your own plug-in class by implementing the `org.apache.struts.action.PlugIn` interface rather than extend the `ActionServlet`. The `PlugIn` interface specifies two methods that you need to define: `destroy` and `init`. The interface is shown in Listing 9-1.

Listing 9-1 PlugIn Interface

```
public interface PlugIn
{
    public void destroy();
    public void init(ActionServlet servlet,
                     ModuleConfig config)
        throws ServletException;
}
```

At startup, the `ActionServlet` checks to see whether any plug-in classes need to be called. If there are any plug-in classes, the `init` method of each plug-in is called. Similarly, when the Web container notifies the `ActionServlet` of an impending shutdown, the `ActionServlet` calls the `destroy` method of all plug-in classes in its list.

Implementing and Configuring Your Own Plug-in

You can create your own plug-in simply by implementing the `destroy` and `init` methods of the PlugIn interface. Listing 9-2 shows an example of how to implement a plug-in for the MusicCollection Web application in Chapter 14. Don't worry if you don't understand what's happening in the two methods, because they're specific to this particular application. What is important to know is that `init` is called at startup and `destroy` is called at shutdown.

Listing 9-2 Plug-in for a Purchase Order Web Application

```
public class StartupManager implements PlugIn
{
    Log log = LogFactory.getLog(StartupManager.class);
    ServletContext sc;  // reference to servlet context for destroy()

    /**
     * initializes resources at application startup
     * @param arg0
     * @param arg1
     * @throws ServletException
     */
    public void init(ActionServlet arg0, ModuleConfig arg1)
        throws ServletException
    {
        // save the servlet context for shutdown needs
        sc = arg0.getServletContext();

        // define the lists and place in the application context
        // set up the years
```

```
        log.info("Initializing years.");
        ArrayList years = new ArrayList();
        int year = Calendar.getInstance().get(Calendar.YEAR);
        for(int i=0; i < 50; i++)
        {
            years.add(String.valueOf(year-i));
        }
        sc.setAttribute("years",years);

        // set up the album types
        // better solution would be to retrieve these values from a database.
        log.info("Initializing types.");
        ArrayList types = new ArrayList();
        types.add("CD");
        types.add("LP");
        types.add("MP3");
        types.add("Tape");
        sc.setAttribute("types",types);

        // set up the album catagories
        log.info("Initializing categories.");
        ArrayList categories = new ArrayList();
        categories.add("Classical");
        categories.add("Country");
        categories.add("Easy Listening");
        categories.add("Heavy Metal");
        categories.add("Jazz");
        categories.add("New Age");
        categories.add("Pop/Rock");
        categories.add("R & B");
        categories.add("World");
        sc.setAttribute("categories",categories);
    }

    /**
     * releases resources at application shutdown
     */
    public void destroy()
    {
        // shut down the dbcp
        log.info("Shutting down the DataSource connection pool.");
        DataSource dbConnMgr = (DataSource)sc.getAttribute("musiccollection");
        dbConnMgr = null;
        sc.removeAttribute("musiccollection");

        // final message
        log.info("Music.com has shutdown.");
    }
}
```

You need to be aware of a couple of things when implementing a plug-in. The `init` method can take two parameters: a reference to `ActionServlet` and `ModuleConfig`. You can use `ActionServlet` to get any resources that it might help you control or get information for your initialization process. In line 6, we use `ActionServlet` to get a reference to `ServletContent`, which is the application scope, to get and set resources in that scope. We also save the reference to `ServletContext` to make use of it in the `destroy` method.

The `ModuleConfig` parameter can contain a reference to the module currently being initialized. Referencing the module is useful if your Web application has multiple modules, because you may want to perform different initialization actions depending on the module. If you are using only the default module, you can safely ignore this parameter.

The `destroy` method takes no parameters. If `destroy` needs a resource that you gathered in the `init` method, be sure to save the resource as an instance variable. In lines 34–36, the destroy method accesses `ServletContent` to reference `DataSource` and gracefully shut it down.

After you create a plug-in, the next step is to notify Struts that the plug-in is ready for use, which you do in the `struts-config.xml` file. Configuring plug-ins in `struts-config.xml` is simple and straightforward. In the "Plug-in Configuration" section of Chapter 7, we describe the use of the `<plug-in>` tag in the configuration file. This simple tag has only one required attribute, `className`. You must specify the fully qualified class name of the plug-in that you want to use.

The only other tag that you may include in the `<plug-in>` tag is the `<set-property>` tag. Use this tag to pass initialization parameters to the plug-in, if needed. Here is an example of configuring the plug-in described in Listing 9-1:

```
<plug-in className="dummies.struts.music.StartupManager" />
```

Be sure to remember that the sequence of elements in the `struts-config.xml` file is important. The plug-in element is the last element defined.

Working with the Validator Plug-in

The Validator plug-in comes with the Struts framework. You use this plug-in to validate form data in a declarative manner instead of using the standard `validate` method in `ActionForm`. (See Chapter 6 for information on using the `validate` method.)

The Validator plug-in has the following advantages over using the `validate` method:

- You can add, modify, or remove validation rules for form fields without changing the source code.
- One text file centrally contains validation rules for all form fields.

- The plug-in provides many common validation rules.
- You can use the plug-in with DynaActionForms.

Configuring the Validator plug-in

The Validator requires two xml configuration files: validation.xml and validator-rules.xml. You might think that the validation.xml file is more interesting because that is where you define the forms and fields to validate as well as the rules to use when validating those fields. The actual rules that perform the validation are defined in validator-rules.xml.

The validation.xml and validator-rules.xml files share the same DTD. (For details on DTD, see "Editing the Web Container Configuration File" in Chapter 7.) In practice, however, each .xml file uses a different subset of the DTD syntax.

The Validator configuration files have a DTD file that defines the grammar acceptable in the configuration. Each file should begin with a DOCTYPE indicating the version of the DTD that you're using. The following example specifies version 1.0.1 of the Validator DTD:

```
<!DOCTYPE form-validation PUBLIC
     "-//Apache Software Foundation//DTD Commons Validator Rules Configuration
           1.0.1//EN"
     "http://jakarta.apache.org/commons/dtds/validator_1_0_1.dtd">
```

The root tag — and therefore the first tag — in Validator configuration files is <form-validation>. The DTD syntax for the <form-validation> tag follows:

```
<!ELEMENT form-validation (global*, formset*)>
```

We show examples of using the DTD throughout this section.

Using the Validator plug-in

To use the Validator plug-in, you need to do the following:

1. **Create your form class by extending** org.apache.struts.validator.ValidatorActionForm **instead of the normal** org.apache.struts.action.ActionForm.
2. **Configure the Validator plug-in in the** struts-config.xml **file.**
3. **Define the validation rules to apply to your form fields by configuring the** validation.xml **file.**
4. **Tweak the** struts-config.xml **file and message resources.**

We explain each of these steps in detail by modifying the Login example from Chapter 3.

Extending the ValidatorForm class

Rather than creating `LoginForm` by extending the `ActionForm` class, you should extend the `ValidatorForm` class. What does this accomplish? Essentially, you'd have a prebuilt validate method that takes advantage of the validation rules that you defined in the `validation.xml` file. Therefore, you would not need a validate method in `LoginForm`. Listing 9-3 shows how `LoginForm` should look when you extend the `ValidatorForm` class.

Listing 9-3 LoginForm for Use with the Validator Plug-in

```
public class LoginForm extends ValidatorForm
{
    private String userName;
    private String password;

    public void reset(ActionMapping mapping, HttpServletRequest request)
    {
        password = "";
        userName = "";
    }

    public String getPassword() {
        return password;
    }

    public String getUserName() {
        return userName;
    }

    public void setPassword(String string) {
        password = string;
    }

    public void setUserName(String string) {
        userName = string;
    }
}
```

Compare this code to Listing 3-4 in Chapter 3. Notice the lack of a `validate` method. This method is no longer needed because the `ValidatorForm` we are extending already has one. The validate method in the `ValidatorForm` class knows how to perform validation based on the `validation.xml` and `validator-rules.xml` files. These files are described in the next section.

Configuring the Validator plug-in in the config file

The next step in setting up the Validator plug-in is to configure the plug-in in the struts-config.xml file. The configuration is just like the previous plug-in definition (see the "Configuring Plug-ins" section) with one addition — you need to add one parameter to pass to the plug-in. The Validator needs to know the context-relative paths so it can find the validation.xml and validator-rules.xml configuration files. You typically place these files in the WEB-INF folder. Here is the configuration information that you would add to the struts-config.xml file in the Login project example:

```
<!-- ========== Plug-in Definitions
          ============================== -->
<plug-in
  className="org.apache.struts.validator.ValidatorPlugIn">
    <set-property property="pathnames"
                  value="/WEB-INF/validator-rules.xml,
                         /WEB-INF/validation.xml"/>
</plug-in>
```

Defining the fields to validate

The original Login project example (in Chapter 3) did not use the Validation plug-in and therefore did not include the Validation configuration files, validation.xml and validator-rules.xml. However, when you use the Validator plug-in, you must place the two configuration files in the WEB-INF folder because that is the location that the plug-in configuration specifies.

The third step for using the Validator is to define the forms, fields, and rules to apply to the fields in the validation.xml file. To find out how to do this, note the DTD for the configuration files:

```
<!ELEMENT form-validation (global*, formset*)>
```

The form-validation element is the root element for both of the configuration files; it can contain one or more global elements and one or more formset elements. We discuss the formset element here and cover the global element later in this chapter, in the "Looking more closely at validation.xml" section.

The syntax for defining formset follows:

```
<!ELEMENT formset (constant*, form+)>
<!ATTLIST formset language     CDATA #IMPLIED
                  country      CDATA #IMPLIED
                  variant      CDATA #IMPLIED >
```

The formset element defines at least one or more forms to be validated for a particular Locale. If you don't use any of the attributes, formset represents the default Locale. Otherwise, you can specify different formsets for a different Locale language, country, variant, or any combination. The formset element can also contain constant definitions, which we explain in the "Looking more closely at validation.xml" section.

The syntax used to define a form follows:

```
<!ELEMENT form     (field+ )>
<!ATTLIST form     name          CDATA #REQUIRED>
```

The form element is used to define the fields of a form to be validated. The name attribute is required and corresponds to the name of the form as defined in the struts-config.xml file.

A field is defined using the following syntax:

```
<!ELEMENT field    (msg|arg0|arg1|arg2|arg3|var)*>
<!ATTLIST field    property CDATA #REQUIRED
                   depends  CDATA #IMPLIED
                   page     CDATA #IMPLIED
                   indexedListProperty CDATA #IMPLIED >
```

The field element defines the properties to be validated. In a Web application, a field could also correspond to a control on an HTML form. To validate the properties, the Validator works through a JavaBean representation, the specified ActionForm. The field element can accept up to four attributes:

- property: The property in the JavaBean corresponding to this field element. This attribute is required.
- depends: The comma-delimited list of validators to apply against this field. For the field to succeed, all validators must succeed. *Validators* represent the rules against which the value of the field will be tested.
- page: The JavaBean corresponding to this form may include a page property. Only fields with a page attribute value that is equal to or less than the page property on the formbean are processed. This attribute is useful when using a wizard approach to completing a large form, to ensure that a page is not skipped. The default value is 0.
- indexedListProperty: The method name that returns an array or a Collection that retrieves the list of indexed properties and then loops through the list performing the validations for this field.

The msg element is defined using this syntax:

```
<!ELEMENT msg      EMPTY>
<!ATTLIST msg      name     CDATA #IMPLIED
                   key      CDATA #IMPLIED
                   resource CDATA #IMPLIED >
```

The msg element defines a custom message key to use when one of the validators for this field fails. Each validator has a default message property (which we explain in the next section) that is used when a corresponding field msg is not specified. Each validator applied to a field may have its own msg element. The msg element accepts up to three attributes:

- name: The name of the validator corresponding to this msg.
- key: The key that returns the message template from a resource bundle.
- resource: Determines whether the key is a literal value or a message resource bundle key. If you set this attribute to false, the key is a literal value rather than a message resource bundle key. The default value is true.

You can specify up to four args for a field. The following is the syntax to define each of them:

```
<!ELEMENT arg0-3    EMPTY>
<!ATTLIST arg0-3    name      CDATA #IMPLIED
                    key       CDATA #IMPLIED
                    resource CDATA #IMPLIED >
```

The arg0-3 (arg0, arg1, arg2, arg3) elements define the first through fourth replacement value to use with the message template for this validator or this field. Each of the arg0-3 elements accepts up to three attributes:

- name: The name of the validator corresponding to this msg.
- key: The key that will return the message template from a resource bundle.
- resource: Determines whether the key is a literal value or a bundle key. If you set this attribute to false, the key is a literal value rather than a bundle key. The default is true.

The last element that can be included in a field definition is var. The following is the syntax for defining it:

```
<!ELEMENT var (var-name, var-value)>
```

The var element can set parameters that a field may need to pass to one of its validators, such as the minimum and maximum values in a range validation. These parameters may also be referenced by one of the arg0-3 elements using a shell syntax: ${var:var-name}.

The var-name element is the name of the var parameter to provide to a field's validators. This element has the following syntax:

```
<!ELEMENT var-name  (#PCDATA)>
```

Regular expressions

A *regular expression* is a concise way to describe and search for complex string patterns. The term originated in the UNIX environment, but regular expressions are now available in many languages, including Java. Fortunately, regardless of the language, you use the same syntax to create a regular expression. If you've never used regular expressions, we suggest that you take some time to find out about them. The following Web sites offer tutorials:

```
www.regular-expressions.info/
    tutorial.html
java.sun.com/docs/books/
    tutorial/extra/regex
```

History buffs might be interested in knowing that the origins of regular expressions came from physiology and mathematics, not computer science. According to Jeffrey E. F. Friedl, in the forties Warren McCulluch and Walter Pitts created neuron-level models of how the nervous system operated. Mathematician Stephen Kleene later described these models using mathematical notation that he called regular expressions. Ken Thompson incorporated that system of notation into qed (the grandfather of the UNIX ed). Since then, regular expressions have appeared in UNIX and UNIX-like utilities.

The `var-value` element is the value of the `var` parameter to provide to a field's validators. This element has the following syntax:

```
<!ELEMENT var-value (#PCDATA)>
```

Now that you know the grammar for the `validation.xml` file, it's time to look at its sister file, `validator-rule.xml`.

The `validator-rules.xml` file has a number of predefined validators that you can use in the `validation.xml` file to perform various checks on the value of specified fields. The following is a current list of each of the validators and their function. Note that `var` refers to the `var` element defined in the `field` element. You can get the `validator-rules.xml` file from the Struts distribution `lib` directory.

- `required`: Checks that the field isn't null and that length of the field is greater than zero, not including white space.
- `validWhen`: Checks to see that certain conditions exist for the field to be validated. You must specify `var` as `test` with the value consisting of an expression that evaluates to a boolean value. The expression must evaluate to `true` for the validation to succeed.
- `minlength`: Checks whether the field's length is greater than or equal to the minimum value. Specify `var` as `minlength` with the minimum value allowed. The value should be an integer.
- `maxlength`: Checks whether the field's length is less than or equal to the maximum value. Specify `var` as `maxlength` with the maximum value allowed. The value should be an integer.

- `mask`: Checks whether the field matches the regular expression in the `mask` attribute of the field. Specify the `var` as `mask` as a regular expression. For more information on regular expressions, see the "Regular expressions" sidebar.
- `byte`: Checks whether the field can safely be converted to a byte primitive.
- `short`: Checks whether the field can safely be converted to a short primitive.
- `integer`: Checks whether the field can safely be converted to an integer primitive.
- `long`: Checks whether the field can safely be converted to a long primitive.
- `float`: Checks whether the field can safely be converted to a float primitive.
- `double`: Checks whether the field can safely be converted to a double primitive.
- `date`: Checks whether the field is a valid date.
- `intRange`: Checks whether a field's value is within a range. Specify `vars` as `min` and `max` with the beginning and ending values allowed. The values should be integers.
- `floatRange`: Checks whether a field's value is within a range. Specify `vars` as `min` and `max` with the beginning and ending values allowed. The values should be of the type `float`.
- `creditCard`: Checks whether the field is a valid credit card number. Confirms a credit card number as a valid American Express, Visa, Master Card, or Discover credit card.
- `email`: Checks whether a field has a valid e-mail address.

Now that you know about `validators` and the syntax of the `validation.xml` file, you can create your own `validation.xml` to validate `LoginForm`. The `LoginForm` example has two fields to validate: `userName` and `password`. Listing 9-4 shows the entire `validation.xml` file.

Listing 9-4 validation.xml File for the Login Application

```
<?xml version="1.0" encoding="ISO-8859-1" ?>
<!DOCTYPE form-validation PUBLIC
     "-//Apache Software Foundation//DTD Commons Validator Rules Configuration
           1.0.1//EN"
     "http://jakarta.apache.org/commons/dtds/validator_1_0_1.dtd">
<form-validation>
    <!-- ========= Form Definitions ==================== -->
    <formset>
```

(continued)

Listing 9-4 *(continued)*

```
4        <form name="loginForm">
5            <field property="userName"
6                   depends="required">
7               <arg0   key="error.username.required"/>
8            </field>

9            <field property="password"
10                  depends="required,minlength">
11              <arg0   key="error.password.required"/>
12              <arg1   key="${var:minlength}" name="minlength"
           resource="false"/>
13              <var>
14                  <var-name>minlength</var-name>
15                  <var-value>5</var-value>
16              </var>
17           </field>

18           <field property="password"
19                  depends="maxlength">
20              <arg0   key="error.password.required"/>
21              <arg1   key="${var:maxlength}" name="maxlength"
           resource="false"/>
22              <var>
23                  <var-name>maxlength</var-name>
24                  <var-value>8</var-value>
25              </var>
26           </field>
27       </form>
28   </formset>
29</form-validation>
```

Note the following lines in Listing 9-4:

- Line 4: You must define each form that the Validator needs to validate with a `<form>` tag. This line specifies that the `loginForm` is to be validated.
- Lines 5–8: You need to define each field in the form that needs validating with a `<field>` tag. These lines accomplish this definition for the `userName` field.
- Line 6: The `userName` field is defined as a required field, nothing more. The `depends` attribute on this line is equal to `required`, the name of the rule to invoke when validating the field. The `required` validator checks to make sure that the value of the field is neither null nor an empty string.
- Line 7: Specifies argument one to be passed to the default message resource. The default message resource is

  ```
  errors.required={0} is required.
  ```

  Therefore, the `arg0` value functions as a key to look up a message in the default message resource bundle. Instead of `{0}`, the user sees that message in the default error message.

- Line 9: Defines the password field i as the next field to validate. This field has two validators, required and minlength. Both tests have to pass before the field is validated. The required validator does the same function as for the previous username field. The minlength validator checks to make sure that the length of the string is greater than or equal to some minimum length. The minimum length is specified with a <var> tag. var-name has to be minlength. var-value must be an integer value indicating the minimum length to check against. The default error message for minlength is

  ```
  errors.minlength={0} can not be less than {1} characters.
  ```

- Lines 11 and 12: The default message takes two parameters, a field name and a minimum length. These lines define these two parameters. The interesting point here is the dual use of the arg0 value. Because the code specifies two validators, the arg values must apply to them both. As luck would have it, arg0 can fit for the default error message for either the required validator or the minlength validator.
- Lines 13–16: Define the minimum length of the password to be 5 characters.
- Lines 18–26: Define the maximum length of the password field to be 8 characters. We defined the password field twice because we also wanted to use the maxlength validator. However, the default messages for minlength and maxlength both specify {1} as the length value. The dilemma is that arg1 can take only one value. To get around this thorny problem, we chose to define the password field twice. The second time we applied only the maxlength validator and gave the maximum allowed value for the arg1 value.

The validation.xml file is now complete and ready to use with the updated Login application.

Tweaking other files

You must check a couple of other files to make sure that they're ready for the Validator. The action definition in the struts-config.xml file that's using the form to be validated must not have the validate attribute set to false (true is the default value). Otherwise, the validate method of the ValidateAction superclass will not get called.

In the message resources file, you need to include the error message definitions that the Validator uses. The ApplicationResources file used for the Login project in Chapter 3 did not have these messages. You can find the list of error messages at the beginning of the validator-rules.xml file. The error messages are as follows:

```
# Struts Validator Error Messages
errors.required={0} is required.
errors.minlength={0} can not be less than {1} characters.
errors.maxlength={0} can not be greater than {1} characters.
errors.invalid={0} is invalid.

errors.byte={0} must be a byte.
errors.short={0} must be a short.
errors.integer={0} must be an integer.
errors.long={0} must be a long.
errors.float={0} must be a float.
errors.double={0} must be a double.

errors.date={0} is not a date.
errors.range={0} is not in the range {1} through {2}.
errors.creditcard={0} is not a valid credit card number.
errors.email={0} is an invalid e-mail address.
```

You need to add these messages to the `ApplicationResources` file.

Try out the modified Login application

To try out the modified Login application, replace the three original files in your IDE with the newly modified ones: `LoginForm`, `struts-config.xml`, and `ApplicationResources.properties`. Then add the two validation configuration files, `validation.xml` and `validator-rules.xml`, to the `WEB-INF` folder. Copy the entire `Login` folder to the `webapps` folder of Tomcat, replacing the existing `Login` folder (if it exists).

When you run the application, you can test that the new validation is working by entering any username and then a password of less than five characters. You should see an error message indicating that the password field cannot be less than five characters, as shown in Figure 9-1. This shows that the `minlength` validator caught the error.

Looking more closely at validation.xml

We skipped over some of the important features of configuring the `validation.xml` file to keep the Login example as simple as possible. In this section, we cover all the additional parts of the grammar we missed earlier.

You can use the `constant` element in either the `formset` element or the `global` element. The grammar is as follows:

```
<!ELEMENT constant (constant-name, constant-value)>
<!ELEMENT constant-name  (#PCDATA)>
<!ELEMENT constant-value (#PCDATA)>
```

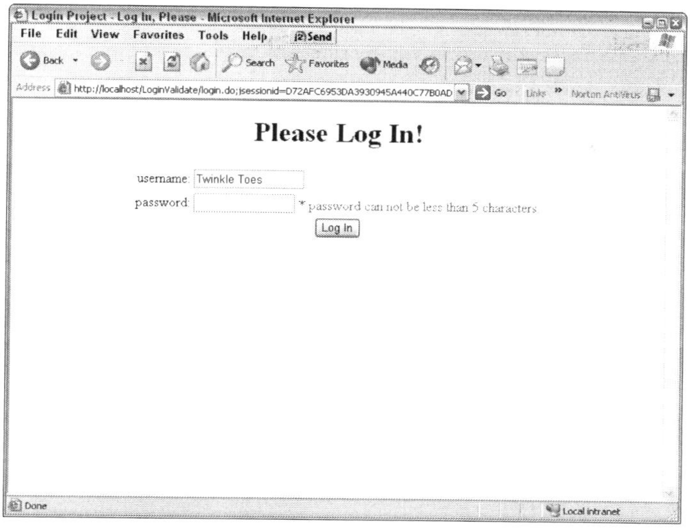

Figure 9-1: Login page with a password error message.

The `constant` element defines a static value that you can use as replacement parameters in `field` elements. The `constant-name` and `constant-value` elements define the constant's reference ID and replacement value, respectively.

An example might help clarify the use of `constant`. Suppose you want to validate a telephone field using the `mask` validator. The `mask` validator takes a regular expression and applies it to the field to be validated. Here is an example of verifying that the phone field has the form *nnn-nnn-nnnn*, where *n* is a digit:

```
<field property="vendorPhone"
        depends="required,mask">
    <arg0   key="vendor.phone.label"/>
     <var>
        <var-name>mask</var-name>
        <var-value>^\d{3}-\d{3}-\d{4}$</var-value>
    </var>
</field>
```

Rather than using the regular expression in the `var-value` tag, you could define a constant with that value and then reference the constant in the `var-value` tag. Listing 9-5 shows an example of using the `constant` element.

Listing 9-5 Example Using the constant Element

```
<constant>
    <constant-name>phone</constant-name>
    <constant-value>^\d{3}-\d{3}-\d{4}$</constant-value>
</constant>
```

(continued)

Listing 9-5 *(continued)*

```
5 <field property="vendorPhone"
6       depends="required,mask">
7     <arg0   key="vendor.phone.label"/>
8     <var>
9        <var-name>mask</var-name>
10       <var-value>${phone}</var-value>
11    </var>
12 </field>
```

Lines 1-4 define the constant with a reference ID of `phone`, and the constant's value is the regular expression that you want phone numbers to conform to. Now when defining the value for the `mask` var, you can simply reference the `phone` constant instead of entering the regular expression itself, as shown in Line 10.

The use of constants is valuable when you need to use the same value many times. For example, you may have many phone numbers to validate, such as `mainPhone`, `nightPhone`, `personalPhone`, `faxPhone`, `cellularPhone`, and `alternatePhone`. All would be expected to be the same format; therefore the `phone` constant could be used as shown in Line 10. Then, if the format changed (such as changing the dash to a blank between the area code and the remaining numbers), all you'd need to do is change the regular expression in the `phone` constant.

Now that you know how to use the `constant` element, where can you use it? There are two acceptable places: the `formset` element and the `global` element. Here is the grammar for both the `formset` and `global` elements:

```
<!ELEMENT form-validation (global*, formset*)>
<!ELEMENT global (validator*, constant*)>
<!ELEMENT formset (constant*, form+)>
```

If you use `constant` in the `formset` element, all `fields` defined in that `formset` can reference it. To make it available in all `formsets`, define `constant` in the `global` element.

Using the Validator with DynaActionForms

If you're using `DynaActionForms` instead of `ActionForms`, you can still use the Validator. However, you need to make the following changes:

1. **When you define** `DynaActionForm` **in the** `struts-config.xml` **file, the** `type` **attribute should be** `org.apache.struts.validator.DynaValidatorForm` **instead of the standard** `org.apache.struts.action.DynaActionForm`.
2. **Make sure that the form fields referenced in the** `validation.xml` **file match the** `form-property` **names defined for the form in question.**

Chapter 10

Getting a Helping Hand with Tag Libraries

In This Chapter

- Finding out how to use tag libraries
- Understanding Expression language
- Working with the Struts-EL tag library
- Using the JSTL tag library
- Discovering other Struts tag libraries
- Creating user interfaces with Java Server Faces

When creating JavaServer Pages, one of the prime considerations is to eliminate or at least minimize the use of scriptlets in the pages. When scriptlets clutter up the page with Java code, making sense of the page is much more difficult. In addition, in larger projects, JSP pages belong more to the realm of user-interface designers and graphic artists. The use of Java logic in your pages mixes programming and design — a definite no-no.

Custom tags were invented to alleviate this problem. They encapsulate higher level functionality in the form of a JSP tag. Usually a tag library consists of a family of tags that are all related to one area, such as formatting or using JavaBeans.

The following two components make up the JSP Tag library architecture:

- **Tag support classes:** These Java classes are responsible for implementing the functionality of the tags in the library. Essentially, these classes represent the functionality of the scriptlet but don't need to appear themselves in the JSP page. Tag support classes are generally packaged in a JAR file.
- **Tag Library Descriptor (TLD) XML file:** An XML file describes all the tags that go to make up the tag library — names, attributes, and support classes. The JSP engine uses this file to determine how to process the tags.

Using Tag Libraries

You need to follow several generic steps to take to make use of any tag library. These steps are as follows:

1. **Move the TLD file for the library into the `WEB-INF` folder.**

   You could place the TLD file into any folder in the Web application's folder. However, most users place it in the `WEB-INF` folder.

2. **Move the library's JAR file into the `WEB-INF/lib` folder.**

3. **Define the tag library in the `web.xml` file.**

   To define the tag library, use the JSP directive tag:

   ```
   <taglib>
        <taglib-uri>could be any distinct text</taglib-uri>
        <taglib-location>content relative path to the TLD</taglib-location>
   </taglib>
   ```

   As with all `web.xml` tags, the `<taglib>` tag is position dependent. Here is an example that defines the JSTL Core library:

   ```
   <taglib>
        <taglib-uri>jstl-c</taglib-uri>
        <taglib-location>/WEB-INF/c.tld</taglib-location>
   </taglib>
   ```

   The URI to reference the Core library is `jstl-c`. You could have just as easily used `bugaboo`. However, it is good practice to keep the URI relevant to the library's name. The content-relative path to the TLD is `/WEB-INF/c.tld`. Whenever you want to reference the library in the JSP file, you use the URI, as explained in the next step.

4. **Reference the TLD of the tag library in each JSP page that uses the library's tags.**

   To reference the TLD, use the following JSP directive tag:

   ```
   <%@ taglib prefix="some prefix" uri="uri defined in the web.xml file" %>
   ```

   Here's an example of referencing the JSTL Core library defined in Step 2:

   ```
   <%@ taglib prefix="c" uri="jstl-c" %>
   ```

   Use the prefix when you use a particular tag from the tag library. For example, the JSTL Core library has a `set` tag. When using that tag, you must add the prefix you have defined for this library. In this case, you would use `c`, as in:

   ```
   <c:set ... \>
   ```

A common practice is to place all `taglib` directives in a single JSP file and `include` this file in the other JSP pages. In this way, you have only one file to edit when you want to add or remove additional tag library references.

5. **Add the desired tags to the JSP page.**

   You can now successfully use the tags defined in the tag library.

Expressing with the Expression Language

The developers of Struts have recommended that you no longer use the standard Struts tag library, which was based on the older *runtime expressions* to evaluate attribute values of tags. Instead, they have created a new library called Struts-EL which uses *expression language* (EL) for evaluating attribute values. Struts-EL uses the expression evaluation engine provided by the JSP Standard Tag Library (JSTL) 1.0.

Runtime expressions are of the form `<%= expression %>`. The *expression* represents some Java language expression. This is the standard way of evaluating expressions in JSP 1.2 and below. Beginning with JSP 2.0, the EL syntax is the preferred expression language because the EL syntax is simpler to learn than Java syntax. EL provides the users of the libraries a more flexible, intuitive, and powerful way to create expressions.

The basic form for an EL expression is

```
<some tag  value='${expression}' \>
```

Here is an example of an EL expression. This tag outputs the value of the `userName` attribute that is stored in the session scope:

```
<c:out value='${sessionScope.userName}' />
```

EL evaluates and coerces the expression into the type expected by the `value` attribute. You can use either single or double quotation marks to delimit the EL expression.

You can also intersperse text with expressions when the resulting type that the attribute expects is text:

```
<a tag value='${expression1} any text ${expression2} more
         text' \>
```

Here is an example of the preceding syntax. Assume the `now` variable contains the current date and time:

```
<c:out value='${sessionScope.userName} logged on at ${now}' />
```

This example results in the String result of *expression1* concatenated with *any text* concatenated with the String result of *expression2* concatenated with *more text*.

Expressions can contain any of the following items:

- Identifiers
- Literals
- Operators
- Implicit objects

These items are discussed in the next few sections.

Identifiers

If a named variable exists in one of the four scopes (page, request, session, or application), the EL expression can retrieve the value of the variable. All identifiers function as a *key* that can return a *value*. So the expression

```
<some tag value='${product}' \>
```

produces a lookup like this:

```
pageContext.get("product");
```

The EL engine searches each of the four scopes in turn (starting with the page scope) until it finds the value. If the search doesn't find the value, it returns a null.

Literals

Literals can be one of four types or be null. The four types are

- **String**: Any text enclosed in single or double quotes
- **Boolean:** The unquoted text, `true` or `false`
- **Integer:** Any digit from 0 through 9, optionally prefixed with the + (plus) or – (minus) sign
- **Floating point:** Any normal decimal number

See the JSTL 1.0 specification for exact definitions of the form literals can take. You can get the specification from `java.sun.com/products/jsp/jstl`.

Operators

The operators available are the standard arithmetic, relational, and logical operators you would expect to find in a modern programming language. However, EL also adds a few new operators.

The [ ] (square bracket) and . (period) operators

Two of the operators that EL adds are the [ ] (square bracket) and . (period) operators. These two operators are similar but the [ ] operator has a wider number of uses than the . operator.

You can use the . operator much like the Java . operator, except rather than calling a method, the . operator accesses a property of a bean and is used on a variable that references a bean. For example, suppose you have a bean named `PurchaseOrder` that has a property named `vendorName`. Furthermore, the bean is referenced by a variable named `po`. You could use an EL expression like the following to access `vendorName`. (We are using JSTL tags in our examples, although we do not explain the JSTL tags until the "Core library" section later in this chapter.)

```
<c:out value='${po.vendorName}' />
```

You could also use the [ ] operator to access `vendorName` by using this type of expression:

```
<c:out value='${po["vendorName"]}' />
```

However, the . operator is limited to properties of beans, but the [] operator can also access values stored in arrays, Lists, and Maps.

The empty operator

The `empty` operator solves the problem of an identifier being non-null yet essentially empty, such as a zero-length string. Using the unary `empty` operator on an identifier returns `true` if the identifier is either null or has an empty value. This applies to Strings, arrays, Maps, and Lists. Here is an example of its use:

```
<c:if test='${empty po.vendorName}' />
```

Implicit Objects

The EL engine has numerous objects available that you can use in expressions to retrieve values. You reference the implicit objects by name. Here are their names and descriptions:

- `pageContext`: The `PageContext` object
- `pageScope`: A `Map` object that maps page-scoped attributes to their values
- `requestScope`: A `Map` object that maps request-scoped attributes to their values
- `sessionScope`: A `Map` object that maps session-scoped attributes to their values
- `applicationScope`: A `Map` object that maps application-scoped attributes to their values
- `param`: A `Map` object that maps parameter names to a single String value
- `paramValues`: A `Map` object that maps parameter names to a String array of all values
- `header`: A `Map` object that maps header names to a single String value
- `headerValues`: A `Map` object that maps header names to a String array of all values
- `cookie`: A `Map` object that maps cookie names to a single Cookie object
- `initParam`: A `Map` object that maps context-initialization parameter names to their `String` parameter value

For example, to retrieve a value from a session attribute called `userName`, you would use the following:

```
< c:out  value="${sessionScope.userName}" \>
```

To retrieve the value of a request parameter named `action`, you would use

```
< c:out  value="${param.action}" \>
```

Using the Struts-EL Tag Library

The Struts-EL library is designed to work with the Struts framework. The implementations of the tags “know” about the configuration of your Struts application and make reference to various Struts components when generating the page content. You can find the complete syntax for all the Struts-EL tags in Appendix A.

Getting the Struts-EL tag library

To use the Struts-EL library, you must include the standard Struts tag library, because the Struts-EL library classes are inherited from the Struts library classes. You also need to include the JSTL tag libraries because Struts-El uses the expression engine from the JSTL libraries. The libraries `struts.jar`, `struts-el.jar`, `jstl.jar`, and `standard.jar` come with the Struts 1.1 distribution in the `contrib\struts-el\lib` folder.

If you intend to use the tags in any of the JSTL libraries — and you should — you need to include also the libraries that JSTL needs. You need to download these additional libraries separately by retrieving the JSTL implementation from the Jakarta Taglibs Web site at

```
jakarta.apache.org/taglibs/doc/standard-1.0-doc/intro.html
```

An implementation of JSTL version 1.1 is available, but we have chosen to use version 1.0 because version 1.1 requires a Web container that supports the JSP 2.0 specification. Tomcat 5.0 supports JSP 2.0, but it is still in beta testing at the time of this writing.

To summarize, to use Struts-EL and JSTL, be sure that you include the following twelve JAR files in your `WEB-INF/lib` folder.

- `struts.jar`: The standard Struts tag library, as well as the Struts framework class files
- `struts-el.jar`: The EL version of the standard tag library
- `jstl.jar`: The JSTL API classes
- `standard.jar`: The JSTL standard taglib implementation
- `dom.jar`: Library needed by JSTL
- `jaxen-full.jar`: Library needed by JSTL
- `jaxp-api.jar`: Library needed by JSTL
- `jdbc2_0-stext.jar`: Library needed by JSTL
- `sax.jar`: Library needed by JSTL
- `saxpath.jar`: Library needed by JSTL
- `xalan.jar`: Library needed by JSTL
- `xercesImpl.jar`: Library needed by JSTL

The Struts-EL library consists of three separate tag libraries. Each library encompasses a particular set of functionality. The Beans-EL tag library is for handling JavaBeans. The largest library is HTML-EL, which contains Struts-related HTML tags. Finally, Logic-EL provides functionality for performing certain logical operations.

Beans-EL library

The Beans-EL library contains five tags. The common convention is to reference them with the prefix `bean`, as follows:

- `<bean:>`: Renders an internationalized message string to the response. The JSTL `fmt:message` tag offers the same functionality, so we recommend you use it instead of `bean:message`.
- `<bean:page>`: Exposes a specified item from the page context as a bean. The JSTL `c:set` tag offers the same functionality plus a whole lot more and therefore should be used instead.
- `<bean:resource>`: Loads a Web application resource and makes it available as a bean. The JSTL `c:import` tag performs the same functionality, so we recommend its use instead of `bean:resource`.
- `<bean:size>`: Defines a bean containing the number of elements in an array, Collection, or Map. The `size` tag is useful because EL doesn't support calling a bean's method directly. For example, you can find the number of elements in a Collection by calling the `size` method of the Collection. Because `size` is not a standard getter method (otherwise it would be called `getSize`), you can't get the number of elements in the Collection directly through an EL expression. Therefore, the Beans-EL `size` tag offers functionality that JSTL does not.
- `<bean:struts>`: Exposes a named Struts internal configuration object as a bean. The `struts` tag has no equivalent in JSTL because it doesn't directly know about Struts components. By using the `struts` tag, you may copy a formbean, forward, or mapping object into the page scope and reference it through an `id` variable.

HTML-EL library

A reasonable question might be why you use a special tag to insert standard HTML tags. Why not just write the HTML tags directly? The answer is that the HTML-EL tags know about the Struts application configuration and can therefore fill out the HTML tag attributes at runtime. The HTML-EL tags are commonly referenced with the prefix `html`.

You might specify an HTML form, for example, by using the `html:form` tag from the HTML-EL library. It might look like this:

```
<html:form action="polist.do" >
```

Notice that we listed only the one required attribute, `action`. Yet when the page is generated, the resulting HTML tag is

```
<form name="poListForm"
      method="post"
      action="/webpurchasing/polist.do">
```

The `name` attribute is looked up in the action-mappings in the `struts-config.xml` file. The `method` attribute uses `"post"` as the default. And the `action` attribute URI has the Web application context prefixed to be relative to the Web container context. The other HTML-EL tags also cooperate in this fashion with the Struts framework.

The HTML-EL library is by far the largest of the Struts-EL collection, with 28 tags. All HTML-EL tags and their syntax are listed in Appendix A.

Logic-EL library

The Logic-EL library adds commonly used logic to the JSP page without requiring scriptlets of Java code. The common convention is to prefix Logic-EL tags with `logic`. The tags that make up the Logic-EL library are

- `<logic:forward>`: Forwards control to the page specified by the specified `ActionForward` entry.
- `<logic iterate>`: Repeats the nested body content of this tag over a specified collection.
- `<logic match>`: Evaluates the nested body content of this tag if the specified value is an appropriate substring of the requested variable.
- `<logic messagesNotPresent>`: Generate the nested body content of this tag if the specified message is not present in this request.
- `<logic messagesPresent>`: Generates the nested body content of this tag if the specified message is present in this request.
- `<logic notMatch>`: Evaluates the nested body content of this tag if the specified value is not an appropriate substring of the requested variable.
- `<logic notPresent>`: Generates the nested body content of this tag if the specified value is not present in this request.
- `<logic present>`: Generates the nested body content of this tag if the specified value is present in this request.
- `<logic redirect>`: Renders an HTTP redirect.

All the logic tags are unique with the exception of `iterate`, `present`, and `notPresent`. The `iterate` tag has an equivalent JSTL tag in `c:forEach`. You can render the `present` and `notPresent` tags using the `c:if` tags.

Working with the JSP Standard Tag Library

The JavaServer Pages Standard Tag Library (JSTL) simplifies the life of a page author by encapsulating the most commonly used functionality into a set of JSP tags. The addition of a simplified Expression Language makes it easier to retrieve or set values in application data.

JSTL offers a lot to the page author. In this section, we review all the tags that make up JSTL, offering a synopsis of each tag and an example of how the tag might be used. In Appendix A, we provide the syntax for each tag in the library.

JSTL 1.0 has two versions of JSTL: the EL version, which uses the EL expression language, and the RT version, which uses the older runtime expression language. All our examples use only the EL version.

JSTL is considered one library, but the implementation divides JSTL into four separate libraries: Core, Formatting, SQL, and XML. Each library encompasses a particular set of functionality.

Core library

The Core tag library provides general functionality that page developers commonly need most. The convention is to reference all tags in the Core library with the prefix `c`.

General-purpose tags

The general-purpose tags consists of four tags that you use to manipulate *scoped variables* (variables that exist in one of the four scopes — page, request, session, or application). They are

- `<c:out>`: The `out` tag evaluates an expression and outputs the result to the current JSPWriter (responsible for writing out the page contents). The following example outputs the value of the `vendorName` property found in the `po` object stored in the session:

  ```
  The vendor is <c:out value="${sessionScope.po.vendorName}"/>.
  ```

- `<c:set>`: The `set` tag sets the value of a scoped variable or a property of a target object. For example, use the following to set a scoped variable named `"currentResident"`:

  ```
  <c:set var="currentResident" value="${sessionScope.customer.name}"/>
  ```

To set the "city" property of the "customer.address" target object, use the following:

```
<c:set target="${customer.address}" property="city" value="${po.city}"/>
```

- <c:remove>: The remove tag removes a scoped variable from the scope. To remove the "currentResident" variable from the page scope, use the following:

```
<c:remove var="currentResident"/>
```

- <c:catch>: The catch tag catches an exception (java.lang.Throwable) in a nested block. For example, to catch an exception in a set of tags, use the following:

```
<c:catch var="theException">
    <c:out value="${po.poNumber}" />
    ... other tags ...
</c:catch>
<c:if test="${theException != null}">
    Oops! An error occurred.
</c:if>
```

The theException variable holds an Exception if one is thrown in the c:catch body.

Conditional tags

Conditional tags support the conditional execution of various enclosed page elements based on the evaluation of one or more expressions. Two basic tags are available, a simple conditional tag and a mutually exclusive tag:

- <c:if>: The simple conditional is the if tag. If the expression evaluates to true the body of the if tag is executed. For example:

```
<c:if test="${customer.accesses == 1}">
    This is your first access. Welcome to the Blah-Blah Web site.
</c:if>
```

- <c:choose>, <c:when>, **and** <c:otherwise>: In the body of choose you define the mutually exclusive conditions by using the when tag. If none of the when conditions are true, the optional otherwise tag is executed. For example:

```
<c:choose>
    <c:when test="${po.tag == 'save'}">
        ...
    </c:when>
    <c:when test="${po.tag == 'update'}">
        ...
    </c:when>
    <c:when test="${po.tag == 'delete'}">
        ...
```

```
    </c:when>
    <c:otherwise>
        ...
    </c:otherwise>
</c:choose>
```

Iterator tags

The iterator tags provides a looping mechanism to iterate over a wide variety of collections of objects. Two very flexible tags are available to accomplish this:

- **<forEach>:** The `forEach` tag repeats the body content once for each element in the collection of objects it is iterating over. The collection of objects can be any implementation of `java.util.Collection`, `java.util.Map`, `java.util.Iterator`, `java.util.Enumeration`, an array, and even a `String` of comma-separated values. Here is an example iterating over a collection of purchase orders and writing out the purchase order number of each purchase order:

  ```
  <table>
      <c:forEach var="po" items="${purchaseorders}">
          <tr><td><c:out value="${po.poNumber}"/></td></tr>
      </c:forEach>
  </table>
  ```

  Here is a similar iteration, but this time the collection of objects is of the type `java.util.Map`. Each item from the map will be of type `java.util.Map.Entry` and have two properties, `key` and `value`. The example outputs the `value` property:

  ```
  <table>
      <c:forEach var="ponumber" items="${ponumbers}">
          <tr><td><c:out value="${ponumber.value}"/></td></tr>
      </c:forEach>
  </table>
  ```

  You may also use the `forEach` tag to iterate over a particular range of numbers, with a starting and ending number as well as a number to increment by. Here is an example that iterates 11 times, from number 100 to 110.

  ```
  <c:forEach var="i" begin="100" end="110">
      <c:out value="${i}"/>
  </c:forEach>
  ```

  Finally, you may need to know the particular iteration number you are currently on. You may define the `varStatus` attribute and retrieve the `count` property from that variable. Here is an example:

```
<table>
    <c:forEach var="purchaseorder" items="${purchaseorders}"
          varStatus="status">
        <tr>
            <td><c:out value="${status.count}"/></td>
            <td><c:out value="${purchaseorder.poNumber}"/></td>
        </tr>
    </c:forEach>
</table>
```

- `<c:forTokens>`: The `forTokens` tag is similar to the `forEach` tag except `forTokens` iterates over a set of *tokens* (user-defined entities) that are separated by the delimiters supplied as an attribute. The set of tokens are enclosed in a `String`. Here is an example of using `forTokens` with a `";"` delimiter:

```
<table>
    <c:forTokens var="alphavalue" items="a;b;c;r,s;w;z" delims=";">
        <tr><td><c:out value="${alphavalue}"/></td></tr>
    </c:forEach>
</table>
```

URL-related tags

Four URL tags support linking, importing, and redirecting:

- `<c:import>`: The import tag is designed to overcome some of the memory-related inefficiencies of the `<jsp:include>` tag. Using the `import` tag, you may import a context-relative URL, a page-relative URL, a foreign-context URL (in a different Web application but in the same Web container), or an absolute URL. The contents of the imported resource are written out as text to the current JSPWriter. This example imports a resource with a relative URL from the same context:

```
<c:import url="/header.html" />
```

  This example imports a resource with a relative URL from a different context in the same Web container:

```
<c:import url="/footer.jsp" context="/sample" />
```

  This example imports a resource with an absolute URL:

```
<c:import url="http://www.othenos.com/polist?accept=true" />
```

- `<c:url>`: The `url` tag takes care of rewriting URLs, if necessary, and prefixing the context to context-relative URLs.

Rewriting URLs is a technique used to a change a URL for various purposes. The `url` tag rewrites the URL when a browser does not accept cookies because you need to store session information about the user. The `url` tag embeds the session information (specifically, the session ID) in the URL. In this way, when the browser submits a request, the session information is sent also.

Here is an example of using the `url` tag to process a URL and then using that processed URL in an `href` tag:

```
<c:url value="/polist" var="theUrl" />
<a href='<c:out value="${theUrl}"/>'>Purchase Order</a>
```

- `<c:redirect>`: The `redirect` tag sends an HTTP redirect request to the browser for a new URL, as in this example:

```
<c:redirect url="http://www.mum.edu/registrar" />
```

- `<c:param>`: The three previous tags (`import`, `url`, and `redirect`) can accept parameters in the body content of the tag. You use the `param` tag to specify those parameters. You must specify a `name` and `value` attribute for each parameter. Here is an example of the `param` tag used with the `url` tag:

```
<c:url value="/polist" var="theUrl" >
    <c:param name="user" value="${user.userName}"/>
    <c:param name="country" value="${user.country}"/>
</c:url>
<a href='<c:out value="${theUrl}"/>'>Register</a>
```

The parameter attributes are also encoded as part of the processing.

URL encoding refers to the process of encoding special characters in a string. For example, you must encode a space in a URL parameter string as a '%20', as in this example:

```
webpurchasing/polist?user=Tom%20Jones&country=United%20Kingdom
```

Most often you represent the offending character as `%hh`, where `hh` are two hexadecimal digits representing the US ASCII value of the character (assuming that you're using the US ASCII character set). Only the following characters may appear in URLs without encoding:

`0` through `9`, `a` through `z`, `A` through `Z`, and `$ - _ . + ! * ' ( ) ,`

Formatting library

The tags available in the Formatting library, especially the internationalization tags, provide the page author with a simple mechanism to internationalize the page. The prefix used for the Formatting library is most commonly `fmt`. (We discuss I18N issues in Chapters 3 and 6, so we won't discuss them in detail here.)

Internationalization tags

The six tags in the internationalization grouping deal explicitly with I18N issues. These tags use Locales and Resource Bundles to do their work, as we discuss in Chapter 6:

- `<fmt:setLocale>`: This tag sets the locale for subsequent internationalization tags. If you use this tag, browser-based locale setting capabilities are disabled. Here is an example of setting the locale:

  ```
  <fmt:setLocale value="en_US" />
  ```

  The value can be either a 2 letter language code (and optionally an underscore followed by a 2-letter country code) or a `java.util.Locale` object. When using this tag, be sure to set it at the beginning of the page because all the other internationalization tags depend on it.

- `<fmt:bundle>`: The `bundle` tag allows you to set a specific resource bundle for use in a narrow context, the body of the `bundle` tag. For example:

  ```
  <fmt:bundle basename="Labels">
      <fmt:message key="polist.find.label"/>
      <fmt:message key="polist.find.all"/>
  </fmt:bundle>
  ```

  In the body of the `bundle` tag, the messages will look up their keys in the resource bundle named `"Labels"`.

- `<fmt:setBundle>`: The `setBundle` tag specifies the resource bundle to use globally in the page, request, session, or application scope. Once set, all messages use that resource bundle to look up their keys and retrieve the message text. The only exceptions are `message` tags enclosed in a `bundle` tag. Here is an example of setting a resource bundle:

  ```
  <fmt:setBundle basename="Errors" var="errorBundle" />
  ```

  In this example, the resource bundle named `Errors` is used to retrieve messages. This particular localization context (the Locale and Resource Bundle being used) can be referenced by the `errorBundle` variable. The use of the `var` attribute is optional.

- `<fmt:message>`: You may output an I18N message using the `message` tag. This tag retrieves the message content based on the supplied key and the current resource bundle, as in the following example:

  ```
  <fmt:message key="errors.db.connection"/>
  ```

- `<fmt:param>`: You can add parameters to messages to provide specific information to the user. You can pass these parameters to the message by using the `param` tag in the `message` tag's body. For example:

  ```
  <fmt:message key="errors.db.connection">
      <fmt:param value="${user.userName}"/>
  </fmt:message>
  ```

The message associated with the "error.db.connection" key might be

```
errors.db.connection=A connection error occurred for {0}
```

- <fmt:requestEncoding>: When a browser encodes a response's form data using a character set other than the default character set, you will likely have trouble with the form's data. This is because most browsers don't handle the content type properly. Use of the requestEncoding tag ensures that the encoding is correct. Use this tag when you're expecting nondefault character-set encoding:

```
<fmt:requestEncoding />
```

Formatting tags

The following six tags enable you to format dates, times, and numbers in a locale-specific or customized manner:

- <fmt:timeZone>: This tag specifies the time zone to apply to the formatting tag that you place in the body of the timeZone tag. An example of this tag is shown here:

```
<fmt:timeZone value="GMT+1:00">
    <fmt:formatDate value="${now}" type="both" dateStyle="full"
            timeStyle="full"/>
</fmt:timeZone>
```

  The now variable is assumed to represent a Date object. The timeZone value attribute can be a string with a time zone ID, a string with a custom ID supported by the Java language, or a java.util.TimeZone object. See the documentation on java.util.TimeZone for more information.

- <fmt:setTimeZone>: This tag sets the default time zone for the page, request, session, or application scope. It replaces the previous default time zone. The setTimeZone tag is similar to the timeZone tag except there is no body and you can specify the scope, if desired. The following example sets the time zone as U.S. Pacific Time in the session scope. The default scope is page:

```
<fmt:setTimeZone value="America/Los Angles" scope="session"/>
```

- <fmt:formatNumber>: The fmtNumber tag can format a number, currency, or a percentage in a locale-specific or custom manner, as shown in this example:

```
    <fmt:formatNumber value="9876543.21" type="currency"/>
```

  This example formats the number 9876543.21 in a currency format specific to the current locale for the page. If the locale were en_US, the number would appear as

```
$9,876,543.21
```

However, if the locale were fr_CH (French, Switzerland), the number would appear as

```
SFr. 9'876'543.21
```

The value attribute is the only required attribute if there's no body to the tag. Otherwise, value can appear in the body. Eleven other attributes offer you complete control over how the number is formatted.

- <fmt:parseNumber>: The parseNumber tag is the opposite of the formatNumber tag. It takes a String as input and produces a Number. You would want to use this tag when you have to perform calculations on a number that exists as a String. The following is an example of its use:

```
<fmt:parseNumber value="${cur}" type="currency" var="money"/>
```

  This example parses the String representation in the cur variable and stores the resulting number in the money variable. The type of formatting used is currency.

- <fmt:formatDate>: The formatDate tag formats dates and times into a locale-specific or custom format. For example:

```
<jsp:useBean id="now" class="java.util.Date" />
<fmt:formatDate value="${now}" timeStyle="long" dateStyle="long"/>
```

  The example produces the following output for the U.S. locale:

```
October 31, 2003 11:00:03 AM CST
```

  and this for the French locale:

```
31 octobre 2003 11:00:03 GMT-07:0
```

  Many options for formatting are available, including specifying a pattern as used in java.text.SimpleDateFormat.

- <fmt:parseDate>: The parseDate tag is the opposite of formatDate. It expects a String value of a Date and creates a java.util.Date object that's stored in a variable or output with JSPWriter:

```
<jsp:useBean id="now" class="java.util.Date" />
<fmt:formatDate value="${now}" dateStyle="long" var="rightNow"/>
<fmt:parseDate value="${rightNow}" var="realDate"/>
```

  This example takes the rightNow Date String created by the formatDate tag and stores it as java.util.Date in the realDate variable.

SQL library

The SQL Library provides the page author with a means to access an SQL database directly from the JSP page. Of course, this technique breaks all the rules about separation of concerns, the encapsulation of database operations in the Model layer, and many other good programming practices. Yet, in some circumstances you may find it useful to have direct SQL access, such as in very small applications, prototyping, or just trying out a creative idea. Six tags make up the SQL library. Together they provide the basic functionality to interact with a SQL database, such as establishing a connection, querying, updating, deleting and inserting data, and transactions. The SQL library most commonly uses `sql` for its prefix.

You are required to establish a data source before you can use the tags in the SQL library. You can establish a data source in a simple way by declaring the JDBC parameters for your database in the tag you're using. This means specifying the URL, driver, username, and password when setting the data source using the `setDataSource` tag.

If you've already configured a data source in Struts, another possibility is to create a startup class (by extending the `PlugIn` interface — see "Implementing Your Own Plug-in" in Chapter 9) that adds the data source to the JSTL configuration file. The `init` method would have code like the following:

```
// assume we have a reference to the ServletContext in "sc"
// assume your data-source is named "mssql" in struts-config
// get a reference to the data source
DataSource dbConnMgr = (DataSource)sc.getAttribute("mssql");
// set the data source into the JSTL Config file
Config.set(sc, Config.SQL_DATA_SOURCE, dbConfigMgr);
```

This code has the advantage of not having to bother with specifying a data source in any of the SQL tags.

The six tags of the SQL library are

- `<sql:query>`: The `query` tag allows you to specify an SQL query string and return the results in a variable whose type is `javax.servlet.jsp.jstl.sql.Result`. You can then iterate the results to extract the values. Here is an example of a `query` tag and then extracting the results:

```
<sql:query var="purchaseorders" >
    SELECT * FROM purchaseorders
    WHERE country = 'France'
    ORDER BY lastname
</sql:query>
<table>
    <c:forEach var="row" items="${ purchaseorders.rows}">
        <tr>
            <td><c:out value="${ purchaseorders.vendorName}"/></td>
            <td><c:out value="${ purchaseorders.address}"/></td>
            <td><c:out value="${ purchaseorders.phone}"/></td>
        </tr>
    </c:forEach>
</table>
```

- <sql:update>: To insert, update, or delete data from the database, you use the update tag. You may use ? in the SQL as a parameter placeholder in the same manner as with the java.sql.PreparedStatement class. See the Java API for more details. This example supplies two parameters to the SQL statement by using the param tag:

```
<sql:update>
        UPDATE account
        SET Balance = Balance - ?
        WHERE accountNo = ?
    <sql:param value="${transferAmount}"/>
    <sql:param value="${accountFrom}"/>
</sql:update>
```

  See the section on the param and dateParam tags for further explanation.

- <sql:transaction>: The transaction tag provides transaction capabilities to query and update tags. The transaction tag encloses one or more query tags, or update tags, or both. If no exception is detected, the transaction is *committed,* or saved. Otherwise, the transaction is *rolled back* (all actions are reversed). Here is an example:

```
<sql:transaction dataSource="${dataSource}">
    <sql:update>
            UPDATE account
            SET Balance = Balance - ?
            WHERE accountNo = ?
        <sql:param value="${transferAmount}"/>
        <sql:param value="${accountFrom}"/>
    </sql:update>
    <sql:update>
            UPDATE account
            SET Balance = Balance + ?
            WHERE accountNo = ?
        <sql:param value="${transferAmount}"/>
        <sql:param value="${accountTo}"/>
    </sql:update>
</sql:transaction>
```

- <sql:setDataSource>: This tag sets the data source for the page, request, session, or application depending on the scope you choose. Page scope is the default. You may specify the data source using JDBC parameters, as in the following example, or you may use an instance of javax.sql.DataSource:

```
<sql:setDataSource url="jdbc:JTurbo://localhost/Purchasing"
                   driver="com.ashna.jturbo.driver.Driver"
                   user="webpurchaser"
                   password="purcha$e" />
```

- <sql:param> **and** <sql:dateParam>: Both tags supply values to parameter markers (?) in an SQL statement used in the query and update tags. The `param` tag provides any value except a `java.util.Date` type; that value is provided by the `dataParam` tag. The sequence of the `param` and `dateParam` tags in the body of the `query` and `update` tags must match the use of `?` in the SQL string.

XML library

The XML library handles XML documents and is based on XPath, a W3C (World Wide Web Consortium, the official standards body for the Web) recommendation for selecting and specifying the parts of an XML document. The use of XPath for XML documents expands on the expression language used by the other libraries of JSTL. The description of XPath is beyond the scope of this book. For a nice tutorial on XPath, go to

```
www.w3schools.com/xpath/default.asp
```

The XML library provides many of the same functions for XML documents as described previously in this section: core tags for commonly used functionality, flow control tags for conditional and iterative functions, and transform tags for transforming XML documents with XSLT. The prefix `x` is the convention for the XML Library tags.

XML core tags

The XML core tags follow:

- `<x:parse>`: Parses an XML document and stores the resulting object into a scoped variable.
- `<x:out>`: Evaluates an XPath expression and outputs it to the current JSPWriter.
- `<x:set>`: Evaluates an XPath expression and stores the result in a scoped variable.

XML flow control tags

All tags in the XML flow control group are identical to the tag in the Core library except that they take XPath expressions instead of EL expressions. The tags are `if`, `choose`, `when`, `otherwise`, and `forEach`.

XML transform tags

The two XML transform tags follow:

- `<x:transform>`: Applies an XSLT stylesheet to an XML document and outputs the resulting transformation.
- `<x:param>`: Used in the transform tag's body to supply transformation parameters.

Other Struts Tag Libraries

Several additional Struts-specific tag libraries are available. We offer a sampling in this section.

Tiles library

The `jsp:include` tag allows the page developer to include or insert other resources into a page at runtime. For example, rather than duplicate common header and footer information on each page of a Web application, the developer can simply use `jsp:include` to insert the pages that contain the header and footer definitions.

The general idea behind the Tiles library is to augment and expand on the `jsp:include` tag by providing ways to

- Define the structure of pages by using a template
- Extend templates through inheritance
- Support internationalization
- Integrate with the Struts framework

In Chapter 11, we show you how to leverage the Tiles library to your advantage.

Struts-Layout library

The Struts-Layout tag library is a powerful, open-source, custom tag library to aid the page author in the creation of user interface elements. It offers:

- Specialized input fields that offer controlled access and display. These input fields are similar to the Struts HTML-EL library but offer additional functionality, such as displaying error messages next to the field and visually marking required fields.
- Powerful and flexible display of collections, including sorting and paging.
- Layout definitions to control the arrangement of elements on the page.
- Control over the page's look-and-feel through *skins* (a way of specifying color combinations and styles for an entire application).
- Custom formatting of text information.

The JSTL and Struts-EL libraries provide some of the functionality found in the Struts-Layout library. However, if you need to format and manage lists of data, you should investigate the use of Struts-Layout.

The Struts-Layout home page is `struts.application-servers.com`.

Display library

Although not specifically made for Struts, the Display tag library focuses exclusively on displaying collections in a table format. The Web site describes the functionality succinctly as, "Give it a list of objects and it will handle column display, sorting, paging, cropping, grouping, exporting, smart linking and decoration of the table in a nice and customizable xhtml style." Figure 10-1 is a sample of the output you could expect.

You can find more information at the Display tag Web site at

```
displaytag.sourceforge.net/index.html
```

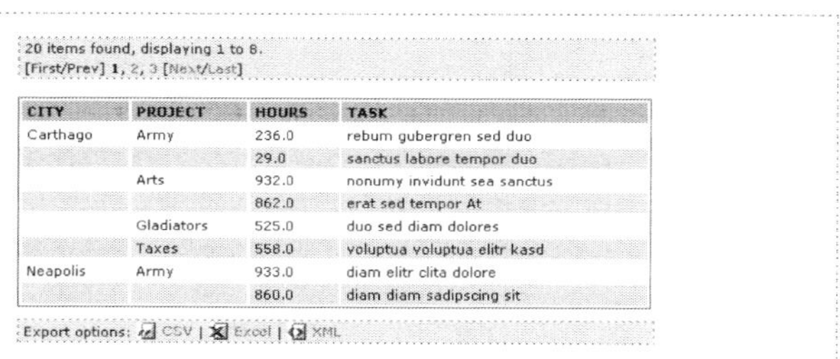

20 items found, displaying 1 to 8.
[First/Prev] 1, 2, 3 [Next/Last]

CITY	PROJECT	HOURS	TASK
Carthago	Army	236.0	rebum gubergren sed duo
		29.0	sanctus labore tempor duo
	Arts	932.0	nonumy invidunt sea sanctus
		862.0	erat sed tempor At
	Gladiators	525.0	duo sed diam dolores
	Taxes	558.0	voluptua voluptua elitr kasd
Neapolis	Army	933.0	diam elitr clita dolore
		860.0	diam diam sadipscing sit

Export options: CSV | Excel | XML

Figure 10-1: Sample table display using the Display library.

Looking at Java Server Faces

Java Server Faces (JSF) is touted as an evolutionary jump in the way J2EE Web applications are created. By standardizing the way developers construct user interfaces (UI) in J2EE Web applications, JSF can make the developer's task a lot easier, as well as make the resulting Web application more flexible.

JSF is a framework that offers the following benefits:

- Provides a rich palette of UI components that are device independent
- Offers a standardized, server-based event handling mechanism for UI components
- Maintains page state automatically
- Includes a validation framework

David Geary, a member of the JSF specification team, likens JSF to a combination of Struts and Swing — the strong lifecycle management capability of the Struts controller married to the rich UI components and event model of Swing.

This brings up the question of how JSF will affect the future of Struts. Will it replace Struts? The answer seems to be a resounding no. As it turns out, one of the two JSF specification lead members is Craig R. McClanahan, the principle developer of Struts. In a recent mailing list posting, Craig stated that Struts will have, ". . . a very clean integration with JSF, so that you can use JSF components in your user interface, but continue to use the controller, Actions, and associated business logic."

To that end, Craig has been developing a library called `struts-faces` that will accomplish the smooth integration between JSF and Struts. You can download this library by downloading the source code for the latest Struts nightly build at

```
archive.apache.org/dist/jakarta/struts/old/release/struts-faces
```

The bad news is that you have to build the JAR file yourself. The good news is that the download provides an Ant build file. (We discussed the Ant development tool in Chapter 2.) The source code and `build.xml` file are in the `contrib/struts-faces` folder.

Currently, the specification for JSF (Java Specification Request 127) is still in the review process. Therefore, the only implementations of the technology are based on a moving target (the changing JSR). The latest reference implementation is labeled EA4. You can download it at

```
java.sun.com/j2ee/javaserverfaces
```

If you're interested in experimenting with Struts and JSF, the Struts Web site contains instructions for integrating the two technologies. See the following for more information:

```
jakarta.apache.org/struts/proposals/struts-faces.html
```

Here are some additional JSF resources that you may find helpful:

- `www.jsfcentral.com/index.html`: A nice JSF portal that links to many JSF resources.
- `www.javaworld.com/javaworld/jw-11-2002/jw-1129-jsf.html`: David Geary has written three very readable articles on JSF. The first one is at this URL. From there, you can find links to the other two articles.
- `java.sun.com/j2ee/javaserverfaces`: The home page for JSF.
- `jcp.org/en/jsr/detail?id=127`: The JSR-127 specification.

Chapter 11

Working with Page Composition Techniques

In This Chapter

- Simplifying page layout
- Using *includes*
- Working with the Tiles Framework

When your Web application starts expanding beyond a few pages into the realm of dozens or even hundreds of pages, maintenance becomes an important issue. With so many pages to keep up to date, you're thinking of ways to do less and accomplish more. One easy way to save work is to isolate content that is repeated on many pages, such as header and footer information. If you can isolate this information into separate files and only reference it on each page, life would be a lot easier, at least when you need to modify a header or footer for the site.

Making Your Page Layout Life Easier

A sample JSP page that is full of opportunities for *refactoring* — rewriting portions of code to make the resulting code simpler, more readable, and more efficient — is shown in Listing 11-1. This page is similar to the `loggedin.jsp` page we created in Chapter 3 except that we added logo and footer information to make the page more representative of a production page. We will use this page to show how you can use page composition techniques to maintain pages more easily.

Listing 11-1 Sample JSP Page, refactor.jsp

```
<!-- begin the taglib definitions -->
<%@ taglib prefix="c" uri="/WEB-INF/c.tld" %>
<%@ taglib prefix="fmt" uri="/WEB-INF/fmt.tld" %>
<%@ taglib prefix="html"
```

```
             uri="/WEB-INF/struts-html-el.tld" %>
5 <!-- end the taglib definitions -->

6 <html:html locale="true"/>
7 <head>
8    <fmt:setBundle basename="ApplicationResources" />
9    <title><fmt:message key="login.title"/></title>
10</head>

11<body>

12    <!-- begin the logo for the application -->
13    <table width="100%">
14        <tr valign="top" align="center">
15            <td>
16                <img src="images/webLogo.gif"
                     name="webLogo"
                     width="425" height="50" border="0">
17            </td>
18        </tr>
19    </table>
20    <!-- end of logo -->

21    <h2>
22        <fmt:message key="loggedin.msg">
23            <fmt:param value='${requestScope.userName}' />
24        </fmt:message>
25    </h2>

26    <!-- begin the footer for the application -->
27    <div align="center">
28        <hr SIZE="1" WIDTH="100%"><br/>
29        Comments or Questions?
30        <a href='mailto:support@othenos.com'>
            Email Othenos Customer Support</a><br/>
31        &copy;2003 Othenos Consulting Group<br/>
32    </div>
33    <!-- end of footer -->

34</body>
35</html>
```

In examining the page makeup in Listing 11-1, three areas stand out as possibilities for common content:

- The definitions of the `taglibs` between lines 1 and 5
- The inserted logo in lines 12-20
- The footer section in lines 26-33

You can assume that other pages in the Web application are similar in structure — they include the same taglib definitions, logo graphics, and footer information. Because these code snippets are common to so many other pages, you could simplify the code a lot by removing these repeated sections and putting them into their own separate files. Then the original pages that contained the snippets could reference this content using the `include` directive and `jsp:include` tag.

You can extract the common features and put them into three separate files, as shown in Listings 11-2, 11-3, and 11-4.

Listing 11-2 taglibs.jsp

```
<%@ taglib prefix="c" uri="/WEB-INF/c.tld" %>
<%@ taglib prefix="fmt" uri="/WEB-INF/fmt.tld" %>
<%@ taglib prefix="html" uri="/WEB-INF/struts-html-el.tld" %>
<%@ taglib prefix="tiles" uri="/WEB-INF/struts-tiles.tld" %>
```

Listing 11-3 logo.jsp

```
<table width="100%">
    <tr valign="top" align="center">
        <td>
            <img src="images/webLogo.gif" name="webLogo"
                 width="425" height="50" border="0">
        </td>
    </tr>
</table>
```

Listing 11-4 footer.jsp

```
<div align="center">
    <hr SIZE="1" WIDTH="100%"><br/>
    Comments or Questions?
    <a href='mailto:support@othenos.com'>
        Email Othenos Customer Support
    </a><br/>
    &copy;2003 Othenos Consulting Group<br/>
</div>
```

Simplifying with Includes

You can use three elements to insert outside content into a JSP page: the `include` directive, the `jsp:include` tag, and the JSTL `c:import` tag.

The JSP `include` directive allows the insertion of static content into the JSP page at the time the page is converted into a Java class by the JSP engine. This directive has the following syntax:

```
<%@ include file="relativeURLspec"%>
```

Highlights of the tag follow:

- The tag can place only static content in a JSP file, such as an HTML or JSP file.
- The tag is processed only when JSP is converted into a Java class, not at request time.
- If the included file is updated, JSP containers are not required to change the converted page to include new content.

Listing 11-2 shows the use of the `include` directive to insert the `taglibs.jsp` segment into the `loggedin.jsp` page. You must include the `taglibs.jsp` in the page before the page is converted to the Java class because the tags that the page uses (`html`, `c`, `fmt`, `tiles`) require that you define the library before the conversion can occur. The library definition is in the `taglibs.jsp` file. Inserting `taglibs.jsp` at request time would be too late. Here is how you would insert it before the page is converted:

```
<!-- begin the taglib definitions -->
<%@ include file="taglibs.jsp" %>
<!-- end the taglib definitions -->
```

To include content at request time, you can use the `jsp:include` tag. This tag can insert both static and dynamic content into the page when the page is requested. The following is the syntax for `jsp:include`:

```
<jsp:include page="relativeURLspec" flush="true|false"/>
```

Highlights of the tag are as follows:

- The tag can include static (for example, HTML) or dynamic (for example, JSP) content.
- Inclusions are processed at request time.
- You can pass parameters to the included content.
- The JSP container is aware when an included resource changes and generates new content based on the new file.
- The `flush` attribute defaults to `false`. If set to `true`, it indicates that the page, if buffered, should be flushed (written out) before including the new resource.

The `logo.jsp` and `footer.jsp` segments (Listings 11-3 and 11-4) are candidates for including with the `jsp:include` tag. Here is how they would look if you included them with `jsp:include`:

```
<!-- begin the logo for the application -->
<jsp:include page="logo.jsp" flush="true" />
<!-- end of logo -->

<!-- begin the footer for the application -->
<jsp:include page="footer.jsp" flush="true" />
<!-- end of footer -->
```

You may want to use the `c:import` tag from the JSTL library instead of `jsp:include`. The `c:import` tag claims to reduce some of the buffering inefficiencies found in the `jsp:include` tag. Another feature of the tag is its ability to retrieve resources from any URL. The `jsp:include` tag is limited to resources in the same context as the current page. The simplest syntax for the `c:import` tag is

```
<c:import url="url" />
```

Here is how you might use the `c:import` tag instead of `jsp:include` in the preceding example:

```
<!-- begin the logo for the application -->
<c:import url="logo.jsp" />
<!-- end of logo -->

<!-- begin the footer for the application -->
<c:import url="footer.jsp" />
<!-- end of footer -->
```

You can use `c:import` or `jsp:include` interchangeably, depending on the tag libraries you prefer.

In Listing 11-5 we show how the original JSP in Listing 11-1 looks after refactoring and using `includes` to retrieve the common information. We use the `c:import` tag for including, with the exception of including the `taglibs.jsp` (line 2). `Taglibs.jsp` must be included when the page gets converted to a Java class because other tags in the page depend on the tag library definitions found in `taglibs.jsp`. Therefore the JSP `include` directive must be used.

Listing 11-5 Simplified JSP Using includes

```
<!-- begin the taglib definitions -->
<%@ include file="taglibs.jsp" %>
<!-- end the taglib definitions -->
<html:html locale="true"/>
<head>
    <!-- begin the header for the application -->
    <fmt:setBundle basename="ApplicationResources" />
    <title><fmt:message key="login.title"/></title>
   <!-- end of header -->
</head>

<body>

    <!-- begin the logo for the application -->
    <c:import url="logo.jsp" />
    <!-- end of logo -->

    <H2>
    <fmt:message key="loggedin.msg">
        <fmt:param value='${requestScope.userName}' />
    </fmt:message>
    </H2>

    <!-- begin the footer for the application -->
    <c:import url="footer.jsp" />
    <!-- end of footer -->

</body>
</html>
```

You can use `includes` to refactor all the JSP pages in the application that have a similar structure. By doing so, you dramatically reduce the amount of effort necessary to make changes to the common parts of the pages because you need to edit only one copy of each common segment. Any change to common content automatically ripples through every page that includes the segment. See Figure 11-1 for a graphical representation of the process.

Although refactoring and using `includes` offer many advantages to the alternative of all-in-one JSP pages, the resulting pages still have a maintenance problem. The structure or layout of the page is defined in the page. In other words, each JSP page must define how it will be laid out. If that layout changes (and it will over time), all pages need to be reworked to accommodate the new arrangement. Fortunately, a solution to that problem exists: the Tiles framework.

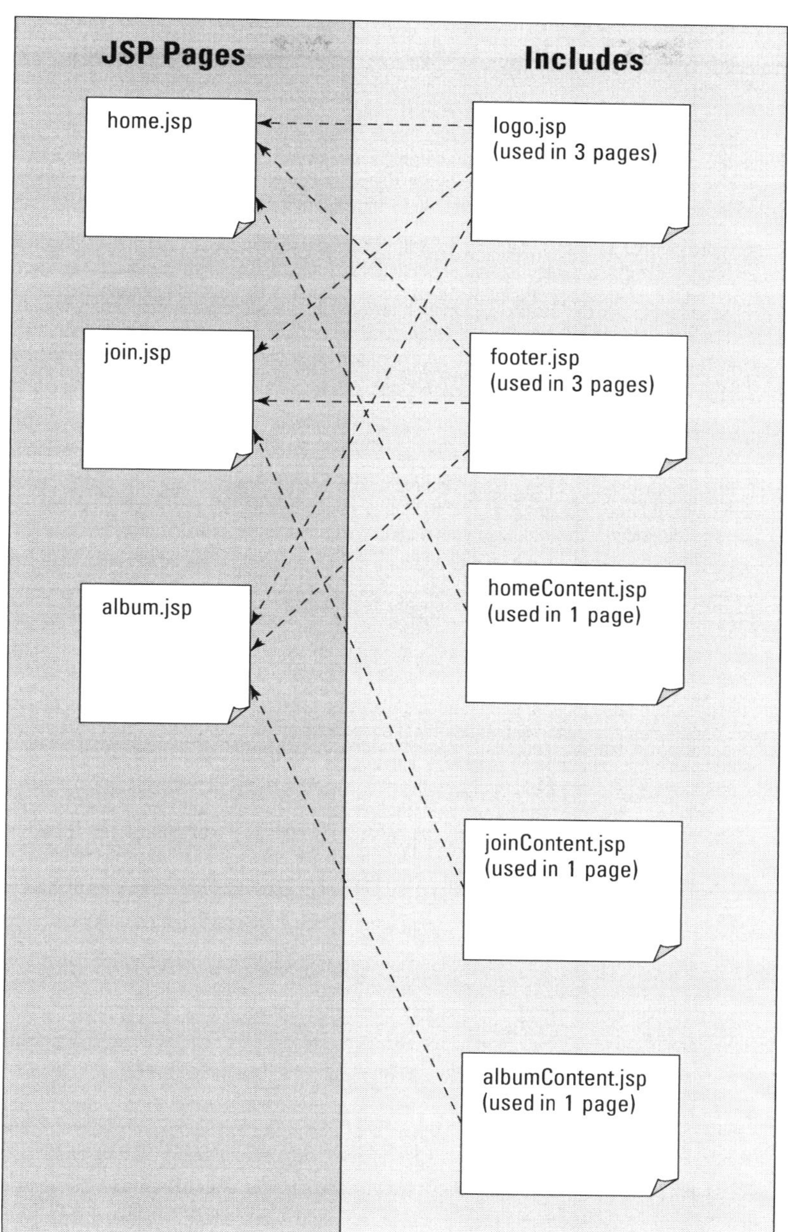

Figure 11-1: Diagram showing page composition using the includes mechanism.

Using the Tiles Framework

The Tiles framework expands on the use of `includes` by providing the developer a way to define a common look-and-feel in a template (sometimes called a *layout*). The *template* defines how the page should look but not what content should go into it. The template includes the page markup that describes the structure of the page, as well as names the additional segments that the page should include as content. These additional segments are called *tiles*.

If you want a JSP page to take advantage of the Tiles framework, you reference the template to use the template's structure as the page's own. You then choose tiles that should be inserted into the structure as content. The resulting page displays the structure as defined by the template along with the content as defined by the tiles it uses.

An example will help clarify how the Tiles framework works. For this example, we use the final JSP page from the preceding section (Listing 11-5) as the starting point. This page contains the structure of how the page should be presented and references most of the content required to fill the structure. The only content that is part of the page is the body, which consists of lines 15-19. To make a general structure, you can remove lines 15-19 and create a new page segment called `loggedinBody.jsp` as shown in Listing 11-6. Notice the `include` directive on the first line to add tag library definitions. You need the `include` directive because of the custom tags in the page. Each tile that is a JSP page must be complete enough that the JSP engine can convert the code in the tile to a Java class.

Listing 11-6 loggedinBody.jsp

```
<%@ include file="taglibs.jsp" %>
<H2>
    <fmt:message key="loggedin.msg">
        <fmt:param value='${requestScope.userName}' />
    </fmt:message>
</H2>
```

Now you can use the structure to create a template. To do so, you need to understand a couple of the Tiles tags, in particular, the `tiles:insert` and the `tiles:getAsString` tags. The `tiles:insert` tag is used specifically in the template page. This tag tells the Tiles framework to insert a tile identified by the `name` attribute into the structure at a specific point. Note that the `name` attribute is not the name of a tile or page segment, but an ID that the JSP page that references the template will use.

The `tiles:getAsString` tag allows you to pass a value to the structure and substitute that value for the tag. In a sense, this tag is a parameter-passing mechanism for templates. To understand the functionality of both of these tags, look at the JSP page that uses the template, as shown in Listing 11-7.

Listing 11-7 Simplified JSP Structure Defined as a Tiles Template, mainTemplate.jsp

```
1 <!-- begin the taglib definitions -->
2 <%@ include file="taglibs.jsp" %>
3 <!-- end the taglib definitions -->

4 <html:html locale="true"/>
5 <head>
6     <!-- begin the header for the application -->
7     <fmt:setBundle basename="ApplicationResources" />
8     <title><tiles:getAsString name="title"/></title>
9
10</head>

11<body>

12    <!-- begin the logo for the application -->
13    <tiles:insert attribute='logo'/>

14    <!-- begin the body -->
15    <tiles:insert attribute='body'/>

16    <!-- begin the footer for the application -->
17    <tiles:insert attribute='footer'/>

18</body>
19</html>
```

In examining this example, notice that it is a valid JSP page. The JSP page defines a structure that all pages that reference the template will contain. In addition:

- Line 8: Specifies a parameter with the name of `title` that should be converted to a `String` (if necessary) and inserted at this point.
- Lines 13, 15, and 17: Tell the Tiles framework that these are named insertion points for content that will be provided by a JSP page that uses the template.

When you have defined the template, you can create JSP pages that will use the template to flesh out the page. Continuing with the preceding example, Listing 11-8 shows a `loggedin.jsp` page using Tiles and the template that we defined in Listing 11-7. This page has the same look and feel, content, and functionality as the page described in Listing 11-5, which uses `includes`. But notice the difference in size between Listing 11-8 and 11-5.

Listing 11-8 loggedin.jsp Page Using Tiles

```
1 <%@ include file="taglibs.jsp" %>
2
3 <tiles:insert page='mainTemplate.jsp' flush='true'>
4     <tiles:put name="title">
5         <fmt:setBundle basename="ApplicationResources" />
6         <fmt:message key="loggedin.title"/>
7     </tiles:put>
8     <tiles:put name='logo'   value='logo.jsp'/>
9     <tiles:put name='body'   value='loggedinBody.jsp'/>
10    <tiles:put name='footer' value='footer.jsp'/>
11</tiles:insert>
```

This example uses the template (`mainTemplate.jsp`) that we defined in Listing 11-7 to provide the structure for the page. Note the following items in Listing 11-8:

- Line 3: The `tiles:insert` tag references the template with the `page` attribute. Everything in the body of the `tiles:insert` tag is used to flesh out the template with content.
- Lines 4–7: Define an attribute whose name is `"title`" and whose value will be the result of evaluating the two tags (lines 5 and 6) in the `tiles:put` body. As with other similar examples in this book, you will end up with a message string.
- Lines 8–10: Define the content to associate with the `"logo"`, `"body"`, and `"footer"` attributes, respectively. This content will replace the corresponding `tiles:insert` tags in the template. With the exception of `loggedinBody.jsp`, the JSP files are the same ones (Listings 11-3 and 11-4) defined in the preceding section. The `loggedinBody.jsp` of Listing 11-6 consists of the specific body content found in the example in Listing 11-5.

In Figure 11-2 we represent graphically how this process might work when considering multiple presentation pages using one template and sharing various tiles.

The beauty of the Tiles approach is in the following benefits:

- **Guaranteed consistency in the look-and-feel of the Web application:** Because all pages in the site get their structure from one template or another, the page appearance is consistent with the appearance defined in the template. Changing the look-and-feel is as simple as modifying the underlying template file.
- **Ease of maintenance:** Changing the content is also easy. Modifying a tile used everywhere (such as `footer.jsp`) pushes those changes to all pages that reference the tile. Changing the content used by only one page (for example `loggedinBody.jsp`) is also easier because that information is isolated from other content.

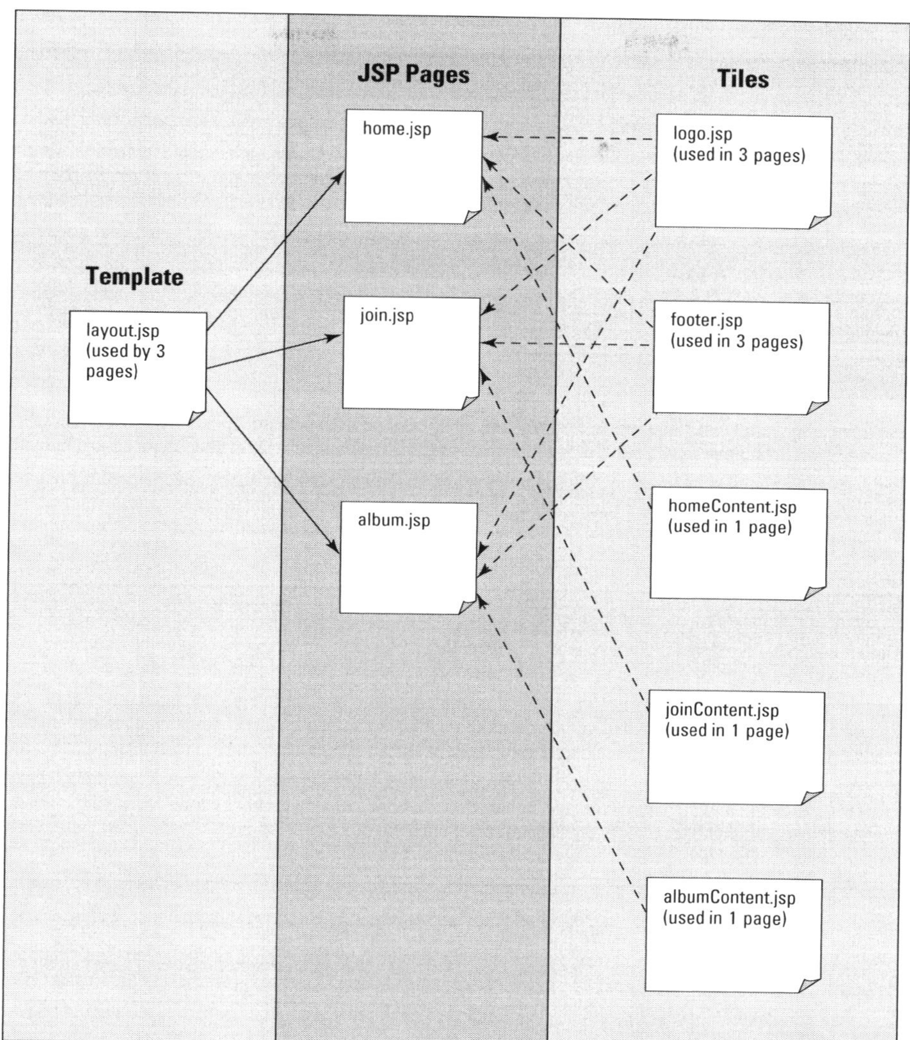

Figure 11-2: Diagram showing page composition using the Tile framework.

Configuring Tiles

You need to attend to a few configuration issues to use the Tiles framework with Struts. The Tiles library is already included in the Struts framework, so that is one less thing to worry about. But you do need to perform the following steps:

1. **Put the tiles TLD file (`struts-tiles.tld`) in with all the other TLD files, usually in the `WEB-INF` folder.**

You can find this file in the `tiles-documentation.war` file that comes with the Struts 1.1 distribution.

2. **Update the `web.xml` file to include a reference to the `struts-tiles.tld` file.**

   Here's an example of what a reference might look like:

   ```
   <taglib>
     <taglib-uri>/WEB-INF/struts-tiles.tld</taglib-uri>
     <taglib-location>/WEB-INF/struts-tiles.tld</taglib-
           location>
   </taglib>
   ```

3. **Include a tiles `taglib` reference in any page that uses Tiles tags.**

One thing that you may have noticed is that this technique requires two pages for each presentation page in the application. One page is the page definition (such as `loggedin.jsp`) and the other is the unique content (such as `loggedinBody.jsp`). This can be an added maintenance issue with large sites. Fortunately, the Tiles framework has a solution called *definitions,* which allow you to specify all the attributes that go to make up a Tile in a reusable structure.

Tiles definitions

A Tile definition page is remarkably similar in structure to a root Tile page. The principle difference is the use of the `tiles:definition` tag instead of the `tile:insert` tag. Listing 11-9 shows an example of a definition in a JSP page.

Listing 11-9 Tile Definition Using JSP

```
1 <%@ include file="taglibs.jsp" %>
2
3 <tiles:definition id="loggedin" page='mainTemplate.jsp'>
4     <tiles:put name="title">
5         <fmt:setBundle basename="ApplicationResources" />
6         <fmt:message key="loggedin.title"/>
7     </tiles:put>
8     <tiles:put name='logo'   value='logo.jsp'/>
9     <tiles:put name='body'   value='loggedinBody.jsp'/>
10    <tiles:put name='footer' value='footer.jsp'/>
11</tiles:definition>
```

The definition is mostly the same as the Tile defined in Listing 11-8. The only difference is in line 3. In Listing 11-9, line 3 contains the `tiles:definition` tag along with one attribute named `id`. The `id` attribute enables you to reference the definition in other places. After the Tiles framework processes a definition, the definition is placed into the page scope (different scopes can be specified) as a JavaBean. From there, other pages can use the definition with the `tiles:insert` tag.

Here is an example of using the bean for creating a Tile:

```
<tiles:insert beanName="loggedin" flush="true" />
```

The result is a page that's identical to the page from Listing 11-8. That is well and good if you want to create a `loggedin` page, but what if you want to use different content for the title and body? No problem. You simply override the default `puts` with new ones. For example:

```
<tiles:insert beanName="loggedin" flush="true" >
    <tiles:put name="title>
        <fmt:setBundle basename="ApplicationResources" />
        <fmt:message key="musiclist.title"/>
    </tiles:put>
    <tiles:put name='body' value='musicListBody.jsp'/>
</tiles:insert>
```

This example replaces the definition's `puts` for the title and body with ones more appropriate for the desired page.

You can also create definitions that inherit from another definition. This makes reuse of definitions a reality. Listing 11-10 is an example of creating a root definition named `"main"` and a child definition named `"loggedin"`. The `"loggedin"` definition inherits all the properties that belong to `"main"` and extends it by adding two additional properties, `"title"` and `"body"`.

Listing 11-10 Tile Definition Using JSP with Example of Inheritance

```
<%@ include file="taglibs.jsp" %>

<tiles:definition id="main" page='mainTemplate.jsp'>
    <tiles:put name='logo'   value='logo.jsp'/>
    <tiles:put name='footer' value='footer.jsp'/>
</tiles:definition>

<tiles:definition name="loggedin" extends="main" >
    <tiles:put name="title">
        <fmt:setBundle basename="ApplicationResources" />
        <fmt:message key="loggedin.title"/>
    </tiles:put>
    <tiles:put name='body'   value='loggedinBody.jsp'/>
</tiles:definition>
```

Admittedly, using a JSP page to create definitions is a bit awkward, and it doesn't really address the issue of reuse very well. You could put all the Tile definitions into a single JSP file (much like we did with tag library definitions) and include the JSP file for each Tile that you want to create using definitions. This works but is inefficient, because each time you load a page, the loading mechanism recreates the definitions. A better method is to use an XML document to create the definitions and then load and build them when the Web application starts.

Using XML for Tile definitions

The syntax for creating a definition in XML and in JSP is remarkably similar. For example, Listing 11-11 duplicates the definitions shown in Listing 11-9 using JSP.

Listing 11-11 Tile Definition Using an XML Configuration File Named tileDefinitions.xml

```
<?xml version="1.0" encoding="ISO-8859-1" ?>

<!DOCTYPE tiles-definitions PUBLIC
     "-//Apache Software Foundation//DTD Tiles Configuration
           1.1//EN"
    "http://jakarta.apache.org/struts/dtds/tiles-
           config_1_1.dtd">
<tiles-definitions>

  <!-- main definition -->
  <definition name="main " path="/mainTemplate.jsp">
      <put name="logo"   value="logo.jsp" />
      <put name="footer" value="footer.jsp" />
  </definition>

  <!-- loggedin definition -->
  <definition name="loggedin" extends="main">
      <put name="title"  value="loggedinTitle.jsp" />
      <put name="body"   value="loggedinBody.jsp" />
  </definition>

</tiles-definitions>
```

Besides the small syntax changes and the use of a slash (/) in front of the `path`, we had to write another small JSP page to get the proper title information, as shown in Listing 11-12. You can't know what the proper title string should be in the XML file because the string is `Locale` dependent.

Listing 11-12 Defining the Title, loggedinTitle.jsp

```
<%@ include file="taglibs.jsp" %>
<fmt:setBundle basename="ApplicationResources" />
<fmt:message key="loggedin.title"/>
```

To make use of the Tiles configuration file, you need to adjust the Struts configuration a little bit by adding a new plug-in. The `TilesPlugin` processes definitions in a centralized file. In its simplest form, the `TilesPlugin` takes no parameters. The plug-in assumes that the Tiles configuration XML file is named `"tileDefinitions.xml"`. Here is the line to add to the `struts-config.xml` file:

```
<plug-in className="org.apache.struts.tiles.TilesPlugin" />
```

After you decide to use XML Tiles definitions, you also commit to using the special Tiles version of the `RequestProcessor` class, `TilesRequestProcessor`. You don't have to do anything more — the plug-in takes care of everything. However, if you've already replaced `RequestProcessor` with your own custom class, your class needs to extend `TilesRequestProcessor` instead of `RequestProcessor`.

The final step in this process that makes it all worthwhile is changing the `forward`s in the actions in `struts-config.xml`. Normally, `forward`s refer to a destination JSP file where control will be forwarded to when an action has completed. However, now we can specify also a definition of where control should be forwarded to. For example, instead of the normal `success forward` in our `Login` action, you use this:

```
<forward name="success" path="loggedin"/>
```

The `path` is the name of the Tile definition where control should be forwarded.

To summarize, to use Tile definitions in an XML format, you should do the following:

1. **Create your definitions in** `tileDefinitions.xml`**.**

   This file should be in the `WEB-INF` folder. Other names for the file could be used, but you must notify the system of those names when defining `TilesPlugin`.

2. **Add the** `TilesPlugin` **class as a plug-in to the** `struts-config.xml` **file.**

   Remember that if you've already defined a custom `RequestProcessor`, the custom class must extend `TilesRequestProcessor` instead of `RequestProcessor`.

3. **For each forward element that you want to forward to a Tiles definition, modify the path to refer to the definition ID.**

Using Tile definitions allow you to eliminate the need for a presentation JSP page, such as `loggedin.jsp`. Instead you can use an XML Tile definition as a replacement.

We've just covered the basics of the Tiles framework. This framework offers a robust and comprehensive solution to enforcing consistency and reducing maintenance for Struts applications. If you're interested in further details, look at the references found at the bottom of the Tiles documentation page on the Struts Web site:

```
jakarta.apache.org/struts/userGuide/dev_tiles.html
```

Chapter 12

Securing Your Application

In This Chapter

- Making your application responsible for security
- Handing over security responsibility to the container

If you're developing an application that has any pages or other resources that need restricted access, you need to decide on how to approach the issue of security. You can take one of two broad approaches to managing security in a Web application. You can make the application responsible for its own security issues or leave security issues to the Web container. As you see in the following sections, both approaches have their advantages and disadvantages.

In the issue of security, you need to be concerned with two matters:

- **Limiting access to a certain subset of users:** When users make a request and are granted permission to see the page or perform the operation, we say that they're *authorized.*
- **Making sure users are who they say they are:** When users have been verified to be who they say they are, we say that they've been *authenticated.*

Therefore, the two issues of security are authorization and authentication.

Making the Application Responsible

When the application is responsible for its own security, it must ensure that the user has been authenticated and is authorized to view the page or perform the action before allowing access to that page or operation. The application can respond in one of the following ways:

- If the user is authenticated but not authorized, the application denies access to the user and forwards the user to a "You can't do that" page.
- If the user has not yet been authenticated, the application forwards the user to a login page.

Logging in and authenticating a user

When a user requests or is referred to a login page, he or she enters the appropriate username and password for the Web site. When the user submits the form, the application uses the values in the username and password fields to authenticate the user by testing the values against a list of valid username and passwords. This list could be in memory, in an SQL database, in an LDAP (Lightweight Directory Access Protocol) server, or just about anywhere else on the network you could think of.

When the application has authenticated the user, the authentication information is typically stored somewhere (usually in the session). Then the next time the user requests a protected page, the security mechanism can first check to see whether the user has already been authenticated. If so, the application processes the requested page. Otherwise, the application forwards the user to the login page.

Authorizing a user

After authentication, the next task is authorization. In many Web applications, authentication and authorization may be the same — pages and operations are open to all authenticated users. After authentication is complete, further authorization is unnecessary.

However, if you have many levels or classes of users, each of whom can view different pages or perform different operations, you need an authorization procedure when those requests come up.

Authentication and authorization in Struts

You need to perform authentication and authorization checks, each time a user requests a protected page or operation. What is an effective way to manage these checks in a Struts application?

One approach is to insert an authentication check at the beginning of any `Action` class that you need to protect. Here is a code segment that shows how you can perform this check:

```
HttpSession session = request.getSession();
User user = (User) session.getAttribute("user");
// ensure that user has been authenticated
if (user == null)
{
    return (mapping.findForward("login"));
}
```

When a user is authenticated, a `User` object representing the user is placed in the user's session with the key, `"user"`. In this way, whenever you need to check a user's authentication, you just need to get the `User` object out of the session (Lines 1 & 2). If the `User` object is available (Line 3), you can assume that the user was previously authenticated. If the User object is not available (Line 3), you know that the user needs to be authenticated and can forward him or her to the login page (Line 4).

Authorization, if necessary, requires that you consider the permissions that have been granted to the user in relation to the requested page or operation. This means that before performing an operation, the code must check to see whether the current user is authorized to perform that operation.

One approach is to encapsulate the permissions granted to the user into the `User` object created at login time. These could take the form of boolean values for the possible permissions. For example, you could have a Web application that has three levels of users, each of which is allowed to view different pages in the application. Besides the standard user, suppose that you have department head users and administrative users. Therefore, you can have two boolean properties in the `User` object that indicate this, `departmentHead` and `administrator`. You can reference them with the methods `isDepartmentHead` and `isAdministrator`.

Now when you want to check the authorization level of the user before displaying a page, you can do something like the following in the `Action` class:

```
1 HttpSession session = request.getSession();
2 User user = (User) session.getAttribute("user");
  // authenticate the user
  ...

  // ensure that user is an administrator authorized
  // to perform this operation
3 if (!user.isAdministrator())
  {
4     return (mapping.findForward("unauthorized"));
  }
  // begin modification of logins
  ...
```

This is a reasonable approach if you have a small Web application that's not going to get much bigger. If the application does become much larger, however, the drawbacks are considerable because you have authorization code interspersed throughout many `Action` classes.

Customizing the RequestProcessor Class

For larger Web applications, another approach is to centralize the authentication process in one class.

The RequestProcessor class is one of the key classes in the Controller layer. (For more information about the RequestProcessor class, see "Processing Requests" in Chapter 4.) This class handles all requests for the Struts application and is therefore an ideal location to place an authentication function. The Struts developers must have had this use in mind when they added an *extension point* (a dummy method made to be overridden in a subclass) to the class.

The RequestProcessor class has a method named processPreprocess that does nothing in the class (other than return true) and exists only to be overridden by you. Here is the method signature:

```
protected boolean processPreprocess(HttpServletRequest request,
                                    HttpServletResponse response)
```

Each time RequestProcessor processes a request, it calls the process Preprocess method. Normally, nothing happens. However, here is an ideal place to add any kind of preprocessing actions that you would like to occur for each request — such as authentication.

Listing 12-1 shows how you might extend the RequestProcessor class and override the processPreprocess method to include authentication. We subclass the RequestProcessor class to create CustomRequestProcessor.

Listing 12-1 Overriding the processPreprocess Method of the CustomRequestProcessor Class

```
protected boolean processPreprocess(HttpServletRequest request,
                                    HttpServletResponse response)
{
  boolean continueProcessing = true;    // assume success
  // Test if the request is a login request
  try
  {
      HttpSession session = null;
      // ensure that the user's session has not timed out
      if(request.isRequestedSessionIdValid())
          session = request.getSession();
      else    // user's session has timed out, make them login again
          response.sendRedirect("login.jsp");
      // get the current request's path
      String path = processPath(request, response);
      // don't do any testing if user is logging on
      if ( !path.equals((String) "/login"))
      {
          // get the user bean
          User user = (User) session.getAttribute("user");
          // ensure that user has logged on
          if (user == null)    // else make them login first
          {
```

```
23                try
24                {
25                    response.sendRedirect("login.jsp");
26                }
27                catch(Exception ioe)
28                {
29                    log.error("problem redirecting in processPreprocess - " +
                                ioe.getMessage());
30                }
31                continueProcessing = false;
32            }
33        }
34    }
35    catch(Exception ioe)
36    {
37        log.error("problem processing path - " + ioe.getMessage());
38        continueProcessing = false;
39    }
40    return continueProcessing;
41}
```

Here's how this code works:

- Line 9: The overridden `processPreprocess` method first makes sure that the user's session has not timed out and is still valid.
- Line 12: If the session has timed out, the user is redirected to the `login.jsp` page to log on again.
- Line 14: We get the current request path to determine whether the user may be trying to log on right now. The `processPath` method is inherited from the superclass `RequestProcessor`. If the user is trying to log on, we skip all the authentication code in Lines 16-33 and just let the request go through.
- Lines 19 and 21: If the request is anything other than the login page, we ensure that we have a `User` object before continuing.
- Line 25: If we do not have a user object, the user has not yet logged on, so we redirect the user to the `login.jsp` page.

Every request handled by Struts executes this code. The approach used in Listing 12-1 may not be an appropriate solution if you have a mixture of protected and unprotected pages handled by Struts, because in that case you need to disregard requests for unprotected pages. If you have HTML pages or non-Struts JSP pages that need protection, this approach will not work because it handles only requests that come through the Struts controller. Furthermore, this approach does not address the issue of authorization specific to particular lines of code in the `Action` class.

The final step is to inform Struts of the new RequestProcessor by adding it to the struts-config.xml file, as shown here.

```
<!-- ========== Controller Definition ========================== -->
<controller processorClass="dummies.struts.CustomRequestProcessor" />
```

The controller definition comes right after the action-mappings definition in the configuration file.

Declaring Security in Your Web Container

The J2EE specification defines a *declarative security* mechanism in which application security is expressed in a declarative syntax in the configuration files. Using declarative security, Web containers can provide both authentication and authorization services for Web applications running in the Web container. You can use these services with Struts applications.

Four basic steps need to happen for the container's declarative security to work. We discuss each of these steps in detail in this section.

Step 1 — Setting up the roles

The first step is to define the roles that your application will use. Roles are a way of grouping users. A *role* represents a set of permissions that you want to apply to a certain group of users. For example, a purchasing Web application might have three categories of users: Regular users create purchase orders, department heads approve purchase orders, and administrators add and delete users from the system. Regular users and department heads should not be able to add or remove users. Regular users and administrators should not be able to approve purchase orders. To accommodate these three types of users, you might define a role for each group of users — standard, depthead, and admin.

Step 2 — Defining the realms

The second step is to define a realm in the Web container's server.xml file. A *realm* identifies a set of users, their passwords, and their associated roles. Four types of realms are possible, depending on how you set up your user information:

- **UserDatabaseRealm:** The simplest but least flexible and secure choice. In this scenario, usernames, passwords, and roles are kept in a static file that is loaded into the Web container's memory at startup. For Tomcat, this file defaults to `tomcat-users.xml`.
- **JDBCRealm:** If you keep your username, passwords, and roles in an SQL or other database, using `JDBCRealm` makes sense. You must have two tables for user information: one for usernames and passwords and the other for the associated roles given to users.
- **JNDIRealm:** Use this realm if you use an LDAP (Lightweight Directory Access Protocol) server. JNDI (Java Naming and Directory Interface) is the standard for Java access to LDAP servers. `JNDIRealm` gives you all the options you need to look up usernames, passwords, and roles from the LDAP server.
- **JAASRealm:** JAAS (Java Authentication and Authorization Service) provides an implementation of the PAM (Pluggable Authentication Module) framework that allows applications to remain independent of the authentication and authorization implementation. You can find this service in J2EE SDK 1.4 and above.

Suppose that you have a database that contains all your users, their login names, and their passwords. Because `JDBCRealm` covers this type of database, you would choose `JDBCRealm` in the `server.xml` file. To accommodate the roles, you need to create a new database table to hold the same login names and their associated roles. If a user has more than one role, you need one row containing the user name and role for each role. The table structures would look like Figure 12-1.

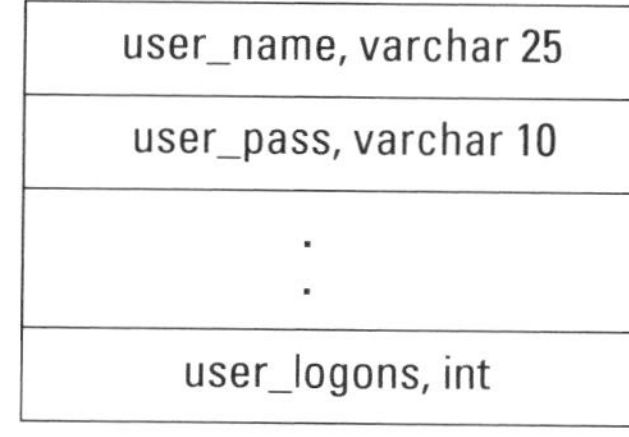

Figure 12-1: Table structures for users and roles.

Here are some example rows of data for each table:

users table

user_name	*user_pass*
bjohnson	indigo
clrook	lucy12$

userRoles table

user_name	*role_name*
bjohnson	admin
clrook	depthead

After you defined and populated the tables, you need to define JDBCRealm for the database you're using in the server.xml file. The server.xml file already has definitions (commented out) for several of the most common databases — MySQL, Oracle, and the generic database connected with ODBC. In Listing 12-2, we modify the sample JDBCRealm definition for MySQL and put it into use.

Listing 12-2 JDBCRealm Definition for MySQL in server.xml

```
1 <Realm  className="org.apache.catalina.realm.JDBCRealm"
2         debug="99"
3         driverName="com.mysql.jdbc.Driver"
4         connectionURL="jdbc:mysql://localhost/Purchasing"
5         connectionName="webpurchasing"
6         connectionPassword="bigmoma2"
7         userTable="users"
8         userNameCol="user_name"
9         userCredCol="user_pass"
10        userRoleTable="userRoles"
roleNameCol="role_name" />
```

Note the following lines from Listing 12-2:

- Line 1: Specifies the fully qualified class name of the realm that we're defining — in this case, JDBCRealm.
- Line 2: Sets the debug level to the lowest possible setting.
- Lines 3 and 4: Specify the database driver and connection URL, respectively.
- Lines 5 and 6: Specify the username and password used to connect to the database.
- Line 7: Names the table that contains the username and password information.
- Lines 8 and 9: Name the username and password column names.
- Line 10: Names the table that contains the user roles.
- Line 11: Names the column that contains the role. The column in this table that contains the username must have the same name as the column that contains the username in the user table. In this case, the column in this table that contains the username is named "user_name".

All of these definitions let the container know how to access the user and role information for authentication and authorization. Because the container is managing security and we are using the JDBCRealm, the database driver must be available. Therefore, the driver should be placed somewhere on the container's classpath. For Tomcat, place the driver in the common/lib folder.

You can define only one realm for the Web container. Every application that uses container-based security must use that same realm.

Step 3 — Specifying authorization areas

The third step in the process is to declare the areas in the application that you want to protect by modifying the application's `web.xml` file. When using Struts applications, you can make these declarations in two areas: in the `struts-config.xml` file to protect Struts actions and in the `web.xml` file to protect other resources, such as JSP, HTML, and image files.

Struts use of user roles for authorization

You can protect a Struts `Action` in the container-based security scheme using the `roles` attribute in the `action` tag. `RequestProcessor` always checks to see whether an `Action` is protected with a role. If it is protected, `RequestProcessor` checks to make sure that the user's role matches one of the permitted roles before `Action` is called. Note that you do not have to subclass `RequestProcessor` using this security approach.

Here is a code snippet from a `struts-config.xml` file:

```
<action path="/acctlist"
        type="com.othenos.purchasing.struts.AcctListAction"
        name="acctListForm"
        scope="session"
        input="/acctlist.jsp"
        roles="admin,depthead">
    <forward name="errors" path="/acctlist.jsp"/>
    <forward name="success" path="/acctlist.jsp"/>
</action>
```

Note the `roles` attribute in the `action` definition. This attribute specifies that only users who have either `admin` or `depthead` roles may execute this `action`.

General-purpose authorization

Use the `web.xml` file to protect all the other resources that you can't protect with `struts-config`. The purpose of the `security-constraint` tag is to define an area in the Web application that should be protected from general use. The syntax for the `security-constraint` tag follows:

```
<!ELEMENT security-constraint (display-name?, web-resource-collection+,
                              auth-constraint?, user-data-constraint?)>
<!ELEMENT display-name (#PCDATA)>
<!ELEMENT web-resource-collection (web-resource-name, description?, url-
            pattern*,
                                  http-method*)>
```

```
<!ELEMENT web-resource-name (#PCDATA)>
<!ELEMENT description (#PCDATA)>
<!ELEMENT url-pattern (#PCDATA)>
<!ELEMENT http-method (#PCDATA)>
<!ELEMENT auth-constraint (description?, role-name*)>
<!ELEMENT description (#PCDATA)>
<!ELEMENT role-name (#PCDATA)>
<!ELEMENT user-data-constraint (description?, transport-guarantee)>
<!ELEMENT description (#PCDATA)>
<!ELEMENT transport-guarantee (#PCDATA)>
```

The syntax is not quite as complex as it might first appear. Many of the elements are optional. For each area that you want to protect, you use a `security-constraint` tag to define the area. For each `security-constraint` tag, you need at least one `web-resource-collection` tag that describes the area to be protected.

Suppose that you want to protect a folder (`/admin`) that contains some JSP pages for use by users in only the `admin` role. It might look like this:

```
<security-constraint>
    <web-resource-collection>
        <web-resource-name>
            Administrative Area
        </web-resource-name>
        <url-pattern>
            /admin/*.jsp
        </url-pattern>
    </web-resource-collection>
    <auth-constraint>
        <role-name>admin</role-name>
    </auth-constraint>
</security-constraint>
```

The sequence of tags in configuration files in important. Refer to Chapter 7 for information on a particular tag.

The `web-resource-name` tag is used only for identification for human readers. The `url-pattern` tag defines the context-relative portion of the URL that indicates a protected area. To protect all resources in the `admin` folder, don't include `.jsp`. The `auth-constraint/role-name` tag defines which user roles may have access to these protected resources.

To find out more about the `security-constraint` tag, browse or download the J2EE 1.4 Tutorial at `java.sun.com/j2ee/1.4/docs`.

Step 4 — Defining authentication methods

The last step is defining the authentication mechanism to use. When a user accesses a protected area, the container first determines whether the user has been authenticated. If not, the container performs authentication based on one of the four authentication methods selected. The four possible authentication methods are:

- **BASIC:** If you choose BASIC authentication, the Web container uses the standard HTTP basic authentication. This means the Web browser asks the user for a username and a password. The password goes across the network in base64-encoded text.
- **DIGEST:** The DIGEST form of authentication uses a more robust encryption method to send the passwords across the network. However, this form of authentication is more complex to set up and prone to problems with the current 4.*x* versions of Tomcat.
- **FORM:** In the FORM style of authentication, you provide both the login form and the error form (in case the login has problems). Unless you're using SSL (Secure Sockets Layer, that is, HTTPS), passwords go across the network unencrypted.
- **CLIENT-CERT:** This form of authentication requires the use of SSL. During authentication, the browser is asked to present an X.509 client certificate in lieu of the user typing a username and password combination. CLIENT-CERT is a complex topic, so we do not discuss it in detail. To read more about this and other forms of authentication, look at the J2EE tutorial at java.sun.com/j2ee/1.4/docs.

The web.xml file has a login-config tag that you use to define the authentication method. Here is the syntax of the tag:

```
<!ELEMENT login-config (auth-method?, realm-name?, form-login-config?)>
<!ELEMENT auth-method (#PCDATA)>
<!ELEMENT realm-name (#PCDATA)>
<!ELEMENT form-login-config (form-login-page, form-error-page)>
<!ELEMENT form-login-page (#PCDATA)>
<!ELEMENT form-error-page (#PCDATA)>
```

The auth-method tag refers to one of the four possible authentication methods: BASIC, DIGEST, FORM, or CLIENT-CERT. The realm-name tag is the name that will be displayed on the browser-supplied login form in BASIC or DIGEST forms of authentication.

If you choose the FORM type of authentication, you also need to supply the forms to display using the form-login-config tag. Specify the login form to use with the form-login-page tag. The error page should be defined in the form-error-page tag. Both the login and error pages are required if you use FORM based authentication.

Examples of declaring authorization and authentication

To integrate the information in this chapter, this section provides two examples of authorization and authentication.

Protecting the entire application with BASIC authentication

In the first example, we assume that every page of the application is protected from all users, except those who have the role of `admin`. We use the `BASIC` form of authentication, letting the browser display the login form. Here is the code snippet from `web.xml`:

```
<security-constraint>
    <web-resource-collection>
        <web-resource-name>
            All of Application
        </web-resource-name>
        <url-pattern>
            /*
        </url-pattern>
    </web-resource-collection>
    <auth-constraint>
        <role-name>admin</role-name>
    </auth-constraint>
</security-constraint>

<login-config>
    <auth-method>BASIC</auth-method>
    <realm-name>Login Sample Application</realm-name>
</login-config>
```

The `url-pattern` tag specifies that all resources of the application should be protected. The use of the `role-name` tag with the `admin` role specifies that only users with that role can access the pages. Figure 12-2 shows an example of a login form using BASIC authentication. Notice that the realm name is displayed in the login form.

Figure 12-2: BASIC authentication login screen.

Restricting access to two folders

In this example, we assume that a group of pages in the admin folder should be protected from all except those with admin roles. In addition, a group of accounting pages in the acct folder should be restricted to those users with the depthead or admin role. Again, we use the BASIC form of authentication, letting the browser display the login form. Here is the code snippet from web.xml:

```
<!--Security for Administrative pages -->
<security-constraint>
    <web-resource-collection>
        <web-resource-name>
            Administration
        </web-resource-name>
        <url-pattern>
            /admin/*
        </url-pattern>
    </web-resource-collection>
    <auth-constraint>
        <role-name>admin</role-name>
    </auth-constraint>
</security-constraint>

<!--Security for Accounting pages -->
<security-constraint>
    <web-resource-collection>
        <web-resource-name>
            Accounting
        </web-resource-name>
        <url-pattern>
            /acct/*
        </url-pattern>
    </web-resource-collection>
    <auth-constraint>
        <role-name>depthead</role-name>
        <role-name>admin</role-name>
    </auth-constraint>
</security-constraint>

<!-- Authorization BASIC -->
<login-config>
    <auth-method>BASIC</auth-method>
    <realm-name>Login Sample Application</realm-name>
</login-config>
```

The two secure areas are constrained so that only users with the proper roles can view them. One interesting thing to note is that we can switch realms in the server.xml file without having to change any settings in the web.xml file. So you could initially use UserDatabaseRealm and then change to JDBCRealm with no side effects on the security configuration in web.xml.

The steps in setting up container-based, declarative security can be summarized in these four steps:

1. Decide on the roles in which to group users based on the pages and actions each group should be able to access or perform.
2. Determine the authentication method to use — define the realm in the `server.xml` file. Make sure the appropriate user data is configured in the data source you are using.
3. Define the authorization areas in the application by configuring the `struts-config.xml` file. To define authorization on non-Struts resources, such as HTML files, use the `web.xml` file.
4. Set up the authentication method for the application in the `web.xml` file.

Part IV

Putting It All Together

The 5th Wave By Rich Tennant

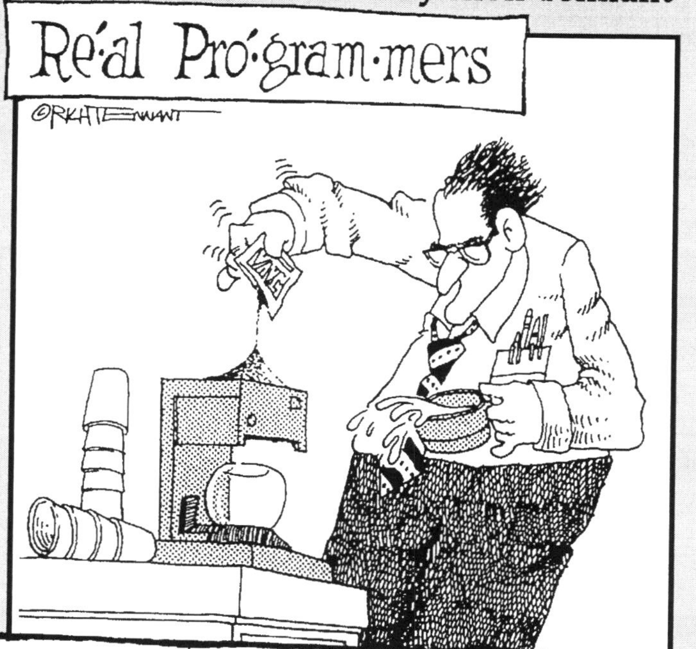

Real Programmers know plenty about Java but never know how to use the coffee machine.

In this part . . .

This is where we put together all the knowledge in the book into an example Web application. In Chapter 13, we explain the tools in Struts for creating a log that you can use to troubleshoot problems. (Of course, you never have any problems, right?) In Chapter 14, we explain the code that you need to create MusicCollection.com, an application that lets users create, store, and edit a list of their favorite albums online. Users need to register the first time they visit the site and log on for subsequent visits. Then they retrieve their list of albums from the database and add, edit, or delete entries. When they are finished, they can log off. After completing this application, you should be off and running, creating your own Web applications.

Chapter 13

Logging Your Actions

In This Chapter

- Advantages of logging
- Working with Commons logging
- Trying out Java 1.4 logging
- Getting familiar with Log4J

When an application is running, many events occur that would be valuable for you to know about. Some events might be in the area of security, such as knowing when and how frequently users log on and off. You might also want to know when error conditions occur. The benefits of logging are limited only by the creativity and imagination of the developer.

One way to track all this information is to write messages about the events in a place where you can look at them. Writing these messages on the system console, on a file on disk, in an e-mail message, or just about any place you can think of — is defined as *logging* the messages.

Logging for Everyone

Logging has been described as a low-tech debugging mechanism. That may be true, but logging can also be much more. Using logging, the developer can do the following, all without changing code:

- Provide useful information about the runtime state of the application
- Increase or decrease the amount of logging detail provided
- Vary the format of the logging information
- Send the logging information to a different destination
- Create multiple logs
- Turn logging on or off

Using Commons Logging

Fortunately, Struts provides the developer with a lot of flexibility when it comes to logging through the inclusion of the Commons Logging library — another of the many Jakarta projects — in the Struts library files.

Commons Logging is a lightweight framework that provides a common logging interface to any one of the many actual logging packages, such as Log4J and Java 1.4. This common interface enables you, the developer, to pick and choose the logging package that you want to use without having to worry about changing your code.

To use Commons Logging, make sure that the `commons-logging.jar` file is in your `WEB-INF/lib` directory. Import the `Log` and `LogFactory` classes in the source files that you want to include logging using the following:

```
import org.apache.commons.logging.Log;
import org.apache.commons.logging.LogFactory;
```

The two classes of interest in the Commons Logging package are the `Log` class, which performs the logging function, and the `LogFactory` class, which knows how to get an instance of the `Log` class. After you import the two logging classes, you need to get an instance of a `Log` from the `LogFactory` by passing the Class that is invoking the logger, using the following:

```
Log log = LogFactory.getLog(Login.class);
```

The `LogFactory` determines what type of logger to get based on the following steps:

1. Look for an attribute named `org.apache.commons.logging.Log` in the `common-logging.properties` file. If the attribute exists, use the associated value to choose the logger class. Otherwise, go to the next step. In this way you can explicitly define which logger implementation to use. For Log4J, use `org.apache.commons.logging.impl.Log4JLogger`. If you want the Java 1.4 logger, use the `org.apache.commons.logging.impl.Jdk14Logger` class.
2. Look for a system property named `org.apache.commons.logging.Log`. If the property is found, use the associated value to choose the logging implementation; the value should be one of the logger classes listed in Step 1. Otherwise, go to the next step.
3. If the Log4J logging system is available in `classpath`, use the corresponding `Log4JLogger` wrapper class. Otherwise, go to the next step.
4. If the application is running with JDK 1.4 or above, use the corresponding `Jdk14Logger` wrapper class. Otherwise, go to the next step.

5. Use the simple built-in logger called `SimpleLog`. `SimpleLog` sends all messages `to System.err`. You can configure this logger by setting various system properties. See the `org.apache.commons.logging.impl.SimpleLog` API documentation for further details. You may find the API documentation for the Commons Logging package at `jakarta.apache.org/commons/logging/api/index.html`.

You use the log instance to write messages to the log file. The messages are written based on the priority of the message. Following are the possible priorities from most severe to least severe:

- **Fatal:** Severe errors that cause termination of the application
- **Error:** Other runtime errors or unexpected conditions
- **Warn:** Use of deprecated APIs, poor use of API, other errors or situations that are unexpected but not necessarily wrong
- **Info:** Interesting runtime events, such as initialization or shutdown actions
- **Debug:** Detailed information on the flow of events in the application
- **Trace:** More detailed information than the Debug level

Each priority has a method by the same name with two different method signatures. For example, for the fatal priority, the methods are:

```
log.fatal(Object message);
log.fatal(Object message, Throwable t);
```

Each of the other priorities has method signatures like `fatal`. The determination whether or not to write the message to the log comes only when the method is called. The logger configuration specifies the lowest level of severity to write out. For example, if you choose the WARN level, the log file will contain only log messages with priorities of FATAL, ERROR, and WARN. In this way, you have control over how much information you log.

The ability to control the quality of logging information in the configuration file means that you can leave the logging code in the application without much of a performance effect. Only when you need more detailed information do you need to turn on the lower-level logging features.

The one disadvantage of leaving the log statements in the code is that a certain amount of overhead occurs when calling the methods even if the logging does not take place. To reduce that overhead, *code guard* methods are available to test the logging level and skip the calling of logging methods if that level is not enabled. The code guard methods are

```
logIsFatalEnabled()
logIsErrorEnabled()
logIsWarnEnabled()
logIsInfoEnabled()
```

```
logIsDebugEnabled()
logIsTraceEnabled()
```

Following is an example of using a code guard:

```
if (logIsInfoEnabled())
{
    log.info("Starting mail server.");
}
```

Using Java 1.4 Logging

By default, the configuration file for Java 1.4 logging is `logging.properties` in the `JRE/lib` directory. You can use an alternative means of reading the configuration file by specifying the file location and name in the `java.util.logging.config.file` system property. Look at the Java API documentation for the `java.util.logging.LogManager` class for further information on logging configuration.

You can set the following features in the configuration file:

- The priority level to log messages. INFO is the default.
- The handler to use when logging. The standard is to log to the console. An optional handler is available to log to a file. Other handlers are available to write to memory, an output stream, or a network stream.
- A SimpleFormatter or XML formatter. Use a formatter to format the log records.

The Java 1.4 logging offers more features than the `SimpleLog` implementation in Commons Logging but fewer features than Log4J.

Working with the Log4J Package

Log4J is a mature, industrial-strength logging package with a multitude of options. Chances are that this package will do everything you need and then some. Log4J is one of the many Jakarta open-source projects.

The configuration file for the Log4J logging package is `log4j.properties`. You usually place this file in the `WEB-INF/classes` folder. In addition, the Log4J library file, `log4j.jar`, needs to be present in the `WEB-INF/lib` folder. You may download the library file as well as sample configuration files from the Log4J Web site at jakarta.apache.org/log4j/docs/index.html

Documentation is also available at the site.

Log4J offers more logging options than the Java 1.4 logger, including where you write the files and how you format them. Listing 13-1 shows a sample of a Log4J configuration file that outputs to the console and to a rolling log file.

Listing 13-1 Sample Configuration File for Log4J

```
1 # The root category uses two appenders called stdout and R.
2 # The root category assumes the INFO priority for root.
3 # If the priority is not specified, it is DEBUG. The root
4 # category is the only category that has a default priority.

5 log4j.rootCategory=INFO, stdout, R

6 # stdout is set to be a ConsoleAppender which outputs to std out.

7 log4j.appender.stdout=org.apache.log4j.ConsoleAppender

8 # Configure stdout appender to use the PatternLayout
9 log4j.appender.stdout.layout=org.apache.log4j.PatternLayout

10 # Pattern to output the caller's filename and line number
11 log4j.appender.stdout.layout.conversionPattern =%d{DATE} %5p [%t] (%F:%L) -
            %m%n

12 # R is the RollingFileAppender that outputs to a rolling log
# file called rolling_log_file.log.

13 log4j.appender.R=org.apache.log4j.DailyRollingFileAppender
14 log4j.appender.R.File=${catalina.base}/logs/wp_log_file.log
15 log4j.appender.R.DatePattern='.'yyyy-MM-dd'.txt'

16 # Define a pattern layout for the file.
17 # For more information on conversion characters (i.e. d,p,t,c,l,m,n)
18 # please see the PatternLayout class of the Log4j API.

19 log4j.appender.R.layout=org.apache.log4j.PatternLayout
20 log4j.appender.R.layout.conversionPattern =%d{DATE} %5p [%t] (%F:%L) - %m%n
```

In Listing 13-1, note the following lines:

- Line 5: Specifies the priority of `INFO` using two appenders, `stdout` and `R`, which are defined later.
- Line 7: Specifies that `ConsoleAppender` be used with `stdout`. This means all messages will be written to the system console.
- Lines 9 and 11: Specify the format to use when writing out messages to `stdout`.

- Lines 13–15: Define the `R` appender as `DailyRollingLogAppender`. This means that for each 24-hour period, a new file will be created and the old one closed. You specify the file name and location, as well as the suffix that you want to append to the file after it has been rolled over. In this case, the suffix is the date followed by the `.txt` extension (such as 2003-11-27.txt).
- Lines 19–20: Specify that the format for the `R` appender will be identical to the `stdout` appender.

The configuration of Log4J offers many options. For detailed information on configuration issues, visit the Log4J Web site at `jakarta.apache.org/log4j/docs` and review the documentation.

Chapter 14

Creating the MusicCollection.com Application

In This Chapter

- Introducing the MusicCollection application
- Creating the database schema
- Configuring the data source
- Creating the pages
- Logging on
- Creating a user account
- Displaying albums
- Creating, editing, and deleting albums
- Logging off the program
- Handling exceptions in different ways
- Running the program

This chapter shows you how to create a complete application using Jakarta Struts. To create this demonstration application. you need to apply most of the concepts and techniques we have explored throughout the book. You don't need to retype the code — you can find the complete code for the MusicCollection.com application at the *Jakarta Struts For Dummies* Web site at `www.dummies.com/go/jakarta`.

Description of the Application

The hypothetical MusicCollection.com application enables registered users to create and maintain a list of their favorite music. In the application, we call each listing an *album*.

The prospective user must *join* the Web site by entering a small amount of personal information, such as name, e-mail address, and a password. Subsequent visits to the site require users to log on using their e-mail address and password.

After the user has logged on, the application retrieves a list of his or her albums from the database and displays this list. The user may modify or delete an album or create one. The application immediately updates all changes or additions in the database and displays the resulting album list.

When finished, users may log off to remove their connection to the system. If an error should occur during the processing of a request, the application displays an appropriate error page.

Figure 14-1 shows the various pages and relationships that go to make up the application.

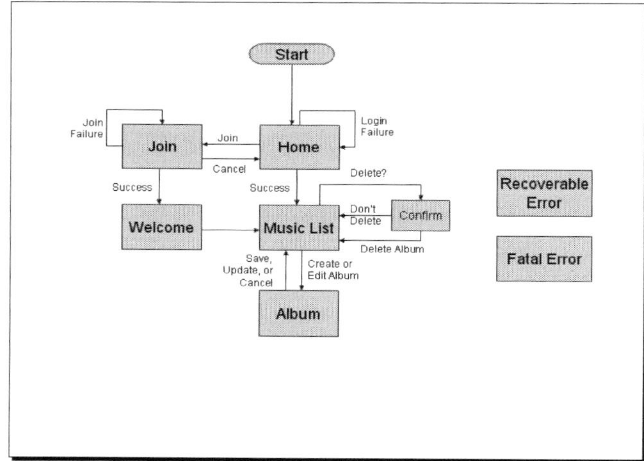

Figure 14-1: High-level view of the application's Web site.

To maximize your exposure to the various capabilities and techniques discussed throughout the book, we have made several design decisions about what should go into the application. These decisions are to

- Develop the pages with a common look-and-feel through the page composition technique of using `includes` (Chapters 6 and 11)
- Use I18N throughout the application (Chapter 6)
- Maximize the use of the JSTL and Struts-EL tag libraries (Chapter 10)
- Let Struts handle the creation of `ActionForms` by using its dynamic form capability (Chapter 6)

- Use the Validator plug-in to perform validation on the forms that need it (Chapter 9)
- Use a database to hold all application data (Chapter 5)
- Interact with the database using a `DataSource` managed by Struts (Chapter 5)
- Handle exceptions through the Struts declarative mechanism (Chapter 8)
- Write a custom `ExceptionHandler` to provide better exception logging (Chapter 8)
- Provide a common authorization mechanism implemented in a customized `RequestProcessor` (Chapter 12)
- Perform initialization actions during application startup and cleanly close the `DataSource` before application shutdown by creating a custom plug-in (Chapter 9)

Creating the Database Schema

One of the first steps in creating the application is defining the database scheme that you want to use. The primary purpose of the site is to manage lists of albums for individual users, so you can use one table for that purpose. We named the table `albums`. This table contains information about the albums, such as name, artist, year of release, type of media, and category of music. (You could add additional fields to the record structure if you want to track other types of data.) In addition, each database record has a unique ID, the user's ID, and the date and time of the record's creation. You see this table in Figure 14-2.

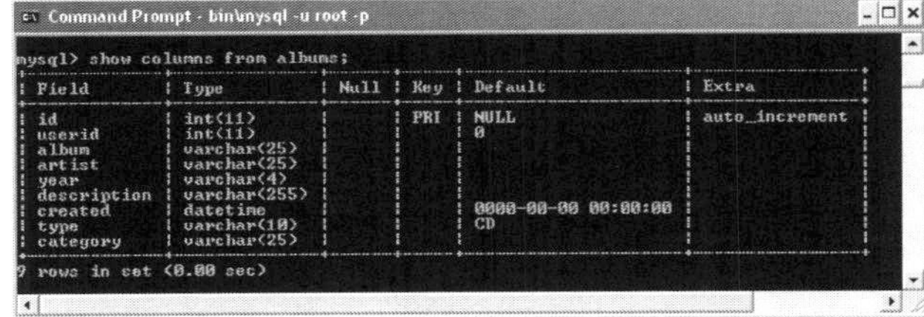

Command Prompt - bin\mysql -u root -p

mysql> show columns from albums;

Field	Type	Null	Key	Default	Extra
id	int(11)		PRI	NULL	auto_increment
userid	int(11)			0	
album	varchar(25)				
artist	varchar(25)				
year	varchar(4)				
description	varchar(255)				
created	datetime			0000-00-00 00:00:00	
type	varchar(10)			CD	
category	varchar(25)				

9 rows in set (0.00 sec)

Figure 14-2: The album table structure.

Because this site is for only registered users, you need a table to keep track of those who have registered. We called the table `users`. The primary information consists of the first and last name of the user, e-mail address, and password. In addition, we want to keep track of how often users log on, the last time they logged on, when records were created, and the unique ID for each the user. Figure 14-3 shows the structure of the `users` table.

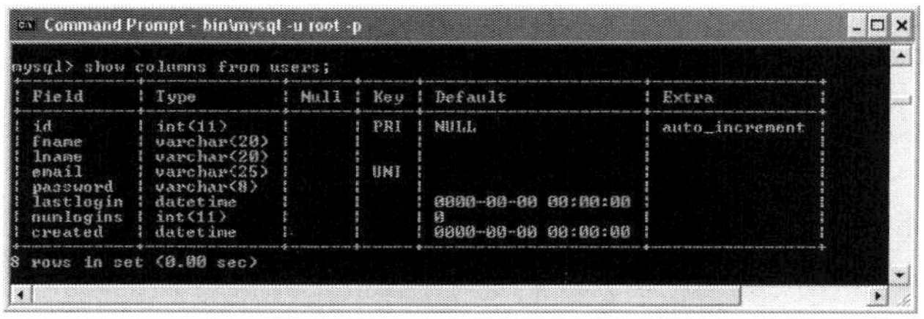

```
Command Prompt - bin\mysql -u root -p

mysql> show columns from users;
+-----------+-------------+------+-----+---------------------+----------------+
| Field     | Type        | Null | Key | Default             | Extra          |
+-----------+-------------+------+-----+---------------------+----------------+
| id        | int(11)     |      | PRI | NULL                | auto_increment |
| fname     | varchar(20) |      |     |                     |                |
| lname     | varchar(20) |      |     |                     |                |
| email     | varchar(25) |      | UNI |                     |                |
| password  | varchar(8)  |      |     |                     |                |
| lastlogin | datetime    |      |     | 0000-00-00 00:00:00 |                |
| numlogins | int(11)     |      |     | 0                   |                |
| created   | datetime    |      |     | 0000-00-00 00:00:00 |                |
+-----------+-------------+------+-----+---------------------+----------------+
8 rows in set (0.00 sec)
```

Figure 14-3: The users table structure.

Configuring DataSource

Because you're using a database to store user and album information, it makes sense to take advantage of the capability Struts has to manage `DataSources`, as discussed in Chapter 5. You may need to make slight modifications to the following configuration, depending on your database, driver, username, and password. Here is the definition of `DataSource` in the `struts-config` file for use with the MySQL database:

```
<!-- ========== DataSource Definitions =================================== -->
<data-sources>
    <data-source key="musiccollection"
            type="org.apache.commons.dbcp.BasicDataSource">
    <set-property property="description" value="Music Collection Database"/>
    <set-property property="driverClassName" value="com.mysql.jdbc.Driver"/>
    <set-property property="username" value="webuser"/>
    <set-property property="password" value="bigmoma"/>
    <set-property property="url" value="jdbc:mysql://localhost/musiccollection" />
    <set-property property="maxCount" value="8"/>
    <set-property property="minCount" value="2"/>
    </data-source>
</data-sources>
```

Creating the Pages and Associated Files

The application overview in Figure 14-1 shows that at least three pages have form data needing validation: `Login`, `Join`, and `Album`. As it turns out, the `MusicList` page also needs a form, although validation is not necessary.

For those three pages using the form validation features of the `Validator` plug-in, the dynamic forms will be of the `DynaValidatorForm` class. The `MusicList` dynamic form will be a `DynaActionForm` class, because it doesn't need validation.

The Web site should have a similar look-and-feel on every page. To achieve that goal, you can use one of the page composition techniques that we discuss in Chapter 11. Instead of using the Tiles technology, we have elected to use the `includes` technique to keep things simple. We will define common header and footer JSP files for each page of the Web site.

We use an iterative development process to build the example application. You could take many approaches to construct the various components. However, we find it useful to start with one page and implement as many of the related parts as reasonable (for example, `ActionForms`, Actions, beans, and configurations). The general steps to do this follow:

1. **Define and create the page.**

   Analyze the data needed for the page and create the JSP. All JSP pages should use the JSTL and Struts-EL tag libraries when needed. I18N should be included for every page.

2. **Configure the dynamic form, if necessary.**

   If the page contains form fields, define the associated dynamic form in the `struts-config` file. The dynamic form is either a `DynaValidatorForm` or a `DynaActionForm` class, depending on whether or not field validation is needed.

3. **Add the validation rules to `validation.xml`, if needed.**

   If a dynamic form needs a field or fields to be validated, define the field validators in the `validation.xml` file.

4. **Create the `Action` class, if needed.**

   All pages that need processing should have an `Action` class. Some pages may have two or more possible actions (for example, "new" and "update") that need to be handled in the `Action` class.

5. **Create the `Bean` class for the `Action`, if needed.**

   Pages that interact with the Model layer need to have a bean whose responsibility is to encapsulate all the interactions with the database. In most cases, you also need to create a Data Transfer Object (DTO).

6. **Configure action mapping for the `Action` class, if needed.**

   If an `Action` class is created, you need to define the action-mapping configuration in the `struts-config` file.

7. **Repeat steps 1 through 6 for each page in the Web site.**

Let's begin by looking at each of the pages that make up the Web site, starting with the `Home` page.

Logging On from the Home Page

The `Home` page serves an entry point for both registered and prospective users. As such, this page provides a form for the user to log on as well as a mechanism for prospective users to create a user account.

Because of the logon function, the `Home` page requires the following additional components:

- A dynamic form for the logon fields
- Validation of the fields using the `Validator` plug-in
- A `LoginAction` class to process the logon
- A `LoginBean` to interact with the database to authorize the user
- The use of a common authorization mechanism so that after the user is authorized, each page request easily verifies the user's status

Home page design

Let's sketch the content of the `Home` page to see what fields you need to include for user input. Clearly, you need to have fields available for the user to enter an e-mail address and a password. Furthermore, you need a button for the user to click to submit the information for logging on.

However, if the user has not yet registered for the `MusicCollection.com` service, the user needs to fill out a registration form to get a user account. Although a different page (the `Join` page) will gather this information, the `Home` page needs a button for the user to click to indicate the desire to join MusicCollection.com. Clicking the button should take the user to the `Join` page.

That is about all we need on the Login page. However, for eye appeal, you probably want to add some marketing text as well as images to the body of the page.

Because this application uses the `includes` page composition technique, the main page (`home.jsp`) defines the structure of the page and includes the header, footer, and body information from other files. The header and footer are common to all pages and reside in the `logo.jsp` and `footer.jsp` files, respectively. The body of the page will go into a separate JSP page named `homeContent.jsp`. We follow this convention in creating all JSP pages.

Figure 14-4 shows how the `Home` page looks.

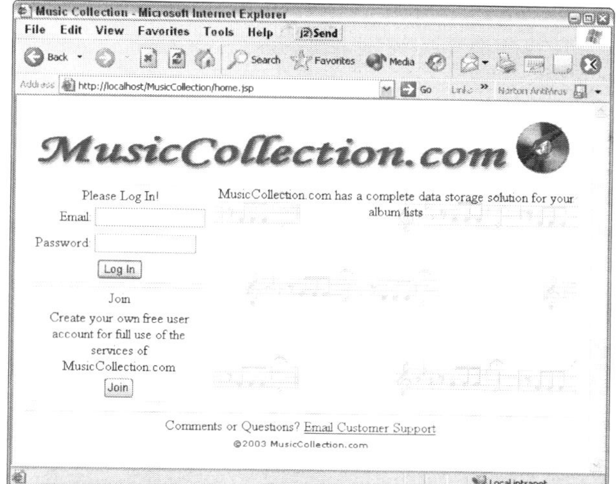

Figure 14-4: The Home page.

LoginForm

The next step is to define the dynamic form associated with the Login page. You define the dynamic `loginForm` in the `struts-config` file, as we explain in Chapters 6 and 9. The `loginForm` has only two fields associated with it: the `email` and `password` fields. The following code segment is the definition for `loginForm`:

```
<form-bean name="loginForm"
           type="org.apache.struts.validator.DynaValidatorForm">
    <form-property name="email"
                   type="java.lang.String"
                   initial=""/>
    <form-property name="password"
                   type="java.lang.String"
                   initial=""/>
</form-bean>
```

LoginValidation and validation.xml

You need to perform declarative validation on the two fields in `loginForm`. The `email` field is required and should look like an e-mail address. The `password` field is also required. In the `validation.xml` file, you specify the `validators` for the `loginForm` as follows:

```
<form name="loginForm">
    <field property="email"
           depends="required,email">
```

```
    <arg0  key="error.email.required"/>
    </field>

    <field property="password"
           depends="required">
    <arg0  key="error.password.required"/>
    </field>
</form>
```

LoginAction

The basic idea behind `LoginAction` is to take the user's `email` and `password` values and give them to `LoginBean` for authorization. If authorization is successful, `LoginAction` saves the user information in the session and forwards control to the `MusicList` page. If authorization fails, `LoginAction` creates an error message and returns control back to the `Home` page.

Because the user can also request to sign up for an account, you should add another button for joining. This button is actually a Cancel button that, when clicked, submits the login form and puts an attribute (`org.apache.struts.action.CANCEL`) with a value of `true` into the request. `LoginAction` looks for this attribute-value pair. If `LoginAction` finds this pair, it forwards control to the `join.jsp` page.

You could put a link on the `Home` page instead of a Cancel button. However, using a link exposes the URL of the `join.jsp` page to the public. Listing 14-1 shows the body of the execute method of `LoginAction`.

Listing 14-1 Body of the execute Method of LoginAction

```
// did the user click the Join button?
Boolean bCancel =
             (Boolean)request.getAttribute("org.apache.struts.action.CANCEL");
if(bCancel != null)
    if(bCancel.booleanValue())
        return (mapping.findForward("join"));

// create a new LoginBean passing the datasource
LoginBean lb = new LoginBean(getDataSource(request, "musiccollection"));

// check to see if this user/password combination are valid
// will return a non-null UserDTO if valid
UserDTO user = lb.validateUser((String)((DynaValidatorForm)form).get("email"),
                               (String)((DynaValidatorForm)form).get("password"));
if(user != null)
{
    // save UserDTO in session
    request.getSession().setAttribute("user",user);
    return (mapping.findForward("success"));
```

```
}
else   // username/password not validated
{
    // create ActionError and save in the request
    ActionErrors errors = new ActionErrors();
    ActionError error = new ActionError("error.login.invalid");
    errors.add("login",error);
    saveErrors(request,errors);
    return (mapping.findForward("failure"));
}
```

LoginBean, model layer, and exception handling

The purpose of LoginBean is to authorize the user. Therefore, when the LoginBean is instantiated, a reference to DataSource is passed to LoginBean. That reference is saved in an instance variable for use by the validateUsermethod.

To perform authorization, the validateUsermethod must query the database's user table for a record that matches the given e-mail and password values. If the validateUsermethod finds a record, it validates the user and returns a DTO for the user. The UserDTO is a class that holds user information in an object form, specifically the user's lname, fname, email, and id. If the user is not found in the user table, a null value is returned, indicating authorization failure.

Any exception that gets caught in the method is logged and, in turn, throws a ModuleException that is propagated up the calling stack until it reaches the ExceptionHandler for RequestProcessor.

Listing 14-2 shows the validateUser method of LoginBean.

Listing 14-2 validateUser Method of LoginBean

```
public UserDTO validateUser(String email, String password) throws
               ModuleException
{
    UserDTO user = null;
    Connection con = null;
    Statement stmt = null;
    ResultSet rs = null;
    String sQuery = "";
    try
    {
        con = dataSource.getConnection();
        stmt = con.createStatement();
```

(continued)

Listing 14-2 *(continued)*

```
        sQuery = "SELECT * FROM Users " + "WHERE email = '"
        sQuery += email + "' " + "AND password = '" + password + "'";
        rs = stmt.executeQuery(sQuery);
        if (rs.next())
        {
            // Create new user transfer object
            user = new UserDTO();
            user.setFirstName(rs.getString("fname"));
            user.setLastName(rs.getString("lname"));
            user.setId(rs.getInt("id"));
            user.setEmail(rs.getString("email"));

            // update user login information
            sQuery = "UPDATE Users SET lastlogin=now(),numlogins=numlogins+1
               where id="
            sQuery += user.getId();
            int result = stmt.executeUpdate(sQuery);
        }
    }
    catch (SQLException se)
    {
        log.error("Error in validating user.");
        log.error("SQL statement = " + sQuery);
        se.printStackTrace();
        ModuleException me = new ModuleException("error.db.sql");
        throw me;
    }

    finally
    {
        .
        . finally code omitted
        .
    }
    return user;
}
```

Action mapping configuration

Configuring the `struts-config` file for the `LoginAction` is straightforward. You have to make sure to turn on validation by setting the `validation` attribute to `true`.

You can take three possible directions from `LoginAction`:

- If authorization fails, return to the `home.jsp` page.
- If authorization succeeds, go to the `musiclist.do` action.
- If the user asks to join MusicCollection.com, go to the `join.jsp` page.

Here is the action mapping for LoginAction:

```
<action    path="/home"
           type="dummies.struts.music.LoginAction"
           name="loginForm"
           scope="request"
           input="/home.jsp"
           validate="true">
    <forward name="failure" path="/home.jsp"/>
    <forward name="success" path="/musiclist.do"/>
    <forward name="join" path="/join.jsp"/>
</action>
```

Continued User Authentication

Once the user has been authenticated, the application must continue to check the user's authorization for each protected page requested. As it turns out, every page except the Home and Join pages are protected.

To accomplish this, we use our example of how to write a custom Request Processor found in Chapter 12, "Customizing the RequestProcessor Class." You can use the processPreprocess method in that example as a place to start. As a reminder, the processPreprocess method is called for each request that comes through the Struts controller. If the request is not for the Home or Join pages, then you need to verify that the user has been previously authenticated by looking for a UserDTO object in the session. If the UserDTO object is not there, the user has not yet been authenticated and you need to redirect the request to the Home page so the user can log on.

Listing 14-3 shows the processPreprocess method.

Listing 14-3 processPreprocess Method of Custom RequestProcessor

```
protected boolean processPreprocess(HttpServletRequest request,
                                    HttpServletResponse response)
{
    boolean continueProcessing = true;

    // Test if the request is a login request
    try
    {
        HttpSession session = null;
        // make sure session has not timed out
        if(request.isRequestedSessionIdValid())
            session = request.getSession();
        else
            response.sendRedirect("home.jsp?invalid=yes");
```

(continued)

Listing 14-3 *(continued)*

```
        // get the current request path
        String path = processPath(request, response);

// if user is not trying to logon or join, make sure user has been authenticated
        if ((!path.equals((String) "/home"))&&( !path.equals((String) "/join")))
        {
            // get the user bean
            UserDTO user = (UserDTO) session.getAttribute("user");

            // insure user has logged on
            if (user == null)// else make them logon first
            {
                try
                {
                    response.sendRedirect("home.jsp?invalid=yes");
                }
                catch(Exception ioe)
                {
                    log.error("problem redirecting in processPreprocess - " +
                              ioe.getMessage());
                }
                continueProcessing = false;
            }
        }
    }
    catch(Exception ioe)
    {
        log.error("problem processing path - " + ioe.getMessage());
        continueProcessing = false;
    }

    return continueProcessing;
}
```

Struts is to be notified about the `CustomRequestProcessor` by adding it to the `struts-config` file, as follows:

```
<!-- ================== Controller Definition ============================ -->
<controller processorClass="dummies.struts.music.CustomRequestProcessor" />
```

Creating a User Account

In order to use the services of MusicCollection.com a prospective user must create an account. The `Join` page contains a form that the user fills out to create the account.

Join page

From the Home page, a prospective user can create an account by clicking the Join button and going to the Join page. The Join page provides a form for the prospective user to enter the personal information necessary to create the account. The necessary fields are first name, last name, e-mail, and password. Since the password value is always hidden while typing, it is always a good practice to have the user enter the password twice to reduce the possibility of typing errors. Therefore, you can also include one additional password validation field.

After entering all the information, the user clicks on the Join button to submit the form. If the account is successfully created, the Welcome page is displayed. If the user decides not to join, a Cancel button takes the user back to the Home page. See Figure 14-5.

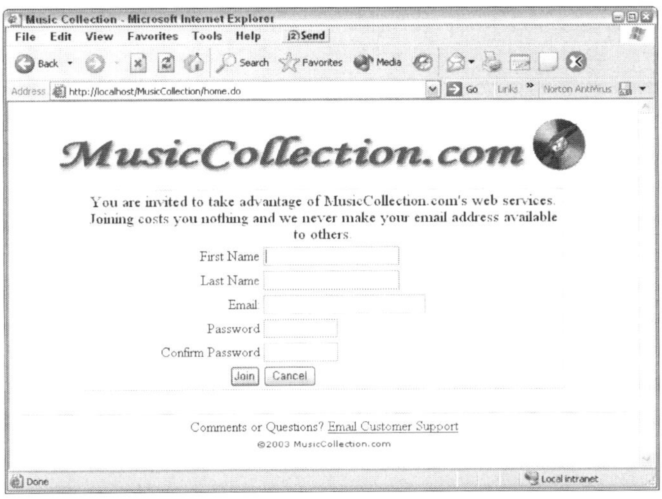

Figure 14-5: The Join page.

The Join form

The Join page requires a dynamically generated ActionForm and is validated using the Validator plug-in. Here you see the code segment that defines the ActionForm in the struts-config file:

```
<form-bean name="joinForm"
      type="org.apache.struts.validator.DynaValidatorForm">
   <form-property name="email"
                  type="java.lang.String"
                  initial=""/>
```

```
    <form-property name="password"
                   type="java.lang.String"
                   initial=""/>
    <form-property name="password2"
                   type="java.lang.String"
                   initial=""/>
    <form-property name="fname"
                   type="java.lang.String"
                   initial=""/>
    <form-property name="lname"
                   type="java.lang.String"
                   initial=""/>
</form-bean>
```

Join validation

Declarative validation is necessary for all the fields in the joinForm. Each field is required and the email field should look like an e-mail address. The content of the password field should be between 5 and 8 characters in length. Furthermore, the password2 field should match the contents of the password field to reduce the chances of a typographical error.

We covered the creation of the necessary validators in the previous "LoginValidation" section except the requirement that password should match password2. With Struts 1.1, there is no out-of-the-box validator that provides this capability. (The validWhen validator will do what you need but will only be available in later versions of Struts.) So you have a choice of performing that validation within the JoinAction class or writing your own custom validator. While it is not too difficult to write a validator, we did not cover it when discussing the Validator plug-in in Chapter 9. Therefore, we have chosen to implement the password comparison test within the JoinAction code.

In the validation.xml file you need to specify the validators for the joinForm as follows:

```
<form name="joinForm">
    <field property="fname"
           depends="required">
    <arg0 key="error.fname.required"/>
    </field>
    <field property="lname"
           depends="required">
    <arg0 key="error.lname.required"/>
    </field>
    <field property="email"
           depends="required,email">
    <arg0 key="error.email.required"/>
    </field>
```

```
    <field property="password"
           depends="required,minlength">
    <arg0 key="error.password.required"/>
    <arg1 key="${var:minlength}" name="minlength"
              resource="false"/>
    <var>
        <var-name>minlength</var-name>
        <var-value>5</var-value>
    </var>
    </field>

    <field property="password"
           depends="maxlength">
    <arg0 key="error.password.required"/>
    <arg1 key="${var:maxlength}" name="maxlength"
              resource="false"/>
    <var>
        <var-name>maxlength</var-name>
        <var-value>8</var-value>
    </var>
    </field>
</form>
```

JoinAction

The `JoinAction` is straight-forward, performing the following steps:

1. Checks to see whether the user cancelled the action. If the user did request to cancel, return directly to the `Home` page.
2. Compares the `password` and `password2` fields to make sure they match. If they do not, creates an `ActionError` and returns it to the `Join` page.
3. Creates a `JoinBean`, passing the `DataSource` reference.
4. Calls a method in `JoinBean`, passing all user information, to create the user record in the database and return a populated `UserDTO`. The `JoinBean` will create a `UserDTO` only after attempting to insert the user's information in the user table. The operation fails if there's an existing record with the same e-mail address.
5. Puts the `userDTO` object into the session, logging the user onto MusicCollection.com.
6. Forwards control to the Welcome page.

Listing 14-4 shows the `JoinAction` execute method.

Listing 14-4 Body of the JoinAction execute Method

```
Boolean bCancel =
            (Boolean)request.getAttribute("org.apache.struts.action.CANCEL");
if(bCancel != null)
    if(bCancel.booleanValue())
        return (mapping.findForward("cancel"));
// compare password with password2
if(((String)((DynaValidatorForm)form).get("password2")).equals((String)((DynaVal
            idatorForm)form).get("password")))
{
    // create a new JoinBean passing the datasource
    JoinBean jb = new JoinBean(getDataSource(request, "musiccollection"));
    // create an account for the user
    UserDTO user = jb.createUser((String)((DynaValidatorForm)form).get("fname"),
                          (String)((DynaValidatorForm)form).get("lname"),
                          (String)((DynaValidatorForm)form).get("email"),
                          (String)((DynaValidatorForm)form).get("password"));
    if(user != null)
    {
        // save UserDTO in session
        request.getSession().setAttribute("user",user);
        return (mapping.findForward("success"));
    }
    else// could not add the use. Must be because already exists.
    {
        // create ActionError and save in the request
        ActionErrors errors = new ActionErrors();
        ActionError error = new ActionError("error.join.exists");
        errors.add("join",error);
        saveErrors(request,errors);
        return (mapping.findForward("failure"));
    }
}
else// passwords did not match
{
    // create ActionError and save in the request
    ActionErrors errors = new ActionErrors();
    ResourceBundle bundle = ResourceBundle.getBundle("ApplicationResources");
    ActionError error = new ActionError("error.join.passmismatch",
                                    bundle.getString("join.password2"),
                                    bundle.getString("join.password"));
    errors.add("password2",error);
    saveErrors(request,errors);
    return (mapping.findForward("failure"));
}
```

JoinBean

The `JoinBean` gives the `JoinAction` the means to create a new user account by taking user information from the `joinForm` and inserting a new row in the `users` table. The table has a unique index on the `email` column, thereby throwing an error if an attempt is made to insert a new row with an email value already in the table. The JoinBean tests for that possibility and returns a null value for the UserDTO if the error occurs. If the insertion of the new row is successful, then a fully populated UserDTO is returned. If any other error occurs, the method throws a ModuleException.

Listing 14-5 shows the createUser method of the JoinBean.

Listing 14-5 createUser Method of JoinBean

```
public UserDTO createUser(String fname, String lname, String email, String
               password) throws ModuleException
{
    UserDTO user = null;
    Connection con = null;
    Statement stmt = null;
    ResultSet rs = null;
    String sQuery = "";
    try
    {
        con = dataSource.getConnection();
        stmt = con.createStatement();
        sQuery = "INSERT INTO Users (fname,lname,email,password,
                                    lastlogin,numlogins,created)";
        sQuery += " values('" + fname + "','" + lname + "','" + email + "','" +
               password ;
        sQuery += "',now(),1,now())";
        int result = stmt.executeUpdate(sQuery);
        if(result == 1)// insertion went ok, retrieve record to get id
        {
            sQuery = "SELECT * FROM Users " + "WHERE email = '" + email + "' ";
            sQuery += "AND password = '" + password + "'";
            rs = stmt.executeQuery(sQuery);
            if (rs.next())
            {
                // Create new user transfer object
                user = new UserDTO();
                user.setFirstName(rs.getString("fname"));
                user.setLastName(rs.getString("lname"));
                user.setId(rs.getInt("id"));
                user.setEmail(rs.getString("email"));
            }
        }
    }
    catch (SQLException se)
    {
        if(se.getLocalizedMessage().indexOf("Duplicate") == -1)
        {
            log.error("Error in creating user.");
            log.error("SQL statement = " + sQuery);
            se.printStackTrace();
```

(continued)

Listing 14-5 *(continued)*

```
            ModuleException me = new ModuleException("error.db.sql");
            throw me;
        }
    }

    finally
    {
    .
    . finally code omitted
    .
    }
    return user;
}
```

Configuring the action mapping for JoinAction

When a user tries to join, three possibilities can occur. As a result, there are three possible directions to take from the `JoinAction`.

- If a user account gets created, go to the `welcome.jsp` page.
- If a user account fails to be created, return to the `join.jsp` page.
- If the user cancels the registration process, go back to the `home.jsp` page.

Make sure to turn on validation by setting the `validation` attribute to `true`. Here is the action mapping for `JoinAction`:

```
<action path="/join"
        type="dummies.struts.music.JoinAction"
        name="joinForm"
        scope="request"
        input="/join.jsp"
        validate="true">
    <forward name="cancel" path="/home.jsp"/>
    <forward name="failure" path="/join.jsp"/>
    <forward name="success" path="/welcome.jsp"/>
</action>
```

The Welcome page

The Welcome page is displayed after the user successfully creates an account. This page presents a personalized welcome message along with a link to take the user to the main music display page. Figure 14-6 shows the Welcome page.

Figure 14-6: The Welcome page.

Displaying the User's Albums

When a user has logged on, the application retrieves the user's album information from the database and displays it in a list. From this page, the user can create, edit, or delete an album. There is also a Logoff button for the user to invalidate the user's session.

The MusicList page

On the `MusicList` page, we'll be displaying a collection of items, namely albums. This means we need to dig a little deeper into the JSTL tag library to discover some of the iterative tags.

For each album displayed, we will show the following information:

- A number representing the row number of the album in the current list
- The album name, which is also a link to the entire album record for editing and viewing
- The individual or group who recorded the album
- The year the album was released
- A delete link that enables the user to delete the album from the collection

In addition, the page has two buttons, as shown in Figure 14-7. The first is used to add a new album to the list, and the second is used to log off MusicCollection.com. Clicking the `Add an Album` button results in

MusicListAction forwarding the request to AlbumAction. For the Logoff button, the MusicListAction redirects the request to LogoffAction.

Figure 14-7: The MusicList page.

The MusicList form

Because the MusicList page has no input fields, you might conclude that no form is necessary. However, several functions can be used from the page, namely creating a new album and logging off. (You can also edit and delete an album, but these actions are handled directly by AlbumAction, not MusicListAction). Therefore, you need to have a way of specifying the particular action to MusicListAction.

To do so, you can create a hidden field named action that specifies the requested action. When the page is submitted, the value in the action field determines what function needs to be performed.

The two actions are new, to create a new album, and logoff, to invalidate the user's session. Here is the form definition in the struts-config file:

```
<form-bean name="musiclistForm"
          type="org.apache.struts.action.DynaActionForm">
    <form-property name="action"
                   type="java.lang.String"
                   initial=""/>
</form-bean>
```

MusicListAction

MusicListAction needs to handle three situations that can arise from a user's action. The first is displaying the user's list of albums. When MusicListAction is called, the action form variable determines what action should be performed. If action is null or empty, the request displays all the user's albums. MusicListBean does all the work to retrieve the album list. MusicListAction just needs to instantiate the bean and pass it the user object. The bean returns the list of albums in a Collection, which MusicListAction puts into the session for use by the MusicList page for display.

If the action form variable's value is add, the user is requesting to create an album. AlbumAction handles the creation of the new album. Therefore, control is forwarded to newalbum ActionForward.

The third possibility is when the action form variable equals logoff, which indicates that the user wants to log off the MusicCollection.com Web site. Control is forwarded to logoff ActionForward, which is the LogoffAction class.

Listing 14-6 lists the code for MusicListAction.

Listing 14-6 MusicListAction Code

```
public ActionForward execute( ActionMapping mapping,
                 ActionForm form,
                 HttpServletRequest request,
                 HttpServletResponse response)
                 throws Exception
{
    // determine the action. choices should be null, add, logoff
    String action = (String)((DynaActionForm)form).get("action");
    if((action == null)|(action.equals("")))
    {
        // get the session object
        HttpSession session = request.getSession();
        // get the user object
        UserDTO user = (UserDTO)session.getAttribute("user");
        // create a new LoginBean passing the datasource
        MusicListBean mlb = new MusicListBean(getDataSource(request,
              "musiccollection"));
        // get the music records for the user
        Collection ml = mlb.getMusic(user);
        // save MusicDTO collection in session
        session.setAttribute("musiclist",ml);
    }
    else if (action.equalsIgnoreCase("add"))    // add a new album
    {
```

(continued)

Listing 14-6 *(continued)*

```
        return (mapping.findForward("newalbum"));
    }
    else if (action.equalsIgnoreCase("logoff"))    // logoff
    {
        return (mapping.findForward("logoff"));
    }
    return (mapping.findForward("success"));
}
```

MusicListBean

MusicListBean retrieves the albums that belong to a user and bundles them into a Collection. To do so, a DTO class, AlbumDTO, is created to hold the album information. However, because the MusicList page displays only the album, artist, and year fields, only those fields load into the AlbumDTO. The album id doesn't display but is needed when a user requests to edit, view, or delete an album.

Should an SQLException occur during processing, MusicListBean logs the offending error and throws a new ModuleException. Listing 14-7 shows the getMusic method of MusicListBean.

Listing 14-7 MusicListBean getMusic Method

```
public Collection getMusic(UserDTO user) throws ModuleException
{
    Collection albums = new ArrayList();
    Connection con = null;
    Statement stmt = null;
    ResultSet rs = null;
    String sQuery = "";
    try
    {
        con = dataSource.getConnection();
        stmt = con.createStatement();
        sQuery = "SELECT * FROM albums WHERE userid=" + user.getId();
        sQuery += " ORDER BY album";
        rs = stmt.executeQuery(sQuery);
        while (rs.next())
        {
            // Create new user transfer object
            AlbumDTO album = new AlbumDTO();
            album.setAlbum(rs.getString("album"));
            album.setArtist(rs.getString("artist"));
            album.setId(rs.getInt("id"));
            album.setYear(rs.getString("year"));
```

```
            // save the album in the collection
            albums.add(album);
        }
    }
    catch (SQLException se)
    {
        log.error("Error in retrieving albums.");
        log.error("SQL statement = " + sQuery);
        se.printStackTrace();
        ModuleException me = new ModuleException("error.db.sql");
        throw me;
    }

    finally
    {
    .
    . finally code omitted
    .
    }
    return albums;
}
```

Configuring action mapping for MusicListAction

You don't need to perform validation on `MusicListForm`, so you should turn it off in the action mapping by setting the `validation` attribute to `false`. Three possible directions can be taken from `MusicListAction`, so three forwards need to be defined in the action mapping:

- If the user requests to log off, go to the `logoff.do` action.
- If the user requests a new album, go to the `album.do` action.
- To display the list of albums, go to the `musiclist.jsp`.

Here is the action mapping for `MusicListAction`:

```
<action path="/musiclist"
        type="dummies.struts.music.MusicListAction"
        name="musiclistForm"
        scope="request"
        input="/musiclist.jsp"
        validate="false">
    <forward name="logoff" path="/logoff.do"/>
    <forward name="newalbum" path="/album.do"/>
    <forward name="success" path="/musiclist.jsp"/>
</action>
```

Creating, Editing, or Deleting an Album

On the Album page, users can view the details of any album, add an album, or delete an album that they no longer want on their list. Therefore, you need a section of the application to handle the following:

- Displaying the details of an album
- Ensuring that the data is acceptable
- Creating album database records
- Deleting album database records

The Album page

The Album page contains the complete set of information about the album. In addition to the album name, artist, and year of release (displayed as a Select list), the Album page also contains information not normally displayed in the MusicList page, as follows:

- type: The album can be recorded on vinyl, tape, CD, or MP3. The type is displayed as an HTML Select list.
- category: The category describes the genre or category of music that the album belongs to. Choices are Classical, Country, Easy Listening, Heavy Metal, Jazz, New Age, Pop/Rock, R & B, and World. The category is displayed as an HTML Select list.
- description: This is a free-form comment field that enables the user to add a comment about the album. The description is displayed as TextArea.

The user can accept changes made to the page (Save button) or discard changes (Cancel button) by clicking the appropriate button. Figure 14-8 shows the Album page.

AlbumForm

The AlbumForm form has the normal assortment of properties — one for each field displayed on the Album page. Because we also have three Select lists for years, types, and categories, we need additional properties to contain the arrays that populate the Select tags.

To create these three arrays, you can use a custom plug-in designed to initialize various application parameters at startup with the StartupManager plug-in. (See the next section for details.)

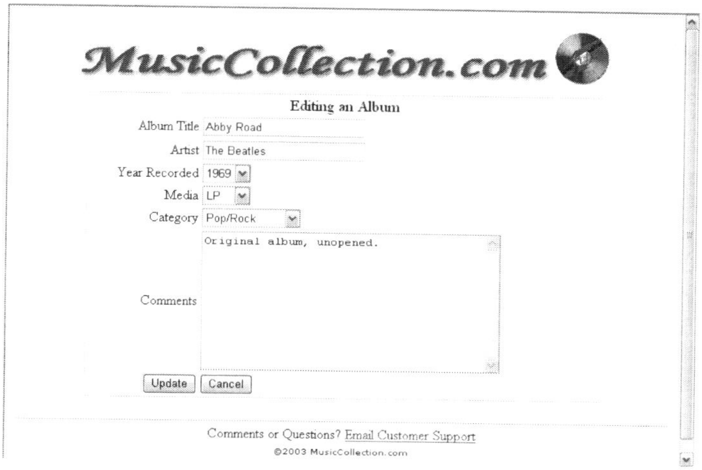

Figure 14-8: The Album page.

Furthermore, you need to keep track of the `id` (album), `userid`, and whatever `action` needs to be performed. Therefore, these fields are also present in the `albumForm`, as shown here:

```
<form-bean name="albumForm"
          type="org.apache.struts.validator.DynaValidatorForm">
    <form-property name="album"
                   type="java.lang.String"
                   initial=""/>
    <form-property name="artist"
                   type="java.lang.String"
                   initial=""/>
    <form-property name="year"
                   type="java.lang.String"
                   initial=""/>
    <form-property name="type"
                   type="java.lang.String"
                   initial=""/>
    <form-property name="category"
                   type="java.lang.String"
                   initial=""/>
    <form-property name="description"
                   type="java.lang.String"
                   initial=""/>
    <form-property name="userid"
                   type="java.lang.String"
                   initial=""/>
    <form-property name="id"
                   type="java.lang.String"
                   initial=""/>
    <form-property name="action1"
                   type="java.lang.String"
                   initial=""/>
```

```
    <form-property name="years"
                   type="java.util.ArrayList"/>
    <form-property name="medias"
                   type="java.util.ArrayList"/>
    <form-property name="categories"
                   type="java.util.ArrayList"/>
</form-bean>
```

StartupManager

In Chapter 9 we provide an example of a custom plug-in called `StartupManager` that initializes various application resources at startup and releases resources in an orderly way at shutdown. You can use `StartupManager` in this application to initialize the arrays needed by the `Album` page and to release the `DataSource` resources when the application shuts down.

Be sure to add the plug-in to the `struts-config` file like this:

```
<plug-in className="dummies.struts.music.StartupManager" />
```

AlbumValidation

Many of the fields do not need validation because they are HTML `Select` lists that are guaranteed to have a valid value. Furthermore, the `Description` field is optional and may contain anything. That leaves just the `album` and `artist` fields that should be filled in before the page is accepted. Here is `validation.xml` for `albumForm`:

```
<form name="albumForm">
    <field property="album"
           depends="required">
        <arg0 key="error.album.required"/>
    </field>

    <field property="artist"
           depends="required">
        <arg0 key="error.artist.required"/>
    </field>
</form>
```

AlbumAction

To allow users to manage their album list, `AlbumAction` has to be able to handle six actions:

- Creating an album
- Editing an album
- Deleting an album
- Saving a new album
- Updating an album
- Canceling the editing or creation of an album

Because of the various tasks involved, `AlbumAction` is the most complex class in the application. Consequently, we examine this class in sections.

Determining the requested action

The first thing to consider is how the `execute` method determines what action needs to be performed. Requests can come from two sources — directly or indirectly from the `MusicList` page (create, edit, and delete actions) and from the `Album` page itself (save, update, or cancel). To handle these various sources, `AlbumAction` needs to look at two action properties. One property comes as a form property from the `Album` page. The other comes as a request parameter when the `AlbumAction` is being called from the `MusicList` page directly:

```
// determine the action. values can be null, 'save', 'update', or 'cancel'
String action = (String)((DynaValidatorForm)form).get("action1");
// action2 can be either null, empty or contain 'view' or 'delete'
// comes directly from musiclist
String action2 = (String) request.getParameter("action2");
if(action2!=null)
    if(!action2.equals(""))
        action = action2; // replace action with action2 if action2 is not empty
```

The preceding code segment, at the beginning of `AlbumAction`, determines which action to take. Notice that `action2` comes from the `request` parameter. If `action2` is not empty, you can assume that the request came directly from the `MusicList` page and is either `'view'` or `'delete'`. You replace the current value of `action` with the value in `action2`. If `action2` is empty, you keep the value of the `action1` parameter that was put in the `action` variable.

Creating an album

If `action` is null or empty, the request is to create an album. The following code segment shows how this is accomplished:

```
if((action == null)|(action.equals(""))) // request came from musiclist to
               create an Album
{
    ServletContext sc = this.getServlet().getServletContext();
    ((DynaValidatorForm)form).set("years",(ArrayList)sc.getAttribute("years"));
```

```
    ((DynaValidatorForm)form).set("types",(ArrayList)sc.getAttribute("types"));
    ((DynaValidatorForm)form).set("categories",
                                (ArrayList)sc.getAttribute("categories"));
    return (mapping.findForward("new"));
}
```

This code populates the `years`, `types`, and `categories` arrays of `albumForm` from the application scope, where the arrays were stored by `StartupManager` during the startup phase. Control then passes to the new `ActionForward`, which points to the `album.jsp` page. Notice the use of the Map key-value pair mechanism for getting and setting values in `DynaValidatorForm` (likewise for `DynaActionForm`).

Editing or viewing an existing album

The next possibility that you need to check for is viewing an album. The following code segment performs that task:

```
else if(action.equalsIgnoreCase("view")) // request came from musiclist to edit
              an Album
{
    // get the id of the album
    int id = convertID((String) request.getParameter("id"));
    if(id > 0)
    {
        // create a new AlbumBean passing the datasource
        AlbumBean ab = new AlbumBean(getDataSource(request, "musiccollection"));
        AlbumDTO album = ab.findAlbum(id);
        ServletContext sc = this.getServlet().getServletContext();
        xferToForm(album,form,sc);
    }
    return (mapping.findForward("new"));
}
```

If the request is to view an album, the first thing to do is to retrieve the request parameter `id`. The `convertID` method then converts it from a `String` to an `int`. Here is the `convertID` code:

```
private int convertID(String id) throws ModuleException
{
    int idNum = 0;
    if(id != null)// id should contain the id of the album to delete
        if(!id.equals(""))// then user is request to delete an album
        {
            // convert the String id to int id
            try
            {
                idNum = Integer.parseInt(id);
            }
```

```
            catch(NumberFormatException nfe)
            {
                log.error("error in converting string to a number");
                log.error(nfe.getLocalizedMessage());
                ModuleException me = new ModuleException("error.nfe.message");
                throw me;
            }
        }
    return idNum;
}
```

After a valid ID is returned, `AlbumBean` is created. The `findAlbum` method of `AlbumBean` is passed the album `id`, returning the album in the form of a DTO named `AlbumDTO`. The `AlbumDTO` data is inserted in `albumForm` through the use of the private `xferToForm` method, as follows:

```
private void xferToForm(AlbumDTO album, ActionForm form, ServletContext sc)
{
    ((DynaValidatorForm)form).set("album",album.getAlbum());
    ((DynaValidatorForm)form).set("artist",album.getArtist());
    ((DynaValidatorForm)form).set("description",album.getDescription());
    ((DynaValidatorForm)form).set("year",album.getYear());
    ((DynaValidatorForm)form).set("category",album.getCategory());
    ((DynaValidatorForm)form).set("type",album.getType());
    ((DynaValidatorForm)form).set("id",String.valueOf(album.getId()));
    ((DynaValidatorForm)form).set("userid",String.valueOf(album.getUserid()));
    ((DynaValidatorForm)form).set("years",(ArrayList)sc.getAttribute("years"));
    ((DynaValidatorForm)form).set("types",(ArrayList)sc.getAttribute("types"));
    ((DynaValidatorForm)form).set("categories",
                                (ArrayList)sc.getAttribute("categories"));
}
```

For the most part, this method just moves the properties from `AlbumDTO` into `albumForm`. However, to populate the three array properties used for the HTML `Select` lists, you need to retrieve the arrays from the application scope. Hence you need to pass the `ServletContext` reference to the method.

Finally, the `AlbumAction` code returns the `new ActionForward` object, which passes control to the `album.jsp` page.

Deleting an album

The final action that can come from the `MusicList` page is to delete an album. The code is a little simpler than editing an album because there is no need to transfer data to the form:

```
else if(action.equalsIgnoreCase("delete"))// request from musiclist to delete an
                Album
{
    // get the id of the album
    int id = convertID((String) request.getParameter("id"));
```

```
    if(id > 0)
    {
        // create a new AlbumBean passing the datasource
        AlbumBean ab = new AlbumBean(getDataSource(request, "musiccollection"));
        ab.deleteAlbum(id);
    }
}
```

As with editing an album, you use a `request` parameter to pass the album `id` data. If the `id` is valid, a new `AlbumBean` is created and the `deleteAlbum` method is called with the album `id`. `ActionForward` used is the general `success` forward at the end of the `execute` method.

Canceling the creation or editing of an album

The next three requests are `cancel`, `save`, or `update` an album. These requests come from the `Album` page itself. Here is the code when a `cancel` action is detected:

```
else if (action.equalsIgnoreCase("cancel")) // abandon adding/modifying an album
{
    return(mapping.findForward("cancel"));
}
```

The `cancel` forward returns control to the `MusicList` page.

Saving or updating an album

The final two requests are handled in one section of code. The only difference is whether album data is inserted new into the database (saving) or an existing record is updated. Here is the code:

```
else if ((action.equalsIgnoreCase("save"))|(action.equalsIgnoreCase("update")))
{
    ActionErrors errors = ((DynaValidatorForm)form).validate(mapping,request);
    if(errors.isEmpty())
    {
        // get the session object
        HttpSession session = request.getSession();
        // get the user object
        UserDTO user = (UserDTO)session.getAttribute("user");
        // initialize a fresh AlbumDTO
        AlbumDTO album = new AlbumDTO();
        // move form info to album
        xferToBean(form,album,action,user);
        // create a new AlbumBean passing the datasource
        AlbumBean ab = new AlbumBean(getDataSource(request, "musiccollection"));
        // if action == save, insert the new album
        if(action.equalsIgnoreCase("save"))
            ab.saveAlbum(album);
        else // must need to update existing album
            ab.updateAlbum(album);
```

```
        }
        else  // there were validation errors
        {
            saveErrors(request, errors);
            return (mapping.findForward("failure"));
        }
    }
```

The first thing you might notice is that the code performs validation manually. We do this because we forward directly to `album.do` in the `MusicList` page rather than forward to the `album.jsp` page, thus avoiding having a JSP file show up in the URL. The downside is that you can't have the validator automatically perform validation because initially the form's properties are empty, an unacceptable state for the validation process. Therefore, we manually call the `validate` method only when we know that the properties of the form are populated.

You could eliminate this nonstandard mechanism by removing the `<A HREF>` tag and using JavaScript to process an `onclick` condition. The JavaScript code could then perform a forward to the `album.jsp` page without changing the current URL. (We didn't use this technique because it would have added more complexity than would have been suitable for this example application.)

If validation errors are detected, the errors are saved in the request and control returns to the `Album` page.

If no validation errors are returned, you get the `UserDTO` object from the session to pass to the `xferToBean` method. You create an empty `AlbumDTO` object to hold the form properties and call the private `xferToBean` method to transfer all the form's properties to `AlbumDTO`. Listing 14-8 shows the `xferToBean` method.

Listing 14-8 xferToBean Method

```
private void xferToBean(ActionForm form, AlbumDTO album, String action, UserDTO
                user) throws ModuleException
{
    album.setAlbum((String)((DynaValidatorForm)form).get("album"));
    album.setArtist((String)((DynaValidatorForm)form).get("artist"));
    album.setDescription((String)((DynaValidatorForm)form).get("description"));
    album.setYear((String)((DynaValidatorForm)form).get("year"));
    album.setType((String)((DynaValidatorForm)form).get("type"));
    album.setCategory((String)((DynaValidatorForm)form).get("category"));
    if(action.equalsIgnoreCase("update"))
    {
        try
        {
            album.setUserid(Integer.parseInt(
                            (String)((DynaValidatorForm)form).get("userid")));
```

(continued)

Listing 14-8 (continued)

```
            album.setId(Integer.parseInt((String)((DynaValidatorForm)form).
               get("id")));
        }
        catch(NumberFormatException nfe)
        {
            log.error("error in converting string to a number");
            log.error(nfe.getLocalizedMessage());
            ModuleException me = new ModuleException("error.nfe.message");
            throw me;
        }
    }
    else// assume creating a new album, so no userID or ID available in form
    {
        album.setUserid(user.getId());
        album.setId(0);
    }
}
```

The `xferToBean` method simply transfers the form properties to the DTO. If the action is `update`, the `userid` and album `id` already exist in the form and can be transferred directly to the DTO. If the action is `save`, the `userid` and album `id` values will not exist in the form. Therefore, it is necessary to get the `userid` from the `UserDTO` and set the album `id` to 0.

When the `AlbumDTO` has been populated, an `AlbumBean` is created which, depending on the action, calls either the `saveAlbum` or `updateAlbum` method, passing the `AlbumDTO` object.

The `ActionForward` used is the general `success` forward at the end of the `execute` method, which returns control to the `MusicList` page.

AlbumBean

`AlbumBean` performs all the database interactions involving single albums. For this purpose, you can use four methods:

- `findAlbum`
- `deleteAlbum`
- `updateAlbum`
- `saveAlbum`

These methods are discussed in the following sections.

Finding an album

The `findAlbum` method receives an album `id` and uses that `id` to search for the album. The method is shown in Listing 14-9.

Listing 14-9 findAlbum Method

```
public AlbumDTO findAlbum(int id) throws ModuleException
{
    Connection con = null;
    Statement stmt = null;
    ResultSet rs = null;
    String sQuery = "";
    AlbumDTO album = null;
    try
    {
        con = dataSource.getConnection();
        stmt = con.createStatement();
        sQuery = "SELECT * FROM albums WHERE id=" + id;
        rs = stmt.executeQuery(sQuery);
        if(rs.next())
        {
            album = new AlbumDTO();
            album.setAlbum(rs.getString("album"));
            album.setArtist(rs.getString("artist"));
            album.setDescription(rs.getString("description"));
            album.setId(rs.getInt("id"));
            album.setUserid(rs.getInt("userid"));
            album.setYear(rs.getString("year"));
            album.setType(rs.getString("type"));
            album.setCategory(rs.getString("category"));
        }
    }
    catch (SQLException se)
    {
        log.error("Error in finding album.");
        log.error("SQL statement = " + sQuery);
        se.printStackTrace();
        ModuleException me = new ModuleException("error.db.sql");
        throw me;
    }

    finally
    {
        .
        . finally code omitted
        .
    }
    return album;
}
```

The query is for an album with the specified album `id`. If an album record is found, `AlbumDTO` is populated with the album data and returned. The code logs any `SQLException` and throws a `ModuleException`.

Deleting an album

An album id is passed to the deleteAlbum method, just like in findAlbum. Other than not returning a value, the only difference between deleteAlbum and findAlbum is in the try block:

```
try
{
    con = dataSource.getConnection();
    stmt = con.createStatement();
    sQuery = "DELETE FROM albums WHERE id=" + id;
    int result = stmt.executeUpdate(sQuery);
}
```

The SQL statement requests deletions of an album with the same id as the passed album id.

Saving an album

The saveAlbum method, like the deleteAlbum method, does not return a value. This method, however, receives an AlbumDTO instead of an album id. The following try block sets it apart from the other methods of AlbumBean:

```
try
{
    con = dataSource.getConnection();
    stmt = con.createStatement();
    sQuery = "INSERT INTO albums (album,artist,year,type,category,";
    sQuery += "description,userid,created)";
    sQuery += " values('" + filter(album.getAlbum()) + "','";
    sQuery += filter(album.getArtist()) + "','";
    sQuery += album.getYear() + "','";
    sQuery += album.getType() + "','";
    sQuery += album.getCategory() + "','";
    sQuery += filter(album.getDescription()) + "',";
    sQuery += album.getUserid() +",";
    sQuery += "now())";
    int result = stmt.executeUpdate(sQuery);
}
```

The SQL INSERT statement is created with the values of the AlbumDTO properties. For those String properties that a user may enter by hand, you use a quick filter to replace any single quotes with a pair of single quotes. You need the two single quotes to avoid causing errors in the SQL statement:

```
private String filter(String value)
{
    return value.replaceAll("'","''"); // replace 1 single quote with 2 single
            quotes
}
```

Updating an album

Finally, the updateAlbum method also receives an AlbumDTO as a parameter and returns nothing. Its try block looks like this:

```
try
{
    con = dataSource.getConnection();
    stmt = con.createStatement();
    sQuery = "UPDATE albums ";
    sQuery += "SET album='" + filter(album.getAlbum()) + "',";
    sQuery += "artist='" + filter(album.getArtist()) + "',";
    sQuery += "year='" + album.getYear() + "',";
    sQuery += "type='" + album.getType() + "',";
    sQuery += "category='" + album.getCategory() + "',";
    sQuery += "description='" + filter(album.getDescription()) + "',";
    sQuery += "userid=" + album.getUserid() ;
    sQuery += " WHERE id =" +album.getId();
    int result = stmt.executeUpdate(sQuery);
}
```

The SQL statement updates an existing album record that has the album id found in AlbumDTO. Again you can use the filter method on some properties to escape (render harmless) single quotes.

Configuring action mapping for AlbumAction

AlbumAction performs validation manually for reasons explained in the "AlbumAction" section earlier in this chapter. You turn automatic validation off by setting the validation attribute to false.

There are four possible directions that AlbumAction can take:

- If the user cancels the edit or creation of an album, go to the musiclist.do action.
- If the user updates the edit or saves the creation of an album, go to the musiclist.do action.
- If the user wants to create a new album, go to the album.jsp page.
- If validation errors are detected when the user submits the albumForm, return to the album.jsp page.

Here is the action mapping for AlbumAction:

```
<action path="/album"
        type="dummies.struts.music.AlbumAction"
        name="albumForm"
        scope="request"
```

```
        input="/album.jsp"
        validate="false">
    <forward name="cancel" path="/musiclist.do"/>
    <forward name="success" path="/musiclist.do"/>
    <forward name="new" path="/album.jsp"/>
    <forward name="failure" path="/album.jsp"/>
</action>
```

Logging Off

Logging the user off the Web site is important for both security and resource reasons. The MusicList page has a Logoff button that forwards control to the execute method in LogoffAction.

LogoffAction

LogoffAction is primarily responsible for invalidating the user's session, but it also provides some useful information for the application log file. Here is the body of the execute method for LogoffAction:

```
// retrieve the user object
HttpSession session = request.getSession();
UserDTO user = (UserDTO) session.getAttribute("user");
// write logoff info to application log
if (user != null)
{
    log.info("LogoffAction: User '" + user.getFirstName() + "' logged off in
              session " + session.getId());
}
else
{
    log.info("LogoffActon: User logged off in session " + session.getId());
}
// make the session invalid
session.invalidate();
// Forward control to the specified success URI
return (mapping.findForward("success"));
```

When the UserDTO object is retrieved from the session, you can log a message about the user. Invalidating the user's session really performs the act of logging the user off. Control then passes to the Home page.

Configuring action mapping for LogoffAction

The standard procedure after logging off is to return to the `Home` page. Here is the action mapping for `LogoffAction`:

```
<action path="/logoff"
        type="dummies.struts.music.LogoffAction"
        scope="request"
        validate="false">
    <forward name="success" path="/home.jsp"/>
</action>
```

Handling Exceptions

This application makes use of many of the error-handling features discussed in Chapter 8. The exception choices require very little in the way of implementation because `CustomExceptionHandler` is written in Chapter 8.

Our own exception

We use `ModuleException` for the application exceptions, as we do in Chapter 8. `ModuleException` allows you to pass a resource key that will create an `ActionError` object stored in `ModuleException`. In this way, you can provide I18N support in your exception error messages.

The custom ExceptionHandler

To provide more data on exceptions, the application uses `CustomExceptionHandler`, which is developed in Chapter 8. (To check it out, see the "Exception Information" section in Chapter 8.) `CustomExceptionHandler` provides complete logging of the exception stack trace, including chained exceptions. Struts is notified of its existence by adding one or more exception tag definitions that reference it (as detailed next).

Declarative exception handling

We declare two exceptions to be global: ModuleException and RuntimeException. ModuleException is an application-thrown exception used for errors that we detect during execution. The infamous RuntimeException is a nonrecoverable error thrown by the runtime system. Rather than showing a stack trace to the user, you can catch the error and display your own, more friendly error page. Here's the code:

```
<!--==========GlobalExceptionDefinitions=========================-->
<!---key value will be taken from the ModuleException instance------->
<global-exceptions>
    <exception bundle="ApplicationResources"
               key=""
               path="/error.jsp"
               handler="dummies.struts.music.CustomExceptionHandler"
               type="org.apache.struts.util.ModuleException"/>
    <exception bundle="ApplicationResources"
               key="error.RuntimeException"
               path="/baderror.jsp"
               handler="dummies.struts.music.CustomExceptionHandler"
               type="java.lang.RuntimeException"/>
</global-exceptions>
```

Both exceptions use CustomExceptionHandler, which we created for better error logging. ModuleException uses the error.jsp page to display its error messages; RuntimeException uses the baderror.jsp page.

Error pages

Because you are handling two types of exceptions (ModuleException and RuntimeException), you need to display two error pages.

For ModuleException, the error.jsp page contains the error message that the application stores in ModuleException. This message should be as clear and nontechnical as possible, because it needs to tell the user what happened and how to proceed. A link on the page enables the user to return to the page containing the list of albums, which is not too helpful if this is the page causing the exception. A second link allows the user to log off the MusicCollection.com Web site if the first link causes another exception. Figure 14-9 show how the page looks.

If a more serious error occurs (that is, RuntimeException), the user should just log off immediately. A standard error message appears, indicating the seriousness of the situation. Figure 14-10 shows the baderror.jsp page.

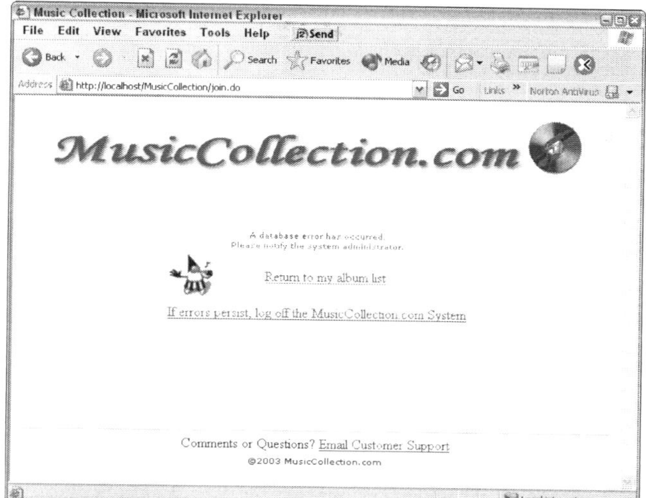

Figure 14-9: The error.jsp page.

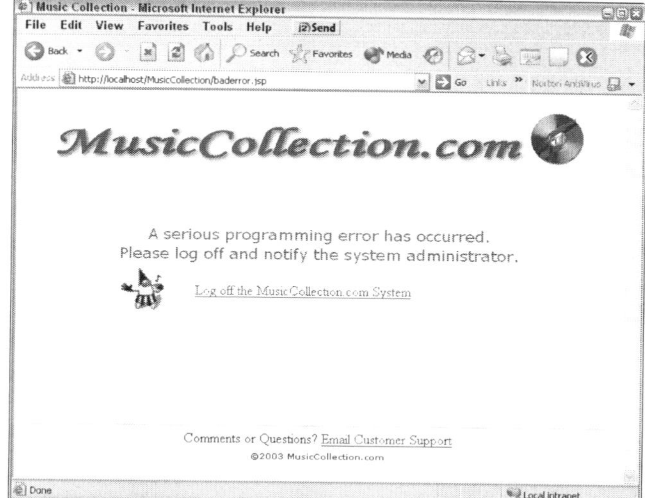

Figure 14-10: The baderror.jsp page.

Running the Application

At the Web site for this book (`www.dummies.com/go/jakarta`), you can download this application as a compressed or uncompressed archive. The archive includes all files necessary to run the application, including all the library files. It also contains the SQL script for creating the database and tables in a MySQL database.

To run the example, you should need to do only the following:

1. **Set up your database schema as described in the beginning of this chapter.**
2. **Modify `DataSource` in the `struts-config` file to accommodate the particulars of your database connection.**
3. **If you use a different database driver than the one we provide, replace our driver with yours in the `WEB-INF/lib` folder.**

   You will also need to modify the DataSource definition in the `struts-config.xml` file to specify your database driver.

The intention of the MusicCollection.com application is to give you exposure to the various features and extensibility of the Struts framework. By working through the example, you should gain familiarity with the power and flexibility Struts can offer you. To see a running version of the MusicCollection.com application, go to

`www.othenos.com/musiccollection/`

Be sure to include the last slash. Good luck!

Part V
The Part of Tens

In this part . . .

Part V is the famous Part of Tens contained in every *For Dummies* book. In Chapter 15 we offer ten helpful extensions to Struts to make your programming go more smoothly. In Chapter 16 we list ten ways to find more information on Struts, including the Struts Web site, discussion groups, articles, resource Web sites, and sample applications. You'll find lots of helpful material here.

Chapter 15

Ten Helpful Extensions to Struts

In This Chapter

- ImageButtonBeanManager
- Struts Spring plug-in
- Hibernate
- Expresso
- SSLExt
- Struts Action Scripting
- StrutsDoc
- StrutsTestCase for JUnit
- Struts workflow extension
- Easy Struts plug-in

After a product gains a following, improvements and additions are sure to follow. Struts has been downloaded hundreds of thousands of times over the past several years, so that qualifies as popular! As developers create diverse applications with Struts, they also develop solutions to common (and not so common) problems. Sometimes these solutions are general enough to be of use to other people. And sometimes the developers see fit to generously make these solutions available to others through the open-source process.

In this chapter, we describe a sampling of these open-source solutions that you can use. Not all of these packages were developed specifically for Struts, but they're all useful nevertheless.

ImageButtonBeanManager

ImageButtonBeanManager is a niche package, but if you have the need, it fills the bill quite nicely. ImageButtonBeanManager is a Struts extension that supports the `Image` tag in the Struts HTML tag library and the `org.apache.struts.util.ImageButtonBean` class. This support is like the support provided by the `LookupDispatchAction` class for multiple Submit buttons (as discussed in Chapter 4). With this extension, the `LookupDispatchAction` class can recognize when the user has selected one of many images and pass control to the appropriate handler method.

The documentation for this package is complete and useful. To download ImageButtonBeanManager, visit

```
sourceforge.net/projects/imagebuttonbean
```

Struts Spring Plug-in

Computer scientists are always trying to find ways to reduce dependencies in code. In other words, they attempt to have the loosest coupling possible. Loose coupling creates code that exhibits a high degree of flexibility and is resilient to changes elsewhere in the application. The Struts Spring plug-in allows developers to take greater advantage of this principle by integrating the Inversion of Control (IoC) mechanism from Spring's J2EE framework into Struts. IoC is also known as The Hollywood Principle — don't call us, we'll call you — and effectively reduces dependencies in classes. With this plug-in, a Struts application can take advantage of IoC with little or no references to Spring.

Documentation for Spring's J2EE framework is extensive. You can read more about Spring's J2EE framework at their Web site at

```
www.springframework.org
```

To download the Struts Spring plug-in, go to

```
struts.sourceforge.net/struts-spring
```

The plug-in documentation is sparse, but the downloaded package includes an example application using the plug-in.

Hibernate

Hibernate is an open-source project designed to take the work out of getting Java objects to and from a relational database. Hibernate provides a transparent persistence mechanism for Java objects as well as a flexible ORM (Object Relational Mapping) tool for use with a large selection of open-source and commercial databases. In addition, Hibernate implements it own Hibernate Query Language as an object-orientated extension to Standard Query Language (SQL). Hibernate developers claim that the Hibernate plug-in is the most widely-used ORM tool in the Java marketplace.

Because Hibernate concerns only the persistence of Java objects, it integrates easily with Struts. To see some examples of Struts applications that use Hibernate, look at the hibernate link at

```
sourceforge.net/projects/struts
```

To read more about Hibernate or to download the code, visit

```
www.hibernate.org
```

Expresso

Expresso, like Struts, is a large, open-source, Java-based application framework. In fact, Expresso contains Struts.

Expresso focuses on providing an implementation of the Model layer of the MVC pattern. This plug-in comes already integrated with Struts and adds many new capabilities to the Struts framework. The Expresso framework includes 16 separate but integrated components. You may choose to use one or all of them, as you see fit. Expresso adds to or supplements Struts capabilities in the following areas:

- Security
- Robust object-relational mapping
- Background job handling and scheduling
- Self-tests
- Logging integration
- Automated table manipulation
- Database connection pooling
- E-mail connectivity
- Event notification
- Error handling
- Caching
- Internationalization
- XML automation
- Testing
- Registration objects

- Configuration management
- Workflow
- Automatic database maintenance

For further information on Expresso, visit

```
www.jcorporate.com/index.html
```

SSLExt

If you'd like to use the *https protocol* (http protocol with the Secure Socket Layer protocol underneath) to secure some but not all pages in your Struts application, consider using the SSLExt plug-in. SSLExt allows developers to configure Struts applications to automatically switch between the http and https protocols. You define this configuration in the `struts-config.xml` file.

You can find succinct documentation at `sslext.sourceforge.net`. To download the plug-in, go to

```
sourceforge.net/projects/sslext
```

Struts Action Scripting

If you're proficient in any of the myriad of scripting languages, you may be wishing you could use that skill for writing Struts `Action` classes. Wish no longer — IBM's Alphaworks provides a solution that they call Struts Action Scripting.

Struts Action Scripting is a Struts plug-in that allows you to develop Struts actions with almost any scripting language. The plug-in provides a Struts `Action` class called `ScriptedAction`. The `ScriptedAction` class uses the BSF (Bean Scripting Framework) to enable Struts developers to create a Struts `Action` in the language of their choice, including JavaScript, Python, TCL, ActiveScript, and PerlScript.

The Bean Scripting Framework is an open-source project supported by IBM. BDF can be used not only by the Struts Action Scripting plug-in, but with any Java application or applet to incorporate scripting. You can find it at

```
www-124.ibm.com/developerworks/projects/bsf
```

Take a look at

```
secure.alphaworks.ibm.com/tech/strutsscripting
```

to find out more about Struts Action Scripting.

StrutsDoc

Would you like to see your Struts application configuration represented as a JavaDoc-like document? Then the StrutsDoc package is what you're looking for. StrutsDoc is an Ant task that generates the documentation from reading the `struts-config.xml` file. (See `ant.apache.org` for further information on Ant.) StrutsDoc currently supports only the 1.1 version of Struts.

See Figure 15-1 for a sample of the document. The sample is taken from the MusicCollection application created in Chapter 14. This package can create a useful form of documentation, especially for larger projects. We briefly explain Ant in the "Choosing Your Development Environment" section of Chapter 2. For more information, visit the Web site at

```
struts.sourceforge.net/strutsdoc
```

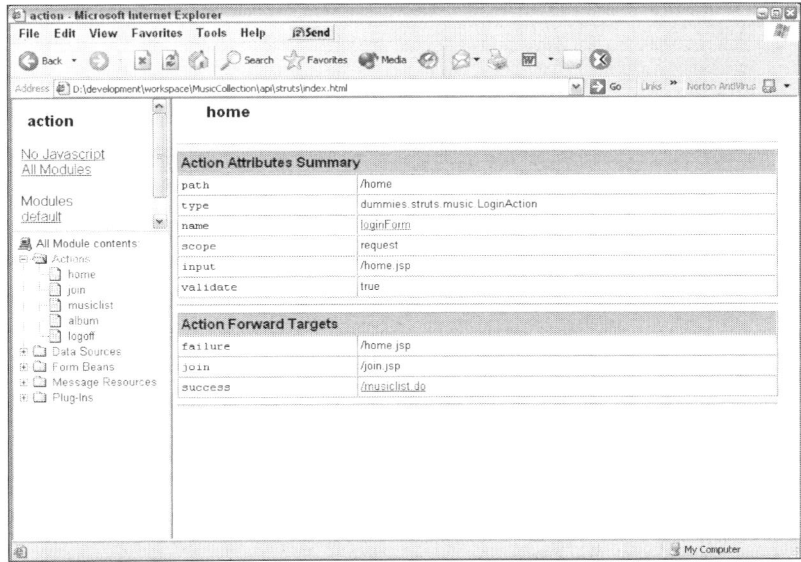

Figure 15-1: StrutsDoc view of the home Action.

Here is the Ant build.xml file we used to generate the document shown in Figure 15-1.

```
<project name="musiccollection" default="run-strutsdoc"
         basedir=".">
    <taskdef name="strutsdoc" classname="strutsdoc.Main"
             classpath="WEB-INF/lib/strutsdoc-0.4.jar"/>
    <target name="run-strutsdoc">
        <strutsdoc destdir="api/struts" configdir="WEB-INF"
                   webxml="WEB-INF/web.xml"/>
    </target>
</project>
```

StrutsTestCase for JUnit

If you already use JUnit, StrutsTestCase for JUnit will be of immediate interest to you. If you don't currently use JUnit or have never heard of it, a little explanation is needed. JUnit is a popular testing framework for developing unit tests for Java code. It was developed by Erich Gamma and Kent Beck and is available as open-source software. JUnit is closely associated with the programming methodology called eXtreme Programming (XP). The underlying philosophy — eXtremely simplified! — is that you should write the tests for a class before you write the class itself. You can find more about JUnit and XP at

```
www.junit.org/index.htm
```

StrutsTestCase for JUnit is an extension of the standard JUnit TestCase class, which provides facilities for testing code based on the Struts framework. StrutsTestCase provides two approaches to running ActionServlet: a mock approach and an in-container approach. The mock approach runs the Struts ActionServlet without requiring a Web container. With the in-container approach, tests are run while running the Web container. Because StrutsTest Case uses the ActionServlet controller to test your code, you can test not only the implementation of your Action objects, but also your mappings, formbeans, and forwards declarations. And because StrutsTestCase already provides validation methods, it's quick and easy to write unit test cases.

For further information on StrutsTestCase for JUnit, visit their Web site at

```
strutstestcase.sourceforge.net
```

Struts Workflow Extension

The problem with Web applications is the ability of the user to do unusual actions that tend to screw up the natural flow of things. For example, suppose a user has just pressed the Reload button after he or she has submitted a form, which results in the form being submitted again. Another example might be performing actions out of sequence through the creative use of the Back button. These are real problems that Web application developers have to face. The Struts Workflow Extension deals these problems.

The Struts Workflow Extension addresses these issues by doing the following:

- Disallows the user to accidentally do double submits, such as by pressing the browser's reload button.
- Makes the user follow a prescribed sequence of steps when required.
- Supports the implementation of reusable action sequences. For example, you can display a confirmation dialog box when the user is about to delete something.
- Cleans up session attributes such as by removing session scope forms, when the user finishes or breaks out of a sequence of actions.
- Prevents the user from deviating from a sequence of actions. For example, you may want the user to answer a dialog box with only yes or no, not allowing any other option.

The Struts Workflow Extension does not require the modification of any application classes, just the `action` definitions in the `struts-config.xml` file. The Extension provides the workflow services by extending the Struts `ActionMapping` and `RequestProcessor` classes.

The providers of this open-source solution did a great job providing thorough documentation to go with their product. To find out more, visit LivingLogic's Web site at

```
www.livinglogic.de/Struts
```

Easy Struts Plug-in

Easy Struts is a plug-in for your development environment that promises to aid in the development process by providing a specialized editor for modifying the `struts-config.xml` file and various wizards to help you construct entries for the config file. Easy Struts is available as a plug-in for the Eclipse and JBuilder IDEs (Integrated Development Environments).

The editor for the struts-config.xml is extensive, as shown in Figure 15-2.

To download the plug-in, visit the Easy Struts Web site at

```
easystruts.sourceforge.net
```

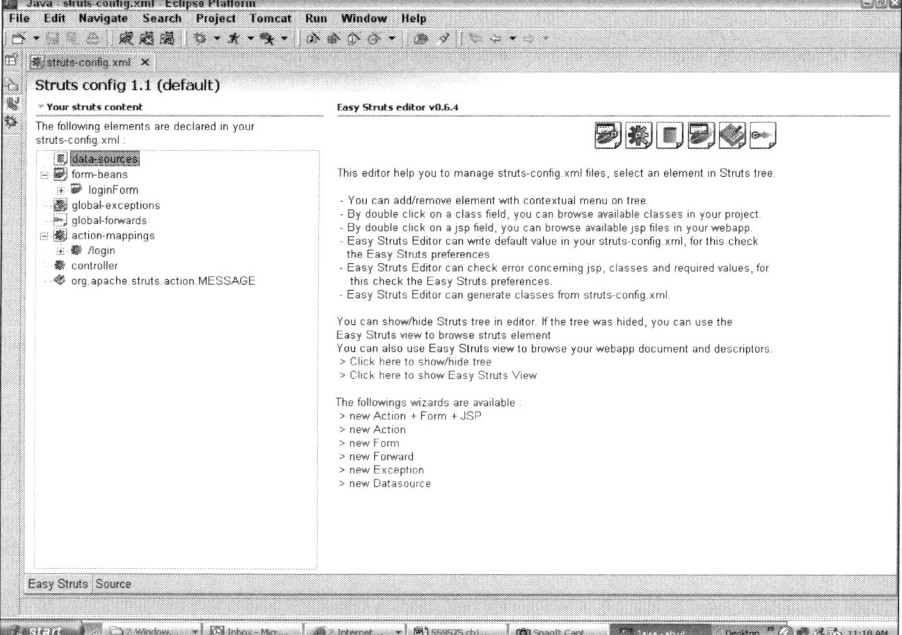

Figure 15-2: The Easy Struts plug-in editor for the Eclipse IDE.

Chapter 16

Ten Ways to Find More Information

In This Chapter

- The Struts Web site
- The Struts mailing lists
- Articles
- Tutorials
- Consultants
- Classes
- Training resources
- Sample applications
- The documentation
- Friends and colleagues

When you're informed, you have a better chance of success in any project that you undertake. In this chapter, we provide some pointers to help you achieve success. Most of these resources are available on the Web, although some may be hard to find. The key to finding good information is in sifting the wheat from the chaff, so to speak. Luckily, we did the hard work for you.

Struts Web Site

You should consider `jakarta.apache.org/struts/` as the definitive source of information for Struts — the Struts portal. Here you can find the latest binary and source code for Struts, documentation, history, planned enhancements, bug reports, as well as many other resources. Be sure to click the Resources link under the Community heading for a long list of helpful article, tutorials and examples.

Struts Mailing Lists

If you run into problems that you can't resolve by reading this book or by reading the documentation, the next place to go is to the Struts mailing lists. Mailing lists provide a forum for Struts users (developers who use Struts to build Web applications) to ask and answer development questions. Experienced Struts developers monitor the list and try to provide help and guidance.

You can take advantages of the Struts Users mailing list in several ways. The first way is to search the mailing list archives at

```
nagoya.apache.org/eyebrowse/SummarizeList?listId=42
```

to see whether your problem or question has already been answered. More than likely, it has. The second way is to join the Struts User mailing list (or the shorter mailing list digest that comes out once a day). To join the mailing list, go to

```
jakarta.apache.org/site/mail2.html#Struts
```

When you become a member of the mailing list, you can post your question directly to the list.

One disadvantage of joining the mailing list is the number of e-mails you receive. If you want to post messages without joining the mailing list, use the Struts newsgroup at

```
www.beanbase.com
```

An alternate site for examining mailing list archives is

```
www.mail-archive.com
```

You may find this site useful if the Apache Web site is too slow or cumbersome. You can also search other mailing lists here.

If you get to the point where you would like to contribute to the development of Struts by adding to the code base, documentation, or test cases, join the developers mailing list. You can join at

```
jakarta.apache.org/site/mail2.html#Struts
```

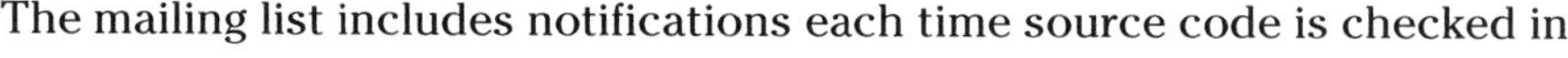

The mailing list includes notifications each time source code is checked in.

Do not use the developer's mailing list for questions or problems related to using Struts unless you want to incur the wrath of the developers on the list.

Articles

A wide range of articles are available for your edification and enjoyment. Many of these articles are written by the same people who helped develop the Struts framework. In this section, we list a few that we think are particularly interesting and useful.

An interview by ServerSide.com with the Struts creator, Craig McClanahan, is particularly enlightening. You can select questions that were asked of Mr. McClanahan during the interview and see his responses in full-motion video. To see the interview, go to the following:

```
www.theserverside.com/events/videos/CraigMcClanahan/dsl/
          interview.html
```

You should have a high-speed connection to take advantage of the video.

Another good article is "Jakarta Struts: Seven Lessons from the Trenches" by Chuck Cavaness. In this article, Mr. Cavaness shares the best practices that he gleaned from developing Struts applications for his company. These valuable lessons can save you a lot of development time and make your application more robust. You can read the article at

```
www.onjava.com/pub/a/onjava/2002/10/30/jakarta.html
```

You can find a long list of articles and presentations by visiting the Struts Web site at

```
jakarta.apache.org/struts/resources/articles.html
```

Tutorials

Several tutorials offer a step-by-step walkthrough of the process involved in building a Struts application. A fairly complete tutorial is offered by Stephen Weisner. This tutorial is in PDF format and has a well-organized table of contents. Go to

```
rzserv2.fhnon.de/~lg002556/struts/Struts_Tutorial.pdf
```

If you would like to try your hand at creating a Struts application that uses the iBATIS persistence mechanism, try the tutorial by Rick Reumann at

```
www.reumann.net/do/struts/main
```

The application that you create in this tutorial is a little more real-world than most — you build the structure to input and retrieve information from a database.

When you consider yourself to be well-versed in Struts programming and lore, you can take a short quiz (just for fun) to test how detailed your knowledge is. You can find the quiz at

```
developer.java.sun.com/developer/Quizzes/misc/struts.html
```

You can find a fairly diverse list of tutorials and examples at the Struts Web site, at

```
jakarta.apache.org/struts/resources/tutorials.html
```

Consultants

You can conduct an Internet search for "Struts Consultants" to find a list of consultants who have their shingles out on the Web. For another useful resource, look at StrutsProjectPages on the Apache Wiki Web site. (If you want to know what a Wiki is, see the "What's a Wiki?" sidebar.) You can find the Apache Wiki at

```
nagoya.apache.org/wiki/apachewiki.cgi?HomePage
```

When you get to StrutsProjectPages, you can choose the StrutsConsultants link to get a list of Struts consultants by geographical location.

Anyone can create a Web page claiming to be a Struts expert. If you're considering hiring a consultant for help in developing a Web application, be sure to ask for references and examples of completed work.

What's a wiki?

According to the original wiki site at `c2.com/cgi/wiki`, "Wiki is a composition system, it's a discussion medium, it's a repository, it's a mail system, it's a chat room, it's a tool for collaboration." It was originally called WikiWiki (Hawaiian for quick). The first wiki site was established in 1995 at the link just mentioned. The creators of the open-source wiki software have a Web site at

```
wiki.org/wiki.cgi?WelcomeVisitors
```

Go there to read about their book, *The Wiki Way,* download the software, and find out more about wiki.

Classes

Many companies and individuals offer various levels of training in Struts development. A casual search on Google found 43,600 hits for the words "Struts training." You can choose from the various offering of companies in your geographical area. You might also find online training classes.

Here are a couple of listings of companies that offer Struts training courses in the United States:

- Accelebrate at `www.accelebrate.com/struts/`
- Themis, Inc. at `www.themisinc.com/courses/index.asp?categoryid=34`

For a training company in Europe, you can go to

```
www.sharedskills.com/softwaredev/strutscourse.html
```

You can download a Struts training video for free at

```
www.middleware-company.com/offer/6may-thanks.shtml
```

The Struts Web site lists several potential sources for training at

```
jakarta.apache.org/struts/resources/seminars.html
```

Struts Resources Web Sites

Because of the popularity of Struts, lots of developers are busy creating tools, add-ons, and other software to complement the Struts framework. We covered some of these packages in Chapter 15, but you can find many more. For a comprehensive list, go to

```
jakarta.apache.org/struts/resources/extensions.html
```

Many tools are also available to help the developer create Struts applications. One such commercial tool is called Struts Studio from Exadel. Struts Studio is a plug-in that you use with the Eclipse development environment. Struts Studio offers a visual development environment for Struts applications. Exadel offers several editions, including a free community version that runs as a stand-alone Java application. Although we have never used this tool, we are impressed with its potential time-saving features. The plug-in versions aren't free, but you should not let that be a deciding factor. If you develop with Struts a lot, the time that you save with these tools could easily save your company a tidy sum of money in your salary alone. At least, that's the argument you can use with your boss. You can look at the product description or download it at

```
www.exadel.com/products_strutsstudio.htm
```

We discussed the Sysdeo Tomcat Launcher plug-in Chapter 2. Nevertheless, we remind you that this Eclipse plug-in is extremely useful. You can find it at www.sysdeo.com/eclipse/tomcatPlugin.html.

The following page has a comprehensive list of plug-ins and standalone tools to use with Struts:

```
jakarta.apache.org/struts/resources/tools.html
```

If you're using the Eclipse development environment, several plug-ins, while not directly related to Struts, make Struts development easier. For example, having an XML plug-in makes it easier to edit web.xml and struts-config.xml files. In addition, many external frameworks that can be used with Struts have Eclipse plug-ins for easier use. The primary site that we recommend to search for Eclipse plug-ins is

```
eclipse-plugins.2y.net/eclipse/
```

The site has organized the plug-ins into various categories that make it easy to find the ones that are of interest.

Sample Applications

What better way to understand Struts that to look at example applications built on Struts? You get a chance to look through the code and see how other programmers have used the Struts features. Most example applications are simple enough that you won't have to invest a long time trying to understand what they're trying to do.

The Struts binary download comes complete with the struts-example application. To run this application, just drag the struts-example.war file from the jakarta-struts-1.1/webapps folder into the Tomcat/webapps folder. You can access the application through the following URL:

```
http://localhost/struts-example
```

You can read the description of the application by clicking the A Walking Tour of the Example Application link. This example application is based on Struts 1.0. You can find an interesting cross-referenced listing of files used in the example application at

```
www.projectrefinery.com/StrutsCrossReference.pdf
```

To see a wide range of sample and example Struts applications, look at

```
sourceforge.net/project/showfiles.php?group_id=49385
```

Many of the applications provide examples of how to integrate other frameworks (such as Velocity, Cocoon, or Hibernate) into a Struts application. You won't find a lot a lot of documentation explaining the application. However, if you download the project, additional documentation may be included with the download. Another sourceforge site that has a variety of sample Struts applications is

```
struts.sourceforge.net
```

Finally, the Struts Web site offers its own list of sample applications. You can find the sample application list at

```
jakarta.apache.org/struts/resources/examples.html
```

Struts Documentation

The Struts documentation is better than most open-source documentation. This material is essentially a local copy of the Struts Web site. The documentation is provided as a Struts application called `struts-documentation.war`. To install `struts-documentation.war`, simply copy it from the `jakarta-struts-1.1/webapps` folder to the `Tomcat/webapps` folder. Almost everything that you find at the live Web site can be found also in the `struts-documentation` application. You can access the application through the following URL:

```
http://localhost/struts-documentation
```

The User and Developer Guides link on the home page provides an overview of the architecture of Struts with some insights into the historical background of the project. Some readers might find Chapter 6, "Getting Started," of particular interest. You can also find useful information on installing Struts on a variety of Web containers. In addition, the section on "Release Notes" can provide insight into the evolution of the product.

The FAQs and HowTos link on the Struts home page provides additional help on getting started with Struts, as well as instructions on several Struts usage topics not covered in the main documentation.

Friends and Colleagues

Possibly the best resource you can find is closer than you think. Friends who are in the programming business as well as the other programmers you work with may already have experience with Struts. Nothing is better than being able to talk face-to-face with someone who knows more than you do (at least about Struts). For that matter, even if someone is less experienced with Struts than you are, discussing issues and questions with a like-mined person can stimulate the creative and problem solving processes. Who knows what solutions you can create?

The 5th Wave
By Rich Tennant
©RICHTENNANT
YOU KIDDING!! TRUE INTERACTIVE CONTENT?! ME CAN'T WAIT, PULL LEVER, OPEN SCREEN!

In this part . . .

Appendix A lists all the Struts and JSTL tag libraries, what they do, and their syntax. This appendix is a great reference to help you find the tag that you need, when you need it. Appendix B is a glossary to help you with some of the more obscure terms that Struts and Java programmers use.

Appendix A

Struts-EL and JSTL Tag Library Syntax

Tags from the Struts-EL and JSTL tag libraries are used throughout this book during discussing the creation of JSP pages. This appendix provides the complete syntax for each of the tags in the libraries. This material appears courtesy of and is copyrighted by Sun Microsystems, Inc.

Struts-EL and JSTL libraries actually consist of numerous separate libraries, each organized according to function. Struts-EL has the Beans-EL, HTML-EL, and Logic-EL libraries. JSTL consists of the Core, Formatting, SQL, and XML libraries.

Beans-EL Library Syntax

The Beans-EL library provides tags for defining and using beans available to the JSP page.

<bean:message> Renders an internationalized message string to the response.

```
<bean:message [arg0="message argument 0"]
[arg1="message argument 1"]
[arg2="message argument 2"]
[arg3="message argument 3"]
[bundle="resourceBundle"]
[key="messageKey"]
[locale="localeBean"]
[name="beanName"]
[property="propertyName"]
[scope="{page|request|session|application}"]/>
```

<bean:page> Exposes a specified item from the page context as a bean.

```
<bean:page id="variableName"
property="{config|response|request|session|application}"/>
```

<bean:resource> Loads a Web application resource and makes it available as a bean.

```
<bean:resource id="variableName"
name="resourceName"
[input="anyValue"]/>
```

<bean:size> Defines a bean containing the number of elements in a Collection or Map.

```
<bean:size id="variableName"
[collection="theCollection"]
[name="beanName"]
[property="propertyName"]
[scope="{page|request|session|application}"]/>
```

<bean:struts> Exposes a named Struts internal configuration object as a bean.

```
<bean:struts id="variableName"
[formBean="actionForm"]
[forward="actionForward"]
[mapping="actionMapping"]/>
```

HTML-EL Library Syntax

The HTML-EL library can create Struts forms as well as most of the HTML tags used in generating a user interface.

<html:base> Renders (generates) an HTML `<base>` element.

```
<html:base [target="windowTarget"]
[server="serverName"]/>
```

<html:button > Renders a Button Input field.

```
<html:button property="requestParamName"
[accessKey="keyboardChar"]
[alt="altTextString"]
[altKey="altResourceKey"]
[disabled="{true|false}"]
[indexed="{true|false}"]
[onblur="JavaScript function"]
[onchange="JavaScript function"]
[onclick="JavaScript function"]
[ondblclick="JavaScript function"]
[onfocus="JavaScript function"]
[onkeydown="JavaScript function"]
[onkeypress="JavaScript function"]
[onkeyup="JavaScript function"]
```

```
[onmousedown="JavaScript function"]
[onmousemove="JavaScript function"]
[onmouseout="JavaScript function"]
[onmouseover="JavaScript function"]
[onmouseup="JavaScript function"]
[style="cssStyle"]
[styleClass="cssClass"]
[styleId="identifier"]
[tabindex="taborder"]
[title="advisoryTitle"]
[titleKey="advisoryTitleKey"]
[value="label"]/>
```

<html:cancel> Renders a Cancel button.

```
<html:cancel [accessKey="keyboardChar"]
[alt="altTextString"]
[altKey="altResourceKey"]
[disabled="{true|false}"]
[onblur="JavaScript function"]
[onchange="JavaScript function"]
[onclick="JavaScript function"]
[ondblclick="JavaScript function"]
[onfocus="JavaScript function"]
[onkeydown="JavaScript function"]
[onkeypress="JavaScript function"]
[onkeyup="JavaScript function"]
[onmousedown="JavaScript function"]
[onmousemove="JavaScript function"]
[onmouseout="JavaScript function"]
[onmouseover="JavaScript function"]
[onmouseup="JavaScript function"]
[property="requestParamName"]
[style="cssStyle"]
[styleClass="cssClass"]
[styleId="identifier"]
[tabindex="taborder"]
[title="advisoryTitle"]
[titleKey="advisoryTitleKey"]
[value="label"]/>
```

<html:checkbox> Renders a Checkbox input field.

```
<html:checkbox property="requestParamName"
[accessKey="keyboardChar"]
[alt="altTextString"]
[altKey="altResourceKey"]
[disabled="{true|false}"]
[indexed="{true|false}"]
[name="beanName"]
[onblur="JavaScript function"]
[onchange="JavaScript function"]
[onclick="JavaScript function"]
```

```
[ondblclick="JavaScript function"]
[onfocus="JavaScript function"]
[onkeydown="JavaScript function"]
[onkeypress="JavaScript function"]
[onkeyup="JavaScript function"]
[onmousedown="JavaScript function"]
[onmousemove="JavaScript function"]
[onmouseout="JavaScript function"]
[onmouseover="JavaScript function"]
[onmouseup="JavaScript function"]
[style="cssStyle"]
[styleClass="cssClass"]
[styleId="identifier"]
[tabindex="taborder"]
[title="advisoryTitle"]
[titleKey="advisoryTitleKey"]
[value="valueTransmitted"]/>
```

<html:errors> Conditionally displays a set of accumulated error messages.

```
<html:errors [bundle="messageResource"]
[locale="localeKey"]
[name="actionErrorsKey"]
[property="actionErrorsProperty"]/>
```

<html:file> Renders a File Select input field.

```
<html:file property="requestParamName"
[accessKey="keyboardChar"]
[accept="contentTypes"]
[alt="altTextString"]
[altKey="altResourceKey"]
[disabled="{true|false}"]
[indexed="{true|false}"]
[maxlength="maxCharsToAccept"]
[name="beanName"]
[onblur="JavaScript function"]
[onchange="JavaScript function"]
[onclick="JavaScript function"]
[ondblclick="JavaScript function"]
[onfocus="JavaScript function"]
[onkeydown="JavaScript function"]
[onkeypress="JavaScript function"]
[onkeyup="JavaScript function"]
[onmousedown="JavaScript function"]
[onmousemove="JavaScript function"]
[onmouseout="JavaScript function"]
[onmouseover="JavaScript function"]
[onmouseup="JavaScript function"]
[size="sizeOfFileSelectionBox"]
[style="cssStyle"]
[styleClass="cssClass"]
[styleId="identifier"]
```

```
[tabindex="taborder"]
[title="advisoryTitle"]
[titleKey="advisoryTitleKey"]
[value="fieldValue"]/>
```

<html:form> Defines an `Input Form` element.

```
<html:form action="URL"
[enctype="encoding"]
[focus="fieldName"]
[focusIndex="indexInGroup"]
[method="httpMethod"]
[name="actionForm"]
[onreset="JavaScript function"]
[onsubmit="JavaScript function"]
[style="cssStyle"]
[styleClass="cssClass"]
[styleId="identifier"]
[target="windowTarget"]/>
```

<html:frame> Renders an HTML frame element.

```
<html:frame [action="actionName"]
[anchor="anchorTag"]
[forward="forwardName"]
[frameborder="{0|1}"]
[frameName="frameName"]
[href="URL"]
[longdesc="longDescriptionURI"]
[marginheight="marginHeightPixels"]
[marginwidth="marginWidthPixels"]
[name="beanName"]
[noresize="{true|false}"]
[page="transferPath"]
[paramId="requestParam"]
[paramName="beanName"]
[paramProperty="beanProperty"]
[paramScope="page|request|session|application"]
[property="beanProperty"]
[scope="page|request|session|application"]
[scrolling="{yes|no|auto}"]
[style="cssStyle"]
[styleClass="cssClass"]
[styleId="identifier"]
[title="advisoryTitle"]
[titleKey="advisoryTitleKey"]
[transaction="{true|false}"]/>
```

<html:hidden> Renders a Hidden field.

```
<html:hidden property="inputFieldName"
[accessKey="keyboardChar"]
[alt="altTextString"]
```

```
[altKey="altResourceKey"]
[indexed="{true|false}"]
[name="beanName"]
[onblur="JavaScript function"]
[onchange="JavaScript function"]
[onclick="JavaScript function"]
[ondblclick="JavaScript function"]
[onfocus="JavaScript function"]
[onkeydown="JavaScript function"]
[onkeypress="JavaScript function"]
[onkeyup="JavaScript function"]
[onmousedown="JavaScript function"]
[onmousemove="JavaScript function"]
[onmouseout="JavaScript function"]
[onmouseover="JavaScript function"]
[onmouseup="JavaScript function"]
[style="cssStyle"]
[styleClass="cssClass"]
[styleId="identifier"]
[title="advisoryTitle"]
[titleKey="advisoryTitleKey"]
[value="fieldValue"]
[write="{true|false}"]/>
```

<html:html> Renders an HTML `<html>` element.

```
<html:html [xhtml="{true|false}"]/>
```

<html:image> Renders an input tag of type `image`.

```
<html:image [accessKey="keyboardChar"]
[alt="altTextString"]
[altKey="altResourceKey"]
[border="borderWidth"]
[bundle="resourceBundle"]
[disabled="{true|false}"]
[indexed="{true|false}"]
[locale="locale"]
[onblur="JavaScript function"]
[onchange="JavaScript function"]
[onclick="JavaScript function"]
[ondblclick="JavaScript function"]
[onfocus="JavaScript function"]
[onkeydown="JavaScript function"]
[onkeypress="JavaScript function"]
[onkeyup="JavaScript function"]
[onmousedown="JavaScript function"]
[onmousemove="JavaScript function"]
[onmouseout="JavaScript function"]
[onmouseover="JavaScript function"]
[onmouseup="JavaScript function"]
[page="imagePath"]
[pageKey="imagePathKey"]
```

```
[property="propertyName"]
[src="imageURL"]
[srcKey="imageURLKey"]
[style="cssStyle"]
[styleClass="cssClass"]
[styleId="identifier"]
[tabindex="taborder"]
[title="advisoryTitle"]
[titleKey="advisoryTitleKey"]
[value="valueSubmitted"]/>
```

<html:img> Renders an HTML `img` tag.

```
<html:img [align="{left|right|top|middle|bottom|texttop|absmiddle|absbottom}"]
[alt="altTextString"]
[altKey="altResourceKey"]
[border="borderWidth"]
[bundle="resourceBundle"]
[height="imageHeight"]
[hspace="horizontalSpace"]
[imageName="localName"]
[ismap="serverSideMap"]
[locale="locale"]
[name="beanName"]
[onclick="JavaScript function"]
[ondblclick="JavaScript function"]
[onkeydown="JavaScript function"]
[onkeypress="JavaScript function"]
[onkeyup="JavaScript function"]
[onmousedown="JavaScript function"]
[onmousemove="JavaScript function"]
[onmouseout="JavaScript function"]
[onmouseover="JavaScript function"]
[onmouseup="JavaScript function"]
[paramId="requestParam"]
[page="imagePath"]
[pageKey="imagePathKey"]
[paramName="beanName"]
[paramProperty="beanProperty"]
[paramScope="page|request|session|application"]
[property="propertyName"]
[scope="page|request|session|application"]
[src="imageURL"]
[srcKey="imageURLKey"]
[style="cssStyle"]
[styleClass="cssClass"]
[styleId="identifier"]
[title="advisoryTitle"]
[titleKey="advisoryTitleKey"]
[useMap="mapName"]
[vspace="verticalSpace"]
[width="imageWidth"]/>
```

<html:javascript> Renders JavaScript validation based on the validation rules loaded by the Validator plug-in.

```
<html:javascript [cdata="{true|false}"]
[dynamicJavascript="{true|false}"]
[formName="formName"]
[method="altJavaScriptMethod"]
[page="currentPage"]
[src="value"]
[staticJavascript="{true|false}"]
[htmlComment="{true|false}"]/>
```

<html:link> Renders an HTML anchor or hyperlink.

```
<html:link [accessKey="keyboardChar"]
[action="actionName"]
[anchor="anchorTag"]
[forward="forwardName"]
[href="URL"]
[indexed="{true|false}"]
[indexId="indexName"]
[linkName="anchorName"]
[name="beanName"]
[onblur="JavaScript function"]
[onclick="JavaScript function"]
[ondblclick="JavaScript function"]
[onfocus="JavaScript function"]
[onkeydown="JavaScript function"]
[onkeypress="JavaScript function"]
[onkeyup="JavaScript function"]
[onmousedown="JavaScript function"]
[onmousemove="JavaScript function"]
[onmouseout="JavaScript function"]
[onmouseover="JavaScript function"]
[onmouseup="JavaScript function"]
[page="transferPath"]
[paramId="requestParamName"]
[paramName="beanName"]
[paramProperty="beanProperty"]
[paramScope="{page|request|session|application}"]
[property="propertyName"]
[scope="{page|request|session|application}"]
[style="cssStyle"]
[styleClass="cssClass"]
[styleId="identifier"]
[tabindex="taborder"]
[target="windowTarget"]
[title="advisoryTitle"]
[titleKey="advisoryTitleKey"]
[transaction="{true|false}"]/>
```

<html:messages> Conditionally displays a set of accumulated messages.

```
<html:messages id="beanName"
[bundle="resourceBundle"]
[locale="localeBean"]
[name="messagesBeanName"]
[property="propertyName"]
[header="headerKey"]
[footer="footerKey"]
[message="{true|false}"]/>
```

<html:multibox> Renders a Checkbox input field.

```
<html:multibox property="requestParamName"
[accessKey="keyboardChar"]
[alt="altTextString"]
[altKey="altResourceKey"]
[disabled="{true|false}"]
[name="beanName"]
[onblur="JavaScript function"]
[onchange="JavaScript function"]
[onclick="JavaScript function"]
[ondblclick="JavaScript function"]
[onfocus="JavaScript function"]
[onkeydown="JavaScript function"]
[onkeypress="JavaScript function"]
[onkeyup="JavaScript function"]
[onmousedown="JavaScript function"]
[onmousemove="JavaScript function"]
[onmouseout="JavaScript function"]
[onmouseover="JavaScript function"]
[onmouseup="JavaScript function"]
[style="cssStyle"]
[styleClass="cssClass"]
[styleId="identifier"]
[tabindex="taborder"]
[title="advisoryTitle"]
[titleKey="advisoryTitleKey"]
[value="valueTransmitted"]/>
```

<html:option> Renders a Select Option.

```
<html:option value="valueSubmitted"
[bundle="resourceBundle"]
[disabled="{true|false}"]
[key="messageKey"]
[locale="localeBean"]
[style="cssStyle"]
[styleClass="cssClass"]
[styleId="identifier"]/>
```

<html:options> Renders a Collection of Select Options.

```
<html:options [collection="beanName"]
[filter="{true|false}"]
[labelName="labelBean"]
[labelProperty="labelProperty"]
[name="beanName"]
[property="beanProperty"]
[style="cssStyle"]
[styleClass="cssClass"]/>
```

<html:optionsCollection> Renders a Collection of Select Options (more consistently than the `<html:options>` tag).

```
<html:optionsCollection [filter="{true|false}"]
[label="beanProperty"]
[name="beanName"]
[property="formBeanProperty"]
[style="cssStyle"]
[styleClass="cssClass"]
[value="beanProperty"]/>
```

<html:password> Renders a Password input field.

```
<html:password property="requestParamName"
[accessKey="keyboardChar"]
[alt="altTextString"]
[altKey="altResourceKey"]
[disabled="{true|false}"]
[indexed="{true|false}"]
[maxlength="maxInputChars"]
[name="beanName"]
[onblur="JavaScript function"]
[onchange="JavaScript function"]
[onclick="JavaScript function"]
[ondblclick="JavaScript function"]
[onfocus="JavaScript function"]
[onkeydown="JavaScript function"]
[onkeypress="JavaScript function"]
[onkeyup="JavaScript function"]
[onmousedown="JavaScript function"]
[onmousemove="JavaScript function"]
[onmouseout="JavaScript function"]
[onmouseover="JavaScript function"]
[onmouseup="JavaScript function"]
[readonly="{true|false}"]
[redisplay="{true|false}"]
[style="cssStyle"]
[styleClass="cssClass"]
[styleId="identifier"]
[size="allocatedInputChars"]
```

```
[tabindex="taborder"]
[title="advisoryTitle"]
[titleKey="advisoryTitleKey"]
[value="label"]/>
```

<html:radio> Renders a Radio button input field.

```
<html:radio value="tagValue"
[accessKey="keyboardChar"]
[alt="altTextString"]
[altKey="altResourceKey"]
[disabled="{true|false}"]
[idName="beanName"]
[indexed="{true|false}"]
[name="beanName"]
[onblur="JavaScript function"]
[onchange="JavaScript function"]
[onclick="JavaScript function"]
[ondblclick="JavaScript function"]
[onfocus="JavaScript function"]
[onkeydown="JavaScript function"]
[onkeypress="JavaScript function"]
[onkeyup="JavaScript function"]
[onmousedown="JavaScript function"]
[onmousemove="JavaScript function"]
[onmouseout="JavaScript function"]
[onmouseover="JavaScript function"]
[onmouseup="JavaScript function"]
[style="cssStyle"]
[styleClass="cssClass"]
[styleId="identifier"]
[tabindex="taborder"]
[title="advisoryTitle"]
[titleKey="advisoryTitleKey"]/>
```

<html:reset> Renders a Reset button input field.

```
<html:reset [accessKey="keyboardChar"]
[alt="altTextString"]
[altKey="altResourceKey"]
[disabled="{true|false}"]
[onblur="JavaScript function"]
[onchange="JavaScript function"]
[onclick="JavaScript function"]
[ondblclick="JavaScript function"]
[onfocus="JavaScript function"]
[onkeydown="JavaScript function"]
[onkeypress="JavaScript function"]
[onkeyup="JavaScript function"]
[onmousedown="JavaScript function"]
[onmousemove="JavaScript function"]
```

```
[onmouseout="JavaScript function"]
[onmouseover="JavaScript function"]
[onmouseup="JavaScript function"]
[property="inputFieldName"]
[style="cssStyle"]
[styleClass="cssClass"]
[styleId="identifier"]
[tabindex="taborder"]
[title="advisoryTitle"]
[titleKey="advisoryTitleKey"]
[value="label"]/>
```

<html:rewrite> Renders a URI.

```
<html:rewrite [action="actionName"]
[anchor="anchorTag"]
[forward="forwardName"]
[href="URL"]
[name="beanName"]
[page="transferPath"]
[paramId="requestParamName"]
[paramName="beanName"]
[paramProperty="beanProperty"]
[paramScope="{page|request|session|application}"]
[property="propertyName"]
[scope="{page|request|session|application}"]
[transaction="{true|false}"]/>
```

<html:select> Renders a Select element.

```
<html:select property="requestParamName"
[alt="altTextString"]
[altKey="altResourceKey"]
[disabled="{true|false}"]
[indexed="{true|false}"]
[multiple="anyValue"]
[name="beanName"]
[onblur="JavaScript function"]
[onchange="JavaScript function"]
[onclick="JavaScript function"]
[ondblclick="JavaScript function"]
[onfocus="JavaScript function"]
[onkeydown="JavaScript function"]
[onkeypress="JavaScript function"]
[onkeyup="JavaScript function"]
[onmousedown="JavaScript function"]
[onmousemove="JavaScript function"]
[onmouseout="JavaScript function"]
[onmouseover="JavaScript function"]
[onmouseup="JavaScript function"]
[style="cssStyle"]
[styleClass="cssClass"]
```

```
[styleId="identifier"]
[title="advisoryTitle"]
[titleKey="advisoryTitleKey"]
[value="tagValue"]/>
```

<html:submit> Renders a Submit button.

```
<html:submit [accessKey="keyboardChar"]
[alt="altTextString"]
[altKey="altResourceKey"]
[disabled="{true|false}"]
[indexed="true|false}"]
[onblur="JavaScript function"]
[onchange="JavaScript function"]
[onclick="JavaScript function"]
[ondblclick="JavaScript function"]
[onfocus="JavaScript function"]
[onkeydown="JavaScript function"]
[onkeypress="JavaScript function"]
[onkeyup="JavaScript function"]
[onmousedown="JavaScript function"]
[onmousemove="JavaScript function"]
[onmouseout="JavaScript function"]
[onmouseover="JavaScript function"]
[onmouseup="JavaScript function"]
[property="requestParamName"]
[style="cssStyle"]
[styleClass="cssClass"]
[styleId="identifier"]
[tabindex="taborder"]
[title="advisoryTitle"]
[titleKey="advisoryTitleKey"]
[value="label"]/>
```

<html:text> Renders an input field of type Text.

```
<html:text property="inputFieldName"
[accessKey="keyboardChar"]
[alt="altTextString"]
[altKey="altResourceKey"]
[disabled="{true|false}"]
[indexed="{true|false}"]
[maxlength="maxInputChars"]
[name="beanName"]
[onblur="JavaScript function"]
[onchange="JavaScript function"]
[onclick="JavaScript function"]
[ondblclick="JavaScript function"]
[onfocus="JavaScript function"]
[onkeydown="JavaScript function"]
[onkeypress="JavaScript function"]
[onkeyup="JavaScript function"]
```

```
[onmousedown="JavaScript function"]
[onmousemove="JavaScript function"]
[onmouseout="JavaScript function"]
[onmouseover="JavaScript function"]
[onmouseup="JavaScript function"]
[readonly="{true|false}"]
[size="allocatedInputChars"]
[style="cssStyle"]
[styleClass="cssClass"]
[styleId="identifier"]
[tabindex="taborder"]
[title="advisoryTitle"]
[titleKey="advisoryTitleKey"]
[value="initValue"]/>
```

<html:textarea> Renders a Textarea element.

```
<html:textarea property="inputFieldName"
[accessKey="keyboardChar"]
[alt="altTextString"]
[altKey="altResourceKey"]
[cols="numColsDisplayed"]
[disabled="{true|false}"]
[indexed="{true|false}"]
[maxlength="maxInputChars"]
[name="beanName"]
[onblur="JavaScript function"]
[onchange="JavaScript function"]
[onclick="JavaScript function"]
[ondblclick="JavaScript function"]
[onfocus="JavaScript function"]
[onkeydown="JavaScript function"]
[onkeypress="JavaScript function"]
[onkeyup="JavaScript function"]
[onmousedown="JavaScript function"]
[onmousemove="JavaScript function"]
[onmouseout="JavaScript function"]
[onmouseover="JavaScript function"]
[onmouseup="JavaScript function"]
[readonly="{true|false}"]
[rows="numRowsDisplayed"]
[style="cssStyle"]
[styleClass="cssClass"]
[styleId="identifier"]
[tabindex="taborder"]
[title="advisoryTitle"]
[titleKey="advisoryTitleKey"]
[value="initValue"]/>
```

<html:xhtml > Renders HTML tags as XHTML.

```
<html:xhtml/>
```

Logic-EL Library Syntax

The Logic-EL library consists of tags useful for conditionally generating the output of page text.

<logic:forward> Forwards control to the page specified by the `ActionForward` entry in the `name` attribute.

```
<logic:forward name="forwardName"/>
```

<logic:iterate> Repeats the nested body content of this tag over a specified collection.

```
<logic:iterate id="beanName"
[collection="Collection"]
[indexId="beanName"]
[length="maxNumEntries"]
[name="beanName"]
[offset="startingPoint"]
[property="propertyName"]
[scope="{page|request|session|application}"]
[type="javaClassName"]/>
```

<logic:match> Evaluates the nested body content of this tag if the specified value is an appropriate substring of the requested variable.

```
<logic:match [cookie="cookieName"]
[header="headerName"]
[location="{start|end}"]
[name="beanName"]
[parameter="requestParam"]
[property="propertyName"]
[scope="{page|request|session|application}"]
[value="constant"]/>
```

<logic:messagesNotPresent> Generates the nested body content of this tag if the specified message is not present in this request.

```
<logic:messagesNotPresent [name="messageKey"]
[property="propertyName"]
[message="{true|false}"]/>
```

<logic:messagesPresent> Generates the nested body content of this tag if the specified message is present in this request.

```
<logic:messagesPresent [name="messageKey"]
[property="propertyName"]
[message="{true|false}"]/>
```

<logic:notMatch> Evaluates the nested body content of this tag if the specified value is not an appropriate substring of the requested variable.

```
<logic:notMatch [cookie="cookieName"]
[header="headerName"]
[location="{start|end}"]
[name="beanName"]
[parameter="requestParam"]
[property="propertyName"]
[scope="{page|request|session|application}"]
[value="constant"]/>
```

<logic:notPresent> Generates the nested body content of this tag if the specified value is not present in this request.

```
<logic:notPresent [cookie="cookieName"]
[header="headerName"]
[name="beanName"]
[parameter="requestParam"]
[property="propertyName"]
[role="securityRole"]
[scope="{page|request|session|application}"]
[user="userName"]/>
```

<logic:present> Generates the nested body content of this tag if the specified value is present in this request.

```
<logic:present [cookie="cookieName"]
[header="headerName"]
[name="beanName"]
[parameter="requestParam"]
[property="propertyName"]
[role="securityRole"]
[scope="{page|request|session|application}"]
[user="userName"]/>
```

<logic:redirect> Renders an HTTP Redirect.

```
<logic:redirect [anchor="anchorTag"]
[forward="forwardName"]
[href="URL"]
[name="beanName"]
[page="transferPath"]
[paramId="requestParamName"]
[paramName="beanName"]
[paramProperty="beanProperty"]
[paramScope="{page|request|session|application}"]
[property="propertyName"]
[scope="{page|request|session|application}"]
[transaction="{true|false}"]/>
```

JSTL Core Library Syntax

The Core library provides the basic functionality needed to handle common tasks in a JSP page: outputting text, manipulating beans, logical operations, flow control, and managing URL resources.The syntax for all the JSTL libraries was taken from Sun Microsystems JSTL specification document, version 1.0 dated June 2002.

<c:out> Evaluates an expression and outputs the result to the current JspWriter object.

Syntax 1: Without a body.

```
<c:out value="value"
[escapeXml="{true|false}"]
[default="defaultValue"] />
```

Syntax 2: With a body.

```
<c:out value="value" [escapeXml="{true|false}"]>
default value
</c:out>
```

<c:set> Sets the value of a scoped variable or the property of a target object.

Syntax 1: Set the value of a scoped variable using the attribute `value`.

```
<c:set value="value" var="varName"
[scope="{page|request|session|application}"]/>
```

Syntax 2: Set the value of a scoped variable using body content.

```
<c:set var="varName" [scope="{page|request|session|application}"]>
body content
</c:set>
```

Syntax 3: Set the property of a target object using the attribute `value`.

```
<c:set value="value" target="target" property="propertyName"/>
```

Syntax 4: Set a property of a target object using body content.

```
<c:set target="target" property="propertyName">
body content
</c:set>
```

<c:remove> Removes a scoped variable.

```
<c:remove var="varName" [scope="{page|request|session|application}"]/>
```

<c:catch> Catches a `java.lang.Throwable` thrown by any of its nested actions.

```
<c:catch [var="varName"]>
nested actions
</c:catch>
```

<c:if> Evaluates the body content if the expression specified with the `test` attribute is `true`.

Syntax 1: Without body content.

```
<c:if test="testCondition" var="varName" [scope="{page|request|session|
              application}"]/>
```

Syntax 2: With body content.

```
<c:if test="testCondition" [var="varName"]
              [scope="{page|request|session|application}"]>
body content
</c:if>
```

<c:choose> Provides the context for mutually exclusive conditional execution.

```
<c:choose>
body content (<when> and <otherwise> subtags)
</c:choose>
```

<c:when> Represents an alternative within a `<c:choose>` action.

```
<c:when test="testCondition">
body content
</c:when>
```

<c:otherwise> Represents the last alternative within a `<c:choose>` action.

```
<c:otherwise>
conditional block
</c:otherwise>
```

<c:forEach> Repeats the nested body content over a collection of objects, or repeats it a fixed number of times.

Syntax 1: Iterate over a collection of objects.

```
<c:forEach [var="varName"]
items="collection"
[varStatus="varStatusName"]
[begin="begin"]
[end="end"]
[step="step"]>
body content
</c:forEach>
```

Syntax 2: Iterate a fixed number of times.

```
<c:forEach [var="varName"]
[varStatus="varStatusName"]
begin="begin"
end="end"
[step="step"]>
body content
</c:forEach>
```

<c:forTokens> Iterates over tokens, separated by the supplied delimiters.

```
<c:forTokens items="stringOfTokens"
delims="delimiters"
[var="varName"]
[varStatus="varStatusName"]
[begin="begin"]
[end="end"]
[step="step"]>
body content
</c:forEach>
```

<c:import> Imports the content of a URL-based resource.

Syntax 1: Resource content inlined or exported as a String object.

```
<c:import url="url"
[context="context"]
[var="varName"]
[scope="{page|request|session|application}"]
[charEncoding="charEncoding"]>
optional body content for <c:param> subtags
</c:import>
```

Syntax 2: Resource content exported as a Reader object.

```
<c:import url="url"
[context="context"]
varReader="varReaderName"
[charEncoding="charEncoding"]>
body content where varReader is consumed by another action
</c:import>
```

<c:url> Builds a URL with the proper rewriting rules applied.

Syntax 1: Without body content.

```
<c:url value="value"
[context="context"]
[var="varName"]
[scope="{page|request|session|application}"]/>
```

Syntax 2: With body content to specify query string parameters.

```
<c:url value="value"
[context="context"]
[var="varName"]
[scope="{page|request|session|application}"]>
<c:param> subtags
</c:url>
```

<c:redirect> Sends an HTTP redirect to the client.

Syntax 1: Without body content.

```
<c:redirect url="value" [context="context"]/>
```

Syntax 2: With body content to specify query string parameters.

```
<c:redirect url="value" [context="context"]/>
<c:param> subtags
</c:redirect>
```

<c:param> Adds request parameters to a URL. Nested action of `<c:import>`, `<c:url>`, `<c:redirect>`.

Syntax 1: Parameter value specified in attribute `value`.

```
<c:param name="name" value="value"/>
```

Syntax 2: Parameter value specified in the body content.

```
<c:param name="name">
parameter value
</c:param>
```

JSTL Formatting Library Syntax

The Formatting library provides tags to implement I18N support for both language and customs.

<fmt:setLocale> Stores the specified locale in the `javax.servlet.jsp.jstl.fmt.locale` configuration variable.

```
<fmt:setLocale value="locale"
[variant="variant"]
[scope="{page|request|session|application}"]/>
```

<fmt:bundle> Creates an i18n localization context to be used by its body content.

```
<fmt:bundle basename="basename" [prefix="prefix"]>
body content
</fmt:bundle>
```

<fmt:setBundle> Creates an i18n localization context and stores it in the scoped variable or the `javax.servlet.jsp.jstl.fmt.localizationContext` configuration variable.

```
<fmt:setBundle basename="basename"
[var="varName"]
[scope="{page|request|session|application}"]/>
```

<fmt:message> Looks up a localized message in a resource bundle.

Syntax 1: Without body content.

```
<fmt:message key="messageKey"
[bundle="resourceBundle"]
[var="varName"]
[scope="{page|request|session|application}"]/>
```

Syntax 2: With a body to specify message parameters.

```
<fmt:message key="messageKey"
[bundle="resourceBundle"]
[var="varName"]
[scope="{page|request|session|application}"]>
<fmt:param> subtags
</fmt:message>
```

Syntax 3: With a body to specify key and optional message parameters.

```
<fmt:message [bundle="resourceBundle"]
[var="varName"]
[scope="{page|request|session|application}"]>
key
optional <fmt:param> subtags
</fmt:message>
```

<fmt:param> Supplies a single parameter for parametric replacement to a containing `<fmt:message>` action.

Syntax 1: Value specified via attribute `value`.

```
<fmt:param value="messageParameter"/>
```

Syntax 2: Value specified via body content.

```
<fmt:param>
body content
</fmt:param>
```

<fmt:requestEncoding> Sets the request's character encoding.

```
<fmt:requestEncoding [value="charsetName"]/>
```

<fmt:timeZone> Specifies the time zone in which time information is to be formatted or parsed in its body content.

```
<fmt:timeZone value="timeZone">
body content
</fmt:timeZone>
```

<fmt:setTimeZone> Stores the specified time zone in a scoped variable or the time zone configuration variable.

```
<fmt:setTimeZone value="timeZone"
[var="varName"]
[scope="{page|request|session|application}"]/>
```

<fmt:formatNumber> Formats a numeric value in a locale-sensitive or customized manner as a number, currency, or percentage.

Syntax 1: Without a body.

```
<fmt:formatNumber value="numericValue"
[type="{number|currency|percent}"]
[pattern="customPattern"]
[currencyCode="currencyCode"]
[currencySymbol="currencySymbol"]
[groupingUsed="{true|false}"]
[maxIntegerDigits="maxIntegerDigits"]
[minIntegerDigits="minIntegerDigits"]
[maxFractionDigits="maxFractionDigits"]
[minFractionDigits="minFractionDigits"]
[var="varName"]
[scope="{page|request|session|application}"]/>
```

Syntax 2: With a body to specify the numeric value to be formatted.

```
<fmt:formatNumber [type="{number|currency|percent}"]
[pattern="customPattern"]
[currencyCode="currencyCode"]
[currencySymbol="currencySymbol"]
[groupingUsed="{true|false}"]
[maxIntegerDigits="maxIntegerDigits"]
[minIntegerDigits="minIntegerDigits"]
[maxFractionDigits="maxFractionDigits"]
```

```
[minFractionDigits="minFractionDigits"]
[var="varName"]
[scope="{page|request|session|application}"]>
numeric value to be formatted
</fmt:formatNumber>
```

<fmt:parseNumber> Parses the string representation of numbers, currencies, and percentages that were formatted in a locale-sensitive or customized manner.

Syntax 1: Without a body.

```
<fmt:parseNumber value="numericValue"
[type="{number|currency|percent}"]
[pattern="customPattern"]
[parseLocale="parseLocale"]
[integerOnly="{true|false}"]
[var="varName"]
[scope="{page|request|session|application}"]/>
```

Syntax 2: With a body to specify the numeric value to be parsed.

```
<fmt:parseNumber [type="{number|currency|percent}"]
[pattern="customPattern"]
[parseLocale="parseLocale"]
[integerOnly="{true|false}"]
[var="varName"]
[scope="{page|request|session|application}"]>
numeric value to be parsed
</fmt:parseNumber>
```

<fmt:formatDate> Allows the formatting of dates and times in a locale-sensitive or customized manner.

```
<fmt:formatDate value="date"
[type="{time|date|both}"]
[dateStyle="{default|short|medium|long|full}"]
[timeStyle="{default|short|medium|long|full}"]
[pattern="customPattern"]
[timeZone="timeZone"]
[var="varName"]
[scope="{page|request|session|application}"]/>
```

<fmt:parseDate> Parses the string representation of dates and times that were formatted in a locale-sensitive or customized manner.

Syntax 1: Without a body.

```
<fmt:parseDate value="dateString"
[type="{time|date|both}"]
[dateStyle="{default|short|medium|long|full}"]
```

```
[timeStyle="{default|short|medium|long|full}"]
[pattern="customPattern"]
[timeZone="timeZone"]
[parseLocale="parseLocale"]
[var="varName"]
[scope="{page|request|session|application}"]/>
```

Syntax 2: With a body to specify the date value to be parsed.

```
<fmt:parseDate [type="{time|date|both}"]
[dateStyle="{default|short|medium|long|full}"]
[timeStyle="{default|short|medium|long|full}"]
[pattern="customPattern"]
[timeZone="timeZone"]
[parseLocale="parseLocale"]
[var="varName"]
[scope="{page|request|session|application}"]>
date value to be parsed
</fmt:parseDate>
```

JSTL SQL Library Syntax

The SQL library allows the JSP author to directly access an SQL database through the tags it provides.

<sql:query> Queries a database.

Syntax 1: Without body content.

```
<sql:query sql="sqlQuery"
var="varName" [scope="{page|request|session|application}"]
[dataSource="dataSource"]
[maxRows="maxRows"]
[startRow="startRow"]/>
```

Syntax 2: With a body to specify query arguments.

```
<sql:query sql="sqlQuery"
var="varName" [scope="{page|request|session|application}"]
[dataSource="dataSource"]
[maxRows="maxRows"]
[startRow="startRow"]>
<sql:param> actions
</sql:query>
```

Syntax 3: With a body to specify query and optional query parameters.

```
<sql:query var="varName"
[scope="{page|request|session|application}"]
[dataSource="dataSource"]
```

```
[maxRows="maxRows"]
[startRow="startRow"]>
query
optional <sql:param> actions
</sql:query>
```

<sql:update> Executes an SQL INSERT, UPDATE, or DELETE statement. In addition, SQL statements that return nothing, such as SQL DDL statements, can be executed.

Syntax 1: Without body content.

```
<sql:update sql="sqlUpdate"
[dataSource="dataSource"]
[var="varName"] [scope="{page|request|session|application}"]/>
```

Syntax 2: With a body to specify update parameters.

```
<sql:update sql="sqlUpdate"
[dataSource="dataSource"]
[var="varName"] [scope="{page|request|session|application}"]>
<sql:param> actions
</sql:update>
```

Syntax 3: With a body to specify update statement and optional update parameters.

```
<sql:update [dataSource="dataSource"]
[var="varName"] [scope="{page|request|session|application}"]>
update statement
optional <sql:param> actions
</sql:update>
```

<sql:transaction> Establishes a transaction context for <sql:query> and <sql:update> subtags.

```
<sql:transaction [dataSource="dataSource"]
[isolation=isolationLevel]>
<sql:query> and <sql:update> statements
</sql:transaction>
isolationLevel ::= "read_committed"
| "read_uncommitted"
| "repeatable_read"
| "serializable"
```

<sql:setDataSource> Exports a data source either as a scoped variable or as the data source configuration variable (javax.servlet.jsp.jstl.sql.dataSource).

```
<sql:setDataSource
{dataSource="dataSource" |
url="jdbcUrl"
```

```
[driver="driverClassName"]
[user="userName"]
[password="password"]}
[var="varName"]
[scope="{page|request|session|application}"]/>
```

<sql:param> Sets the values of parameter markers ("?") in an SQL statement. Subtag of `SQLExecutionTag` actions such as `<sql:query>` and `<sql:update>`.

Syntax 1: Parameter value specified in attribute `value`.

```
<sql:param value="value"/>
```

Syntax 2: Parameter value specified in the body content.

```
<sql:param>
parameter value
</sql:param>
```

<sql:dateParam> Sets the values of parameter markers ("?") in an SQL statement for values of type `java.util.Date`. Subtag of `SQLExecutionTag` actions, such as `<sql:query>` and `<sql:update>`.

```
<sql:dateParam value="value" type="[timestamp|time|date]"/>
```

JSTL XML Library Syntax

The XML library consists of a set of tags designed to make the processing of XML documents easier for the page author.

<x:parse> Parses an XML document.

Syntax 1: XML document specified via a String or Reader object.

```
<x:parse xml="XMLDocument"
{var="var" [scope="scope"]|varDom="var" [scopeDom="scope"]}
[systemId="systemId"]
[filter="filter"]/>
```

Syntax 2: XML document specified via the body content.

```
<x:parse
{var="var" [scope="scope"]|varDom="var" [scopeDom="scope"]}
[systemId="systemId"]
[filter="filter"]>
XML Document to parse
</x:parse>
```

<x:out> Evaluates an XPath expression and outputs the result of the evaluation to the current JspWriter object.

```
<x:out select="XPathExpression" [escapeXml="{true|false}"]/>
```

<x:set> Evaluates an XPath expression and stores the result into a scoped variable.

```
<x:set select="XPathExpression"
var="varName"
[scope="{page|request|session|application}"]/>
```

<x:if> Evaluates the XPath expression specified in the select attribute and renders its body content if the expression evaluates to true.

Syntax 1: Without body content.

```
<x:if select="XPathExpression"
var="varName"
[scope="{page|request|session|application}"]/>
```

Syntax 2: With body content.

```
<x:if select="XPathExpression"
[var="varName"]
[scope="{page|request|session|application}"]>
body content
</x:if>
```

<x:choose> Provides the context for mutually exclusive conditional execution.

```
<x:choose>
body content (<x:when> and <x:otherwise> subtags)
</x:choose>
```

<x:when> Represents an alternative within the <x:choose> action.

```
<x:when select="XPathExpression">
body content
</x:when>
```

<x:otherwise> Represents the last alternative within the <x:choose> action.

```
<x:otherwise>
conditional block
</x:otherwise>
```

<x:forEach> Evaluates the given XPath expression and repeats its nested body content over the result, setting the context node to each element in the iteration.

```
<x:forEach[var="varName"] select="XPathExpression">
body content
</x:forEach>
```

<x:transform> Applies an XSLT stylesheet transformation to an XML document.

Syntax 1: Without body content.

```
<x:transform
xml="XMLDocument" xslt="XSLTStylesheet"
[xmlSystemId="XMLSystemId"] [xsltSystemId="XSLTSystemId"]
[{var="varName" [scope="scopeName"]|result="resultObject"}]/>
```

Syntax 2: With a body to specify transformation parameters.

```
<x:transform
xml="XMLDocument" xslt="XSLTStylesheet"
[xmlSystemId="XMLSystemId"] [xsltSystemId="XSLTSystemId"]
[{var="varName" [scope="scopeName"]|result="resultObject"}]
<x:param> actions
</x:transform>
```

Syntax 3: With a body to specify XML document and optional transformation parameters.

```
<x:transform
xslt="XSLTStylesheet"
xmlSystemId="XMLSystemId" xsltSystemId="XSLTSystemId"
[{var="varName" [scope="scopeName"]|result="resultObject"}]
XML Document to parse
optional <x:param> actions
</x:parse>
```

where `scopeName` is `{page|request|session|application}`

<x:param> Set transformation parameters. Nested action of `<x:transform>`.

Syntax 1: Parameter value specified in attribute `value`.

```
<x:param name="name" value="value"/>
```

Syntax 2: Parameter value specified in the body content.

```
<x:param name="name">
parameter value
</x:param>
```

Appendix B

Glossary

Jakarta Struts uses lots of terms that may not be familiar to you. In this glossary, we collect the terms that we have defined throughout the book and then add some more.

abstract class: A class, such as the `Action` class, that has at least one abstract method and must be subclassed before you can use it.

application context: A name that refers to a particular Web application, including the data logic and resources.

assertion: A statement that evaluates an expression and throws an exception if not true.

attribute: A property of a tag. See ***elements.***

authentication: The process of making sure users are who they say they are.

authorization: The process of granting a user permission to see a page or perform an operation.

chained exception: A mechanism in which one exception is caused by a different exception. You can think of it as exception piggy-backing.

checked exception: An error that the application programmer must catch in a `try/catch` block or throw a similar exception.

collection: An interface and the root definition of a set of classes that hold groups of data objects.

commit: To save a transaction.

component: A small, self-contained program that forms part of a larger application.

custom tag library: Bundles of custom tags that people have created to extend the functionality of JSP through the use of HTML-like tags. They are accompanied by a descriptor file called a *Tag Library Descriptor* (tld). The Struts and Struts-EL tag libraries are examples of this extended functionality.

Data Transfer Object (DTO): An object that carries data from one layer to another in an application.

declarative security: A mechanism in which application security is expressed in a declarative syntax in the Struts configuration files.

definitions, Tile: A mechanism that allows you to specify all the attributes that go to make up a Tile in a reusable structure.

design pattern: A paradigm that structures an application. The Struts design pattern is called Model-View-Controller (MVC) and applies to Web applications.

Document Type Definition (DTD): A definition of the XML grammar used in an XML document

dynamic: Web pages that adapt in response to a user's request.

elements: The part of the grammar in a DTD that defines a tag.

entity: A shortcut to a commonly used value in a DTD. See ***Document Type Definition.***

exception: An event that occurs during the execution of a program that disrupts the normal flow of instructions.

expression language: A scripting language used in JSTL and JSP 2.0 to create expressions for evaluation.

extension point: A dummy method made to be overridden in a subclass. See ***hook.***

formbean: An extension of the `ActionForm` abstract class that provides a consistent container to store the View's form data for presentation to the Controller.

forward: More exactly known as `ActionForward`, a mechanism that defines the passing of control from one module to another.

framework: An application that provides foundational functionality that must be extended for specific needs.

getter: A method that begins with `get` and returns a property's value.

handler: Code that interprets what action to take based on a request.

helper classes: Generic classes that are created by the programmer to provide additional logic or data structure or both for the application. Their purpose is to improve the flexibility and structure of the programming code.

hook: A no-function method designed to be overridden when the class is extended. See ***extension point.***

I18n: A shortcut for internationalization.

implementation: The actual program that functions according to a specification.

implicit objects: Objects already defined by the system and made available to the programmer.

JavaBean: A special form of Java class that follows certain rules, including the methods it uses and its naming conventions.

JavaBeans component architecture: Defines how Beans are constructed and how they interact with the program in which they are used.

JSP/Servlet container: See ***Web container.***

layout: See ***template.***

literal: A constant that is taken at face value and not interpreted, such as the String literal "abcd".

logging: Writing messages about events in an application so that you can look at them later and see what your application actually executed. You might write these message to the system console, a file on disk, or an e-mail message.

map: An interface and root definition of a group of classes that hold data elements against keys. Provide the key, and it will return the piece of data.

module: A set of components in a Web application that are accessed under a different name.

persistence: A situation in which the lifetime of the data exceeds the lifetime of the application. The data continues to exist after the application or even the computer has been shut down. The next time the application starts, the same data is still available.

perspective: In Eclipse, a feature that allows you to change the overall arrangement of the work area to suit your current task.

pipeline: A processing mechanism that moves data and control along a particular path.

plug-in: A class that is added to the main application to provide additional functionality.

public: A property of Java object methods that tell Java they are available to anyone using the Bean or class.

realm: Identifies a set of users, their passwords and their associated roles.

refactoring: Rewriting portions of code to make the resulting code simpler, more readable, and more efficient.

regular expression: A concise way to describe and search for complex string patterns.

resource bundle: A file that contains all the text that the Struts application will display to the user.

roles: A way of grouping users. A role represents a set of permissions that you want to apply to a certain group of users.

rollback: To reverse a transaction.

runtime expression: A Java-based syntax for writing expressions. Used in older tag libraries and JSP version 1.2 and below.

scoped variable: A variable that exists in one of the four scopes — page, request, session, or application.

scriptlets: Short Java code fragments embedded in a JSP page that are executed on the server side to create the dynamic part of the presentation, so that the page can modify its output to reflect the user's request.

separation of concerns: A programming technique to keep from intermingling different functional areas, such as separating the visual layout of a Web page from data.

servlet: A part of a Web application that can take requests from a Web browser and, after some processing, return an assembled Web page. This object is defined by the Java Servlet Specification.

servlet container: A Web application server that adheres to the Java Servlet Specification and can run Java Servlets.

setter: A method that begins with `set` and sets the value of a property.

skin: A color combination and style that control's a page's or application's look — and feel. Also what covers your entire body.

specification: A document that describes all the details of a technology.

tag: In an XML, JSP or HTML document, a definition of an element to appear in the document.

template: A definition of how a page should look but not what content should go into it. The template includes the page markup that describes the structure of the page and names the additional segments that the page should include as content. Sometimes called a *layout.*

template engine: The developer defines templates that describe the look and feel of a page, and the engine merges the page data together with the template to create the presented page. This methodology offers flexibility in site design, easy design development for graphics people, and control of the consistency of site appearance.

thread: A path of execution of the program's code. A Java Web application has multiple paths running simultaneously so that more than one user can use an application at the same time.

thread-safe: Code that doesn't allow conflicts when multiple clients run the code simultaneously.

tiles: In a template, additional segments that the page should include as content.

Web container: A program that manages the components of a Web application, in particular JSP pages and Java Servlets. Sometimes called a JSP/Servlet container.

Index

• Symbols •

• A •

• C •

• D •

• E •

• F •

• L •

• M •

• U •

• V •

• W •

Jakarta Struts For Dummies®

Struts Configuration Tags

Tag	What It Does
`<struts-config>`	Root tag in which all other tags are located
`<datasources>`	Defines a set of datasources
`<datasource>`	Describes a `DataSource` object
`<formbeans>`	Defines a set of formbeans
`<formbean>`	Describes an `ActionForm` subclass
`<global-exceptions>`	Defines a set of exceptions handled for any action
`<exception>`	Describes an `ExceptionHandler` subclass
`<global-forwards>`	Defines a set of forwards available to all actions
`<forward>`	Describes an `ActionForward` subclass
`<action-mappings>`	Defines a set of actions
`<action>`	Describes an `ActionMapping` object
`<forward>`	Describes an `ActionForward` subclass for this action
`<controller>`	Describes a `ControllerConfig` bean
`<message-resources>`	Describes a `MessageResource` object
`<plug-in>`	Describes a general-purpose plug-in object

Principle Struts Classes

Class	What It Does
`ActionServlet`	Handles all requests from client for Struts resources
`RequestProcessor`	Provides general processing for all requests
`Action`	Performs specific processing for a particular request
`ActionForm`	Holds form data for JSP page
`ActionForward`	Provides mapped forwarding information to a URL
`ActionMapping`	Defines mapping from URI to an `Action`

For Dummies: Bestselling Book Series for Beginners

Front

Jakarta Struts For Dummies®

Cheat Sheet

Typical Web Application Folder Structure

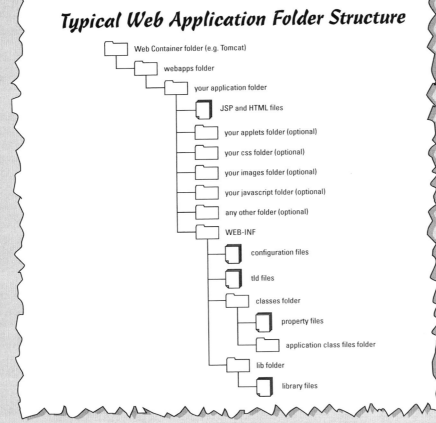

- Web Container folder (e.g. Tomcat)
  - webapps folder
    - your application folder
      - JSP and HTML files
      - your applets folder (optional)
      - your css folder (optional)
      - your images folder (optional)
      - your javascript folder (optional)
      - any other folder (optional)
      - WEB-INF
        - configuration files
        - tld files
        - classes folder
          - property files
          - application class files folder
        - lib folder
          - library files

Optional Jakarta Struts Features

- DataSource: Uses Jakarta Commons-DBCP and Jakarta Commons-Pool implementations to manage database connections and connection pooling
- Logging: Uses Jakarta Commons-Logging implementation to manage log files
- Tiles: Uses Tiles tag library for page composition
- Validator: Uses Validator plug-in for automatic form validation

Common Struts Customization Points

- Overriding `processPreprocess` method of `RequestProcesser` allows you to customize request processing
- Implementing the Plug-in interface enables you to initialize resources at application startup and release resources at application shutdown
- Extending `ExceptionHandler` lets you add more features to exception handling

Item 5957-5.
For more information about Wiley Publishing, call 1-800-762-2974.

9 780764 559570

Printed in Great Britain
by Amazon.co.uk, Ltd.,
Marston Gate.